For Effy + Fin

Making

in London.

Love Bex, Ju, Amber + Olive
x x x x

Making Futures

Making Futures

Marginal Notes on Innovation, Design, and Democracy

edited by Pelle Ehn, Elisabet M. Nilsson, and Richard Topgaard

The MIT Press
Cambridge, Massachusetts
London, England

© 2014 Massachusetts Institute of Technology

This work is licensed to the public under a Creative Commons Attribution-NonCommercial 3.0 license: http://creativecommons.org/licenses/by-nc/3.0/

All rights reserved except as licensed pursuant to the Creative Commons license identified above. Any reproduction or other use not licensed as above, by any electronic or mechanical means (including but not limited to photocopying, public distribution, online display, and digital information storage and retrieval) requires permission in writing from the publisher.

MIT Press books in print format may be purchased at special quantity discounts for business or sales promotional use. For information, email special_sales@mitpress.mit.edu.

This book was set in Stone Sans and Stone Serif by the MIT Press. The print edition was printed and bound in the United States of America.

Library of Congress Cataloging-in-Publication Data

Making futures : marginal notes on innovation, design, and democracy / edited by Pelle Ehn, Elisabet M. Nilsson, and Richard Topgaard
  pages cm
Includes bibliographical references and index.
ISBN 978-0-262-02793-9 (hardcover : alk. paper)
1. Technological innovations. 2. Group work in research. 3. Community development. I. Ehn, Pelle, 1948–, editor of compilation. II. Nilsson, Elisabet M., editor of compilation. III. Topgaard, Richard, editor of compilation.
T173.8.M354 2014
303.48'3—dc23
2014008010
10 9 8 7 6 5 4 3 2 1

Contents

Acknowledgments   vii
Prologue by Laura Watts, Pelle Ehn, and Lucy Suchman   ix

1   Introduction   1
Pelle Ehn, Elisabet M. Nilsson, and Richard Topgaard

I   Designing Conditions for the Social

2   Designing Conditions for the Social   17
Anders Emilson

3   Designing in the Neighborhood: Beyond (and in the Shadow of) Creative Communities   35
Anders Emilson, Per-Anders Hillgren, and Anna Seravalli

4   Connecting with the Powerful Strangers: From Governance to Agonistic Design Things   63
Anders Emilson and Per-Anders Hillgren

II   Opening Production—Design and Commons

5   Opening Production: Design and Commons   87
Sanna Marttila, Elisabet M. Nilsson, and Anna Seravalli

6   While Waiting for the Third Industrial Revolution: Attempts at Commoning Production   99
Anna Seravalli

7   Playing with Fire: Collaborating through Digital Sketching in a Creative Community   131
Mads Hobye

8   How Deep Is Your Love? On Open-Source Hardware   153
David Cuartielles

III   Creative Class Struggles

9   Creative Class Struggles   173
Erling Björgvinsson and Pernilla Severson

10   The Making of Cultural Commons: Nasty Old Film Distribution and Funding   187
Erling Björgvinsson

11   Collaborative Design and Grassroots Journalism: Public Controversies and Controversial Publics   227
Erling Björgvinsson

12   Stories on Future-Making in Everyday Practices from Managers in the Creative Industries   257
Pernilla Severson

IV   Emerging Publics

13   Emerging Publics: Totem-Poling the 'We's and 'Me's of Citizen Participation   269
Per Linde

14   Performing the City: Exploring the Bandwidth of Urban Place-Making through New-Media Tactics   277
Per Linde and Karin Book

15   Publics-in-the-Making: Crafting Issues in a Mobile Sewing Circle   303
Kristina Lindström and Åsa Ståhl

16   Emerging Publics and Interventions in Democracy   323
Michael Krona and Måns Adler

List of Contributors   345
Index   349

Acknowledgments

Our contribution has been to draw this volume together, a modest undertaking in comparison with the contributions made by others. Still, the editors' names are the only ones that appear on the front cover. The many authors, who tell their own stories of being involved in innovation, design, and democracy, have their names in the book. Their stories would, however, not have been possible without the contributions of other participants, human and non-human. Numerous books and articles are among these influential participants. They and their authors are named in lists of references throughout the book. But the most central contributors to these marginal notes—the true makers of this book—are the many direct and indirect participants in the various design encounters. Your toils are the stuff that has made these stories possible. We acknowledge your contributions even though most of your names do not shine from the pages of the book and many are missing from the alphabetical list of participants that follows: Aisha, Alima, Aluma, Amaduh Bah, Amanda Dahllöf, Andrea Botero, Ann Light, Anto Tomic, Archipelago of Futures Workshop 2012, Arduino Boards, Artcom, Attendo, Bambuser, Barbara Andrews, Barbro Lindén, Barn i stan, Behrang Miri, Bertil Björk, Bertil Löwgren, Birgitte Hoffmann, Birthe Muller, Bjarne Stenquist, Björn Wäst, Bo Reimer, Carin Hernqvist, Caroline Lundholm, Catalina Alzate, Centre for Science Studies at Lancaster University, Centrum för publikt entreprenörskap, Charlotte Petersson, Charlotte Ziethen, Cristiano Storni, Christina Merker-Siesjö, Cia Borgström, Coompanion, Cykelköket, David Hakken, Delia Grenville, Do-Fi, DoDream, Ebrima Jameh, Embroidery machine, Endre Dányi, Epsilon, Eva Brandt, Eva Renhammar, Fabriken, Fabriken machines (laser-cutter, CNC mill, sewing machines, overlock machines, saw, belt sander), Fabriken handtools, Feedus, Fiona Winders, Forskningsavdelningen, Fredrik Björk, Fredrik Rakar, Good World, Hanna Sigsjö, Helene Broms, Helene Granqvist, Herrgårds Kvinnoförening, Hjalmar Falk, Hungerprojektet, illutron, Ingemar Holm, Inkonst, Jennie Järvå, Jila Moradi, Joakim Halse, Johan Dahlén, Johan Salo, Jonas Löwgren, Kommission för ett socialt hållbart Malmö, Lars Flygare, Lena Eriksson, Lene Alsbjørn, Leverhulme Trust, Li Jönsson, Lisa Lundström, Louise Brønnum, Lucy's laptop (without which it would all be very different), Luisa Carbonelli, Malmö stad, Malmö University, Maria Foverskov, Marie Aakjer, Maurizio Teli, Medea Collaborative Media Initiative, Media Evolution, Mette Agger Eriksen, Mette Gislev Kjærsgaard, Michaela Green, Miljonprocessen, Mobile phones, Mona Masri, National Federation of Rural Community Centres, Nätverket Göran, Needles, Nicoras Ljogu, Nils Phillips, Nokia N95, Ola Persson, Oyuki Matsumoto, Ozma, Pallets and scrap lying around STPLN, Paula Kermfors, RGRA, Rhefab Management, Righteous Fashion, Röda korset, Sabina Dethorey, Safija Imsirovic, School of Arts and Communication, Selfmade, Skåne stadsmission, Sissel Olander, Social Incubator Workshop, Stefan Löfgren, Stella Boess, STPLN, Studieförbundet vuxenskolan, Svenjohan Davidsson, Swedish Traveling Exhibitions, Tangram Film, Tanja Rosenqvist, TempoS Workshop on Making Futures 2012, Textildepartementet, The Pirate Bay, Thomas Binder, Threads, Tiina Suopajärvi, Tine Damsholt, Tommy Wegbratt, Tösabidarna, Ulrik Jørgensen, Ulrika Forsgren Högman, Unsworn Industries, Vi unga, Viktoria Günes, Xerox PARC (rest in peace), Yanki Lee, Yvonne Dittrich, Åsa Skogström Feldt, Återskapa.

We thank you all.

Pelle Ehn, Elisabet M. Nilsson, and Richard Topgaard
Malmö

Prologue

Laura Watts, Pelle Ehn, and Lucy Suchman

This prologue is carried by a Design Mailboat. It was originally destined for the opening of the 2012 Design and Displacement conference (organized by the Society for Social Studies of Science and the European Association for Studies of Science and Technology) in Copenhagen, where the exchange was performed. Here the Design Mailboat has been redirected, serving as a prologue to the coming marginal notes on innovation, design, and democracy. Mailboats are message-sized vessels, originally sent from remote islands to reach unknown shores, designed to carry words on the tide from one beach to another, to send questions and receive floating replies. The Design Mailboat is one such word-bearing ship. We have been sending it back and forth between three coasts with a passion for design and its futures. The Design Mailboat has floated from the islands of Orkney (off the northeast coast of Scotland), through the Öresund (between Denmark and Sweden), to Silicon Valley (in California). Silicon Valley is the mythic place of origin of the design of the mouse, the graphical user interface, and the big green button on the photocopier. Öresund is a mythic center of Scandinavian Design, the place of origin of the 'white style,' a home of legendary designers and beautiful functional objects, but maybe also the home of the Thing and its agonistic collectives. The islands of Orkney are a mythic place of origin for wave and tidal renewable energy, and for the design of monumental stone circles, built more than 5,000 years ago. From our various locations as the future archaeologist, the collective designer, and the anthropologist of technoscience, we have been asking one another what "design" is in these far-apart places.

From the Future Archaeologist—Message 1

I write this message to be taken in the ocean currents to that far-off continental coast, to that mythic place of Silicon Valley. You echo in the wireless network wind on my cheeks, from the metal chamfers around my keyboard, in logos that litter my web windows, in the very essence and existence of my mouse.

I know your world by its absent presence in mine. You haunt me. Your home haunts me. Where does Silicon Valley not haunt?

Figure P.1
View over the European Marine Energy Centre, wave energy test site, Orkney. Laura Watts (CC:BY-NC).

You live in that place where my future is imagined and rolled-out from, rolled over my bones, over my home, my hills, my islands.

I wonder what you imagine my home looks like (for without imagining there can be no design). What do you know of the islands of Orkney, apart from their location above the northeast coast of Scotland, and their shape, the wings of a diving Osprey? My home is mythic, too. A world center for prehistoric stone circles. A world center for marine renewable energy. But what do you know? What of my home affects your thoughts, your imaginings, your designs for the future?

What does the future mean to you? What does it mean to design a future in your world, on your coast?

But who might you reply to, you may wonder.

So let me introduce myself over the Atlantic flow of the Gulf Stream, which separates us.

I am the future archaeologist.

Yes, an archaeologist, of sorts.

Prologue

Archaeologists reconstruct the past from fragments of found evidence. They make the past from the flotsam and jetsam left behind when people make the world.

I make a *future* from the flotsam and jetsam left behind when people make the world—people like designers, whose choices, whose sociomaterial practices, imaginings, stories, and digital ink, make the world one way and not another.

Maybe you don't see design that way.

I see it as a future-making practice (and Pelle Ehn, a design researcher from Copenhagen and Malmö, would agree with me). Every practice has residues. I just collect those residues from design and paste them together, play with them, try out lots of different ways they go together, and reconstruct them in lots of different ways. If design is a future-making practice, then I reconstruct design futures in lots of different ways. Send me some residues and I'll show you what I mean.

I wish I knew what design is in your world.

Whatever it is, its effects are felt here. Someone, perhaps in an urban, techno-centric place like yours, once designed a broadband wireless network for the islands. But in that designer's world there was no tide, no rising and falling of the sea, no curve of the Earth between wireless antennas. So every time the tide came in, the sea rose and broke the signal. Knowing about tides matters to design here.

Tell me about design in your world, help me understand.

And tell me about you.

Yours, from Orkney,
The future archaeologist

From the Anthropologist of Technoscience—Message 2

Dear future archaeologist,

I was walking on the beach at Pescadero this morning (a rare time out from work—"work hard, play hard" is the program here, but somehow I always seem to implement only the first of those) when I found your message. I had no idea where the islands of Orkney were (before I used Google to find out), but of course I've seen images of those stone circles, and I have a feeling they would be a welcome change from here.

In the twenty years that I've spent here, I've become preoccupied with undoing Silicon Valley—not in the sense of denying its existence or consequence, but in a different sense that sending some messages back and forth might help to articulate. To get started, let me bring in a muse whose voice probably has traveled the distance between us:

A peculiar attitude to history characterizes those who live in the timescape of the technopresent. They (we?) tend to describe everything as new, as revolutionary, as future oriented, as a solution to problems of the past. The arrogance and ignorance of this attitude hardly need comment. ... However, if revolutions here are mostly hype, discontinuities and mutated ways of being are not.

Categories abound in technocultural worlds that did not exist before; these categories are the sedimentations of processual relations that matter. (Haraway 2008, 135)

This "peculiar attitude" expressed itself vividly to me one evening around 1995 as I was driving my car down Hillview Avenue in Palo Alto listening to National Public Radio. "The future arrives sooner here," said the Silicon Valley technologist who was being interviewed. His words constituted a place—a "here"—that, in indexically referencing his location in Silicon Valley, performed the existence of that place once again through the naming of it. And in positing a singular, universal future, his words also reiterated a past, in the form of a diffusionist model of change. The anthropologist Johanes Fabian, in *Time and the Other*, describes this as a form of temporal distancing that "involves placing chronologically contemporary and spatially distant peoples along a temporal trajectory, such that the record of humanity across the globe is progressively ordered in historical time" (Fabian 1983, 13). The kind of spatial and temporal distancing enacted in a statement like this is always, in other words, a colonizing move.

Figure P.2
Manifest Destiny, John Gast, 1872. Public domain.

Prologue   xiii

So I hear this statement as reproducing the geographies of center and periphery, and temporalities of development, that in the mid 1990s underwrote Silicon Valley's figuration as central to the future of everywhere. But postcolonial scholarship has taught us that centers and margins are multiple and relative, and futures can be enacted only in what Anna Tsing (2005, 1–2) calls "the sticky materiality of practical encounters … the makeshift links across distance and difference that shape global futures—and ensure their uncertain status." Locally enacted effects are made to travel less through easy flows than through messy translations, and, as Tsing observes, those who claim to be in touch with the universal are notoriously bad at seeing the limits and exclusions of their own knowledge practices. Postcolonial forms of future-making, it follows, require geographies that have less certain centers (see Redfield 2002, 794).

So one way of relocating future-making, I'm thinking, could be an anthropology of those places now enacted as centers of innovation that shows the provincial contingencies and uncertainties of their own futures, as well as the situated practices required to sustain their reproduction as central. How would that fit, I'm wondering, with your project?

Yours from the Valley,
The anthropologist of technoscience

From the Collective Designer—Message 3

dear archaeologist of the future

and anthropologist of techno-science

this morning

during my daily morning bath

by the sound that

out of denmark, sweden, norway

cut scandinavia

together and apart

your beautiful

immutable mobile mailboat

crossed my path

your mailboat intra-actions

your thoughts on design

and care for futures being made

across the (orkney) islands

and the (silicon) valley

fill me with curiosity

and spark my imagination

but also make me want to share

the futures being made

by the waters where i fare

a collective designer (of sorts)

that's what i am

an oxymoron of course

but please bear with me

there is more to come

in contemporary

techno-science lingua franca

the collective designer

is not the omnipotent maker

of isolated objects (of desire)

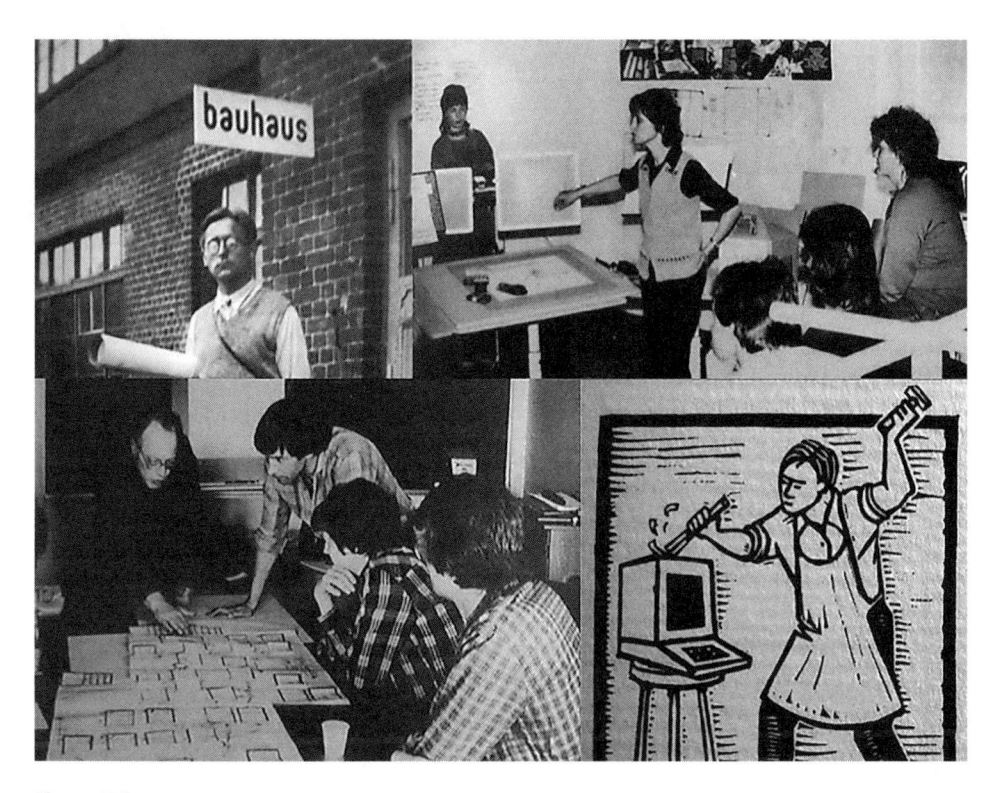

Figure P.3
The collective designer (part of). Upper left: public domain. Upper right and lower left: Copyright Pelle Ehn; published in *Design at Work*. Lower left: Copyright Pelle Ehn; published in *Design at Work*. Lower right: Copyright Pelle Ehn; published in *Work-Oriented Design of Computer Artifacts* (Erlbaum 1988).

but more a passionate participant

among many

in multiple unfolding

things of design

these socio-material

"collectives of humans and non humans"

are designerly appropriations

of ancient nordic things

political assemblies

rituals and places

making futures

through controversial

"agonistic" "matters of concern"

(maybe as it was once

on the islands of orkney)

the contemporary

scandinavian collective designer

some forty years of age or so

norwegian of origin

focusing on democracy

and worker participation

actively searching

alternative futures

through collaborative

design things

at the time when computers

entered the shop floor

threatening to deskill workers

Prologue

and tighten managerial control

pioneered at

"kongsberg weapon factory"

(maybe not the most likely place

for an experiment in

democracy and participation)

but here is another paradox

at that time

the collective designer

traveled over the seas

actually made it to the valley

but not as a

controversial design thing

foregrounding trade unions,

class struggle, and democracy

but as object-oriented design

a computer simulation language

with active data objects

that inherit properties

from data classes

rumors have it

that translated into

the programming environment

"smalltalk"

it became part

of technological futures

being made in the valley

a decade later

the scandinavian collective designer

embarked on travels to "utopia"

not another "nowhere"

but the most socio-material interventions

in the controversial "now here"

a nordic design thing addressing

the potential technological destruction

of the typographer and his union

by an alternative design of

"computer tools for skilled workers"

and "collaborative work organization"

this was in the wake

of the mac apple revolution in the valley

and the collective designer

actually traveled there

for technological inspiration

(yes he was there thirty years ago incognito)

the outcome of "utopia"

resembled the mac as object

with mouse and graphical display

but was a different kind of thing

a participatory design thing

a typographer and designer collaboration

prototyping and exploring

alternative socio-material futures

through technological

class-struggle devices

and political actions

of this utopia

"where workers craft new technology"

the international technical press

wrote with appreciation

and much exaggeration

"today scandinavia

tomorrow perhaps

the rest of the world"

paradoxically

they were partly right

thirty years later

this political utopian

future-making practice

still travels the world

but now politically marginalized

translated into a cornerstone

of mainstream neo-liberal

"user-driven innovation"

today the collective designer

still concerned with matters of

democracy and participation

has moved beyond the workplace

and into ongoing evolving

controversial design things

centered around innovative actors

from the outskirts of the city

and the margins of society

what about the peripheries of

your island and your valley?

yours sincerely

out of scandinavia

the collective designer (part of)

From the Anthropologist of Technoscience—Message 4

Dear future archaeologist and collective designer (part of),

In the Valley it's all about invention and newness. So here's a question: What does it mean to think about invention not through the figure of the light bulb (whether it's in the hands of Thomas Edison or floating in a thought balloon over someone's head), but as an effect of generative connection among things not previously associated? And

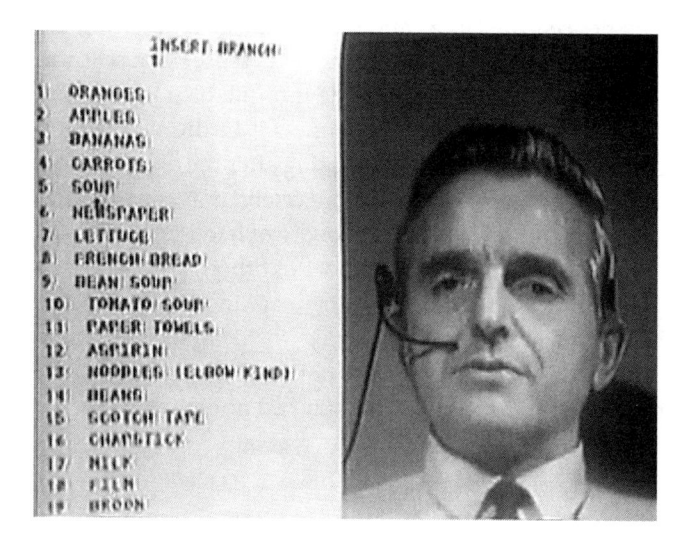

Figure P.4
The moment of invention. Permission granted by SRI International.

to think about newness not as a property, but as a relation? A good strategy is to look for the rhetorical/material practices through which collectives and things are translated as individuals and objects. Within this repertoire, as many of my technoscience studies colleagues have pointed out, the *demonstration* is a pivotal event.

I'm thinking about demos because I just got back (well, in 1998 actually) from an event at Stanford University celebrating the thirtieth anniversary of "The Mother of All Demos." You can watch the original demo yourself online—here's the description:

On December 9, 1968, Douglas C. Engelbart and the group of 17 researchers working with him in the Augmentation Research Center at Stanford Research Institute in Menlo Park, CA, presented a 90-minute live public demonstration of the online system, NLS [standing for oN-Line System], they had been working on since 1962. The public presentation was a session of the Fall Joint Computer Conference held at the Convention Center in San Francisco, and it was attended by about 1,000 computer professionals. ... The mouse was only one of many innovations demonstrated that day, including hypertext, object addressing and dynamic file linking, as well as shared-screen collaboration involving two persons at different sites communicating over a network with audio and video interface.

To characterize the demo as pivotal is not to say that its success is guaranteed; on the contrary, the demo system is always a shaky proposition that has to prove itself in and through its enactment, often in the face of a skeptical audience. At this event in 1998, a panel of speakers—specifically, those who worked with Engelbart to stage the event in 1968—are reflecting on the experience—the labors and the thrills—of configuring the system and making it work on the day of the demo. Which makes sense because it was on that day, I'm suggesting, that the assemblage was made into the oN-Line System, not only by its makers but by those who assembled to witness it in the Convention Center. So how, then, is the system demo positioned as coming after the object, rather than as its founding moment? Other speakers at the Stanford celebration 30 years later recall The Demo's effects. Alan Kay, famous as an early visionary of hand-held computing and credited (along with Abraham Lincoln and a number of others) with the edict that the best way to predict the future is to invent it, puts it succinctly: "This demo changed my life. I was never the same afterwards." If we take the demonstration seriously, it shifts the settlement of questions of newness from objects to events, and to the marks that the latter leave on their participants, both human and nonhuman.

Yours from the Valley,
The anthropologist of technoscience

From the Future Archaeologist—Message 5

We three are kin, it seems. Coastal creatures that thrive at the edge, that seek the periphery where infrastructures of power are more fragile, and can be hacked; here at the edge, the undersea fiber-optic sound of Important Emails from the center can be "transduced," as Adrian Mackenzie (2002) or Stefan Helmreich (2007) might say.

Figure P.5
The Ring of Brodgar stone circle, Orkney. Aaron Watson (CC:BY-NC).

Here, at the periphery, there can still be dragons.

After all, those at the center seek the leading edge, the bleeding edge.

If the future has a place, then it is here, at the edge, where things change form, land to water. The future is a seascape.

But it was ever thus.

Archaeologists, such as Mike Parker Pearson, cite the Ring of Brodgar stone circle as the origin for the design of Stonehenge near London (Parker Pearson et al. 2007). Six thousand years at the leading edge of design and technology. Still there with the European Marine Energy Centre, and the world visiting, eager to learn of its wave and tide energy devices, those moving monuments in the sea.

Orkney has a timescape that is not in the technopresent like Silicon Valley, dear anthropologist of technoscience.

Orkney has a timescape that is mixed—diffracted, since we are borrowing from Donna Haraway (1994). Walk with me through the contemporary heritage management of a World Heritage Site, through a farmer's field sown with ancient organic wheat, and hear your footsteps echo over the concrete remains of a forgotten national wind industry.

The poet George Mackay Brown knew it when he wrote: "The Orkney imagination is haunted by time."

What if "The Mother of All Demos" had taken place here at the edge, where the technopresent is diffracted?

Do such demos require a center, a pivot, a fulcrum, around which to spin outward?

My friends at the European Marine Energy Centre, a test site for demo-ing, would say that it can be otherwise.

We three are kin in other ways, too. We are attentive to collaboration at the edge. You, collective designer, speak of democracy and participation. Here in Orkney some call it 'Orkney PLC', a Public Limited Company, not to invoke cold capitalism, but to invoke the warmth of a company, of people working together to pay the bills, of islanders who know that what we talk about when we talk about money is a future.

Orkney PLC has been around for a while, too.

The stone circles were community-building projects, the archaeologist Colin Richards (2004) argues. Each family, each company in the old sense, brought a stone to a place. Not monument-making but Orkney-PLC-making.

We are still haunted by those community-builders. Most islands have a community development trust with wind turbines that turn fierce tear-your-car-door-off-its-hinges weather into a bank balance for the island community. If the British Crown, owners of the sea, would let them, they'd do the same with wave and tide energy. But the sea is not a local resource, like the stones on shore. Step from the farmer's field into the Atlantic Ocean, get your feet wet, and here there be vast, European Union monsters in the deep. Ask any fisherman.

This far from Brussels, this far from Silicon Valley, you have to work hard or you will sail off the edge of the map and no one will notice. The infrastructure of everyday living gets thin here. One big storm and the lights go out, the Internet goes out. An island community knows the length of copper that thins down their data.

Infrastructures are imagined by the center as centralizing forces. It would be cheaper, more efficient, for us all to live in London or Los Angeles or Beijing. Less copper, fewer oil pipelines, reduced leakage from the water system.

But what might centrifugal infrastructure look like? An infrastructure that was designed to force things to the edge, to the periphery? So that it took work for the center to pull it in?

We three should talk.

We three are kin.

From the Collective Designer—Message 6

dear designboat fellow travelers

i get the point from the valley

that demos are

what make the objects travel

but then again

is not "the mother of all demos"

literally the people

political collective things

and publics in the making?

for the scandinavian

collective designer

this public thing by preference

takes the form of prototyping

in "agonistic" "living labs"

as local activities

collaboratively "rehearsing futures"

making and composing

"matters of concern"

maybe these "living labs"

as performed here by the sound

are more like

the "centrifugal infrastructures"

suggested from the island

then central to such "living labs"

as marginalized and designerly

"infrastructuring" intra-actions

are immigrants like jila moradi

and the herrgård's women's association

counseling on violence in the home

bitterly struggling

for recognition by the city

of their modest but beautiful design

and social innovation prototype

a collective of

displaced and resourceful women

producing catering services

for unaccompanied refugee children

a great offer

the city wasted as of now

another controversial thing

of social innovation

is the design and recomposing

of the city buses

from private advertisement planks

to public places and hubs

for musical exchange and reproduction

as appropriated by

"the voice and face of the street"

a movement of youngsters

from the projects

futures are also being prototyped

and value production reassessed

by "free labor" and in commons

in maker spaces like fabriken

situated in an abandoned shipyard building

opening up and collaboratively exploring

the secret workshop of production

drawing together open software,

electronics, bikes, and textile

in do-it-yourself and craft intra-actions

the collective designer

also takes part in "agonistic" things

not always with a happy ending

like in exploring

new forms of governance

and publics in the making

in designing a city social incubator

drawing together

grassroots movements

local social entrepreneurs

ngos and civil servants

venture capital and politicians

collaboratively prototyping

a future thing to implement

a distributed incubator

out there in the projects

where the action and the demos are

but so far business is as usual

hegemonic power opted out

and left the common thing

implementing their own

incubator vision

a central market driven

new jobs generator

infrastructuring and making things

in cultural production

is neither without friction

in creative class struggles

there is marginalization

but also future-making tactics

things countering capital and state

like the small indie team

behind the film productions

"nasty old people" and

"granny's dancing on the table"

that by crowd-financing

through the "pirate bay"

and collaborating

with the public

in the making

made their dream come through

in the margin

in rural places

there are also demos

coming together through

"centrifugal infrastructures"

like "threads"

a mobile sewing circle

patchworking

traditional craft and mobile phones

stitching together

matters of concern

and prototyping

emerging publics in the making

these are but a few examples

for contemplation

of collective design

and marginal futures

as being made at this location

they may raise questions of power

and design agency distribution

across humans and nonhumans

but there should be more to it

than acts of design delegations

because collective design

it seems

becomes in the very making

in everyday intra-actions

in comings together

in controversial

collaborative composing

preferably performed as

things of design

more kin to ancient political assemblies

on the island and around the sound

than to the new speak of innovation

and the modern object of design?

from the sound

your collective designer

(part of)

From the Anthropologist of Technoscience—Message 7

Dear future archaeologist and collective designer (part of),

I'm inspired by our mailboat exchange to think about questions of time, and how it folds into the work of making the problems for which design offers us its solutions. Here are two images to get us started.

On the left we see Brokaw Road, in San Jose, California, in the first wave of European-American settlement of the valley now known for its silicon, but then famously a place of agricultural abundance, called Santa Clara since its colonization. On the right we see the same place just over 100 years later, in roughly the present moment. I'm making a contrast in setting these two images side by side, of course—a contrast between an agrarian past and a (post?)industrial present, materialized in the shady greenness of organic plant life and the bare grayness of concrete. But I'm most taken by the sign that invites us to "Enter Here' through a door that will grant us access to the home of "Excess Solutions" ("E$"), a reseller of surplus electronics equipment. How did it come to be that we have an excess of solutions? What is the process by which innovation creates its problems, first the need for information technologies, now their disposal?

As we know, disposal is not actually about making things go away, but rather their displacement. The recycling of highly toxic e-waste is a globally though asymmetrically distributed industry, and, as Myra Hird reminds us, landfill is far from an inert source

Figure P.6
An excess of solutions (left: public domain; right: Flickr user mightyohm CC:BY-SA).

of environmental destruction; it is always also a blooming site of becoming for other organisms that thrive on what for us is deadly (Hird 2010, 36–39). But in design imaginaries the present is characterized not by its excesses (that's left to the environmentalists), but rather in terms of the lack or emptiness to which innovation is a necessary and urgent response. The mark of a technological society, Andrew Barry (2001, 201) has suggested, is an orientation that privileges change and then figures change as technological innovation. Innovation, in turn, is embedded within a cultural imaginary that posits a world that is always lagging, always in need of being brought up to date through the intercessions of those trained to shape it—a world in need of design.

Postcolonial scholarship in anthropology, in science and technology studies, and in related fields makes it clear that, far from a universal good, the valorization of newness is a local preoccupation of certain actors invested in particular forms of property, within specific regimes of commodity capitalism. A more performative metaphysics of the new makes it evident that, just as translation invariably produces difference, novelty requires imitation or likenesses to familiar forms. Homi Bhabha (1994, 227) directs our attention to the indeterminate spatiality and temporality of the "in-between" as crucial to a postcolonial figuration of difference—an insight that I take to be generative for thinking about objects as well as subjects, and about relations of old and new so central to discourses of design.

So what if we think about the distance between our islands, valleys, and sounds not as the kind of difference that nostalgia makes, or disenchantment, but in terms of the in-between, and as places and material practices of future-making? "We move into the future," Dorothy Smith writes, "as into a building, the walls, floors and roof of

Prologue   xxxiii

which we put together with one another as we go into it" (1990, 53). This future isn't a temporal period existing somewhere beyond the present, but an effect of discursive and material practices enacted always in the present moment, however much those practices may be haunted by memory or animated by imaginings of things to come. Relocating innovation, as we've explored it together, means putting innovation in its place, in a way that makes evident the multiplicity of places in which different but also potentially related future-making activities occur. (Relocating Innovation is the name of a collaboration among Endre Dányi, Lucy Suchman, and Laura Watts; see http://www.sand14.com/relocatinginnovation/.) This is a strategy that helps us to loosen the grip of unquestioned assumptions regarding what innovation is and where it happens, and to make room for more generative and sustainable forms of future-making.

What does it mean when our dragons turn into machines?

Yours from the Valley,
The anthropologist of technoscience

Figure P.7
The collective designer (part of). Per-Anders Hillgren and Anna Seravalli (CC:BY-NC).

From the Future Archaeologist—Message 8

Collective designer, anthropologist of technoscience (or whoever will intercept this on the predictable lunar tides and Transatlantic currents)...

You speak of dragons turning into machines, anthropologist of technoscience, but which is more mythical, I wonder? I am thinking of Arthur C. Clarke's famous law: any sufficiently advanced technology is indistinguishable from magic. To which I add my own corollary: any magical machine is indistinguishable from advanced technology. Both dragons and magical machines have mythic power, they fly wireless only when severed from their infrastructures, designers, e-waste, and all that keeps them aloft.

Here are the remains of a myth—one perhaps familiar to you, collective designer. It will take you only a few minutes to hike through the cattle and grass, up the hill of Costa Head on the northeast coast of Orkney mainland. There you will look out over the blue sound to the other islands, and on the bog and heather summit you will find a derelict stone shed and a concrete plinth, as though once there were a statue. And you would be right. Here was a monument in 1955. For a while it was a world first in wind energy—a 100-kilowatt wind turbine machine that stood for two years, until the Orkney storms tangled the metal framework. For a while it was the UK's test site for a new renewable energy industry. Now it is a future archaeology. "We blinked," a worried proponent of another new renewable energy test site says. Now it is Denmark that is the home of wind energy.

When I walked up Costa Head, and stood before those cracked stone foundations, I wrote an *in memoriam* and tied it there:

mica encrusted
tomb
to an unknown
turbine

There is no disposal here, only decay. Something mythic, a future renewable energy industry, flew here, for a while, and is now as much heritage as the 5,000-year-old Ring of Brodgar stone circle. Futures are effects of material practices, you say, anthropologist of technoscience. And standing here, in the remains of a future, I agree. Futures leave residues, as I said in my first message. I collect these residues, these fragments, and reconstruct them. Sometimes residues are dispersed. E-waste is just the relocation of archaeological stratigraphy. Machines can be imagined as seascapes, their manufacture from so many parts and materials, and their disposal into different parts, stretched over the sea, from where they are designed to where they decay.

Although drawing on archaeological theory, I am kin to science studies, and I live by the motto "It could be otherwise." I am not interested in reconstructing some nationalistic story of the innovation ownership of wind energy. But I am interested when I talk to the director of the European Marine Energy Centre—the one who did not just say "We blinked" but said it to those who have responsibility for choosing whether to repeat the story for marine energy.

Along with my ethnographic collaborations that remake this past, such as the conversations with the director of EMEC, I collaborated with the poet Alec Finlay and the photographer Alistair Peebles to reconstruct Costa Head online as poetry, as photography, as memorial, as labels tied in the wind (http://skying-blog.blogspot.dk/2011/07/costa-head-orkney.html).

Futures are mythic machines, social and material, designed and made. Reconstructing them is to remember them, to give breath and flame to them. So it can be otherwise. …

The future archaeologist

Figure P.8
View from Costa Head, Orkney, including memorial poem by Laura Watts (CC:BY-NC).

From the Anthropologist of Technoscience—Message 9

Dear collective designer (part of) and future archaeologist

I've left the Valley myself (a purely topographical descriptor for a place transformed into a sprawling cityscape) and moved north to the mountains of British Columbia, so my reports are now retrospective but I hope still timely.

It's perhaps a testimonial to the (re)productive success of Silicon Valley that futures everywhere are now figured (at least by those who imagine themselves as universal future makers) as centers of the IT and media industries, home to an entrepreneurial creative class. Or at least that's the subtext of policy documents, with their apparently unquestioned acceptance of the inevitability of capitalist (rather than post-capitalist) politics. This is a market logic in which proper modes of relation are competitive ones (however much winning might necessitate collaboration), and success in one place requires failures elsewhere.

In Silicon Valley, democracy is taken for granted (as the brand trademarked in 1776 by the United States of America). One consequence is that discussion of the politics of design and innovation are silenced. In this respect, with a few notable exceptions, the Valley is in danger of becoming increasingly marginal (perhaps a good thing?) as it falls behind in the difficult, practical work of crafting durably heterogeneous collectives. The latter requires building long-term relations across the fault lines of social networks. This kind of making is about decentering design, in the sense that designers move outside of their own research-and-development enclosures and in the sense that professional design becomes, if still necessary, not a sufficient practice for future-making.

as ever,
The anthropologist of technoscience

From the Collective Designer—Message 10

dear future archaeologist and anthropologist of technoscience

this is your collective designer

once again by the shore

now contemplating

the gentle lapping of the waves

it is summer in the city

and here up north

those of us that are privileged enough

go to the sea or to the countryside

to enjoy our short summer

with its long light nights

this is also the time to finally get to grips

with some of the books that have piled up

during a hectic working year

this year besides moby dick

god, nature, ocean and the universe

i also grapple with a manuscript

filled with marginal notes

close to my home and heart

exploring design and innovation

as being made by citizens and colleagues

a heterogeneous collective

formerly known as users and designers

now maybe as makers of futures

multiple futures—matters of concern

this manuscript

on future-making practices

localized and peripheral

often marginalized

by major infrastructures

as well as the mainstream

design and technological innovation

that they challenge

these notes

on designing and the social

on opening production

on emerging publics

on creative class struggles

are the design things

the matters of concern

this immutable mailboat mobile carries

keen to find the shores

of your islands and your valley

do they travel well

do they connect

to design and innovation

to publics in the making

to more democratic futures

being made at your locations?

your collective designer (part of)

References

Barry, Andrew. 2001. *Political Machines: Governing a Technological Society*. Athlone.

Bhabha, Homi. 1994. *The Location of Culture*. Routledge.

Fabian, Johannes. 1983. *Time and the Other: How Anthropology Makes Its Object*. Columbia University Press.

Haraway, Donna. 1994. A Game of Cat's Cradle: Science Studies, Feminist Theory, Cultural Studies. *Configurations* 1:59–71.

Haraway, Donna. 2008. *When Species Meet*. University of Minnesota Press.

Helmreich, Stefan. 2007. An Anthropologist Underwater: Immersive Soundscapes, Submarine Cyborgs, and Transductive Ethnography. *American Ethnologist* 34 (4):621–641.

Hird, Myra. 2010. Meeting with the Microcosmos. *Environment and Planning. D, Society & Space* 28:36–39.

Mackenzie, Adrian. 2002. *Transductions: Bodies and Machines at Speed*. Continuum.

Pearson, Parker, and Ros Cleal Mike, et al. 2007. The Age of Stonehenge. *Antiquity* 81 (313):617–639.

Redfield, Peter. 2002. The Half-Life of Empire in Outer Space. *Social Studies of Science* 32:791–825.

Richards, Colin. 2004. A Choreography of Construction: Monuments, Mobilization and Social Organization in Neolithic Orkney. In *Explaining Social Change: Studies in Honour of Colin Renfrew*, ed. J. Cherry, C. Scarre, and S. Shennan. MacDonald Institute.

Smith, Dorothy. 1990. *Texts, Facts, and Femininity: Exploring the Relations of Ruling*. Routledge.

Tsing, Ann. 2005. *Friction: An Ethnography of Global Connection*. Princeton University Press.

1   Introduction

Pelle Ehn, Elisabet M. Nilsson, and Richard Topgaard

Haur du sitt Malmö haur du sitt varden. This was an underdog slogan two decades ago, when the industrial town of Malmö in the south of Sweden was dismantled and its quarter of a million inhabitants were not doing well. Shipyard and plant closures, high unemployment, class and ethnic segregation, crises—no future. In strong colloquial and ironic language, the slogan said "If you have seen Malmö, you have seen the rest of the world." This is the moment when the march toward a more sustainable city started. The bridge to the continent, the new university, the transformation of the deserted harbor into exemplary sustainable architecture and eco-systems and home for a prosperous IT and media industry, successful culture-, design-, and innovation arenas, and a flourishing entrepreneurial creative class.

The international media often depict the city of Malmö less favorably. Sporadic riots in the most vulnerable districts, and numerous gang-related and criminal-network-related killings, form a picture of a violent multi-ethnic segregated town. A perhaps more nuanced scenario is given by the Kommission för ett socialt hållbart Malmö (Commission for a Socially Sustainable Malmö), a group of researchers and practitioners who have been investigating living conditions in the city for two years (Malmökommissionen 2013). They see innovative creativity and the potential in a multicultural city with people from nearly 170 countries, but also deep inequalities, high unemployment, and alienation. The citizens of Malmö have become healthier, and life conditions have improved, but the polarization is increasing. If you live in the low-income and high-unemployment neighborhoods, your life expectancy is five years less than in other parts of the city. The same holds for citizens with shorter versus longer education.

To "close the gap" in health, welfare, and justice, which is fundamental to becoming a socially sustainable city, they suggest a "social investment policy." All of the many suggestions they have come up with to tackle the deep inequalities focus on investments in people that go far beyond a traditional economic growth perspective. They recommend more democratic forms of innovation and governance through citizen participation. They also recommend the building of knowledge alliances between industry and the university, underlining the inclusion of citizens, civil society, and civil servants in those alliances.

This proud but torn city is the context and the main focus of the research on and the experiments in innovation, design, and democracy discussed in this book, and it is where most of the stories told are situated. Furthermore, the interventions conducted and the stories told in the various chapters are very much in line with the mission and vision of the Commission for a Socially Sustainable Malmö and the challenges to which it has pointed.

The authors are all researchers associated with the new university situated in the prosperous Western Harbor area, the turf of the creative class. However, the stories are not primarily about new technology, economic growth, and scalability, but about possible futures for the people who have chosen to engage in changing their conditions. Typically, they are located in the less favored multi-ethnic districts of the city. Whether the designs and innovations concern local services, cultural productions, arenas for public discourse, or technological platforms, the approach is participative, collaborative, and engaging. The starting point is not the search for yet another "killer application," but everyday activities and challenges in people's lives. The main actors are grassroots organizations, non-governmental organizations, and neighborhoods gathering around issues of concern to them. Still, some of the participatory practices, in exemplary ways, travel far and wide through traditional, as well as new, technologies and media.

The stories do not suggest that "if you have seen Malmö, you have seen the rest of the world," but we are convinced that to be able to understand mechanisms behind design and innovation we must situate these practices (Suchman 2002). However, many places in the world face similar challenges. By situating our stories of innovation, design, and democracy, we hope to make them relevant in other places, and we hope that they may travel far and well. *Haur du sitt Malmö haur du sitt varden.*

Values of design and innovation

"Innovation" has become one of the buzzwords of our times, in the public debate as well as in economic and political agendas. Entrepreneurs are being celebrated as if they were rock stars, start-up companies are featured in popular magazines, politicians, executives, and decision makers are forming strategic plans to encourage creative forces and to boost innovation. Less discussed is what actually counts as successful innovation, and how it is being defined and measured. How do things become perceived as "new" and thought of as innovations? Stories that are being framed as "successful" tend, primarily, to be connected to the business world, with a focus on more, faster, larger. Is making it to the market the only thing that really counts?

The discourse about innovation seems, however, to be rather repetitive and uninventive (Suchman et al. 2009). What images of innovation do, in fact, serve as bases for decision makers and policy makers when they formulate standards and legislation that regulate directions, define boundaries, and set the scene for possible futures? What stories about innovation are being told, and by whom?

Design, the sibling of innovation, has received similar notoriety. Design thinking is today a much-favored management approach (Martin 2009; Nussbaum 2009), just as attractive as the creative class (Florida 2003) was a few years ago. By design, we have the potential to tackle major societal problems and to find solutions to fundamental problems of sustainability and survival (Brown 2009; Mau 2004). But who participates in these design endeavors, and is design only about technological change (Barry 2001)?

Much of the hope associated with design and innovation is certainly directed toward the genius of invention—the creative signature designer and the equally creative and omnipotent entrepreneur turning ideas into successful business—but also toward ordinary people, who, as users or consumers, are increasingly seen as potential co-creators (Pralahad and Krishnan 2008). One inspiration for this perspective is the work put forward by Eric von Hippel and his colleagues in management science (von Hippel 2005; von Hippel et al. 2011). Having observed that user-driven and consumer-driven innovations match, and in some countries even exceed, corresponding corporate R&D investments, they call for a paradigm shift.

There is a genuine call for innovation through user-centered design, and even a belief that innovation is getting democratized. At the same time, inventive as it may seem, this new paradigm is surprisingly traditional and managerial. The main challenge put forward is still how large corporations can harvest users' and consumers' innovations into safe and profitable mass-market products. Certainly, cheap production tools and Internet resources for marketing now make it possible for a young man (in most cases) with brave ideas to become a successful entrepreneur without the backing of a large firm, but is that enough to support the claim that innovation has been democratized?

This book is based on the premise that user-driven design and innovation is an approach with great potential, both for producing value and for democratizing such production. We share the observation that users and consumers already are important producers and creators of value, but we believe that the question of what counts as values and for whom should be opened up. We share the ideal of democratizing innovation, but we do so beyond the liberal ideal of the "free individual that can become anything he wants," thus acknowledging that questions of democracy also are power struggles about distribution of resources and rights in which the voices and values of more peripheral but important groups may remain unheard and may not be taken into account.

Current managerial ideology embraces the crowd as a source of innovation—for example in the form of user-driven innovation, crowdsourcing and crowdfunding, and focus-group testing—with a strong rhetoric of accessibility and participation as keys to democratizing innovation. All this is often, however, done from the perspective of the successful corporation and unaltered market logic, which privileges particular crowds and particular places as centers of innovation (Suchman 2008). In this book, we challenge this logic of innovation by exploring the potential of interventions and perspectives that demonstrate a repertoire of situated practices of *future-making*—that is, multiple futures imagined and made locally, in heterogeneous communities, and with marginalized publics (Björgvinsson et al. 2010). Hence, we are exploring more inclusive, collective, and public approaches.

Beyond business as usual

This book tells stories about design and innovation that go beyond business as usual and the seemingly dominating perception of what are counted as successful innovations. Alternative moments of inventions are highlighted, and overlooked innovators and entrepreneurs are acknowledged and put in the spotlight. Thus, these stories represent a critical investigation of the prevailing situation, but not primarily as a conceptual critique. Instead, the focus is on exploring alternatives, on the controversies that surface, and on composing together in and around controversial things (Latour 2010; Binder et al. 2011).

The authors are researchers from the School of Arts and Communication and Medea Collaborative Media Initiative at Malmö University, a digital Bauhaus that for at least ten years has been exploring user-driven design and open innovation, typically with a participatory design approach. (See, for example, Ehn 1998, Nilsson and Topgaard 2012; Löwgren and Reimer 2013.)

The chapters represent a wide spectrum of design and innovation processes, which are generating values that are not easy to measure when applying today's scorecards for successful innovation. The stories exemplify how alternative innovative forces, way beyond the general assumption of what entrepreneurs look like, can become a resource that generate societal value, and contribute to sustainable future-making. However, the book is not a collection of success stories. On the contrary, all of them open up controversies.

The cases and stories are collected under four themes, announced by the titles of the book's four parts.

Designing conditions for the social
As has already been mentioned, the idea that design, especially participatory design, can play a major role in innovations in the everyday life of people is gaining more and more momentum. Under the design umbrella, we find both market-driven social entrepreneurs replacing the role of the welfare state and designers participating in bottom-up formations of collaborative services and creative communities. Our stories are of the latter kind, showing capabilities to improve situations, but also problematic situations

and democratic dilemmas. In chapter 3, we meet a group of immigrant women struggling to be seen and respected by the city and the Swedish society when, as a collective, they are developing and performing collaborative services such as caring for refugee children. In chapter 4, we consider the dilemmas encountered when trying to design, from the bottom up, an incubator for social innovation.

Opening production—design and commons

Makerspaces and fabrication laboratories (fab labs) may be seen as ways to democratize innovation and production by extending open-source strategies into the production of, for instance, open hardware. Fab labs are often seen as open-innovation contexts in which lead users can develop innovation that may become commercial solutions from which companies can profit. But they may also be seen as platforms for broader participation and new ways of collaborative engagement in design and innovation, pointing at alternative forms of user-driven production. The three cases discussed in this part of the book range from experiences with setting up and running a heterogeneous makerspace (chapter 6), to a more artistically oriented lab (chapter 7), to the development of the open-hardware movement (chapter 8). A central question reflected upon in the chapters is in what ways the examples point at robust enough alternatives to business as usual and market-driven production and innovation.

Creative class struggles

In today's innovation discourse, creative industries and the creative class are often seen as major driving forces, foregrounding their economic value production and how they can help brand a city (Florida 2003). The chapters in this part of the book focus on participatory cultural production, especially the conditions for small and independent cultural actors. The creative class is analyzed as being far from homogeneous and as characterized by internal class struggles, displaying complex relations between media industry, the state, and cultural workers. More specifically, chapter 10 explores cultural commons as a foundation for independent and participatory film-making, chapter 11 explores the conditions for grassroots journalism, and chapter 12 takes a closer look at how creative industries' managers look at design, participation, and innovation.

Emerging publics

Design and innovation involving users and consumers, by their very nature, become more and more public. Consequently, the production sphere merges with the public sphere, which traditionally has been the main democratic arena. Conditions for participation become not only a production imperative, but also a predicament for a more inclusive democratic society. The stories that are told in this part of the book explore opportunities and dilemmas in the creation of new kinds of public engagement under these socio-technical conditions. Publics are, with reference to the pragmatist philosopher John Dewey (1927), thought of in the plural and as formed around issues or matters of concern, rather than as crowds to be sourced or counted. The inquiries into such publics, dealing with access to public space and democratic participation, focus on hip-hop youngsters making their music public on the city buses and girls that through skating appropriate the streets and abandoned places of Malmö (chapter 14), sewing circles in rural Sweden where participants embroider mobile-phone text messages and find mundane ways to engage in politics (chapter 15), and activists live-streaming videos of police violence from Tahrir Square in Cairo (chapter 16).

Each of the four parts of the book also features an industry case, which is somewhat different in perspective and style from the other chapters. Two of the industry cases can be described as entrepreneurial reflections on controversial issues encountered when trying to democratize technology. One of these cases involves a small media company enabling citizens to broadcast live video from wherever to whomever (chapter 16); the other is an inside story about controversies associated with making production hardware open to and accessible by the general public (chapter 8). These two cases expose, in different ways, societal and economic forces that are in play when business as usual is challenged by attempts to democratize technology. The third industry case takes a closer look at the creative class as represented by managers in the media and creative industries (chapter 12). What are their perspectives on innovation, participation, and democracy? How deep is their love for democratizing innovation? Part I of the book, the part on design and social innovation, doesn't really have an industry case, but instead has a chapter dealing with the circumstance that the "powerful stranger" from local industry and government, if challenged, has the power to opt out of any collaborative attempt to democratize innovation processes, and thereby independently continue to conduct business as usual (chapter 4).

The book focuses on stories and reflections on practical interventions and doesn't provide a unified theoretical framework for inquiring into design, innovation, and future-making. There are, however, recurring concepts, echoing the prologue, that indicate an orientation, and each of the four parts has an introductory chapter that frames the cases, lays out the issues, and provides some basic concepts for reflecting upon the experiences of innovation, design, and democracy. Quite a few of the basic concepts pertain to multiple themes and multiple chapters. What follows is a short introduction to some of the book's central ideas and references. One such reference is to Scandinavian participatory design, as contemplated by the collective designer (part of) in the prologue. The other major reference is to science and technology studies pondered upon in the prologue by the future archaeologist and the anthropologist of technoscience.

Scandinavian participatory design

Participatory design is a cornerstone of the practice and the theory of the interventions reflected upon by the various authors. For an overview, see the different chapters in *The Routledge Handbook of Participatory Design* (Simonsen and Robertson 2013).

Participatory design started in Scandinavia in the early 1970s as action-research collaborations with local trade unions at the workplace (Sandberg 1976), challenging the use of technology and the management prerogative to define what may count as innovation (Bjerknes et al. 1987; Ehn 1988). Since then, participatory design has been about alternative futures. By being involved in the practice of groups in society, it has, through design practice, endeavored to support democratic changes.

Practically, participatory design started as local knowledge production, typically through collaborative prototyping in struggles about the design, implementation, and use of computers in Scandinavian workplaces (it was then known as the collective resource approach) (Bjerknes et al. 1987). Theoretically, participatory design was done as action-research by appropriating future-workshops methods (Jungk and Müllert 1987), pedagogy-of-the-oppressed tactics (Freire 1970), and object-oriented programming tools (Nygaard and Bergo 1973) into a collaborative prototyping approach. Typically this approach addressed design as "design before use" by involving potential users in the design of their futures (Ehn 2008).

Today, participatory design actions are increasingly taking place beyond the workplace—in public spaces, but also as engagement with non-governmental organizations, grassroots organizations, and other often marginalized groups. This is in line with its democratic tradition, but this new situation also invites researchers and practitioners to re-conceptualize innovation as a form of invention (Barry 1999) and allow them to challenge particular (and often hegemonic) approaches to design and innovation in the corporate workplace.

Local knowledge production and collaborative prototyping are still fundamental to participatory design, but now, typically, this mundane future-making (Suchman et al. 2009) takes place as design in use, not before use, and is often staged to deal constructively with controversies (Mouffe 2000; Latour 2005a).

Science and technology studies

Clearly the book is grounded in values and approaches that have grown out of Scandinavian participatory design, not least the ideas of collaborative prototyping as ways to cross boundaries between different and diverse actors and communities of practice (Lave and Wenger 1991), but there are also clear influences from other fields, especially science and technology studies and feminist techno-science.

The authors make frequent references to Bruno Latour and other actor-network-theory scholars and their suggestions for re-assembling the social as a collective of humans and non-humans (Latour 2005b), to the thing as politics (Latour 2005a), and to a compositionist manifesto that challenges designers to draw things together and work with matters of concern (Latour 2010). The influence of ideas about infrastructuring and about boundary objects as processes and vehicles for design across time and stakeholders, as suggested by Susan Lee Star and colleagues (Star 1989; Star and Ruhleder 1996; Star and Bowker 2002), is also prominent. Several of the chapters have been inspired by the reflections on practice, situated knowledge, and accountability, and on the agency of artifacts and other non-humans, of the feminist techno-science researchers Donna Haraway (1991, 2007) and Lucy Suchman (1987, 2011).

Owing to this theoretical orientation, this book is really not about user-driven design and innovation. In theory and in practice, users are much too often not only taken hostage by neo-liberal capitalism but also patronized by advocates of human-centered design. In social science, it is becoming clear that society is not just social but also material (Latour 2005b). The neglected objects strike back—just think of global environmental crises. With design it might be just the same; we know design cannot be reduced to the shaping of dead objects. But humans should not be reduced to users or to individual subjects living external to objects. The social sciences have had to acknowledge that society is a collective of humans and non-humans. Design may have to do away with both users and objects to remain socially and politically relevant.

Thinking of the interventions discussed in this book as democratic design experiments will shed some light on the work that some of the above-mentioned concepts do.

The ways participation and representation are addressed throughout the book may be viewed as experiments in merging and going beyond political parliaments and scientific laboratories (Latour 2005a). One broad idea that has attracted attention in the field of design research in general, and also in this book, is the re-invention of the ancient Nordic thing (Latour 2005a; Binder et al. 2011).

The etymology of the word 'thing' is of importance to appreciating the re-invention of the thing and to understanding design, innovation, and democracy as acted out between the parliament and the lab. It exposes how the modern understanding of things as objects—entities of matter—was preceded by a more complex socio-material understanding of things as governing assemblies, rituals, and places—an understanding that dealt with matters of concern, with governing of conflicts and controversies, and with the making of decisions. The present-day notion of *design things* (Binder et al. 2011) as explored in this book is inspired by this heterogeneous form of governance and making.

A pragmatic form of the design thing as an experiment in democratic design and innovation is the living lab, a kind of participatory laboratory "in the wild." Living labs come in many shapes, ranging from market-oriented labs for user testing of new products to long-term engagements between designers and diverse groups of citizens and their concerns.

The living labs in Malmö have been of the latter kind and have had three partly overlapping orientations. One lab focuses on experiments in social innovation in neighborhoods in collaboration with local non-governmental organizations and other citizen groups. Issues of citizen participation and controversies related to governance (Swyngedouw 2005; Stigendal 2011) turn out to be of central importance to these experiments, including the tactics of "friendly hacking" (Jégou et al. 2013). (Experiences from this lab are the basis for the reflections in part I and one of the cases in part IV.)

Another lab explores makerspaces as venues where crafts and do-it-yourself practices may challenge more market-driven production processes. Here, the concept of commons (Ostrom 1990; Bauwens 2006) figures in investigations of the potential for economies of scope based on more open forms of production. (These concepts are developed further in part II.)

The third lab also has an orientation toward exploring commons, but in this case the emphasis is on cultural commons, creative class struggles, and ways in which cultural producers lacking strong corporate backing or state support and financing are marginalized by standardized networks or infrastructures (Star 1991). (Experiences from this lab are the basis for the reflections in part III.)

In all the labs, and throughout the book, issues of innovation, design, and democracy are dealt with as processes and events of thinging and infrastructuring rather than as isolated projects. It is argued that the project frame is too narrow and that long-term relations of trust, which is very far from user-testing in labs, have to be built and maintained. The authors attend to this challenge through experimenting with diverse forms of building trust, thinging, and infrastructuring—beyond simple networking—by, for example, sewing together and cutting apart through patchworking or through rhizomatic collisions.

These thinging or infrastructuring activities do not presuppose consensus among the participating stakeholders, but are inspired by the idea of agonistic democracy (Mouffe 2000), aiming to find ways to turn antagonistic relations into adversarial productive and more democratic interactions and outcomes.

These kinds of collaborations are, however, not activities without risk for the participants, marginalized or not. Here the word 'marginal'—as in mentions of those marginalized by hegemonic infrastructures—should be understood not in an absolute sense but rather as a movement from the periphery, striving to acquire a more legitimate position in intertwined communities of practice (Lave and Wenger 1991). Not all participants have the power to opt out of the thinging and go their own way if their basic interests are threatened, and others may not have resources enough to hang in even if they want to continue collaborating.

This is also a challenge for designers and researchers. There is no *a priori* legitimate center from which activities of thinging and infrastructuring can be viewed, governed, or made. Consequently, designers and researchers are stakeholders among many, having to find legitimate peripheral participation and accountable positioning (Lave and Wenger 1991; Suchman 2002).

Travel guide to futures?

If you have seen Malmö, you have seen the rest of the world. Taking this more as a question than as a claim, we organized a design thing at the 2012 international Participatory Design Conference in Denmark. This thing included, in addition to the local cases from Malmö and the challenges discussed in this book, similar future-making experiences with, for example, retired teachers at a Beijing university, young street vendors in Bogota, and collaboration between detention officers and inmates in a Danish prison. During the thing, an archipelago of futures was mapped out from these different design and innovation experiences, and the do-it-yourself zine *Travel Guide to the Futures* was constructed, exploring proximities of some futures, and distances of others, as well as connections and resistances between these multiple forms of innovation practice (Ehn et al. 2012).

This archipelago of futures deviates dramatically from the future colonized by the technological frontrunners and the innovation centers of the world, like in the Silicon Valley, reported on in the prologue by the anthropologist of technoscience. In the stories told in this book, there is no single future arriving first and fastest, only multiple, heterogeneous, and controversial futures that are in the making, composed through the networking, the many entanglements, the ongoing thinging and infrastructuring, the patchworking and collision of intersecting rhizomes, and quite mundane design and innovation activities (Suchman 2008).

The stories are not success stories of innovation, design, and democracy. The stance is more inquiring, perhaps even with a dash of Nordic melancholia, but still with hope for more democratic futures in the making. There is no straightforward travel guide to the futures, but there certainly is a claim that these design and innovation activities—emanating from the people in the city of Malmö—should be legitimate parts of an emerging, controversial, and expanding archipelago of futures beyond business as usual, a place worth traveling both to and from.

References

Barry, Andrew. 1999. Invention and Inertia. *Cambridge Anthropology* 21 (3): 62–70.

Barry, Andrew. 2001. *Political Machines: Governing a Technological Society*. Athlone.

Bauwens, Michel. 2006. The Political Economy of Peer Production. *Post-Autistic Economics Review* 37 (3):33–44.

Binder, Thomas, Giorgio De Michelis, Pelle Ehn, Giulio Jacucci, Per Linde, and Ina Wagner. 2011. *Design Things*. MIT Press.

Bjerknes, Gro, Pelle Ehn, and Morten Kyng, eds. 1987. *Computers and Democracy: A Scandinavian Challenge*. Avebury.

Björgvinsson, Erling, Pelle Ehn, and Per-Anders Hillgren. 2010. Participatory Design and Democratizing Innovation. Paper presented at Participatory Design Conference, Sydney.

Brown, Tim. 2009. *Change by Design: How Design Thinking Transforms Organizations and Inspires Innovation*. HarperCollins.

Dewey, John. 1927. *The Public and Its Enemies*. Holt.

Ehn, Pelle. 1988. *Work-Oriented Design of Computer Artifacts*. Erlbaum.

Ehn, Pelle. 1998. Manifesto for a Digital Bauhaus. *Digital Creativity* 9 (4): 207–216.

Ehn, Pelle. 2008. Participation in Design Things. Paper presented at Participatory Design Conference, Bloomington, Indiana.

Ehn, Pelle, Elisabet M. Nilsson, Richard Topgaard, and Laura Watts eds. 2012. Travel Guide to the Futures. Medea, Malmö University (http://medea.mah.se/2012/08/pdc-making-futures/).

Florida, Richard. 2003. *The Rise of the Creative Class*. Basic Books.

Freire, Paulo. 1970. *Pedagogy of the Oppressed*. Herder and Herder.

Haraway, Donna J. 1991. Situated Knowledges: The Science Question in Feminism and the Privilege of Partial Perspective. In *Simians, Cyborgs, and Women*, ed. D. Haraway. Routledge.

Haraway, Donna J. 2007. *When Species Meet*. University of Minnesota Press.

Jégou, Francois, Stéphane Vincent, Romain Thévenet, and Anna Lochard. 2013. Friendly Hacking into the Public Sector: Co-Creating Public Policies within Regional Governments. Paper presented at Boundary-Crossing Conference on Co-Design in Innovation, Espoo, Finland.

Jungk, Robert, and Norbert Müllert. 1987. *Future Workshops: How to Create Desirable Futures*. Institute for Social Inventions.

Latour, Bruno. 2005a. From Realpolitik to Dingpolitik or How to Make Things Public. In *Making Things Public*, ed. B. Latour and P. Weibel. MIT Press.

Latour, Bruno. 2005b. *Reassembling the Social: An Introduction to Actor-Network-Theory*. Oxford University Press.

Latour, Bruno. 2010. An Attempt at a Compositionist Manifesto. *New Literary History* 41: 471–490.

Lave, Jean, and Etienne Wenger. 1991. *Situated Learning: Legitimate Peripheral Participation*. Cambridge University Press.

Löwgren, Jonas, and Bo Reimer. 2013. *Collaborative Media: Production, Consumption, and Design Interventions.* MIT Press.

Malmökommissionen. 2013. *Malmös väg mot en hållbar framtid: Hälsa, välfärd och rättvisa.*

Martin, Roger L. 2009. *The Design of Business: Why Design Thinking Is the Next Competitive Advantage.* Harvard Business Review Press.

Mau, Bruce. 2004. *Massive Change: A Manifesto on the Future of Design Culture.* Phaidon.

Mouffe, Chantal. 2000. *The Democratic Paradox.* Verso.

Nilsson, Elisabet, and Richard Topgaard, eds. 2012. *Prototyping Futures.* Medea, Malmö University.

Nussbaum, Bruce. 2009. Design Thinking Battle: Managers Embrace Design Thinking, Designers Reject It (http://www.businessweek.com).

Nygaard, Kristen, and Olav Terje Bergo. 1973. Planlegging, styring og databehandling. Grunnbok for fagbevegelse. Norsk Forlag.

Ostrom, Elinor. 1990. *Governing the Commons.* Cambridge University Press.

Prahalad, C. K., and M. S. Krishnan. 2008. *The New Age of Innovation: Driving Co-Created Value through Global Networks.* McGraw-Hill.

Sandberg, Åke. 1976. *The Limits to Democratic Planning.* Liber.

Simonsen, Jesper, and Toni Robertson. 2013. *The Routledge Handbook of Participatory Design.* Routledge.

Stigendal, Mikael. 2011. Malmö—de två kunskapsstäderna. Kommission för ett socialt hållbart Malmö.

Star, Susan L. 1989. The Structure of Ill-Structured Solutions: Boundary Objects and Heterogeneous Distributed Problem Solving. In *Distributed Artificial Intelligence*, volume 2, ed. L. Gasser and M. Huhns. Morgan Kaufman.

Star, Susan L. 1991. Power, Technology and the Phenomenology of Conventions: On Being Allergic to Onions. In *A Sociology of Monsters*, ed. J. Law. Routledge.

Star, Susan L., and Geoffrey C. Bowker. 2002. How to Infrastructure. In *The Handbook of New Media*, ed. L. Lievrouw and S. Livingstone. Sage.

Star, Susan L., and Karen Ruhleder. 1996. Steps toward an Ecology of Infrastructure: Design and Access for Large Information Spaces. *Information Systems Research* 7 (1): 111–134.

Suchman, Lucy A. 1987. *Plans and Situated Actions: The Problem of Human-Machine Communication.* Cambridge University Press.

Suchman, Lucy. 2002. Located Accountabilities in Technology Production. *Scandinavian Journal of Information Systems* 14 (2): 91–105.

Suchman, Lucy. 2008. Striking Likenesses to Difference. Paper presented at 4S/EASST (annual meeting of Society for Social Studies of Science), Rotterdam.

Suchman, Lucy. 2011. Anthropological relocations and the limits of design. *Annual Review of Anthropology* 40: 1–18.

Suchman, Lucy, Endre Danyi, and Laura Watts. 2009. Relocating Innovation: Places and Material Practices of Futuremaking (http://www.sand14.com/relocatinginnovation/download/RelocatingInnovation_ResearchDescription.pdf).

Swyngedouw, Erik. 2005. Governance Innovation and the Citizen: The Janus Face of Governance-Beyond-the-State. *Urban Studies (Edinburgh, Scotland)* 42 (11):1991–2006.

von Hippel, Eric. 2005. *Democratizing Innovation*. MIT Press.

von Hippel, Eric, Susumu Ogawa, and Jeroen P. J. de Jong. 2011. The Age of the Consumer-Innovator. MIT Sloan Management Review 53 (1): 27–35.

I Designing Conditions for the Social

2 Designing Conditions for the Social

Anders Emilson

In recent years, social innovation has been seen as a way to tackle climate change, aging populations, and social exclusion. The U.S. government (SICP 2012), the European Union (Hubert 2011), the Young Foundation, and the Rockefeller Foundation acknowledge social innovation as important. Nicholls and Murdock (2012, 1–2) consider social innovation to be a "sixth wave" of macro-innovation following more technology-based predecessors: the industrial revolution; steam and railways; steel, electricity, and heavy engineering; oil, automobiles, and mass production; and information and telecommunications. Design as a discipline emerged in parallel to these earlier waves of macro-innovations as a response to the need of adapting technological artifacts to human needs, behaviors and measures. Today, design is also one of the creative disciplines that are active in social innovation. In the next two chapters, we look into cases where design methods are applied to create social innovation and into the emerging design discipline known as *design for social innovation*, sometimes referred to as *social design*. Designers are not alone in this field; social innovations can be created by many methods used by such diverse actors as social entrepreneurs, public servants, commercial companies, or activists. Another characteristic of social innovation that will be emphasized is that it often emerges from collaborations between actors from different sectors and disciplines.

One might ask what design methods have to offer in these constellations of diverse actors. Before looking for an answer, let us acknowledge the fact that design has a long history of being involved in shaping the societies we live in. In Europe, the modern movement of the early twentieth century (most strongly symbolized by the German Bauhaus School, with its roots in the British Arts and Crafts movement and social democracy) strove to improve people's living conditions and to build an equal and peaceful world through the use of mass production and a new modernistic design language. In Sweden, designers and architects were involved in articulating the modern welfare state through the means of urban planning, architecture, furniture, and the design of everyday objects according to modernist principles. We all know that many of these well-intentioned designs can be considered failures, most explicitly exemplified with the demolition of the infamous Pruitt-Igoe housing project in St. Louis in 1972.

Pruitt-Igoe, completed in 1955, consisted of 33 rectangular eleven-story apartment buildings. Its design was based on the modernist International Style invented by Le Corbusier, Walter Gropius, and others in the 1920s and the 1930s. In Sweden, about a million apartments were built between 1965 and 1974 following these modernist design principles. The housing situation in Sweden was similar to that in St. Louis: there was a need to replace overcrowded slums with new housing. But soon, as in Pruitt-Igoe, many (though not all) of these new projects became associated with poverty, segregation, and crime. In 1977 the architectural historian Charles Jenks argued that the demolition of Pruitt-Igoe symbolized the failure and death of modernistic architecture (Bristol 1991, 163). Others argued that not all the blame should be put on architectural design alone, and that social and economic factors should be considered. Katharine Bristol claimed that the exaggerated focus on the designers' responsibility in Pruitt-Igoe had diverted attention from the "institutional or structural sources of public housing problems" and had legitimized the architecture profession by "implying that deeply embedded social problems are caused, and therefore solved, by architectural design" (ibid.).

The real lesson to be learned from Pruitt-Igoe, thus, is not about formal design of an object, but that complex societal challenges call for the kind of participatory and cross-disciplinary work that is discussed in the following two chapters. On the other hand, one cannot ignore the fact that problems in many of these modernistic housing areas remain today. At the time of this writing, there have just been week-long riots in several housing areas in various parts of Stockholm. A few years ago there were riots in Malmö. Some of our collaborators live and work in modernistic housing areas, and some of our work targets present-day challenges in these areas—challenges such as social exclusion, unemployment, and the need for renovation. The question, of course, is "Will we make the same mistakes as the well-intentioned designers and social engineers before us?"

A less well known successor to the socially engaged and "democratic design" characterizing the modernist tradition is the Scandinavian Participatory Design tradition that began in the 1970s. But, as the name indicates, this was different than some idealistic designers and architects that considered themselves experts on how people should live and what products they should consume. Instead of designing *for* people, designers within the participatory design tradition involved the people concerned and designed *with* them, starting from their own experiences and desires. Participatory design originates from the social, political, and civil rights movements of the 1960s and the 1970s, when people "demanded an increased say in the decisions that affected many different aspects of their lives" (Robertson and Simonsen 2012, 3). Influenced by these movements, designers began to claim that "if we are to design the futures we wish to live, then those whose futures are affected must actively participate in the design process" (ibid., 5).

This approach fits well with what Mulgan (2012a) considers to be the underlying ethic of collaboration in social innovation: to act *with* rather than *for*. Or, in the words of President José Manuel Barroso of the European Commission: "In a nutshell, social innovation is for the people and with the people." (Barroso 2011, no paging) Designing *with* people is part of a major shift in innovation (Chesbrough 2003; Leadbeater 2008, 2009), going from closed in-house processes to more open and collaborative ones. Murray, Caulier-Grice, and Mulgan (2010, 6) write that innovation itself should be open and social and "welcoming responses from anyone; involving users at every stage as well as experts, bureaucrats and professionals."

To involve and design *with* actors that represent different positions in society is also the basis for Malmö's Living Lab the Neighborhood, which works with participatory design and social innovation in districts in Malmö marked by social exclusion. In our practice (Björgvinsson and Hillgren 2004; Björgvinsson, Ehn, and Hillgren 2010; Hillgren, Seravalli, and Emilson 2011), we put much emphasis on building long-term relationships and on using prototyping as a way to evoke and explore possibilities and dilemmas. Our activities are based on three methodological ideas:

- to set up *collaborative* design processes where diverse stakeholders with complementary skills work side by side and where mutual respect and learning is supported
- to build *long-term relationships* and trust with stakeholders
- to perform early *prototyping* where possibilities are explored in real-life contexts but where potential dilemmas also are highlighted.

Social innovation often demands multiple perspectives (Murray, Caulier-Grice, and Mulgan 2010; den Ouden and Valkenburg 2011), and we collaborate with nongovernmental organizations, municipalities, and private business partners. Over the years, we have worked with associations, small media and design companies, successful ICT companies, public transport and public broadcasting companies, and municipal departments on projects such as using a mobile phone game to explore marginalized neighborhoods, street journalism by youths, and new collaborative tools for city planning. Often we establish relationships with actors separately to explore possibilities related to their respective interests and agendas, getting multiple starting points for potential projects and innovation. At the same time, we also try to see how different interests might be integrated.

Today, when "co-design" and "working *with* people" have become recurring mantras in both social innovation and in design, we know—through 30 years of experience in the participatory design field—that this is not always easy. Conflicting interests, values, or ways of working often threaten to cause projects to collapse, and at times projects are closed down because the different actors do not match with each other as intended. But, we will argue, this is not a reason for giving up; instead it is a reason to see the matching of people and the creation of constellations as a kind of prototyping process: if one match doesn't work, try another. This could be seen as designing the social conditions of the participatory process and also the core of "infrastructuring" (Björgvinsson, Ehn, and Hillgren 2010)—the building of long-term relationships and the matching of actors with complementary resources.

Concepts such as "infrastructuring," "design things," and "agonism" are both analytical and methodological, and such concepts have been central to our research. They have also been important tools in our work with the creation of social conditions—"networks and relations" (Binder et al. 2011, 157)—in the design process.

By *the social*, we mean the interactions and relations between people who are gathered in a constellation or a design project. By *conditions*, we mean the creation of constellations of actors who take part in a mutual learning process guided by designers using tools such as workshops, scenarios, and prototypes. In this way, we try to explore new challenges for designers that are more about people and networks than about technology and objects. Important issues are how to create trust, how to show respect for the opinions of others, and how to facilitate mutual learning in a constellation. We also want to explore the role of the *social* in networks, creative processes, new business models, and new concepts such as collaborative services and collaborative consumption. At the core is dealing with people with different agendas and values. This has the consequence that the designer needs to have competence in dealing with conflicts, dilemmas, power relations, and politics. While this is nothing new for designers working with participatory design, the challenge with social innovation is the new context in which more heterogeneous actors take part, the "place" is a neighborhood rather than a workplace, and the designed artifact is more likely to be a service, a practice, or an organization than a piece of technology. Let us take a quick look at how design is being applied in the field of social innovation.

The field of social innovation

Social innovation as a field has emerged as existing structures, policies, and tools, both from the market and from the state, have proved inadequate for tackling many of today's social and societal challenges. It is a reaction to the previous dominance of technological and business aspects in innovation policy and practice. Social innovation is also a response to the complexity of present-day societal challenges, such as failing welfare systems, that affect both individuals and society as a whole; therefore, it involves heterogeneous actors across sectors and disciplines. Social innovation can be seen as an umbrella concept covering different ways—such as entrepreneurship, financing, and activism—of responding to social demands and societal challenges.

Social innovation is nothing new—individuals and organizations have always developed new solutions and concepts to address social needs. An early Swedish example of a social innovation, one that later became a public institution, is Barnavårdscentraler (child-care centers). They were started in 1901 by the föreningen Mjölkdroppen (2013) (Milk Drop Association) to help poor mothers to provide their children with nutritious milk. At the time, 10 percent of newborns died because breastfeeding frequency was low. In the 1940s this support for mothers and children was taken over by public child-care centers. Mjölkdroppen is an example of how a small initiative undertaken by an association develops into a public institution; it also shows the importance of civil society in developing social innovations. Other examples of public institutions that were first developed by civil society, and not by the state or the market, are fire brigades and libraries. This historical role of civil society tends to be forgotten in discussions of social innovation. Often the focus is on stronger actors in the private sector (social entrepreneurs, philanthropists) and in the public sector.

There is no single definition of social innovation, and we have experienced difficulty in communicating the concept. In trying to embrace both the breadth and the main ideas of social innovation, we turn to acknowledged researchers in the field.

Murray, Caulier-Grice, and Mulgan (2010, 3) describe social innovation as "new ideas (products, services and models) that simultaneously meet social needs and create new social relationships or collaborations" and as "innovations that are both good for society *and* enhance society's capacity to act." Phills, Deiglmeier, and Miller (2008, 39) emphasize that social innovation is a way to meet needs that would not be met otherwise and to create value that would otherwise not be created; thus, they define social innovation as "a novel solution to a social problem that is more effective, efficient, sustainable, or just than existing solutions and for which the value created accrues primarily to society as a whole rather than private individuals." "A social innovation," they write, "can be a product, production process, or technology (much like innovation in general), but it can also be a principle, an idea, a piece of legislation, a social movement, an intervention, or some combination of them. Indeed, many of the best recognized social innovations, such as microfinance, are combinations of a number of these elements."

According to Westley and Antadze (2010, 2), "social innovations involve institutional and social system change, they contribute to overall social resilience, and they demand a complex interaction between agency and intent and emergent opportunity." They define social innovation as "a complex process of introducing new products, processes or programs that profoundly change the basic routines, resource and authority flows, or beliefs of the social system in which the innovation occurs. Such successful social innovations have durability and broad impact."

As the definitions above suggest, and as Nicholls and Murdock (2012) show, social innovation exists on different levels: on an incremental level (with a focus on products and services), on an institutional level (with a focus on markets), and on a disruptive level (with a focus on politics and on system change). Hubert (2011, 43) frames social innovation in a *process dimension* (in which new forms of organization and interactions are developed to respond to social issues) and an *outcome dimension* (in which the meaning of "social" ranges from individual and groups to society as a whole). Hubert (ibid.) describes the outcome dimension through three complementary and interdependent approaches that respond to

social demands that are traditionally not addressed by the market or existing institutions and are directed towards vulnerable groups in society [Approach 1]
societal challenges in which boundaries between "social" and "economic" blurs, and which are directed towards society as a whole [Approach 2]

and

the need to reform society in the direction of a more participative arena where empowerment and learning are sources and outcomes of well-being [Approach 3].

Hubert describes the interdependence between the approaches this way: "[A]n innovation that addresses a social demand (e.g. care of the elderly) contributes to addressing a societal challenge (ageing society) and through its process dimension (e.g. the active engagement of the elderly), it contributes to reshape society in the directions of participation and empowerment." (ibid.)

Howaldt and Schwarz (2010, 21) write that the distinction between social and technical innovation is in the immaterial and intangible structure of social innovations: "The innovation does not occur in the medium of a technical artefact but at the level of social practice." Practice, what people really do, is also fundamental in participatory design (Robertson and Simonsen 2012). Another important characteristic of social innovation, brought up by Murray, Caulier-Grice, and Mulgan (2010, 7), is the role of stakeholder networks. Whereas in business the firm is the main agent of innovation, in social innovation the impetus is more likely to come from a wider network, "perhaps linking some commissioners in public sector, providers in social enterprises, advocates in social movements, and entrepreneurs in business" (ibid.). This insight from social innovation theory fits well with our ambition in the Living Labs of gathering a wider network of heterogeneous actors in order to explore and tackle social and societal challenges.

Our motivations for attaching ourselves to the discourse of social innovation are a belief in democratic principles and an interest in how design can play a part in exploring new possibilities to create a more sustainable, equal, and just world. To be able to reach that goal, we believe, one has to move beyond single solutions in the form of products and services that sustain business as usual or the hegemony of the establishment, and one has to address issues on both an individual level and a systemic level. We believe that the overall objective for social innovation is to reorganize society—to really affect the causes of social problems rather than merely relieve the symptoms, or, in Schulman's (2012, no paging) words, to "shake up the status quo, narrow inequalities, and set new social standards." With that ambition you will get into trouble and experience a lot of painful moments.

Design for social innovation

As has already been mentioned, design has a history of social engagement, from William Morris (1834–1896), socialist artist, designer and leader of the *Arts and Crafts movement*, and Walter Gropius (1883–1969), architect and founder of the *Bauhaus School*, to Victor Papanek (1923–1998), designer and author of *Design for the Real World: Human Ecology and Social Change*. But, as Margolin and Margolin (2002, 24) argue, this has not led to an established "social model" for design. Instead, the "market model" has been dominant, and there has been a lack of research that might "demonstrate what a designer can contribute to human welfare" (ibid., 28). In the last ten years, however, there have been various initiatives to establish a "social model" for design, focusing on how design can contribute to society. Examples include John Thackara's Doors of Perception conferences and blog, Bruce Mau's book *Massive Change* and his Institute Without Boundaries, Cameron Sinclair's non-profit organization Architecture for Humanity, and Emily Pilloton's Project H Design and Design Revolution exhibition.

Also contributing to the development of this "social model" are the designers and design researchers who consider how design methods and tools could support social innovation (Jégou and Manzini 2008; DESIS 2012). Concurrently, design has been recognized as a valid tool by organizations advocating, supporting, and researching social innovation (Murray, Caulier-Grice, and Mulgan 2010; Rockefeller Foundation 2008). In 2011, the Young Foundation hired a "head of social design" to develop a new social design practice as a way to complement their current work (Kimbell 2011). At the Waterloo Institute for Social Innovation and Resilience in Ontario, Frances Westley has begun to explore the concept of social innovation labs, where inspiration from "design labs" plays an important role. Among the other contributors to the emergence of this new design field have been academic design researchers and design practitioners (the latter mainly from service-design companies and from public organizations that support design, like the Design Council in the United Kingdom, or set up their own design led innovation units, like MindLab in Denmark, La 27e Région in France, or the Helsinki design lab in Finland).

At the Politecnico di Milano, Ezio Manzini and François Jégou have led international research projects such as Emerging User Demands for Sustainable Solutions and Creative Communities for Sustainable Lifestyles (SEP 2012). Sustainability was the starting point for those projects, but subsequently the insight that sustainability is not merely a technical issue (new products) but an issue of lifestyles and behavioral changes led to the conclusion that "social innovation could be a powerful driver towards sustainability" (DESIS 2012, no paging). In their book *Collaborative Services: Social Innovation and Design for Sustainability*, Jégou and Manzini (2008) explicitly emphasized the concept of social innovation. Today such research is gathered under the umbrella of the DESIS (Design for Social Innovation and Sustainability) network. Design researchers from this network have identified and collected cases from what they call *creative communities* around the world. Jégou and Manzini (ibid., 30) define creative communities as "groups of people who cooperatively invent, enhance and manage innovative solutions for new ways of living." Generally, the outcomes are collaborative services that are "social services where final users are actively involved and assume the role of service co-designers and co-producers" (ibid.).

In the United Kingdom, several service design companies, among them Live Work, Engine, and ThinkPublic, began to apply design methods to social and societal challenges in the early 2000s. This occurred in parallel with support from the Design Council, which encouraged the exploration of using design in new social and public contexts through research and demonstration projects. One example was the Design Council's RED research unit, which consisted of professional designers and professionals from disciplines such as policy analysis and social sciences (Design Council 2004). Burns et al. (2006) describe the RED unit's approach, called *transformation design*, as based on involving heterogeneous stakeholders from the beginning through participatory design. In 2007, the RED unit became an enterprise called Participle, which, in turn, became the starting point for the design company InWithFor (which closed in 2012).

The Design Council has also initiated demonstration programs. Two such programs were Designs of the Time (Design Council 2012b) and Public Services by Design (Design Council 2008, 2012a). Furthermore, other public institutions in the United Kingdom have initiated projects involving design companies. For example, Engine (2012) has supported the Kent County Council in designing a new platform for co-creation, Live Work (2012) has created services to support hard-to-reach unemployed people, and ThinkPublic (2012, no paging) has used participatory design to engage "local residents in identifying challenges and co-designing responses to better community health and wellbeing."

In the United States too there is growing interest in design for social innovation; it is among the areas of expertise offered by the design firms IDEO, Continuum, and Frog Design. The typical approach to design for social innovation in the United States refers to projects in developing countries (Brown and Wyatt 2010). However, the DESIS Lab at the New School for Design in New York is working more in a European way; it helps local creative communities to develop collaborative services and sustainable lifestyles (DESIS Lab 2012). In the research program known as Public & Collaborative NYC, the DESIS Lab explores what role design can play in building bridges between city government and people in the creation of social innovation (Staszowski, Brown, and Winter 2013). And Project H Design (2012) is bringing design skills into public education in a rural community.

Strengths and weaknesses of design in social innovation

One sign of how design is evolving in social innovation, Geoff Mulgan (2012b, no paging) argues, is that designers are getting "humbler about what can be achieved, and about what they need to learn from others" (ibid.). Mulgan was one of the first people from the field of social innovation to cite both the strengths and the weaknesses of design for social innovation. In 2009, the concept of design for social innovation was primarily associated with hype about "design thinking" and with the design-can-solve-everything attitude of many of the world's leading designers. According to Mulgan, the strengths of design for social innovation include visualization techniques, bringing novel insights, working from a user perspective, and fast prototyping. The weaknesses include lack of economical and organizational skills, inability to drive the implementation process, the cost of design consultants who often do not have a long-term commitment to a project, and the fact that designers sometimes ignore evidence and field experiences and tend to "reinvent the wheel" (Mulgan 2009). Mulgan's (2009, 2012b) critique mostly concerns design methods, but several other critical voices have been heard with regard to the ethics, the values, and the political awareness of designers working in unfamiliar contexts (Cottam 2009; Tonkinwise 2010; DiSalvo 2010; Blyth and Kimbell 2011; Schulman 2012).

The big picture

Social innovation is no longer a concern only for grassroots movements or third-sector organizations (non-governmental organizations, associations, non-profit businesses) fighting inequality or addressing global challenges such as climate change. Today, in North America and in Europe, social innovation is also a concern of governments. In the United States, President Barack Obama has created an Office of Social Innovation and Civic Participation in recognition of the idea that "the best solutions to our challenges will be found in communities across the country" (SICP 2012, no paging). Social innovation has also become a priority of the European Union's innovation policy (European Commission 2010).

According to a report titled *Empowering People, Driving Change: Social Innovation in the European Union* (Hubert 2011, 18), the old belief that economic growth alone could provide all the solutions to social problems has been shown to be incorrect, and social innovation can mobilize people's creativity. That report also suggests that a new form of "enabling welfare state" is emerging, and a change of attitude and the involvement of citizens, public authorities, and private organizations will be necessary if new social responses to our social challenges are to be developed.

Hubert's (2011, 35) description of social innovation as a "process of social interactions between individuals to reach certain outcomes" is interesting. She also refers to lessons learned from the EQUAL initiative in Portugal. That project, with its focus on increasing access to employment, is also interesting in relation to our involvement in designing an incubator for social innovation in Malmö (chapter 4) and our work on how a group of women living on public assistance can develop their activities into a cooperative business (chapter 3). In this chapter, I summarize some of Hubert's (2011) findings, building on the EQUAL project, that are important for an understanding of social innovation processes. These findings have much in common with the ethos of participatory design and with the theme of social conditions in participatory design:

1. Solutions must focus on the beneficiaries and be created with them, preferably by them, and never without them.
2. Focusing on the strengths of individuals and communities rather than on their weaknesses
3. Capitalizing on the diversity of ethnicities, ages, religions, gender, etc. and not just combating discrimination
4. Developing a holistic approach rather than fragmented responses to people's diverse problems
5. Reinforcing and extending partnerships rather than having each organization individually handling its services and its responsibilities
6. Collaborative working and networking as ways to stimulate social innovation

(Hubert 2011, 35)

Design, politics, and some early warnings

Co-creation and collaboration obviously are central to participatory design as well as to social innovation. They are also central to new policies (for example, the British government's "Big Society" vision) that build on citizen involvement and action, using local knowledge and social networks (Coote 2010). The goal is to "devolve power to the lowest possible level" while making "deep cuts in public spending" (ibid., 2). This policy is a huge challenge for designers. The Design Council's Dott Cornwall program has been viewed as a "Big Society laboratory" by Scott Billings (2011, 22), who also asserts that it "is not a version of Big Society where people are left to fend for themselves, but rather one where collaboration is instrumental in addressing social problems in new ways."

Even before the Big Society policy was launched, the social design firm Participle presented a vision of how to design the new welfare state in a manifesto, titled Beveridge 4.0 (Cottam 2008), that emphasizes people's aspirations and their capabilities rather than their needs and advocates involving citizens in collectively designing new responses to societal challenges. When Prime Minister David Cameron presented the Big Society policy, Hilary Cottam (2009), one of the founders of Participle, welcomed it, pointing to the similarities with Participle's agenda, but at the same time showed a political awareness by pointing to "central flaws" in Cameron's argument and criticizing his reluctance to address inequality: "Britain is one of the most unequal societies in the world. Unless we are willing to talk about and address this disparity, neither a re-imagined state nor an army of social entrepreneurs can build Cameron's big society." (Cottam 2009, no paging) Statements of this sort and a willingness to discuss the political contexts and social conditions in which designers are beginning to operate in are most necessary. Reflecting on the situation in the United Kingdom, where designers create new services according to government policy, Cameron Tonkinwise (2010) has brought up the need for an awareness of political and ethical matters:

> Designers are already facilitating social innovations that can replace government services that David Cameron has a mandate to cut the cost of. The rhetoric, as a recent *Economist* article on social innovation made clear, is all about doing services better, but in ways that just happen to also save the government money and, more importantly, withdraw governments irrevocably from such services. (Tonkinwise 2010, no paging)

Simon Blyth and Lucy Kimbell (2011) have also been reflecting on the role of design in relation to the Big Society policy. Emphasizing the importance of how problems are framed and defined and how issues are made public, they argue that design should be viewed as more than problem solving. Asserting that it is important to go beyond the individual (the focus of user-centered design) and to "situate individuals within dynamic social systems" (ibid., 8), they quote the American sociologist C. Wright Mills:

> [W]hen in a nation of 50 million employees, 15 million people are unemployed, that is an issue, and we may not hope to find its solution within the range of opportunities open to any one individual. The very structure of opportunities has collapsed. Both the correct statement of the problem and the range of possible solutions require us to consider the economic and political institutions of the society, and not merely the personal situation and character of a scatter of individuals. (Mills, quoted by Blyth and Kimbell 2011, 8)

Blyth and Kimbell argue that the view of the design process as a collaborative and consensual activity should be challenged, and that contestation and difference are important elements of the process—especially in public or community contexts. Sarah Schulman of the design consultancy InWithFor goes further. Drawing on her experiences in the social field, she calls for more ethical outrage in the design community and urges designers to deal with the moral dilemmas that underpin "social design" work. Those "moral dilemmas," she continues, "have informed our value set—a value set that enables us to make decisions about the projects we choose to take on, the people we choose to work with, and the solutions we co-create" (Schulman 2012, no paging).

The importance of values became evident to Schulman when she was working with a government agency whose internal co-design unit was driven more by values of "innovation" and "efficiency" than by questions regarding inequalities. Even if the methods were new, the "ends" were quite the same. "It's not that I don't believe in 'social design' methods—in starting with people, making ideas real, and iterating those ideas over time," Schulman (2012, no paging) writes, "but I believe in them insofar as they shake up the status quo, narrow inequalities, and set new social standards. The danger comes when these new design methods make social services more palatable, more attractive, and thus more difficult to challenge."

All these reflections on social innovation and *design for* social innovation point to the need for more discussion of the conditions and contexts of social design work—more discussion of *what* to design and *with whom* to design, and not only of *how* to design. It also points to the relevance of making a distinction between what Carl DiSalvo (2010, no paging) calls *design for politics* (with its focus on "improving structures and mechanisms that enable governing") and *political design* (which focuses more on revealing and confronting power relations and on identifying "new terms and themes for contestation and new trajectories for action"). These reflections could also be seen as early warnings that, if we aren't alert, all this well-intentioned democratic design may fail and may deliver outcomes that do more harm than good—again.

"Design things" and "infrastructuring": Two approaches to exploring and designing the conditions of the social?

Among the design methods and practices that could be applied to social innovation are ethnographic studies, early and rapid prototyping, and involving diverse stakeholders in the process of co-creation. However, all these approaches must be challenged and explored further in the specific context of the present discussion. In the following two chapters, my colleagues and I will reflect on our own experiences and on the shortcomings of using design to address social and societal challenges. We will not tell success stories about creating new and life-changing public services. Instead we will offer insights, expressed through concepts such as "infrastructuring," "design things," agonism, and governance, that, we argue, could contribute to the discussion regarding social conditions in participatory design processes and to confronting many of the challenges that were touched upon earlier in the chapter. For example, we will argue that it is fruitful to consider the possibility that the concept of "design things," as developed by Ehn (2008), Björgvinsson, Ehn, and Hillgren (2010), and Binder et al. (2011), could work as a space for what DiSalvo (2010) calls "political design," and the possibility that heterogeneous stakeholders could "make decisions about the projects we choose to take on, the people we choose to work with, and the solutions we co-create" (Schulman 2012, no paging).

Chapters 3 and 4 focus on "infrastructuring" and on the creation and the re-creation of "design things," with diverse stakeholders gathering to discuss, challenge, and reveal one another's values, interests, and agendas and to go through a process of reciprocal learning. The larger framework for both chapters is how Living Lab the Neighborhood, by setting up collaborative design processes, could address social and societal challenges and increase society's capacity to act. Here we can see interesting links between the concepts "infrastructuring" and "design things" and the conclusions reached in the final report of the Kommission för ett socialt hållbart Malmö (Commission for a Socially Sustainable Malmö):

- the need of departing from a holistic perspective
- the importance of problem definition and that a wider circle of actors participate in defining problems and setting objectives
- the need of creating "knowledge alliances," which mean "equal collaborations between researchers and stakeholders from for example public administration, associations and trade and industry"
- the need of building an infrastructure of knowledge alliances for social innovation and urban integration (Stigendal and Östergren 2013, 128–134; translated from Swedish)

We will argue that the concepts "infrastructuring" and "design things" could contribute to the exploration of what an "infrastructure of knowledge alliances" could be. To situate our research in the local context, we will discuss infrastructuring and design things in relation to the findings in the final report of the Commission for a Socially Sustainable Malmö and in relation to research by the political scientist Tove Dannestam on "city politics" and "governance" in Malmö. Tove Dannestam and the sociologist Mikael Stigendal have made important contributions to the understanding of Malmö and will therefore be mentioned often.

In chapter 3, titled Designing in the Neighborhood, we analyze a bottom-up initiative, tell the story of a group of women who wish to start a cooperative business, and consider how the women's knowledge and skills could be transformed into services. The case in question reveals shortcomings in existing support structures (that is, in society's capacity to act) and points to the need to develop a function in society that can take a long-term responsibility for supporting initiatives that do not fit into—or that challenge—existing norms and institutions. Consequently, that chapter's main analytical concepts are "infrastructuring," "prototyping," and "friendly hacking" (Jégou et al. 2013). This is along the lines of Stigendal and Östergren's observation (2013, 48) that "there is a need for an infrastructure within the municipality that is able to utilize the innovation power and knowledge within civil society." (Interestingly, just such a long-term support structure was discussed in the "design thing" that was gathered to address the issue of an incubator for social innovation.)

In chapter 4, titled "Connecting with the Powerful Strangers," we analyze the initial process of developing a support structure for social innovation, the so-called incubator for social innovation—a process that was a top-down initiative by the municipality. The objective was to explore how such a support structure could function and, in Stigendal and Östergren's (2013) words, how to build an infrastructure of knowledge alliances concerned with the issue of an incubator for social innovation. That chapter's main analytical focus is on "design things" in relation to the political concepts "governance" and "agonism."

In these two cases, we have discovered potentials for new forms of work and new support structures, but we also have discovered shortcomings in existing systems and the difficulties designers will face when dealing with complex societal challenges. These two cases point to the need to approach social needs and societal issues from many perspectives, addressing the needs and the desires of individuals and communities and also addressing structural and systemic causes and limitations—the need to work across sectors and disciplines, from the bottom up and from the top down. In these projects, we have experienced both the joy of working with fantastic people and the agony of diving into the social and societal problems of our time.

References

Barroso, José Manuel. 2011. Europe Leading Social Innovation. Speech at Social Innovation Europe Initiative, Brussels (europa.eu/rapid/press-release_SPEECH-11-190_en.pdf).

Billings, Scott. 2011. Dott's Legacy (http://www.designcouncil.org.uk).

Binder, Thomas, Giorgio De Michelis, Pelle Ehn, Giulio Jacucci, Per Linde, and Ina Wagner. 2011. *Design Things*. MIT Press.

Björgvinsson, Erling, and Per-Anders Hillgren. 2004. On the Spot Experiments within Healthcare. In Proceedings of the Eighth Participatory Design Conference, Toronto.

Björgvinsson, Erling, Pelle Ehn, and Per-Anders Hillgren. 2010. Participatory Design and "Democratizing Innovation." In Proceedings of the Eleventh Participatory Design Conference, Sydney.

Blyth, Simon, and Lucy Kimbell. 2011. Design Thinking and the Big Society: From Solving Personal Troubles to Designing Social Problems. Actant and Taylor Haig.

Bristol, Katharine G. 1991. The Pruitt-Igoe Myth. *Journal of Architectural Education* 44 (3): 163–171.

Brown, Tim, and Jocelyn Wyatt. 2010. Design Thinking for Social Innovation (http://www.ssireview.org/articles/entry/design_thinking_for_social_innovation/).

Burns, Colin, Hilary Cottam, Chris Vanstone, and Jennie Winhall. 2006. Transformation Design (http://www.designcouncil.info/mt/RED/transformationdesign/).

Chesbrough, Henry. 2003. *Open Innovation: The New Imperative for Creating And Profiting from Technology*. Harvard Business School Press.

Coote, Anna. 2010. Cutting It: The "Big Society" and the New Austerity (http://s.bsd.net/nefoundation/default/page/-/files/Cutting_it.pdf).

Cottam, Hilary. 2008. Beveridge 4.0 (http://www.participle.net/about/our_mission).

Cottam, Hilary. 2009. On the Big Society (http://www.participle.net/particles/P10/).

den Ouden, Elke, and Rianne Valkenburg. 2011. Balancing Value in Networked Social Innovation. In proceedings of Participatory Innovation Conference, University of Southern Denmark.

Design Council. 2004. RED Is a "Do Tank" That Develops New Thinking and Practice on Social and Economic Problems through Design-Led Innovation (http://www.designcouncil.info/mt/RED/about/).

Design Council. 2008. Design Council Briefing 02: The Role of Design in Public Services (http://www.designcouncil.org.uk/Documents/Documents/Publications/Research/Briefings/DesignCouncilBriefing02_TheRoleOfDesignInPublicServices.pdf).

Design Council. 2012a. *Public Services by Design* (http://www.designcouncil.org.uk/our-work/leadership/).

Design Council. 2012b. Co-designing Ways to Improve How We Live, Work AND Play (http://www.designcouncil.org.uk/our-work/challenges/Communities/Dott-Cornwall1/).

DESIS. 2012. DESIS Network (http://www.desis-network.org).

DESIS Lab. 2012. Amplifying Creative Communities (http://amplifyingcreativecommunities.net).

DiSalvo, Carl. 2010. Design, Democracy and Agonistic Pluralism. In proceedings of 2010 conference of Design Research Society, Montreal (http://www.designresearchsociety.org/docs-procs/DRS2010/PDF/031.pdf).

Ehn, Pelle. 2008. Participation in Design Things. In Proceedings of the Tenth Anniversary Conference on Participatory Design, Indianapolis.

Engine. 2012. Building a Social Innovation Lab to Develop Services (http://enginegroup.co.uk/work/kcc-social-innovation-lab).

European Commission. 2010. Europe 2020 (http://ec.europa.eu).

Hillgren, Per-Anders, Anna Seravalli, and Anders Emilson. 2011. Prototyping and Infrastructuring in Design for Social Innovation. *CoDesign* 7 (3–4): 169–183.

Howaldt, Jürgen, and Michael Schwarz. M. 2010. Social Innovation: Concepts, Research Fields AND International Trends, (http://www.sfs-dortmund.de/odb/Repository/Publication/Doc%5C1289%5CIMO_Trendstudie_Howaldt_Schwarz_englische_Version.pdf).

Hubert, Agnès. 2011. *Empowering People, Driving Change: Social Innovation in the European Union*. Bureau of European Policy Advisers, European Commission.

Jégou, François, and Ezio Manzini, eds. 2008. Collaborative Services: Social Innovation and Design for Sustainability. POLI.design.

Jégou, François, Stéphane Vincent, Romain Thévenet, and Anna Lochard. 2013. Friendly Hacking into the Public Sector: Co-Creating Public Policies within Regional Governments. Presented at Boundary-Crossing Conference on Co-Design in Innovation, Aalto University (http://www.slideshare.net/27eregion/friendly-hacking-into-public-sector).

Kimbell, Lucy. 2011. Why I'm Joining the Young Foundation as Head of Social Design (http://www.youngfoundation.org/blog/social-innovation/why-im-joining-young-foundation-head-social-design).

Leadbeater, Charles. 2008. *We-Think: Mass Innovation, Not Mass Production*. Profile Books.

Leadbeater, Charles. 2009. The Art of With (http://www.charlesleadbeater.net).

Live Work. 2012. Sunderland: Make It Work (http://livework.co.uk).

Margolin, Victor, and Sylvia Margolin. 2002. A "Social Model" of Design: Issues of Practice and Research. *Design Issues* 18 (4): 24–30.

Mjölkdroppen. 2013. Mjölkdroppen—barnavårdscentralernas föregångare (http://www.mjolkdroppen.se).

Mulgan, Geoff. 2009. Strengths, Weaknesses and a Way Forward? (The original blog post at Social Innovation Exchange is gone, but the text can be found at http://blogs.lse.ac.uk.)

Mulgan, Geoff. 2012a. The Theoretical Foundations of Social Innovation. In *Social innovation: Blurring Boundaries to Reconfigure Markets*, ed. A. Nicholls and A. Murdock. Palgrave Macmillan.

Mulgan, Geoff. 2012b. Better by Design (http://www.nesta.org.uk).

Murray, Robin, Julie Caulier-Grice, and Geoff Mulgan. 2010. *The Open Book of Social Innovation*. Young Foundation and Nesta.

Nicholls, Alex, and Alex Murdock, eds. 2012. *Social Innovation: Blurring Boundaries to Reconfigure Markets*. Palgrave Macmillan.

Phills, James, A., Kriss Deiglmeier, and Dale T. Miller. 2008. Rediscovering Social Innovation. *Stanford Social Innovation Review* 6 (4) (http://www.ssireview.org/articles/entry/rediscovering_social_innovation).

Project H Design. 2012. Project H Design (http://projecthdesign.org/).

Robertson, Toni, and Jesper Simonsen. 2012. Challenges and Opportunities in Contemporary Participatory Design. *Design Issues* 28 (3): 3–9.

Rockefeller Foundation. 2008. Design for Social Impact: Workshop (http://www.rockefellerfoundation.org/uploads/files/50371640-262f-415e-ae01-09c60bdd60dc-socialimpact.pdf).

Schulman, Sarah. 2012. Ethical Outrage (http://www.inwithfor.org/2012/04/ethical-outrage/#start).

SEP. 2012. Sustainable Everyday Project—Research (http://www.sustainable-everyday.net/main/?page_id=8).

SICP. 2012. About SICP—The Community Solutions Agenda (http://www.whitehouse.gov/administration/eop/sicp/about).

Staszowski, Eduardo, Scott Brown, and Benjamin Winter. 2013. Reflections on Designing for Social Innovation in the Public Sector: A Case Study in New York City. In *Public and Collaborative*, ed. E. Manzini and E. Staszowski. DESIS Network.

Stigendal, Mikael, and Per-Olof Östergren. 2013. Malmös väg mot en hållbar framtid. Hälsa, Välfärd och rättvisa. Kommision för ett socialt hållbart Malmö, Malmö stad.

Think Public. 2012. Youcankingston (http://thinkpublic.com/case-studies/youcankingston/).

Tonkinwise, Cameron. 2010. Politics Please, We're Social Designers (http://www.core77.com/blog/featured_items/politics_please_were_social_designers_by_cameron_tonkinwise__17284.asp).

Westley, Frances, and Nino Antadze. 2010. Making a Difference: Strategies for Scaling Social Innovation for Greater Impact. *The Innovation Journal* 15 (2): 3–20.

3 Designing in the Neighborhood: Beyond (and in the Shadow of) Creative Communities

Anders Emilson, Per-Anders Hillgren, and Anna Seravalli

Living Lab the Neighborhood was initiated to explore how a platform that could facilitate social innovation and collaborative services could be set up in the city of Malmö. Although a few strategic decisions were made (for example, to adopt a long-term perspective that could go beyond single projects, to take a very inclusive approach to participation, and to build the platform from the needs, capabilities, and assets of local communities), the intention was that the platform should be designed and redesigned continuously in relation to what it encountered.

The platform is labeled as a *living lab*, a concept that originated at the Massachusetts Institute of Technology (Eriksson, Niitamo, Kulkki, and Hribernik 2005) and has been spreading rapidly around the world for about ten years. Today more than 400 labs are members of the European Network of Living Labs (ENOLL). There is no consensus on how to define a living lab (Følstad 2008; Stålbröst 2008), but usually such a lab is described as a long-term environment for open innovation that supports experimentation with real users in real contexts (Følstad 2008). This fits very well with what we see as essential in a platform that could facilitate social innovation. However, most living labs are strongly driven by industry and commercial interests, and that has consequences for how open "open innovation" can be (Kommonen and Botero 2013) and for what is regarded as innovation (Björgvinsson, Ehn, and Hillgren 2010, 2012). More than many other living labs, our platform is design-driven. According to some researchers, it is also one of few living labs driven by the interests of users' or citizen communities (e.g., NGOs) (Nystrom and Leminen 2011).

Living labs resonate with the idea of enabling platforms as formulated by designers in the field of *design for social innovation*. These platforms are looked upon as structures that should respond to the meta-technological demands of grassroots social innovations (Jégou and Manzini 2008). Manzini and Rizzo (2011) call these supporting structures "framework projects" and discuss what implications they might have for designers. According to Manzini and Rizzo, designers can act as facilitators and support ongoing initiatives, or they can act as triggers and start new initiatives. They can also be either design activists or members of co-design teams. We did not define any explicit roles the designer should take when exploring how the Living Lab the Neighborhood could contribute to social innovation, but we would argue that we have been working in all the roles described by Manzini and Rizzo. We have also taken an active role in matchmaking heterogeneous and complementary stakeholders to generate creative encounters. Focusing on different levels of design engagement has been important to our way of operating—we have sometimes zoomed in and paid attention to the details of concrete experiments together with grassroots communities, but when we have encountered obstacles to realizing the potential results of the concrete experiments we have sometimes zoomed out again to elaborate a possible change in the bigger picture by inquiring into more systemic levels by trying to modify regulations, work procedures and cultures, public policy, and indicators of project success.

We are not, however, the only ones who pay attention to these more systemic levels. Recently, several actors have started to explore how design potentially could have an impact on larger systems and, especially, how design could reach into the public sector and into municipal offices (Bason 2010; Christansen and Bunt 2012; Jégou et al. 2013; Staszowski et al. 2013). One inspiring example is La 27e Région, an independent innovation organization that explores how design approaches can influence policy development within the public sector in France. La 27e Région's strategy, which they have characterized as *friendly hacking*, builds on embedding multidisciplinary teams, including designers, who—for shorter or longer periods—can empower civil servants within diverse public organizations. They use the term 'hacking' because it "signifies the intent to challenge the robustness of public policy instruments" (Jégou et al. 2013, 6). "The hacking," they add, "is friendly, not destructive." Although most of our design interventions are based on concrete interventions at the community level, the concept of friendly hacking resonates well with how Living Lab the Neighborhood, as a meta-design platform, has focused more and more on building alliances within the public sector with the aim of having an impact on a systemic level. Our starting point has been quite different from that of La 27e Région. Since the beginning, they had several politicians sitting on their board, and their friendly hacking is commissioned by the public sector and supported by formal agreements that give them a mandate to work inside these organizations. We, by contrast, started far from power centers and rooted our initial work within local communities.

Apart from the more systemic recent engagements, the lab activities have focused on a variety of topics, on community needs, and on potential designs that include technology that increases grassroots organizations' visibility and mobile games for urban exploring (see chapters 11 and 14). During these processes, the concepts of *infrastructuring*, *design things*, and *agonistic spaces* have emerged and have helped us to better understand our activities. These concepts are discussed elsewhere in the present volume (e.g., chapters 2, 10, 11 on infrastructuring, chapters 2 and 14 on design things, and chapters 11 and 13 on agonism) and in recently published research papers by Björgvinsson, Ehn, and Hillgren (2010, 2012) and by Hillgren, Seravalli, and Emilson (2011). In this chapter we will focus on long-term infrastructuring, because the story we tell here is probably one of our most significant examples of such a process.

Surprising findings from the city of Malmö

To better understand our focus and what we try to aim for, consider the two quite different perspectives on Malmö that are described in the introduction to this book (see chapter 1). One highlights how the city has gone through an extensive transformation, from an industrial city to a "knowledge city" and a regional growth engine. The other perspective depicts it as a segregated city with a high number of immigrants who live primarily in the southeastern part, which has some of the highest rates of child poverty and unemployment in Sweden. In 2008, when we were engaged in research activities in Malmö's Rosengård district (famous for its social problems), riots were occurring and young people were attacking firefighters and police officers. The riots attracted international media attention.

According to the Kommissionen för ett socialt hållbart Malmö (Commission for a Socially Sustainable Malmö), these riots weren't surprising if one considered the huge differences in health and living conditions between Rosengård and other districts of Malmö. According to Stigendal and Östergren (2013), it is surprising that the tensions and troubles aren't worse.

We will come back to this later, but now we will start to describe the journey of designing Living Lab the Neighborhood. First, we will discuss whom we could collaborate with and how. We will then present a series of design interventions performed on different scales, stretching over several years, and financed by diverse funding schemes. Finally, we will discuss what this means as a design practice.

Beyond (and in the shadow of) creative communities

At the beginning of Living Lab the Neighborhood, two important questions were whom to collaborate with and which actors could have relevant capacity and skills to work creatively with social innovation. Concepts such as *the creative class* (Florida 2004) and *lead users* (von Hippel 2005) mainly bring forward privileged groups, such as engineers, poets, artists, researchers, or designers. These groups are well established and make up a significant percentage of the citizens in the western part of Malmö, where new-media clusters are emerging and where Malmö University is located. However, the starting point for our lab was to try to work with stakeholders and citizens that are living and operating in the southeastern part of the city. Although there are engineers, poets, and artists in these areas, we were particularly interested in locating people and groups that were not on Florida's or von Hippel's list. One promising alternative to the privileged groups—an alternative that inspired us at the time—was the concept of creative communities made up of "professionals of the everyday" (Meroni 2007)—people who have organized themselves to solve a local problem, often focusing on achieving local sustainable solutions.

Whereas the creative class is driven by highly individualistic norms (Florida 2004), the creative communities are driven by a sense of community spirit and by the pleasure of collaborating and building relationships (Meroni 2007). Most of the examples that Meroni brings up are tied to specific categories (for example, commuting, eating, and housing) and are aiming for a specific solution, such as a "walking school bus" (an arrangement by which children walk to school together). Creative communities are also quite visible in the urban landscape. Even if you might find examples in Malmö that more explicitly resemble these cases, we were curious if we could find other resourceful actors that were less visible. As we argued in the introduction to the present chapter, we aim for an inclusive approach that will allow marginalized actors to participate.

What kind of groups could be found "under the radar"? Every time we have asked civil servants about prominent creative groups or stakeholders in these areas, and every time we sent students out to do research, the same answers recurred: the most prominent actors were Drömmarnas Hus (an independent organization focusing on cultural activities such as theater and film, often in collaboration with schools) and Yalla trappan (a cooperative association of formerly unemployed immigrant women who provide catering and housekeeping services). Drömmarnas Hus and Yalla trappan are supported by the municipality, highly visible, and fairly well established.

How can those "under the radar" be reached? We had an infrastructuring process (Björgvinsson, Ehn, and Hillgren 2010, 2012; Hillgren et al. 2011) going on some years before the Neighborhood Lab started. Infrastructuring basically means that we cultivate long-term working relationships with diverse actors and slowly build a designing network. In this process, some stakeholders have been using their social capital to help us approach and enter other networks that are "under the radar" and marginalized. For example, Rörelsen Gatans Röst och Ansikte (RGRA), an organization with which we had been working for a long time, connected us to a marginalized but also highly innovative and skillful group, the Herrgård's Women's Association (HWA).

The Herrgård's Women's Association

HWA was founded in 2002 by five women in the Rosengård district of Malmö as a response to the feeling of being excluded from Swedish society. The organization counts approximately 400 members (200 of them children) with backgrounds in Iran, Iraq, Bosnia, and Afghanistan. Most of the women live on social security, have limited skills in Swedish, are illiterate, and generally lack higher education. HWA fulfills most of the characteristics of a creative community: the members' emotional involvement is tightly connected to a collective approach, and they have organized themselves to develop solutions for challenging problems in their neighborhoods. These problems are, however, slightly different than the ones that have been described by Meroni (2007). They include complex social problems that seldom are visible in the physical environment or outside their community. One issue is social integration, since many immigrants have a hard time being accepted in the Swedish society. Then there are gender issues in patriarchal cultures where the group slowly, but forcefully, has pushed the borders for what a woman is allowed to do. Moreover, through the trust that the women have developed within their networks during many years, they can mediate between family members to prevent honor-related violence and they organize educational events in collaboration with the city around health issues (e.g., sexual health). Here, we would like to connect back to the Commission for a Socially Sustainable Malmö (Stigendal and Östergren 2013) and argue that HWA and similar organizations probably are one of the reasons why riots and social problems aren't worse than they are. Their invisible everyday work mitigates many of the tensions.

In parallel to being engaged in these complex social and societal issues, the women's activities also include cooking, designing textiles, and making carpets and clothing. The core group of five women meets regularly, and, depending of what kinds of activities are carried out, other members sometimes participate.

If we would bring forward some more of the distinguishing qualities that these women possess, it would be the extensive social network and trust they have built in the area. They have the insider's perspective on what problems and opportunities are embedded within their communities. This gives them the ability to be very creative and to devise situated solutions to local problems in ways that outsiders (e.g., civil servants) cannot.

Another distinctive feature that Meroni (2007) assigns to creative communities is a feature that, we argue, applies well to HWA: their aesthetic qualities. Meroni states that creative communities "are not only interesting because they are innovative, but they are also aesthetically 'beautiful': there is something in the way they appear that invokes

Figure 3.1
The Herrgård's Women's Association. Copyright Per-Anders Hillgren (CC:BY-NC).

positive emotions and recalls the straightforward aesthetics of the useful. They are beautiful because they are colorful and they are authentically and surprisingly creative. They express vitality and spirit of initiative: they are the unthinkable made possible." (2007, 9) HWA is certainly colorful, authentic, and vital in the way that Meroni brings forward.

An emerging framework project: Living Lab the Neighborhood

Once we had identified HWA as a promising and challenging partner with a resemblance to a creative community, though much more in the margins, the next question was how we could work together. As Manzini (2007) argues, when you approach creative communities as a designer, you often do not need to design something new. The good ideas are already there, embedded in the practice, and you have to facilitate, support, and scale up what these groups already are doing. To be able to do that, Manzini and Rizzo (2011) argue, you need a *framework project*, a larger supporting structure that could move these local cases out of isolation and increase their capacity to contribute to society. The purpose is to see if these creative communities could inspire others, be replicated, and eventually have a large impact (ibid.). We explored how Living Lab the Neighborhood could become a framework project. However, it wasn't clear to us what should be scaled up or replicated, or if scaling and replication would be the right strategy at all. Rather, we wanted to collaboratively explore what the women wanted to do and, if possible, build relationships and connect them to diverse stakeholders. If strategic design and scenario building has been the central approaches for Manzini and Rizzo (ibid.) to construct framework projects, we have rather started from the local projects and having a framework project emerging bottom up. In line with Nabeel Hamdi's (2004) argument that overdesign often inhibits progress and development, we have tried to create a balance between defining a possible direction and allowing for emergence. Particularly through our processes of *infrastructuring*, we have been building relations with diverse actors through an ongoing matchmaking process, with flexible allocation of time and resources. This more organic approach tries to make use of the creative potential in a heterogeneous city by facilitating opportunities that emerge along the way. Infrastructuring allows the unexpected to emerge by working toward the creation of framework projects, which strive for being open-ended when it comes to constellations of actors (that is, who will participate) and issues (that is, what to explore and how to do it).

Co-designing with HWA—no method, but artful inquiries

Different methods that could spark creativity and organize discussions during workshops are often highlighted as cornerstones within co-design (Brandt 2006). The designer's role within co-design is to provide "tools for ideation and expression" (Sanders and Stappers 2008, 12). One of the arguments behind this focus is that people with different backgrounds and professional languages need tools to mediate and articulate the discussions during the design process. One might think that this would be especially relevant when approaching a multi-ethnic NGO with diverse cultural backgrounds. However, our experience turned out to be contrary to such expectations. Instead, we started our collaboration slowly with informal meetings, sitting down, drinking tea, and discussing one another's practices and everyday activities. They were not rushed and well-structured meetings, nor smart workshop formats, but very casual and open-ended appointments. Our design approach was rooted in the reflective practice of Donald Schön (1983, 1987) rather than in particular methods. During these encounters, we navigated among opportunities through a process of reflection-in-action and reached an understanding of the women's situation by continuously re-framing it. The process can be viewed, according to Schön, as consisting of "artful inquiries" that represent reflective conversations with unique and uncertain situations where standard theories or techniques cannot be applied. Because of language differences and cultural differences, the approach was to take it slow and let understanding develop. Many meetings between the women and representatives of the municipality have broken down, and our understanding is that the breakdowns have been attributable in part to difficulties in communicating and to the fact that civil servants don't have (or take) enough time to sit down and talk to the women and to the fact that they often set the agendas and the protocols for the meetings.

During the very fruitful discussions that took place during our meetings, the women expressed their desire to be more integrated in the Swedish society by finding opportunities for their abilities and skills to be valued. According to them, their activities were most often considered to be "leisure" by the authorities. This spurred our curiosity as to whether we, together with the women, could demonstrate that their activities could be viewed as "professional," and that an immigrant NGO could become a socioeconomic resource for the Swedish society. During this phase, we could have developed scenarios to highlight this possibility, but there were too many questions and potential issues that had to be resolved, and we needed a more explorative approach. The notion of reflective practice is seldom highlighted in the areas of design and social innovation. However, another concept from design, *prototyping*, has spread quite extensively (Burns et al. 2006; Brown and Wyatt 2010). According to Murray, Caulier-Grice, and Mulgan (2010, 12), refining and testing ideas is important in social innovation because "it is through iteration, and trial and error, that coalitions gather strength (for example, linking users to professionals) and conflicts are resolved (including battles with entrenched interests)." Prototyping has played a central role in the work with HWA (Hillgren, Seravalli, and Emilson 2011), and it often turned out to be a quite demanding and complex activity. All HWA interventions required mobilizing a number of stakeholders and

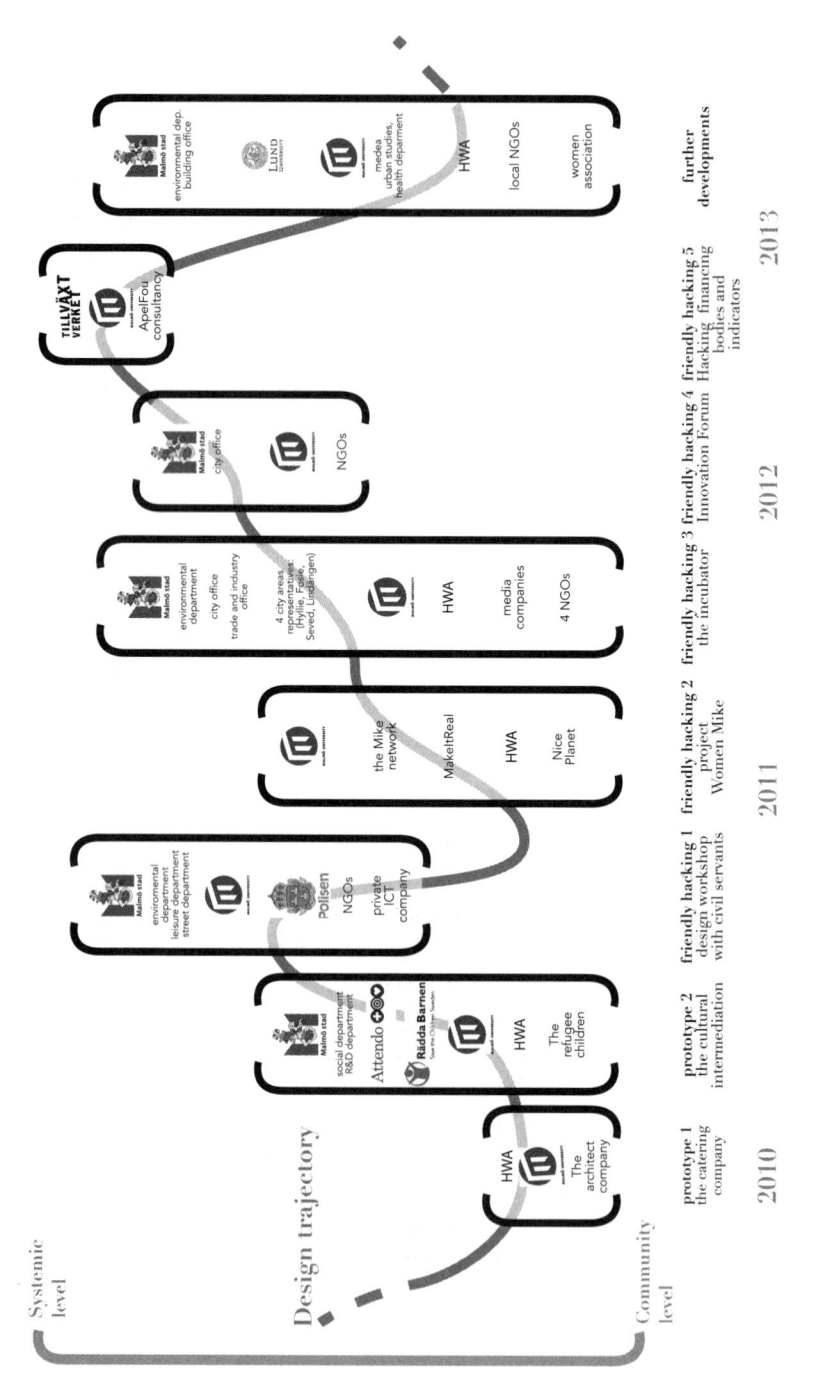

Figure 3.2
The long journey with HWA. Anna Seravalli (CC:BY-NC).

asking them to invest time and resources. This had the implication that the expectations were often quite high, leading to a number of issues related to the actual results of each prototype, with failures being difficult to accept and manage.

In the subsections that follow, we discuss our long-term engagement with HWA and how artful inquiry with the women developed through the use of prototypes and through friendly hacking.

Prototype 1: The catering company
After a suggestion from HWA, our artful inquiry started by developing prototypes around their cooking activities. Initially, we tried to understand how their cooking skills could be developed into a service that besides the food also could include knowledge about the food ingredients and the original cultural context. We also explored if the women could play a more active role when delivering the food than just handing it over. Facilitated by us, the women produced leaflets about the food to be distributed to the clients, and we supported them in getting a few catering orders. For example, we put them in contact with an architectural firm, and we accompanied them to an event at which they provided some tastes of Afghan and Iraqi food to employees at the architectural firm.

The architects clearly expressed their enthusiasm about the additional cultural experience and quickly adopted the Afghan terminology—for example, "Could you please bring me one more Kobbe?" It seemed that both HWA and the architectural firm were satisfied and that the studio would place the order, so we stepped back, leaving the women doing their business. Unfortunately, a few days later HWA informed us that the architects had turned down their offer, apparently because they thought that HWA was too expensive. We phoned the studio and discovered that communication problems had arisen: the company was asking the women to provide a formal offer, stating the menu and the quantity of food they would deliver. The women were not used to these kind of requests, and something went wrong in the communication between the actors: the architects thought that the quantity of food HWA would deliver would not be fair in relation to the price.

In hindsight, it is clear that we should have helped the women to structure and communicate their offer. However, during prototyping with HWA, it has always been problematic to find a balance between the support we should provide them while avoiding making the women feel weak, fragile, and too dependent on us. Nevertheless, the catering activity has developed further and it has become one of the central activities of HWA, even though the women lack access to a professional kitchen and thus have to do the cooking in their homes.

Prototype 2: The cultural intermediation
Early on, the women told us that they would like to try to do something for refugee children in Malmö. These kids, mainly between 13 and 17, are in Sweden without their

families. Malmö has welcomed a lot of Afghan and Iraqi orphans in recent years, and, since they share the same cultural background, the women felt they could offer something to them. However, working with refugee children is a sensitive matter, and we wanted to facilitate the creation of trust between HWA and the responsible department of Malmö's municipal government. Together with us, the women proposed to the city that meetings with the refugee children could be held to explore whether HWA might be able to provide some kind of valuable service for them in the future.

The municipality was positive but didn't want to play an active role. They suggested that we should contact the health-care company Attendo, which provides accommodation for refugee children in Malmö. Attendo was positive and we set up some experiments. We were particularly concerned about the possibility that the prototyping activities might evoke some undesirable memories in the women and the children. We decided to proceed carefully. The first step was simply to invite the kids to HWA's premises for an Afghan meal. They came accompanied by an Attendo employee. It turned out that most of them had not been eating home-made Afghan food since leaving their families, sometimes several years before. It became clear that food could play an important role, and the kids wished that there would be other occasions for meeting the women and eating together. According to the women, several of the children were quite depressed, and to some degree the women were emotionally stirred, but the emotional experience was compensated by the joy of feeling helpful.

The next step was to offer a cooking class to the children. That was done in collaboration with a media company called Nice Planet, which provided access to its kitchen. During this encounter, the children could alternate between cooking with the women and using Nice Planet's computers to explore social media together with some of the company's employees. (See figure 3.3.) The experience was quite positive for all involved (the CEO of Nice Planet said "I feel extremely inspired by meeting the women"). A chance to establish a more solid connection between HWA and Nice Planet emerged, which opened up the possibility for the next step in the artful inquiry with HWA: a possible collaboration between the women and the Mike Network, a Swedish network of businesswomen. (Nice Planet's CEO was a member of the Mike Network.) Making the necessary arrangement with the Mike Network took some time. Meanwhile, we tried to get civil servants from the city of Malmö involved in the effort.

Friendly hacking trial 1: A design workshop with civil servants
A role for designers that often is mentioned in relation to social innovation is to support capacity building, in which communities get empowered with new skills that can facilitate their everyday efforts. When the designer leaves the scene, this capacity will remain within the communities (Burns et al. 2006; Sangiorgi 2011). However, it became more and more clear that the members of HWA, although they might need

Designing in the Neighborhood 45

Figure 3.3
Refugee children cooking with a member of HWA. Per-Anders Hillgren (CC:BY-NC).

some support in doing business, were extremely capable and skillful. The reason why they still were regarded as a societal cost and as acting in the margins must thus be found elsewhere. From our perspective, it would rather be the municipality that needed capacity building and new skills for how to be able to support organizations like HWA. Consequently, from this moment, our attention to where to locate our design interventions shifted from the women toward the municipality, and our first opportunity for friendly hacking emerged. While we were slowly strengthening the women's relations with some civil servants, one of us was asked to participate in an internal municipal development group in the neighborhood in which the HWA members lived and operated. This position was then used to introduce, in the development group, the notion that municipal support for local communities could be valuable, which was received positively by a few civil servants. From this, we got a commission from the municipal government to hold a workshop on design and social innovation. The civil servants prepared the invitation list for the workshop, and HWA's members were not on it, but we sneaked them in by setting up a workshop assignment that was tailored to HWA's needs. The workshop seemed successful and provided many valuable findings for us. First of all, many of the civil servants questioned the vocabulary and practice of both design and social innovation, although some of them had had good experiences with grassroots initiatives. It also became clear that the municipality would have to rethink its practices for how to support NGOs and how to work with social innovation. Some prominent civil servants stated that there was a tension between formal structures and creativity, and that social innovation required them to work across departments. They also argued that there was a need for a more permissive culture, so that civil servants would be allowed to experiment and even to fail. They also discussed how regulations could be stretched, and what could be done without breaking any regulations or laws. Finally, specific scenarios were developed that described how community initiatives (similar to HWA) could be supported by the municipality through an iterative process. Several civil servants seemed very interested in exploring this further, and we expected the process to continue. However, nothing happened, and all our attempts to try to understand why nothing had happened failed. Some civil servants insinuated that the reason nothing had happened was cultural: that civil servants didn't want outsiders to interfere with their business. Although this could be seen as a failure, we learned some valuable things and acquired more allies.

Friendly hacking trial 2: Project Women Mike
While working with the municipality, we continued our conversation with the CEO of Nice Planet. She had been impressed by the women of HWA, and she wanted to find ways to work further with them. We wanted to foster collaborations between HWA and other extraordinary businesswomen, with the aim of strengthening HWA's business competence and, at the same time, challenging established notions of what could be regarded as a company or an entrepreneurial activity.

This new attempt involved the Mike Network (a Swedish organization that promotes peer-to-peer support between career women) and Make It Real (a side project of Nice Planet's CEO—a digital platform for connecting people with diverse competences for the purpose of developing projects). The idea was that Make It Real could facilitate encounters between HWA and the Mike Network with the aim of encouraging peer-to-peer support between the women of the two groups.

We offered to help the founders of Make It Real, since we thought that our long experience with HWA could help. However, they clearly stated that they did not want us to intervene in the project. For Make It Real, the project was a fundamental step in proving that they were able to act as matchmakers; thus, in order to establish their role and state their ownership of the process, they did not want to collaborate with us in structuring the encounters.

The Make It Real founders set up the process as a series of meetings between members of the two organizations. These meetings, mediated by a business coach, were aiming at developing a number of projects from "dreams and aspirations" of the participants.

The first meeting went rather well. The women got to know one another, then organized themselves into five groups focusing on activities that HWA was already carrying out, such as cooking and gardening. After the first day, each group had a series of meetings with the business coach to develop a project plan. In these encounters, it became apparent that it was difficult for HWA members to be able to attend all the planned meetings, because they were involved in several groups at the same time. Another issue was Make It Real's process structure, which was very traditionally business-focused and—already at the early stages—brought up questions such as "Who is your potential client?" and "What is your value proposition?" This approach turned out to be problematic for two reasons. First, it presumed a high commitment from the participants, while they barely knew one another. Second, although these question may sound quite

Figure 3.4
HWA and the Mike Network women out in the woods. Anna Seravalli (CC:BY-NC).

standard and easy to answer, they were completely new to the HWA members, and far from how they were accustomed to framing their everyday activities.

One encounter that went quite well was a day trip organized by one of Make It Real's founders at her house in the middle of a forest. The women spent the day picking herbs and cooking together, getting a chance to get to know one another better. Unfortunately, only a few women of the Mike Network were able to participate in that encounter, since it took place on a working day.

The process continued for a couple of months; then there was a meeting at which the groups were asked to present their proposals. During this meeting, Make It Real stated that each group should develop its projects independently. Consequently, the coach asked the HWA women, who were participating in several groups, to choose one group over the others. This raised concerns among the HWA women, but in the end every participant was on board. Another series of encounters for each group were planned.

A few days after this meeting, someone had forced the door of the small building where HWA met, stolen a binder with the names and addresses of the members in it, and started a fire. This was the third time HWA's meeting place had been burned down, and this time the women were quite scared by the theft of the information about them. HWA asked that the Make It Real project be put on hold.

This break allowed some doubts about the project to emerge. Specifically, HWA members felt that splitting up in separate groups was endangering their NGO, since they were not working as a unit. At the same time, some of the members of the Mike Network complained about the HWA members' lack of commitment in the process—they were not present at all the meetings, they were often late, and they were not very active in formulating and developing the proposals. Through discussions with the participants, we came to understand that there were two main issues: that the process was too fast and that the HWA women considered themselves a collective.

With Make It Real, we discussed the possibility of modifying the process by slowing down its pace. However, the founders of Make It Real found that unacceptable. According to them, the idea of a collective was keeping the women from expressing their full potential. They were also quite frustrated—they had found a potential source of financing for one of the projects, and the break was spoiling their efforts to secure it. In addition, the members of Make It Real were eager to find economical resources that could help them establish their initiative. These tensions, accompanied by the difficulties that HWA had in coping with the consequences of the fire, brought the project to an end.

This experience revealed the challenges and difficulties of "friendly hacking the business", since, when it comes to ideas and formats related to entrepreneurship, there seemed to be very few alternatives to the model of the independent and self-reliant woman. Even worse, there seemed to be no opportunity to experiment with alternative ideas as to what an entrepreneur is and what an enterprise can be. (What if an enterprise is driven by a collective? What if its aim is to generate social values and skills rather than profits?) The possibility of experimenting with alternative notions of enterprise and entrepreneurship was not just a matter of cultural or mental modes (collective vs. individual identity); it was also very much a matter of getting resources for and space within the business sector for experimenting with alternative models of entrepreneurship.

Friendly hacking trial 3: The incubator
The next attempt at friendly hacking was, once more, done within and with the municipality. (It is described in more detail in chapter 4.) Through establishing good relations with a civil servant that were inspired by design approaches through his previous work in the UK, we got the commission to explore how an incubator for social innovation could be structured and how its main features and support functions should be designed. We thought this incubator might make a difference for many invisible but resourceful stakeholders in the city. It was a very promising opportunity to build capacity within the municipality and establish a platform that could collaborate with stakeholders such as HWA. The process, bringing together civil servants, researchers, and grassroots initiatives (including HWA), developed a number of insights that were summed up for the municipality in a policy-briefing note. However, this process was then taken over by other actors. The final result was the establishment of a traditional incubator to support fairly traditional "close to market" business ideas. None of the grassroots initiatives that had been involved in the incubator process could fit into this structure. Although this intervention could also be seen as a severe failure, several civil servants were very disappointed with how the process had unfolded and wanted to continue to fight together with us to see if a structure that could collaborate with and support NGOs such as HWA could be established.

Friendly hacking trial 4: The Innovation Forum
After the incubator process, one of us got the opportunity to be embedded in a team of civil servants that was exploring the establishment of an Innovation Forum in which actors with complementary skills and knowledge could apply design-inspired methods to social challenges. The main task of the Innovation Forum was to develop a municipal structure that could respond to local challenges and initiatives from citizens. The process involved studying local, national, and international examples as well as investigating local grassroots organizations and ongoing municipal initiatives. Practitioners, researchers, and civil servants participated in workshops and seminars. Implementing design approaches within the municipality was regarded as promising; however, it also turned out to pose several challenges, one of which had to do with how some civil servants perceived the vocabulary of design. Insofar as the word 'design' itself

connotes such things as product design and fashion design, using the word as we used it didn't make sense for many civil servants. A serious effort was therefore undertaken to use phrases more appropriate to their language and their culture: "The empathic perspective!" "Collaborative problem formulation!" "Test early and test again!" Finally, a report was produced with concrete suggestions on how to proceed. Once the report had been produced and the municipality owned the process, we believed, the process would lead to the creation of a structure that could finally collaborate with initiatives such as HWA. Again, however, nothing happened.

Friendly hacking trial 5: Hacking financing bodies and indicators
A substantial part of the funding that supported our collaboration with HWA came from Tillväxtverket (the Swedish Agency for Economic and Regional Growth, henceforth abbreviated SAERG), which channels money from EU Structural Funds to regional development projects. Our team was part of a larger project, Malmö Nya Medier, that had very distinct project goals (such as supporting regional growth) and indicators (such as creating a specified number of jobs and companies). During our interventions with HWA, it became obvious that these indicators weren't appropriate. The work with HWA wouldn't easily yield an indicator such as "a new company." At the same time, we could see that HWA had the potential to become a valuable resource for society.

While our project was unfolding, some external evaluators hired by SAERG criticized it severely and argued that our efforts should be more directly targeted toward activities likely to develop commercial businesses. Luckily, we found an ally in a group of researchers that had been assigned by the same financing body to do a meta-study on various projects financed by them. During their study, they could connect the rationale behind our work to a larger context of European policies regarding social cohesion and the connection between social integration and economic growth. According to the researchers, we had succeeded in establishing new forms of collaboration, had utilized unused competences, had empowered people, and had connected stakeholders in ways that had the potential to be models for future efforts: "Here, they have succeeded in something many regard as impossible, but it has not been considered to be valuable." (Stigendal 2012, 49, authors' translation) They concluded that the problem wasn't with how we operated, but with the fact that our activities were measured and evaluated over too short a time span and with indicators that were too limited. We still do not know how much of an impact this report will have, but we hope it will open up more opportunities for similar efforts.

Further developments
We have continued to collaborate with HWA on different projects and funding schemes, though perhaps not as intensively. For example, we did a "tele-crafting" session in which HWA members and some Swedish textile craft groups were connected through

Skype to similar groups of women in Paris. HWA is also connected to two new larger projects in which we are extensively involved. One of these larger projects focuses on new ways of caring for the elderly; the other one takes a systemic perspective on physical and social investments in suburbs. We didn't have to invite HWA to take part in these projects. That group's visibility has increased, at least partly (we would argue) as a result of our stubborn engagement.

When it comes to friendly hacking, the most promising future paths seem to be related to the Commission for a Socially Sustainable Malmö (Stigendal and Östergren 2013), whose final report clearly states that one of the important strategies would be to continue the work that had been done toward establishing an Innovation Forum. The report also argued strongly for the importance of working with NGOs and the civic society. Other promising paths may also emerge from the alliances that we have built with fellow researchers at Malmö University. Thanks to this work, we are now engaged in exploring the possibility of an Institute for Participatory Citizenship, which could become a strong platform for addressing all the issues emerging from the work done with HWA.

HWA and the bigger picture

In this chapter, we have described infrastructuring and prototyping activities aimed at supporting the creative community HWA. The larger framework for this inquiry is how Living Lab the Neighborhood, by setting up collaborative design processes, can contribute to addressing different social challenges and can increase society's capacity to act. Within this framework, we have departed from grassroots efforts in the margins by collaborating with HWA. In this section we will connect the experiences from our collaboration with HWA to the findings of the Commission for a Socially Sustainable Malmö and discuss how HWA creates value and contributes to society and what kind of opportunities our work with them has generated.

First, as was stated above, the work HWA does has a very positive impact on its members and the area in which they live, but unfortunately the establishment doesn't acknowledge their activities. We don't think the prospects of a group such as HWA depend entirely on the members' own capabilities; we think they depend on how society is organized, how the economic system works, what cultural values are held, and what is considered normal. Therefore, in this section we will discuss the bigger picture in relation to HWA—what is considered to be work, what roles culture and civic society play, and what it means to be "integrated in the society."

One of the researchers involved in the Commission for a Socially Sustainable Malmö, the sociologist Mikael Stigendal, asserts the importance of problematizing how the parameters for urban development projects are set—for example, how and by whom a problem is defined, what the objectives are, what counts as results, what is considered normal, what actors are involved, and what is taken for granted:

It has become an established perspective that problems are taken for granted. Unemployed seem not to work, while they in reality work in different forms (taking care of the home, family and relatives). Youngsters without grades seem to be without knowledge, when they rather have a lot of knowledge that we do not count or measure.

The population in some parts of Malmö that are characterized by high unemployment, poverty, and low grades seems to lack everything—while they rather might have and do very much, but things that do not fit into the exclusive community that the Swedish society has developed into. What is the problem? The answer to this question will be essential for the solutions. (Stigendal 2011, 8; translated from Swedish).

Stigendal (2012) argues that achieving social sustainability in Malmö will require questioning the notion of knowledge, the notion of work, and what "to be integrated" entails. He points to the need to take a holistic approach. Rather than working with one isolated problem, or just viewing a problem as rooted in individuals or communities, he argues, we should also consider the systemic and structural factors. He quotes the EU report *Cities of Tomorrow*:

The challenge of moving toward shared visions of holistic, sustainable development models is to a certain extent the challenge of reaching a better and shared understanding of urban realities. Overall objectives need to be understood in wider terms of final objectives—e.g. sustainable quality of life and liveability—and not only in the more narrow terms of the means to get there (e.g. economic growth, employment rate, income levels). (Hermant-de-Callataÿ and Svanfeldt 2011, 61)

The objectives that have been dominant drivers for society at large in the last 30 years, such as economic growth and employment, are more and more put into question. The growth paradigm has been criticized by Jackson (2009) and by Stiglitz, Sen, and Fitoussi (2009), and new objectives such as happiness (Abdallah et al. 2012) and equality (Wilkinson and Pickett 2009) have been proposed as more in line with the ideas of sustainability and quality of life. A major contribution to this field has been made by Amartya Sen (1986), who points out that material well-being is only one of the factors determining a person's quality of life. Specifically, Sen states, the standards of living are based on the possibilities of *being* and *becoming* that someone has. These so-called functionings depend on a person's internal capabilities, such as skills, but also on external things, such as social networks and access to services. In Sen's view, therefore, material well-being is only one of the factors that determine quality of life. Among the others are access to education, opportunity to have a social life, and having a role in one's community.

Stigendal (2012, 8; translated from Swedish) claims that the large-scale urban development programs that have been carried out in Malmö in the last ten years haven't been successful according to objectives like "sustainable growth" and reducing "social, ethnic and discriminating segregation." But, he asks, "what if the objectives were wrong?" (ibid., 28). He means that there has been a lot of innovative work carried out, but that, because it has been concerned with "happiness, meaning of life, community and belonging" (ibid., 30), it has only to a minor degree been taken into account. However, Stigendal views this work as a rich inspirational resource for "developing new forms of work, knowledge, democracy and participation" (ibid.).

We think that it is within this context that the activities of HWA should be considered, along with our collaboration with HWA in exploring "new forms" for contributing to society and for being considered as part of it. Looked at through this lens, HWA seems less problematic, less marginal, and more like a promising initiative with resources and potentials yet to be explored, developed, and acknowledged.

Below we will develop this new perspective by following Stigendal's reasoning regarding work, which is very close to the feminist tradition in economics. Some feminist economists have argued that wage labor and the market economy represent work and production only in part (Waring 1988; Gibson-Graham 1996; Gibson-Graham et al. 2013). They have argued that capitalism focuses only on profit-generating activities and that it ignores non-wage forms of work and production and the fact that these forms of work are essential for wage labor and market labor to exist. According to Gottschlich (2013), household work, caring for family members, and voluntary work within civil society are fundamental for the (re)production of society and for its functioning.

Stigendal (2012, 34) argues that work has been limited to gainful employment and that "other kinds of work," including voluntary work within civil society, studying, household work, and care work, aren't acknowledged. He again cites the *Cities of Tomorrow* report, which claims that "collective goods, i.e. public goods or goods that are not exchanged in the market but are self-produced and exchanged within small groups such as a family, club or social network or association, are of great importance, and are always underplayed in economic analyses that focus on GDP alone," and that "these play a crucial role in quality of life and are often significant in economic development" (Hermant-de-Callataÿ and Svanfeldt 2011, 50).

It is in this sphere that HWA operates, but their *work* doesn't count today. Stigendal (2012, 34) argues that this "other kind of work" could be developed into gainful employment, and that is the kind of exploration we have done with the women, responding to their wishes of becoming more integrated and contributing to society. We would, however, argue that they are already contributing, but their work is neither visible nor properly rewarded and recognized. Stigendal makes an interesting turn when he claims that the kind of work that civil society produces perhaps should not be developed into conventional employment. He means that it may be an "other kind of work" that can contribute to social welfare and cohesion.

But how to make a decent living? Could there be other ways to get acknowledged and paid for the work one does? Is there something in between living on welfare and being employed or running a business? Maybe it is here that our prototypes can make sense. We have failed in developing a conventional business, but we have explored and demonstrated new and alternative forms of work. But this also points to the need for new economic models for this kind of value creation.

We will now discuss how our infrastructuring and prototyping activities have affected HWA in relation to the findings of the Commission for a Socially Sustainable Malmö. First, we will relate infrastructuring to the concept of social capital.

In their discussion paper for the Malmö Commission, Maria Emmelin and Malin Eriksson claim that social capital includes "our social networks, our social support, possibilities to participate in society and degree of social kinship in our neighborhood" (2012, 11; translated from Swedish). Social capital can be an individual resource, but it also can be a collective resource consisting of people's participation in social networks, reciprocity, and trust between people: "When this exists," Emmelin and Eriksson write, "collaboration and mutual efforts between people is easier and leads to a well functioning society." The members of HWA could be said to have a rich "bonding" social capital, being well connected within their 400-member group and in their neighborhood, but they lack "bridging" social capital that might connect them with other groups and networks, institutions, and actors that could provide them with the resources, skills, and knowledge they lack. Here, we claim that our infrastructuring activities—such as connecting HWA with new and complementary actors, and the prototypes that made the women's capabilities visible—increased HWA's bridging social capital. Will Norman (2012) argues that bridging social capital helps an organization to reach beyond its immediate neighborhood, something that is very important if a community is to develop and become innovative.

As was mentioned above, our prototyping activities helped reveal potential in the women's activities and helped to connect them with new actors. Although the prototype with the refugee children and Attendo didn't achieve much, it created a rumor that the women had interesting qualities and had potential for performing such work, and that led the Migrationsverket (the Migration Board) to ask HWA whether it could perform a similar service for single immigrant women. Although that request didn't yield any real results, it shows that prototyping can reveal possibilities and spread them to a wider network of possible stakeholders.

HWA has new facilities and is occasionally doing some catering, but it hasn't yet become a cooperative business. However, doing catering more regularly than in the past, and thus getting a reputation and access to more potential customers, is a good start. Catering is also the most conventional of HWA's activities and perhaps the easiest activity to exploit. Even so, HWA will have to face competition from stronger and better-established actors.

We think that HWA's less conventional qualities and activities, such as the work with refugee children, still has a huge potential and could be developed further. In our view, this represents the real challenge, but also a unique possibility to generate value for the women, the children, and society.

Figure 3.5
Four members of the HWA. Per-Anders Hillgren (CC:BY-NC).

Designing Living Lab the Neighborhood

The design trajectory, our journey, has shown that we couldn't have known from the beginning what kind of lab or *framework project* we would need when we initiated the first explorations. Even though we made a few strategic design decisions, such as explicitly taking an inclusive approach, most of our work has been spent on patchwork efforts to enable initiatives to grow from the bottom up, and on allowing for serendipity. Instead of following pre-defined plans, we navigated step by step among the opportunities and the obstacles we encountered. The whole process of building the lab could be seen as long-term reflective practice in which we have continuously matched different stakeholders and their respective agendas.

At times we were able to invite stakeholders to structured design workshops, but many of the encounters with stakeholders had to take other formats, often as iterative informal appointments. Still, we would argue that these encounters have been very designerly and that they could be seen as "artful inquiries" into the uncertain in which we continuously had to re-frame how situations could be understood and how these re-framings affected our opportunities. The importance of these informal appointments also emerged in the matchmaking between HWA and the Mike Network; for example, the informal herb-picking trip to the woods turned out to be more successful than the structured workshops.

During the process of infrastructuring and building Living Lab the Neighborhood, we have been exploring the boundaries of a *framework project*. This has brought our attention not only to community-based interventions, but also to other levels of design engagements. We have been influenced by La 27e Région's concept of "friendly hacking" aimed at influencing and possibly change the systemic levels of society. Even though more and more opportunities emerged for HWA to become a visible and acknowledged resource for society, the concept of friendly hacking became especially relevant when we could see that those opportunities didn't work within established societal structures.

We and La 27e Région aren't the only ones who argue that designers should take a more transformative role. Several design researchers have recently argued for challenging established structures instead of focusing on productivity, efficiency, experience, or improving services within existing societal structures (Botero and Saad-Sulonen 2013; DiSalvo 2012; Manzini and Staszowski 2013). However, when our design trajectory has reached these systemic levels, practical limitations emerged—for example, the fact that we have no mandate (or funding) to work with systemic change. Rather, we have to work with tactics, on in-between projects, and in informal alliances with civil servants and researchers who share our norms and interests.

Thinking about design and social innovation as long-term collaborations that could stretch between different sub-projects and different funding schemes has been important. Thanks to this long-term perspective, we have been able to build trust between diverse stakeholders, support mutual learning and dared to pick "tough" cases (i.e., cases that do not fit into existing structures and where you might end up without an immediate success story). This has also made it possible to slowly gain authority to work on more systemic levels (as exemplified by the above-mentioned project on physical and social investing in suburbs, in which we have been invited to work in alliances with researchers and civil servants who share an interest in systemic change).

What would be different if we had had a mandate to work on a systemic level from the beginning, as La 27e Région did? Or what if we had been embedded within and owned by the municipal structure, as Mindlab (an innovation unit in Denmark that are owned by and work with three ministries and one municipality) is? We believe that we probably wouldn't have been able to make the choices we made. Now that we are slowly reaching the systemic level, we are still rooted in the communities with which we have been working.

This design trajectory also says something about how we, as design researchers located at a university, can position ourselves. As other design researchers have begun to argue, when you are approaching societal challenges you have to go beyond the traditional design project set-up, with its clear client-consultant relationship, and explore opportunities that may emerge among a variety of stakeholders with diverse agendas and needs (Botero and Saad-Sulonen 2013; Staszowski et al. 2013). This makes the designer role more complex than the role of a traditional innovation lab, such as a corporate lab that is steered and guided by private interests, or an embedded public-sector lab owned and controlled by a public administration (e.g., Mindlab). If a design lab doesn't have a clear client-consultant role, who will decide where and what processes to initiate, with whom, and from what perspective?

Our guiding principles were to be inclusive and to address diverse and conflicting agendas. However, we believe it was important to start with the embedded practices of particular communities. We paid considerable attention to whom we should start our collaboration with, and we tried to find stakeholders who were marginalized but also resourceful and who had extensive social capital within their networks. Although we started from the agendas, needs, and opportunities that we could see in HWA, which always was a point of reference for where we should navigate with our design interventions, we tried to balance their agendas with the interests of other stakeholders, such as the Mike Network or the municipality. This balancing act made the aspect of ownership central. In our work with HWA, we saw the importance of establishing stakeholders' ownership over the processes not only as a way to gain their temporal participation but also as a way to ensure a long-term commitment to the implementation of a new service or solution.

While working with Make It Real and the Mike Network, we stepped back to allow the members of Make It Real to take ownership (because they had an extensive network in the business field). We tried to argue that we could take a more active role because we knew that our experience with HWA could have been very useful in the process. Make It Real turned down our offer and we decided to respect that, although we could see some likelihood that their quite structured and business-focused process would be problematic.

Because different funding opportunities also affect what a lab can focus on, and because research labs depend on external funding, we had to respect the objectives and goals of different research calls from funding bodies. Still, as we saw in friendly hacking trial 5, we also need to challenge these goals and work on our own guidelines. SAERG, the agency that funded our work with HWA, hired external evaluators who during most of the project were quite critical and argued that we were too far from established models of business support. However, in their final report, they surprisingly stated that one of the strengths of our Living Labs was their broad definition of innovation and their strong focus on societal challenges. Their recommendation was that this focus should be developed further and be used to profile innovation in the region.

Given what we have learned, can we still work within the frame of traditional innovation projects dealing only with growth? Engaging in a traditional innovation project would mean accepting a vision that we know may limit our ability to consider what is regarded as legitimate value production within society and what is regarded as work. On the other hand, we know that traditional innovation projects provide a great opportunity to engage with and influence powerful actors such as funding bodies and policy makers. Then should we support pre-defined goals, or should we challenge them? Should we develop solutions that work within existing structures, or should we continue exploring alternatives? Should we continue the "friendly hacking" from within the existing structures?

When, during this long design trajectory, we encountered HWA and explored their capacities not from an existing template but much more freely, they could prove their skillfulness both to us, to refugee children, to other researchers and to (some) civil servants. Since then, HWA has been a point of reference for where we should navigate with our artful inquiries. As long as HWA cannot connect to the rest of society and become a more acknowledged resource, we have to continue the journey.

References

Abdallah, Saamah, Juliet Michaelson, Sagar Shah, Laura Stoll, and Nic Marks. 2012. *The Happy Planet Index: 2012 Report.* New Economics Foundation.

Bason, Christian. 2010. *Leading Public Sector Innovation: Co-creating for a Better Society.* Policy Press.

Björgvinsson, Erling, Pelle Ehn, and Per-Anders Hillgren. 2010. Participatory Design and "Democratizing Innovation." In Proceedings of the Eleventh Participatory Design Conference, Sydney.

Björgvinsson, Erling, Pelle Ehn, and Per-Anders Hillgren. 2012. Agonistic Participatory Design: Working with Marginalised Social Movements. *CoDesign* 8 (2–3): 127–144.

Botero, Andrea, and Joanna Saad-Sulonen. 2013. Peer-Production in Public Services: Emerging Themes for Design Research and Action. In *Public and Collaborative: Exploring the Intersection Of Design, Social Innovation and Public Policy*, ed. E. Manzini and E. Staszowski. DESIS Network.

Brandt, Eva. 2006. Designing Exploratory Design Games—Can They Be the Guiding Framework for the Designer? In Proceedings of the Participatory Design Conference 2006, Trento.

Brown, Tim, and Jocelyn Wyatt. 2010. Design Thinking for Social Innovation. *Stanford Social Innovation Review* (http://www.ssireview.org).

Burns, Colin, Hilary Cottam, Chris Vanstone, and Jennie Winhall. 2006. Transformation Design (http://www.designcouncil.info/mt/RED/transformationdesign/TransformationDesignFinalDraft.pdf).

Christiansen, Jesper, and Laura Bunt. 2012. Innovation in Policy: Allowing for Creativity, Social Complexity and Uncertainty in Public Governance (http://www.nesta.org.uk/publications/assets/features/innovation_in_policy).

DiSalvo, Carl. 2012. *Adversarial Design*. MIT Press.

Emmelin, Maria, and Malin Eriksson. 2012. Kan socialt kapital "byggas in" in våra bostadsområden och därmed förbättra invånarnsa upplevda och mentala hälsa? Kommission för ett socialt hållbart Malmö.

Eriksson, Mats, Veli-Pekka Niitamo, Seija Kulkki, and Karl A. Hribernik. 2005. *State-of-the-Art in Utilizing Living Labs Approach to User-Centric ICT Innovation—A European approach*. Centre for Knowledge and Innovation Research, Helsinki School of Economics.

Florida, Richard. 2004. *The Rise of the Creative Class*. Basic Books.

Følstad, Asbjørn. 2008. Living Labs for Innovation and Development of Information and Communication Technology: A Literature Review. *Electronic Journal for Virtual Organizations and Networks* 10 (7): 99–131.

Gibson-Graham, J. K. 1996. *The End of Capitalism (As We Knew It): A Feminist Critique of Political Economy*. Blackwell.

Gibson-Graham, J. K., Jenny Cameron, and Stephen Healy. 2013. *Take Back the Economy: An Ethical Guide for Transforming Our Communities*. University of Minnesota Press.

Gottschlich, Daniela. 2013. Doing Away with "Labour": Working and Caring in a World of Commons. Keynote speech at Economics of the Commons Conference, Berlin.

Hamdi, Nabeel. 2004. *Small Change: About the Art of Practice and the Limits of Planning in Cities*. Earthscan.

Hermant-de-Callataÿ, Corrine, and Christian Svanfeldt. 2011. Cities of Tomorrow: Challenges, Visions, Ways Forward (http://ec.europa.eu/regional_policy/sources/docgener/studies/pdf/citiesoftomorrow/citiesoftomorrow_final.pdf).

Hillgren, Per-Anders, Anna Seravalli, and Anders Emilson. 2011. Prototyping and Infrastructuring in Design for Social Innovation. *CoDesign* 7 (3–4): 169–183.

Jackson, Tim. 2009. Prosperity without Growth? The Transition to a Sustainable Economy (http://www.sd-commission.org.uk/publications.php?id=914).

Jégou, François, and Ezio Manzini, eds. 2008. *Collaborative Services: Social Innovation and Design for Sustainability*. POLI.design.

Jégou, François, Stéphane Vincent, Romain Thévenet, and Anna Lochard. 2013. Friendly Hacking into the Public Sector: Co-Creating Public Policies within Regional Governments. Presented at Boundary-Crossing Conference on Co-Design in Innovation, Aalto University (http://www.slideshare.net/27eregion/friendly-hacking-into-public-sector).

Kommonen, Kari-Hans, and Andrea Botero. 2013. Are the Users Driving, and How Open Is Open? Experiences from Living Lab and User Driven Innovation Projects. *Journal of Community Informatics* 9 (3).

Manzini, Ezio. 2007. A Laboratory of Ideas: Diffuse Creativity and New Ways of Doing. In *Creative Communites*, ed. A. Meroni. POLI.design.

Manzini, Ezio, and Francesca Rizzo. 2011. Small Projects/Large Changes: Participatory Design as an Open Participated Process. *CoDesign* 7 (3–4): 199–215.

Manzini, Ezio, and Eduardo Staszowski. 2013. Introduction. In *Public and Collaborative: Exploring the Intersection of Design, Social Innovation and Public Policy*, ed. E. Manzini and E. Staszowski. DESIS Network.

Meroni, Anna. 2007. *Creative Communites: People Inventing Sustainable Ways of Living*. Polidesign.

Murray, Robin, Julie Caulier-Grice, and Geoff Mulgan. 2010. *The Open Book of Social Innovation*. Young Foundation and Nesta.

Norman, Will. 2012. *Adapting to Change: The Role of Community Resilience*. Young Foundation.

Nystrom, Anna-Greta, and Seppo Leminen. 2011. Living Lab—A New Form of Business Network. In Proceedings of the 17th International Conference on Concurrent Enterprising.

Sanders, Elisabeth, and Pieter Jan Stappers. 2008. Co-creation and the New Landscapes for Design. *CoDesign* 4 (1): 5–18.

Sangiorgi, Daniela. 2011. Transformative Services and Transformation Design. *International Journal of Design* 5 (2): 29–40.

Schön, Donald. 1983. *The Reflective Practitioner: How Professionals Think in Action*. Basic Books.

Schön, Donald. 1987. *Educating the Reflective Practitioner*. Jossey-Bass.

Sen, Amartya. 1986. The Standard of Living. Tanner Lecture on Human Values, Cambridge University, 1985.

Stålbröst, Anna. 2008. Forming Future IT: The Living Lab Way of User Involvement. Doctoral thesis, Luleå University of Technology.

Staszowski, Eduardo, Scott Brown, and Benjamin Winter. 2013. Reflections on Designing for Social Innovation in the Public Sector: A Case Study in New York City. In *Public and Collaborative: Exploring the Intersection of Design, Social Innovation and Public Policy*, ed. E. Manzini and E. Staszowski. DESIS Network.

Stigendal, Mikael. 2011. Malmö—de två kunskapsstäderna. Kommission för ett socialt hållbart Malmö.

Stigendal, Mikael. 2012. Malmö—från kvantitets- till kvalitetskunskapsstad. Kommission för ett socialt hållbart Malmö.

Stigendal, Mikael, and Per-Olof Östergren. 2013. Malmös väg mot en hållbar framtid. Hälsa, välfärd och rättvisa. Kommission för ett socialt hållbart Malmö.

Stiglitz, Joseph, Amartya Sen, and Jean-Paul Fitoussi. 2009. Report of the Commission on the Measurement of Economic Performance and Social Progress.

von Hippel, Eric. 2005. *Democratizing Innovation*. MIT Press.

Waring, Marilyn. 1988. *If Women Counted: A New Feminist Economics*. Harper & Row.

Wilkinson, Richard G., and Kate Pickett. 2009. *The Spirit Level: Why More Equal Societies Almost Always Do Better*. Allen Lane.

4 Connecting with the Powerful Strangers: From Governance to Agonistic Design Things

Anders Emilson and Per-Anders Hillgren

Social innovation involves—indeed, requires—redistributing power. It's well and good to talk about curing diseases, supporting social innovation, changing poor neighbourhoods, improving education, stimulating economic development, sustaining the environment—but changing the distribution of power? Why would those with wealth and power want to support that?
Frances Westley, Brenda Zimmerman, and Michael Quinn Patton, *Getting to Maybe* (2007, 121)

It is afternoon in Malmö's city hall. We are two design researchers, waiting outside a meeting room to make a presentation of what we can offer in the process of exploring what an incubator for social innovation in Malmö can be. We will meet with a group of civil servants responsible for trade, industry, and economic growth. The door opens and a man exits, having finished his presentation. Later we will realize that we have just met one of the "powerful strangers"—actors with "larger portions of money, authority and access" (Westley, Zimmerman, and Patton 2007, 99)—who will have major roles in what eventually will become an "incubator for new jobs" under the name Growth Malmö. We enter the room and make our presentation. Among other things, we say that we have good connections with innovative grassroots organizations. One of the civil servants replies "We need that!"

The rather trivial response "We need that!" summarizes why people collaborate: they lack something that someone else has. It is also a fact that today, more than in the past, an organization has to collaborate with other organizations to get access to resources (knowledge and skills) it needs if it is to be innovative (Lakhani and Panetta 2007; Lusch, Vargo, and Tanniru 2010). Collaboration is also the "underlying ethic" of social innovation (Mulgan 2012, 61). That was one reason why, when Malmö Living Lab the Neighborhood got the commission from the municipality to run a series of workshops to explore what kind of support structures and functions an incubator for social innovation could have, we gathered a rather diverse group of people representing the private sector, the public sector, and the third sector, as well as academia. In the workshops, knowledge, experiences, and values were shared, but there also was some confrontation. The other reason we wanted to gather a diverse group of actors was purely democratic. An incubator aimed at social innovation and the improvement of well-being of all inhabitants in Malmö is something that concerns everybody, and therefore a wide perspective of people should be able to make their opinions heard, to define issues, and to contribute ideas.

This chapter will tell the story of the incubator process in relation to local democracy and emerging initiatives of social innovation in Malmö, the third most populous city in Sweden. Malmö has a reputation as a world leader in environmental sustainability, but it is struggling with growing social inequalities, child poverty, unemployment, and violence. To meet these challenges and to achieve a balance between all three aspects of sustainability—the social, the environmental, and the economic—the municipality of Malmö has launched two projects: the Områdesprogram för ett socialt hållbart Malmö (Area Programs for a Socially Sustainable Malmö and the Kommissionen för ett socialt hållbart Malmö (Commission for a Socially Sustainable Malmö).

The Area Programs is a five-year project with the objective of improving living conditions, security, and job opportunities in five low-income areas in Malmö. Involving citizens and creating innovations is fundamental to the work of the Area Programs. The idea of an incubator came from a civil servant responsible for the Area Programs who saw the need for a clearer structure for innovative work.

The final report of the Malmö Commission calls for *knowledge alliances*, meaning "equal collaborations between researchers and stakeholders from, for example, administration, associations, and trade and industry" (Stigendal and Östergren 2013, 131; translated from Swedish). But, as this chapter will make clear, such alliances easily fail or fall apart if already powerful actors refuse to take part and refuse to let go of power, resources, and control. Instead of yielding new alliances, new knowledge, and social innovations, the whole project slips back to business as usual and undemocratic processes. However, if the goals are to produce social innovation and to tackle complex challenges such as sustainability, it will be necessary to explore different proposals for how to constitute knowledge alliances and new democratic platforms. Two things that are central to this story are the concept of governance and the fact that political processes now are carried out by informal governance networks that most often consist of "coalitions of economic, socio-cultural or political élites" (Swyngedouw 2005, 1999). Many researchers describe these governance networks as undemocratic. For that reason, there is a need to strengthen the democratic aspect by means of new forms of participation and democratic platforms (Stigendal 2011).

In this chapter we will discuss how local democracy and informal governance networks may be influenced by recent developments in participatory design such as "design things" (Ehn 2008; Binder et al. 2011; Björgvinsson, Ehn, and Hillgren 2010, 2012a), "infrastructuring," and "agonism" (Björgvinsson, Ehn, and Hillgren 2010, 2012a). We will focus on the notion of "agonistic design things" and on whether an agonistic design thing can be a kind of extended knowledge alliance that can include more heterogeneous actors and, consequently, their knowledge and their experiences. We will also argue that an agonistic design thing might be of relevance when engaging in social innovation, and that this requires redistributing power and resources (Westley, Zimmerman, and Patton 2007).

The incubator process consisted of two phases: (1) the workshop series at the university, led by Living Lab the Neighborhood, and (2) the preparation and writing of the decision document for the politicians at the municipality's Trade and Industry Agency. Two types of networks have been active in producing the outcome: (1) the workshop network (with the character of a design thing) and (2) the trade and industry network (with the character of an informal governance network). The only connection between these phases and networks was the written report from Living Lab the Neighborhood (Ehn et al. 2011) and three participants in the workshops. In the transition and translation between these phases and networks, the object of design—the incubator for social innovation—vanished.

Governance and accountability

The concept of governance has got a lot of attention in political theory in recent years and can be seen both as an analytical framework and as a phenomenon. Although the definition of 'governance' has been debated, most often the emphasis is on the idea that a significant part of politics takes place, not within formal governmental institutions, but rather in partnerships with non-governmental actors (Pierre and Peters 2000). One of the more influential contributors to governance theory, Rod Rhodes (1997), has argued that governance is performed mainly through informal self-organized networks, stretching between the public and private sectors. Governance can be seen as a process of "hollowing out the state" whereby privatization of services has increased at the expense of the public sector, which has become smaller and fragmented (ibid.). It can also be seen as the state's ability to adapt to rapid external changes and to find new approaches to steering society in a world where complexity evolves and challenges go beyond what the state alone can solve (Pierre and Peters 2000).

Whatever perspective on governance you choose, it also poses some challenges regarding political accountability. When politics is made in informal networks, one of the consequences is that the boundaries between public and private become blurred, which leads to a blurring of responsibilities and accountability (Stoker 2000). This is not necessarily intentional, but the complexity of the networks makes it difficult for average citizens to understand who is accountable for what or to understand how responsibilities are divided (Pierre and Peters 2000). Finally, and highly relevant from a participatory design perspective, if political power is exercised through informal networks, some actors will always be excluded from these networks (Stoker 2000).

City politics and the political landscape in Malmö

To better understand the role of governance networks in the local context, we turn to the political scientist Tove Dannestam. In her dissertation she examines the political landscape in Malmö and reveals that a significant part of the political processes in the city is executed through informal networks including important key representatives from the business sector and leading civil servants and politicians. According to Dannestam (2009), decisions and consensus are often settled in the corridors before they enter into more public political forums. This has two important implications. One is that it provides the people in these networks with the "ability to act", which make them vigorous and efficient. Dannestam (ibid., 189; translated from Swedish) presents transcripts of interviews in which this becomes evident—for example, the city's former planning director says "In the city of Malmö you can get things done." The same former planning director also argues that these informal networks have evolved and are important because the "municipality's traditional vertical division between units can be paralyzing." However as Dannestam (ibid., translated from Swedish) states, this has some implications for democracy: "On one side you have efficiency and the ability to act, on the other side you have the democratic aspects of planning which tends to be a slow process." Dannestam also describes how these informal governance networks, both in Malmö and other cities around the world, are relevant to what is called "city politics." If the concern of traditional local politics was how to implement welfare services, the aim of city politics is to increase local economic growth and brand cities as attractive, attractiveness being defined mostly from a business perspective. Dannestam writes that city politics have been in favor of the trade and industry's interests and their influence on local politics. Through city politics, a market-economy orientation has been established in the public administration. Another consequence of city politics and governance is that issues that in traditional government were characterized by political conflict are now described as a neutral development in everyone's interest. This consensus between a limited network of actors is considered problematic from a democratic perspective by many researchers. Mikael Stigendal (2011) cites Claude Jaquier's assertion that this consensus hides fundamental conflicts and therefore the democratic aspect needs to be strengthened through new forms of participation.

Networks and social innovation

The kind of networks and resources that are considered to be valuable in social innovation differ sharply from the small, informal, and exclusive governance networks that have been described above. One reason is that social innovation is not limited to market-oriented entrepreneurship, which is favored in governance and city politics. Westley and Antadze (2010, 3) claim that social innovation "does not necessarily involve a commercial interest, though it does not preclude such interest," and that "more definitively, social innovation is oriented towards making a change at the systemic level."

In social innovation theory, the ultimate goal of such innovation is often described as systemic change (Murray, Caulier-Grice, and Mulgan, 2010; Nicholls and Murdock 2012; Westley and Antadze 2010). This disruptive level of social innovation (see chapter 2 in this volume and page 4 of Nicholls and Murdock 2012) involves interaction between diverse elements such as social movements, business models, laws, and new practices (Murray, Caulier-Grice, and Mulgan 2010). Systemic innovation "commonly involves changes in public sector, private sector, grant economy and household sector, usually over long periods of time" (ibid., 13).

Disruptive social innovation will not be content with relieving the symptoms with "band-aid" solutions; it aims for the underlying causes. This often entails challenging established institutions that control the distribution of resources and power. To be able to disrupt and change the broader system, "a social innovation must cross multiple social boundaries to reach more people and different people, more organizations and different organizations, organizations nested across scales (from local to regional to national to global) and linked in social networks" (Westley and Antadze 2010, 5).

Networks that only span between the private sector and the public sector will, consequently, not be sufficient to achieve real system transformation. Rather, collaboration between the establishment and radicals (Westley, Zimmerman, and Patton 2007) will be needed. The powerful established governance networks that often are seen as efficient and as having a strong "ability to act" will not necessarily be the solution, because social change can't be enforced from the top down; rather it is necessary to mobilize resources and create conditions for change to emerge (ibid.). Also, when aiming for social change it is crucial to put inquiry ahead of certitude and to allow paradoxes and multiple perspectives, because "there are no simple formulas—serious and significant social change necessarily involves recognizing and dealing with complex systems" (Westley, Zimmerman, and Patton 2007, ix). This calls for networks built on heterogeneity and explicit inclusion of smaller actors. One such network concept is "the bees and the trees," where the "bees" are bottom-up actors with ideas and the "trees" are top-down actors with resources and power:

Social change depends, in other words, on alliances between what could be called the "bees" and the "trees." The bees are the small organisations, individuals and groups who have the new ideas, and are mobile, quick and able to cross-pollinate. The trees are the big organisations—governments, companies or big NGOs—which are poor at creativity but generally good at implementation, and which have the resilience, roots and scale to make things happen. Both need each other, and most social change comes from alliances between the two, just as most change within organisations depends on alliances between leaders and groups well down the formal hierarchy. (Mulgan 2007, 20)

Here it is relevant to highlight the importance of knowledge as a resource, and the need for different actors to collaborate and exchange different knowledge to be innovative—something that has been emphasized in recent innovation research (Lakhani and Panetta 2007; Lusch, Vargo, and Tanniru 2010). It is also important to emphasize that it's not only the "bees" that needs the resources of the "trees" but that the established and powerful actors also need the resources of weaker actors—the knowledge from the margins. Murray (2009) brings up the shift to a networked paradigm where distributed systems spread complexity from centralized organizations to the margins—to households and front-line workers. These actors at the margins could be seen as closely related to the "bees":

Those at the margins have what those at the center can never have—a knowledge of detail—the specificity of time, of place, of particular events, and in the consumer's and citizens case, of need and desire. This is the potential. But to realise it requires new terms of engagement with users, new relations at work, new terms of employment and compensation. (ibid., 19)

Westley and Antadze (2010, 5) also emphasize the importance of local contributions and viewpoints from marginalized actors: "[S]ocial innovation not only *serves* vulnerable populations, but is *served* by them in turn." With departure in these theoretical accounts, we think it is interesting to explore if participatory design and agonistic design things could be a suggestion for "new forms of participation"—new platforms for gathering heterogeneous stakeholders to deal consciously with societal challenges and social innovation.

Participatory design and agonistic design things

The question "Who should participate?" has always been central to participatory design. Participatory design has paid considerable attention to marginalized actors and power relations. However, when participatory design has moved from a strong focus on "workplace" controversies related to information technology and become more engaged in public spheres and everyday life, the range of who can participate in design processes has expanded. If the former focus was on a fixed user group within a workplace, it is now on heterogeneous and evolving networks that cut across organizational and community borders, very much in line with the kind of networks that social innovation researchers and practitioners, and now also the Malmö Commission, have requested.

This shift has also raised the question of what the central object of design should be. We have argued that it is more crucial to pay attention to designing *things* (sociomaterial assemblies) than "things" (objects) (Ehn 2008; Björgvinsson, Ehn, and Hillgren 2010, 2012a,b). The rationale behind this is that when you stage and set the scene of a development/design project (and what could become larger investments into a future change) it is critical to consider what human and non-human resources could be aligned. By "non-human resources" we mean artifacts, information, and design devices such as sketches and prototypes.

What makes the concept of design things relevant in a discussion about governance and social innovation is the original meaning of the word "Thing" in Nordic and Germanic societies: a governing assembly in which "disputes were solved and political decisions made" (Binder et al. 2011, 1). Thinking of design as assemblies in which heterogeneous actors are gathered into design things puts the focus on the diverse matters of concerns among the participating stakeholders. Still, it is not only the initial gathering of a broad spectrum of actors that discuss matters of concerns that makes a design thing relevant, but also how this discussion continues through collaborative experiments and prototypes (human and non-human) and where the design thing continuously could evolve and move the object of design forward. A design thing should be considered as a process that involves both setting the preconditions for a process of change and opening up opportunities for new design things in which future users and stakeholders can discuss new matters of concern according to changed conditions and re-design the outcomes of previous design things. In this process the design thing also makes the objects of design and the matters of concern public through workshops, exhibitions, public debates, blogs, and videos.

Another concept that has been explored within participatory design in recent years, and one that we believe could be valuable for governance and social innovation, is *agonism* (Björgvinsson, Ehn, and Hillgren 2010, 2012a; DiSalvo 2010, 2012). The concept was brought forward by the political scientist Chantal Mouffe (2000a,b) as a way to approach political hegemony. Marginal actors often are left outside political coalitions that build on consensus. Agonism is best understood in relation to antagonism (the struggle between enemies). Agonism is the struggle between adversaries. An adversary is "somebody whose ideas we combat but whose right to defend those ideas we do not put into question" (Mouffe 2000a, 15). For Mouffe (2000b), "agonistic struggle" is at the core of a vibrant democracy. Democracy should promote a multiplicity of voices, adversaries with opposing views debating matters of concern constructively and passionately. The aim should not be to reach consensus or to support rational decision-making processes, but rather to make the alternative views clearer and more visible.

Merging the concept of *agonism* and the concept of *things* highlights that it is important not only to assemble heterogeneous stakeholders who might aim for a shared vision and agree on a preferred solution, but also to bring out alternative opportunities and allow for a polyphony of voices and for mutually vigorous but tolerant disputes among these stakeholders.

With this as a background, we would argue that, whereas governance researchers have asked for new forms of participation, new inclusive arenas, and platforms (Stigendal 2011), participatory design and agonistic design things could be central elements in what could constitute a political arena. In this way we also position ourselves in relation to a view of social innovation that is more disruptive, focusing on politics and system change and "aiming to change power-relations, alter social hierarchies, and reframe issues to the benefit of otherwise disenfranchised groups" (Nicholls and Murdock 2012, 5). We will therefore return to the process of establishing the incubator for social innovation to see how such an agonistic design thing could emerge in practice.

The incubator workshop as an agonistic design thing

After the meeting in Malmö's city hall, Living Lab the Neighborhood was commissioned by the municipality to conduct three design workshops to explore how the incubator should be structured and how its functions should be designed to be able to support new initiatives in the city. We saw this as an opportunity to explore how an agonistic design thing could be set up. Although this specific case started with the commission, some crucial design work was conducted long before that, making it easier for us to mobilize relevant competences and stakeholders into the workshop process. When we engage in design research, our basic strategy is to go beyond a well-defined design project with pre-defined stakeholders, time lines, and goals. Rather, we aim for a process of *infrastructuring*, focusing on building long-term relationships with diverse stakeholders who have complementary competences. We also aim to work with constellations of actors that are more heterogeneous than the governance networks that usually are active in the political processes in Malmö. In the infrastructuring process, we explore how new opportunities for design interventions can emerge from matchmaking between stakeholder interests and resources (Björgvinsson, Ehn, and Hillgren 2010). Because we had been working with the infrastructuring process before the incubator discussions started, we had been engaged in many ways with NGOs, with social innovators, with small companies, and with civil servants. This involvement had helped us to get a sense of their capabilities and to build mutual trust. All these actors made up a network of potential participants in different design processes.

When choosing whom to invite to the workshops, our strategy was to start with six local initiatives consisting of associations or small companies that could act as potential users of services that the future incubator could provide. Some of them were well-established initiatives, such as *Aluma*, a magazine (now defunct) that was sold by homeless people; others were grassroots organizations, such as the multicultural Herrgård's Women's Association, whose members live and work in the margins but have strong networks and extensive knowledge and ideas about social change. Some started as grassroots initiatives but have been able to grow and become established as a part of the municipality, giving them experience of being both within and outside the more established institutions such as the Kaninhotellet (literally "Rabbit Hotel"), a youth center that also accommodates many small pets. Some have, through our previous design activities, gone into joint collaboration with each other, combining intercultural competences with new-media skills. (One example is Miljonprocessen, a joint business venture between a hip-hop community and a small ICT company.) We also invited Barn i stan (a project run by a Somali association that wanted to use urban farming to connect immigrant kids with Swedish seniors in one of Malmö's toughest areas) and Feed'us (a small group of young adults, tired of making trouble in the streets, who wanted to create a company based on recycling and to become positive role models for children and teenagers). All these stakeholders could be considered as "bees" that needed resources from the "trees," but they also possessed unique resources themselves. Most of them also had a lot of "intercultural competence" or other kinds of knowledge from the margins regarding issues like social exclusion, education, or homelessness, a kind of knowledge that the "trees" need to be able to create relevant change.

All the stakeholders mentioned above had been active in taking initiatives to achieve social change in their local environments and, as said, could be seen as potential users of the incubator. Based on the participatory design standpoint that "those affected by a design should have a say in the design process" (Binder et al. 2011, 162), but also to utilize their knowledge from the margins, we decided to set up a significant part of the workshop around their everyday practices, capabilities, and needs. As a complement, we recruited research colleagues with complementary knowledge, people from organizations supporting social entrepreneurial initiatives, traditional business developers, and civil servants representing different municipal departments. Together, the workshop participants represented a huge resource of complementary competence and perspectives, potentially with agonistic perspectives on what could be an incubator for social innovation.

The workshops
In the first workshop, the six initiatives presented their experiences and issues. Divided into smaller groups, the participants started mapping and discussing the challenges and opportunities of each initiative, trying to identify issues that the future incubator would be able to deal with. In the second workshop, the participants departed from the challenges of the different initiatives and focused on identifying support functions of the incubator and how it could relate to other organizations and society as a whole. Questions regarding trust, ownership, financing, criteria for evaluating ideas, and other matters emerged. The third and last workshop created four scenarios for how the incubator could work.

In the first scenario the concept of a "free zone" was important, and "intermediaries" that could spot ideas and translate dreams into a language that could be accepted by bureaucracy played the most central role. The second scenario was an incubator that was run by the actors that were already active in social innovation and could move around in the city. Here too the idea of a "free zone" was important, and it was suggested that different initiatives should be judged by "crowd judging." The third

Figure 4.1
The participants gathered in a design thing during the workshops at the university.

scenario was a decentralized incubator with a pool of resources. Here the emphases were on the importance of the local context and on the idea that initiatives should be developed locally. The incubator, it was suggested, should work as a test bed, and the issue of power balance was brought up; the consensus was that the social innovators should have as much power as the "big elephants" (municipality, academia, trade, industry). The fourth scenario emphasized that different initiatives need different kinds of support and therefore had to enter into the incubator at different levels. Here too the idea of a "free zone" was emphasized.

Outcomes of the workshops

The breadth and the diversity of the stakeholders was evident in the outcomes of the workshops, which we present below in four recurring categories.

Ownership and mandate   The general view was that not only the municipality should own and run the incubator but that also the actors active in social innovation should take part in running the incubator. The participants clearly expressed their will to take part in the following process of creating and building the incubator and that "we as builders need to be the owners." They also pointed out that the incubator needed to have a "mandate" from those actors who are active within social innovation in Malmö today. That message was repeated in our report (Ehn et al. 2011).

Mental free zone It was agreed that the incubator should be a place where civil servants and social innovators could shift roles, or work in a different mode than they do on an everyday basis; to create a "mental free zone." We would argue that this came about because of the mix of stakeholders and perspectives that were represented in the workshops. A free zone was also discussed in the sense of a safe place to experiment with ideas and challenge economical and juridical frames.

Centralized vs. distributed One of the more interesting outcomes had to do with the set-up and location of the incubator. Traditionally an incubator is viewed as a specific space with staff-members such as business developers and coordinators that support new business initiatives. During the workshops, that structure was questioned. The majority favored a more distributed model, building on existing resources, such as an organization, a company, or a local municipality office that already provided support services, and locating activities in different districts of the city. In the final report, we discussed two contrasting models—the central incubator and the decentralized incubator—and showed how they could fit into the wider social innovation landscape of Malmö. We thought it was important to not only focus on the incubator as such but to try to take a systemic view by embracing the whole chain of innovation. (See figure 4.2.)

Mutual learning process At first many criticisms of the municipality and civil servants were voiced, but quite soon the discussion came to focus on the importance of establishing mutual learning between the stakeholders—between different departments within the municipality as well as between civil servants, citizens, and NGOs. Some self-criticism also was voiced, and one representative of the third sector expressed the opinion that also they needed to renew themselves. The "free zone" was mentioned as a place for mutual learning.

Matchmaking Our initial infrastructuring of the workshop process, in which we aimed for a mix of organizations and competences, created immediate results during the workshops. We could see how different constellations were starting to emerge: the magazine *Aluma* began to negotiate with the interaction design company Do-Fi on how to deal with money transactions in a cashless society, the ideation bureau Artcom helped Feed'us to write a business plan, and the Swedish Red Cross also started a conversation with Feed'us.

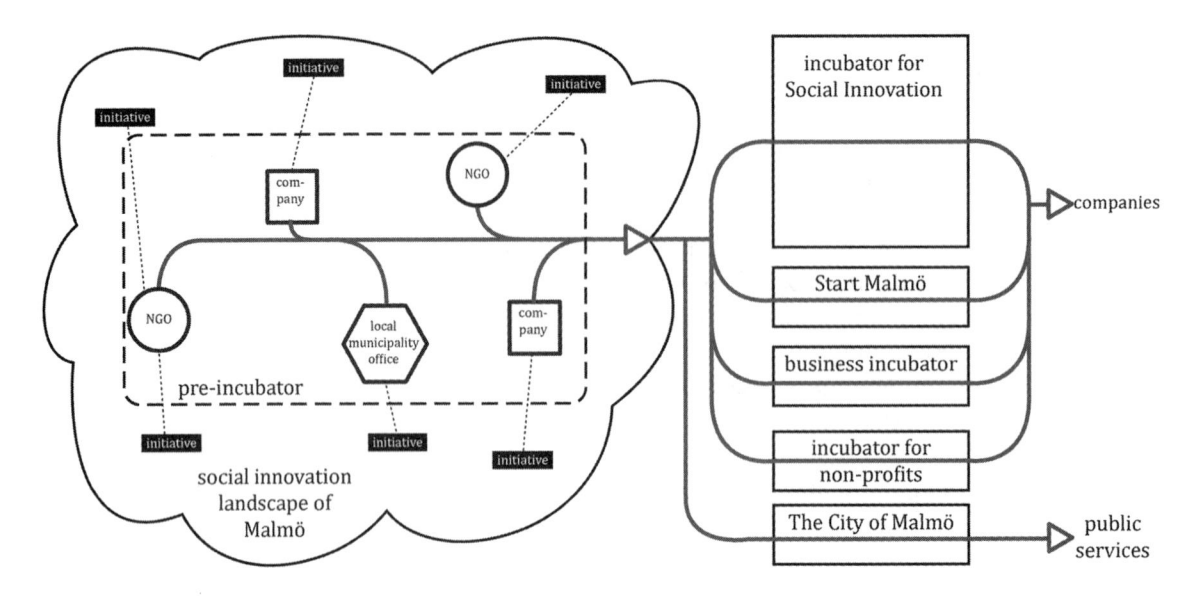

Figure 4.2
The distributed incubator model that emerged during the workshops was transformed into a new model with both a traditional incubator and a distributed pre-incubator. The pre-incubator built on existing resources in the wider social innovation landscape of Malmö, such as a company, an NGO, or a local municipality office that already provided support services. The idea was that the pre-incubator could channel more mature business initiatives to Start Malmö and other established business incubators. However, it would also have the capacity to support initiatives that were far from having traditional business opportunities, but with a potential to create value for society in the form of an association or developing into a public service.

From agonistic design thing to governance by "powerful strangers"

After the three workshops, we summed up the results and had a meeting with the civil servant responsible for the incubator process and the civil servant responsible for writing the official report that would be the basis for further decisions in the City Council. They couldn't really accept the distributed incubator model, to some degree because they could see how hard it would be to get support for such a model in the City Council. However, they realized that a traditional central incubator would need ideas and initiatives coming from the city areas with social challenges, and that, because of the need to mobilize, use, and support existing grassroots resources, it was necessary to consider the whole chain of innovation. During the meeting, these considerations opened up the possibility of a creative act of "bureaucratic translation." The distributed incubator model was transformed into a new model consisting of both a traditional incubator and a pre-incubator, in which the setup of the pre-incubator was based on findings from the workshops. The bureaucratic skills of the civil servants made it possible to translate the workshop findings into a document that presented something new (and slightly radical), but which was still within the City Council's "safe zone." So far, the design thing was still alive.

In a way, the bureaucratic translation continued in the more closed process at the Trade and Industry Agency. Now there were only a few actors, most of them with a business perspective. The exception was the civil servant responsible for the Area Programs, who had come up with the idea of establishing an incubator for social innovation. With the exceptions of that civil servant, the one from the Trade and Industry Agency responsible for the incubator process, and our business developer, the other actors hadn't participated in the workshops, even though some of them had been invited. From here on, these actors will be characterized as *powerful strangers*.

The concept of the powerful stranger is brought forward by Westley, Zimmerman, and Patton (2007, 95), who see power as control of resources ("time, energy, money, talent and social connections") that creating something new requires. Power also means the power to maintain the status quo or the power to change it. Anyone who wish to transform a system has to unlock resources claimed by the status quo. Therefore, a change maker that lacks resources should embrace "the risk and rewards of engaging the powerful stranger":

Early power and resources for change are often found through *connecting*, through joining together with fellow travellers, like-minded individuals whose chief resources are their passion, their time and their energy. If successful at this stage, the community becomes a movement, which opens the door for *confrontation* and possibly conflict as those who control larger portions of money, authority and access resist demands for change. If the system is to be transformed as opposed to overturned, *collaboration* between the radicals and the establishment must be created. If it succeeds, deep shifts in the distribution of resources may occur. (ibid., 99)

The actors in the trade and industry network are powerful in the sense that "they control larger portions of money, authority and access" (Westley, Zimmerman, and Patton, 2007, 99) and are strangers in the sense that they never connected, confronted, or collaborated with the other stakeholders during the workshops. Instead they exercised their power hidden and at a distance from the most important stakeholders—the potential social innovators, entrepreneurs, and front-line workers with knowledge from the margins—the actors the social incubator was originally intended for. The powerful strangers never took part in mutual learning with the other stakeholders.

The trade and industry network prepared a document that included quite a few of the outcomes from the workshops but focused mainly on new jobs. The politicians rejected that document because they didn't understand social innovation. "Some politicians," one civil servant commented, "didn't understand the concepts of social innovation and social entrepreneurship: 'You should not fiddle with the municipal competence.'" "To work with an assignment that is the municipality's by law," the civil servant continued, "that's holy, you can't touch that."

The participants had to compromise. They took out all the sentences that mentioned social innovation, and added, as the aforementioned civil servant put it, that the "activities should not be aimed at assignments that belongs to the municipality by law." Later it became evident that the civil servants who became intermediaries between the design thing and the trade and industry network had struggled with defending the core statements relating to social innovation in the document. One civil servant thought that the participants had gone too far and suggested returning to the original focus on an incubator for social innovation. Again there was a need for "bureaucratic translation" and rewriting, and the result was a compromise. The headline of the new text was now "The establishment of an incubator for entrepreneurs with a focus on social innovations" (Spjut 2011). In the first sentence, that was changed to "an incubator for new jobs and innovation," and that wording dominated the rest of the text. But if one read between the lines, the main message from the workshops—that is, the idea of a local pre-incubator system that could complement a central incubator—was still there. The mentioning of an "innovation system" that could work on two levels was also important. But the most important actors working on the local level—grassroots organizations, non-profit organizations, and NGOs—weren't represented in the trade and industry network that had the power to decide what would become the final decision document and they were mentioned only briefly in the document. From the perspective of participatory design and the wish to create a new innovation system to tackle social challenges, the absence of third-sector representatives and the other "bees" was devastating.

Because we arranged the workshops as a design thing, we wanted there to be a democratic process in which heterogeneous actors could take part. In the first phase of the incubator process (the workshops at the university) we were quite successful in this, but when the invited powerful actors from the trade and industry and the municipality were absent the perspective of the public and that of the third sector dominated. Although we had a very good precondition for a design thing, by losing these powerful actors we also lost some of the expected agonistic struggle and mutual learning. When the powerful strangers took a more active role in the second phase of the incubator process and the actors who should have been preparing a decision document for the politicians narrowed down significantly, the design thing began to fall apart. From that moment on, the incubator was in the hands of a small and elite group consisting mainly of people with a trade and industry perspective—representatives of the established governance networks. We were back to "business as usual."

Discussion

In this chapter we have analyzed the process of exploring what an incubator for social innovation could be. The idea of a social incubator came from a civil servant responsible for the Area Programs who saw the need of a clearer structure for innovative work. However, the outcome of the incubator process was not an incubator for social innovation; it was an organization called Growth Malmö that focuses on supporting existing companies that want to hire more employees. Some of the companies they support are claimed to be social entrepreneurs. In August of 2013, Growth Malmö reported to have contributed to the creation of 1,000 new jobs. Again the governance networks had demonstrated their efficiency and ability to act. Of course, the creation of new jobs is an important contribution to the advancement of welfare and social sustainability in Malmö. But at what cost?

Malmö lost an emerging "knowledge alliance" concerned with supporting social innovation. It also lost a more holistic view of such an innovation system. In the incubator report (Ehn et al. 2011) we sketched an innovation system with many different actors, including the mother organization of Growth Malmö—Start Malmö. But with the establishment of Growth Malmö it seemed that the City of Malmö was satisfied.

The moment the politicians decided to accept the proposal from the trade and industry network, the design thing at the university dissolved and the actors that had been mobilized scattered, going off to work by themselves, and their ability to act with a common purpose became neutralized. Also lost was an emerging new democratic platform—something that, together with knowledge alliances, the Malmö Commission would later emphasize as important in creating social sustainability *along with* new jobs. We will therefore now discuss why knowledge alliances and new democratic platforms are needed.

In trying to understand what happened when the object of design (the issue of the incubator) traveled from the design thing at the university to the governance network at the Trade and Industry Agency, we could observe both a lack of accountability and the exclusivity of small informal networks. As was mentioned earlier, both of these factors have been brought up as major drawbacks by governance researchers who argue that they may threaten democracy (Dannestam 2009; Stoker 2000). Swyngedouw (2005, 1999), who points to the tension between the possibilities of increased democratization through participatory governance and the fact that these governance networks are often led by "coalitions of economic, socio-cultural or political élites," states that governance has "undoubtedly given a greater voice and power to some organizations (of a particular kind—i.e. those who accept playing according to the rules set from within the leading élite networks)." "However," he continues, "it has also consolidated and enhanced the power of groups associated with the drive toward marketisation and has diminished the participatory status of groups associated with social-democratic or anti-privatisation strategies" (ibid., 2003). Stigendal (2011, 31; translated from Swedish) also argues that this exclusiveness raises questions about democracy because governance often involves trade and industry but not "the third sector or representatives of people with low participation in elections," the same group that was excluded in the second phase of the incubator process. Stigendal (2012; translated from Swedish) means that a return to traditional hierarchical government is not a solution; instead, more actors and stakeholders should be able to participate in these networks—a sort of "governance with all." The incubator workshops—the design thing—could be seen as an attempt to experiment with doing "governance with all," even if 100 percent inclusion is impossible.

As has been said, the focus on creating employment is, of course, relevant to tackling the social challenges facing Malmö. But to highlight only the creation of new jobs is to risk losing sight of the fact that the *conditions* for creating new jobs, and social sustainability, depend on many interconnected factors—for example, education, distribution of resources, and how public services work. This complexity was evident in discussions during the workshops and in the Area Programs' deciding to focus on both new jobs *and* education.

The importance of taking a holistic perspective and that of merging different kinds of knowledge so as to be able to tackle complex societal challenges was also emphasized in the final report of the Malmö Commission (Stigendal and Östergren 2013). The commission recommended that new processes of change be based on knowledge alliances and on more democratized governance. It also recommended a change from an emphasis on conditions and results to an emphasis on continuous knowledge and learning processes—a change that would not be about identifying and solving single problems but instead would depart from a holistic perspective and try to solve many problems simultaneously. This, in turn, requires more open processes in which a departure point or a problem is identified by a circle of stakeholders wider than a traditional one. The commission also asserts that in this new processes it is less important to have a final goal clearly defined than to have a direction that allows the exploration of new solutions and the development of new knowledge. Keywords for this new kind of change processes include "creation of new knowledge," "participation," and "system change." One of the gains to be achieved by involving citizens is that a knowledge alliance gets access to both formal and informal knowledge, and in this context the commission mentions the "intercultural competence" that many citizens of Malmö possess.

In regard to social complexity and the idea that social sustainability isn't limited to jobs and companies, it is crucial to bring up the partly unnoticed but important work of the third sector, both in education and in creating a feeling of belonging for many marginalized citizens. This became clear during the workshops. One theme that emerged during the workshops was "people's movement 2.0," which highlighted that some present-day grassroots organizations and youth organizations are organized in a new way, not yet acknowledged, that falls between established categorizations and departments. One consequence of this is that it is difficult for such organizations to get financial support. But they do a lot of important work for society, for example with education. The representative from Miljonprocessen, who also is the leader of the youth organization RGRA, brought up this issue. Two years later this issue was emphasized by Sernhede and Söderman (2013), who noted the importance of this new kind of people's movement, and that of organizations such as RGRA in Malmö, Megafonen in Husby/Stockholm, and Pantrarna in Gothenburg in relation to the 2013 riots in Husby/Stockholm.

Stigendal and Östergren (2013) argue that one explanation for why the situation in Malmö isn't even worse is that the work done by cultural and third-sector organizations is having a positive influence on people's health, their feeling of participation in society, and the creation of trust between people. They also consider the possibility that the third sector has a great potential for creating social sustainability and therefore "should be taken into consideration in many of the political decisions that aim at making the city socially sustainable" (ibid., 48; translated from Swedish). But "people's movement 2.0" and other issues that concerned the third sector would not be a concern or a task of the future incubator as it was further developed by the powerful strangers that dominated the process after the workshops.

Although the politics of Malmö still emphasize economic growth, alternative perspectives seem to emerge from the Malmö Commission. It has to be acknowledged that the small informal governance networks with a strong ability to act have been taking several initiatives that are seen as successful by the majority of citizens (for example, starting the university, initiating the bridge, and the city district known as the Western Harbor). But, as has been argued by many researchers, something else is needed when dealing with complex social issues. The challenge here seems to be how to balance the ability to embrace complexity with the ability to act—how to tackle complex challenges without reducing them to single issues and excluding important actors. This challenge is addressed by Huppé, Creech, and Knoblauch (2012), who argue that governance networks that deal with sustainable development should address the connections between the economy, society, and the natural environment and should try to avoid fragmentation and institutions based on single issues. According to them, these networks will need participants from all sectors from society, including the business sector and the third sector. However, this may create an efficacy paradox: heterogeneity and complex networks may reduce the effectiveness of the process and the ability of participants to reach common goals. The solution suggested by Huppé et al. is to combine processes of opening up the network with processes of closing down the network, in order to avoid paralysis and maintain a strong ability to act and make decisions. Huppé et al. also emphasize the importance in these networks of reflexive learning, whereby stakeholders gain understanding of each other's respective positions and trust and social capital can grow through common activities—something that also was highlighted during the incubator workshops.

Powerful strangers and political design

We started this story with our meeting with one "powerful stranger" in the corridors of Malmö's city hall. This is the usual arena for elite actors and members of the informal governance networks—the corridors of power and boardrooms—and not the kind of inclusive and democratic platform that was our goal in setting up the design thing at the university. The workshops at the university, taking the form of a "design thing", could be seen as an attempt to set up the conditions for connection, confrontation, and collaboration between "the radicals and the establishment." But the powerful actors never turned up. The design thing fell apart, and most participants were excluded from the decision-making phase. However, we would argue that this breakdown explicitly puts the focus on the need for new inclusive governance forms. As we have tried to argue in this chapter, we believe that participatory design and agonistic design things could contribute to the building of democratic governance networks that would be able to tackle complexity and to address issues of sustainability.

To bring design into the political sphere may seem awkward. However, it has long been argued that design is an approach that is well suited to dealing with complexity and with wicked problems (Rittel and Webber 1973). In recent years, design, and specifically design thinking, has gotten a lot of attention as an approach that could contribute fruitfully to governance and to policy development in the public sector (Bason 2010; Christiansen and Bunt 2012; Jégou et al. 2013). Although design approaches have been embraced by many in the public sector, design's practical influence on public policy is still modest. According to Christiansen and Bunt, one reasons for this is that design approaches involve experimentation, which involves the possibility of risk and which for that reason is viewed as less accountable than known bureaucratic procedures with predictable outcomes. Christiansen and Bunt (2012, 18) instead suggest that "informed experimentation" can be seen as "the responsible foundation for decision making in complex settings."

However, it is not only how civil servants set up their everyday work that is challenged. Several researchers rooted in participatory design have, in line with what we are proposing here, argued that design should take a further step into the political (Botero and Saad-Sulonen 2013; Staszowski, Brown, and Winter 2013). Here it is relevant to consider the distinction between what DiSalvo (2010) calls *design for politics*, with its focus on "improving structures and mechanisms that enable governing", and *political design*, which is more focused on revealing and confronting power relations and on identifying "new terms and themes for contestation and new trajectories for action." (ibid., no paging)

DiSalvo (2010) has reviewed some "design for democracy" projects and found that most fit into the established realm of politics. Here DiSalvo is referring mostly to American projects that work as "design *applied* to politics" or "design *for* politics"; however, service-design projects in the United Kingdom, where designers are helping to implement the government's Big Society policy and "are already facilitating social innovations that can replace government services" (Tonkinwise 2010, no paging), could be added to this category. As DiSalvo (2010, no paging) notes, these projects are not "political in an agonistic sense" and "do not represent the range of possible thought and action available to design within the democratic endeavour." According to DiSalvo, an agonistic approach could ask questions and reveal and confront power relations.

The process with the incubator that we have outlined in this chapter brings this view on design up front, especially in regard to the report of the Malmö Commission and the perspectives that the political scientist Tove Dannestam and the sociologist Mikael Stigendal bring to the situation in Malmö.

A design thing can contribute to democratic governance processes by widening the networks and by paying attention to who is included. A design thing explicitly tries to include marginalized and opposing actors and to connect them with stronger more resourceful stakeholders (that is, to connect the "bees" and the "trees"). Also, through a design thing, pre-defined projects are not imposed on other people, and most of the important agendas haven't already been set. Rather, a constellation of diverse stakeholders is assembled to elaborate what could become a future project and what matters of concern that should be elaborated further. A design thing doesn't stop with a group of people and a decision at the workshop table, either. Often it moves beyond producing ideas and deciding which of them to implement, and through phases of collaborative experimentation it explores how diverse ideas can be situated and made sense of. A design thing not only assembles diverse people but also assembles diverse artifacts, prototypes, processes, and sketches to perform collaborative explorations of matters of concern and alternative futures (Björgvinsson, Ehn, and Hillgren 2010, 2012a). During these processes, reports, sketches, and videos are made public—something that is crucial for accountability, and something that is seldom encountered in traditional governance networks.

Our aim was to set up design things in agonistic formats so that disagreements could spur vivid discussions without definitively leading to consensus. That was why we invited people we knew would have very opposing views as to what should constitute an incubator or what was needed to tackle some of the challenges that face Malmö today. However when several of the powerful strangers opted out we also lost some of the agonistic battle that we believe should have produced valuable knowledge about this issue.

We are certainly not against a concrete result such as 1,000 new jobs, but we think such a result is problematic when it is created in the absence of other voices and opinions, continuous inquiries, and the creation of new knowledge. We need both a capacity to act and knowledge about what to act upon. A majority of the research on such knowledge creation points in the direction of diverse constellations such as knowledge alliances and design things rather than in the direction of single-issue-oriented governance networks. The ability to act and to achieve results quickly should be complemented by long-term learning and by experimental processes that embrace complexity and address societal challenges on a systemic level. That is a good reason to continue to explore the potential of design things for becoming a new democratic platform for "governance with all."

References

Bason, C. 2010. *Leading Public Sector Innovation: Co-creating for a Better Society*. Policy Press.

Binder, Thomas, Giorgio De Michelis, Pelle Ehn, Giulio Jacucci, Per Linde, and Ina Wagner. 2011. *Design Things*. MIT Press.

Björgvinsson, Erling, Pelle Ehn, and Per-Anders Hillgren. 2010. Participatory Design and "Democratizing Innovation." In Proceedings of the Eleventh Participatory Design Conference, Sydney.

Björgvinsson, Erling, Pelle Ehn and Per-Anders Hillgren. 2012a. Agonistic Participatory Design: Working with Marginalised Social Movements. *CoDesign* 8 (2–3): 127–144.

Björgvinsson, Erling, Pelle Ehn, and Per-Anders Hillgren. 2012b. Design Things and Design Thinking: Contemporary Participatory Design Challenges. *Design Issues* 28 (3): 101–116.

Blyth, Simon, and Lucy Kimbell. 2011. *Design Thinking and the Big Society: From Solving Personal Troubles to Designing Social Problems*. Actant and Taylor Haig.

Botero, Andrea, and Joanna Saad-Sulonen. 2013. Peer-Production in Public Services: Emerging Themes for Design Research and Action. In *Public and Collaborative: Exploring the Intersection Of Design, Social Innovation and Public Policy*, ed. E. Manzini and E. Staszowski. DESIS Network.

Christiansen, Jesper, and Laura Bunt. 2012. Innovation in Policy: Allowing for Creativity, Social Complexity and Uncertainty in Public Governance (http://www.nesta.org.uk)/publications/assets/features/innovation_in_policy).

Dannestam, Tove. 2009. *Stadspolitik i Malmö: Politikens meningsskapande och materialitet. Lund Political Studies 155*. Lunds Universitet.

DiSalvo, Carl. 2010. Design, Democracy and Agonistic Pluralism. In Proceedings of Design Research Society International Conference, Montreal (http://www.designresearchsociety.org/docs-procs/DRS2010).

DiSalvo, Carl. 2012. *Adversarial Design*. MIT Press.

Ehn, Pelle. 2008. Participation in Design Things. In Proceedings of Participatory Design Conference, Bloomington, Indiana.

Ehn, Pelle, Anders Emilson, Per-Anders Hillgren, and Anna Seravalli. 2011. Inkubatorn finns därute! (http://medea.mah.se/2011/05/inkubatorn-finns-darute).

Huppé, Gabriel A., Heather Creech, and Doris Knoblauch. 2012. The Frontiers of Networked Governance (www.iisd.org/pdf/2012/frontiers_networked_gov.pdf).

Jégou, François, Stéphane Vincent, Romain Thévenet, and Anna Lochard. 2013. Friendly Hacking into the Public Sector: Co-Creating Public Policies within Regional Governments. Presented at Boundary-Crossing Conference on Co-Design in Innovation, Aalto University (http://www.slideshare.net/27eregion/friendly-hacking-into-public-sector).

Lakhani, Karim R., and Jill A. Panetta, J. 2007. The Principles of Distributed Innovation. *Innovations* 2 (3): 97–112.

Lusch, Robert F., Stephen L. Vargo, and Mohan Tanniru. 2010. Service, Value Networks and Learning. *Journal of the Academy of Marketing Science* 38: 19–31.

Mouffe, Chantal. 2000a. Deliberative Democracy or Agonistic Pluralism. Department of Political Science, Institute for Advanced Studies, Vienna.

Mouffe, Chantal. 2000b. *The Democratic Paradox*. Verso.

Mulgan, Geoff. 2007. Social Innovation: What It Is, Why It Matters and How It Can Be Accelerated. Saïd Business School, Oxford University.

Mulgan, Geoff. 2012. The Theoretical Foundations of Social Innovation. In *Social innovation: Blurring Boundaries to Reconfigure Markets*, ed. A. Nicholls and A. Murdock. Palgrave Macmillan.

Murray, Robin. 2009. *Danger and Opportunity: Crisis and the New Social Economy*. Nesta.

Murray, Robin, Julie Caulier-Grice, and Geoff Mulgan. 2010. *The Open Book of Social Innovation*. Young Foundation, Nesta.

Nicholls, Alex, and Alexander Murdock, eds. 2012. *Social Innovation: Blurring Boundaries to Reconfigure Markets*. Palgrave Macmillan.

Pierre, J., and Peters, G. B. 2000. *Governance, Politics and the State*. Macmillan.

Rhodes, R. A. W. 1997. *Understanding Governance: Policy, Networks, Governance, Reflexivity and Accountability*. Open University Press.

Rittel, H. W., and M. M. Webber. 1973. Dilemmas in a General Theory of Planning. *Policy Sciences* 4 (2): 155–169.

Sernhede, Ove, and Johan Söderman. 2013. Kur mot kravaller. *Sydsvenska Dagbladet*, May 24 (http://www.sydsvenskan.se/kultur--nojen/kur-mot-kravaller/).

Spjut, Anders. 2011. Inrättande av en inkubator för entreprenörer med inriktning på sociala innovationer. Stadskontoret, Malmö stad.

Staszowski, E., S. Brown, and B. Winter. 2013. Reflections on Designing for Social Innovation in the Public Sector: A case study in New York City. In *Public and Collaborative: Exploring the*

Intersection Of Design, Social Innovation and Public Policy, ed. E. Manzini and E. Staszowski. DESIS Network.

Stigendal, Mikael., 2011. Malmö—de två kunskapsstäderna. Kommission för ett socialt hållbart Malmö.

Stigendal, Mikael. 2012. Malmö—de två kunskapsstäderna (http://www.youtube.com/watch?v=gk3SRO1XqXY).

Stigendal, Mikael, and Per-Olof Östergren. 2013. Malmös väg mot en hållbar framtid. Hälsa, Välfärd och rättvisa. Kommision för ett socialt hållbart Malmö.

Stoker, Gerry. 2000. Urban Political Science and the Challenge of Urban Governance. In *Debating Governance*, ed. J. Pierre. Oxford University Press.

Swyngedouw, Erik. 2005. Governance Innovation and the Citizen: The Janus Face of Governance-beyond-the-State. *Urban Studies* 42 (11): 1991–2006.

Tonkinwise, Cameron. 2010. Politics Please, We're Social Designers (http://www.core77.com/blog/featured_items/politics_please_were_social_designers_by_cameron_tonkinwise__17284.asp).

Westley, Frances, Brenda Zimmerman, and Michael Quinn Patton. 2007. *Getting to Maybe: How the World Is Changed*. Vintage Canada.

Westley, Frances, and Nino Antadze. 2010. Making a Difference: Strategies for Scaling Social Innovation for Greater Impact. *Innovation Journal* 15 (2): 3–20.

II Opening Production—Design and Commons

5 Opening Production: Design and Commons

Sanna Marttila, Elisabet M. Nilsson, and Anna Seravalli

In recent years, new ways have arisen for organizing and carrying out production in open and collaborative fashions. Here *open production* refers to all value creation, either of intangible (immaterial, digital) or tangible (material, physical) resources, done through open and collaborative processes. It is *open* in that it encourages broader participation in which users often become producers, relying on some forms of shared *commons*. It is *collaborative* in that its sustainability is based on generating new social bonds and alliances, i.e., social capital. Processes of open production often tend to happen outside of traditional social and economic structures, and challenge how value production processes generally are organized. The chapters in part II of the book address issues and questions that this claim generates. The aim is to contribute to the current discussion about open production by providing insights from three cases with different approaches.

In the present chapter, we discuss how the development toward openness and collaboration builds upon, and extends, ideas that are present in participatory design and in the free-software and open-source communities. In these communities, people participate in cumulative peer-to-peer production and are given radically better possibilities to participate in society without middlemen, special skills, or resources.

The three case studies presented in coming chapters—those of Fabriken, Illutron, and Arduino—introduce different approaches to opening design and production. Through practice, design researchers discuss both the opportunities and challenges that openness presents. Special attention is given to processes involving tangible resources, such as physical space and hardware. Among the topics covered in these chapters are the means of opening production, the emergence of open and collaborative design, peer-to-peer cultures, issues related to inclusion, the challenges of collaboration, and difficulties associated with achieving sustainability.

Tracing the open production back to its origins

The rise of open production practices are often associated with the emergence of the free-software and open-source movements. However, their origins can also be traced back to the development of the Participatory Design (PD) approach.

When the PD approach entered workplaces in Scandinavia in the 1970s, the vision was one of making workplaces more democratic and empowering people to fully participate and influence their working conditions, this by establishing more open and collaborative design processes (Bjerknes et al. 1983; Ehn 1988). Since then, the PD community has persistently tried to democratize design and decision-making processes in companies and organizations. In recent years, PD has also moved outside traditional work environments and has engaged with issues in the public realm (Björgvinsson et al. 2010, 2012; Halse et al. 2010). The original premises have not changed; PD is still a matter of letting those involved in the process have a say (Gregory 2003).

Parallel to the emergence of the PD approach, and with a similar political aim, the free/libre/open source software (FLOSS) movement arose. A distributed community of software developers and end users engaged in collaborative design and development processes, applying and developing new tools, methods, and work practices (Raymond 1999; von Hippel 2005).

Until very recently people with no technological expertise or knowledge of specific coding languages or programming skills have had a rather limited opportunity to take part in these ambitious projects due to gaps in competence and abilities, but things are changing rapidly.

New technologies and tools

New communication technologies and new tools for networking and sharing have contributed to the shaping of cultures of participation (Fischer 2011; Castells 1996; Jenkins 2006; Lessig 2004). These new technologies and tools have supported the rise of social networks offering the possibility to process and manage data and information in ways that weren't possible before. According to Yochai Benkler (2006, 60), "the networked environment makes possible a new modality of organizing production: radically decentralized, collaborative and non proprietary; based on sharing resources ... among widely, distributed, loosely connected individuals who cooperate with each other without relying on either market signals or managerial commands."

Today, a wide range of Web-based collaborative media services, channels for knowledge transfer, open-software and open-hardware platforms, do-it-yourself technologies, and prototyping and production platforms allow users to take part in open and collaborative commons-based peer-to-peer production. Peer-to-peer production is viewed as a particular form of collaboration relying on the interaction between the diverse

Opening Production

participants, without any central hub (Bauwens 2006, 2009). Such production processes can include the generation of knowledge, the making of content and artifacts, the enrichment of meaning, and even the construction of individualized applications (Benkler 2006). This development fosters cultures in which users become producers (Toffler 1980; Bruns 2008; Fischer 2011) and everyone can be a designer, not only of content and artifacts, but also of production systems (Gerritzen and Lovink 2010; Schäfer 2011).

Empowerment or free labor?

The open-production movement has also been boosted by the economic success of open-source software, which paved the way for the emergence of an open and democratic innovation paradigm within the business sector (Chesbrough 2003; von Hippel 2005). This development has been generating tension between the idea that opening up production is a way to improve democracy and empower people and the idea that it represents just a way to squeeze out value for profit. Some define commons-based peer production as an alternative model of production, whose sustainability builds on social recognition, relationships between participants, and shared resources (Benkler 2006); others describe how companies are, essentially, harvesting free labor from user-led production (Weber 2004; Kommonen and Botero 2013).

Open production can be viewed and understood from many different angles. From a business angle, it represents a new paradigm for innovation. One claim often put forward is that bringing more people and more ideas into production processes supports innovation (von Hippel 2005). Some companies even have based their business model on open processes, either by creating a system of services around a pool of open and shared resources or by harvesting free labor from participants taking part in open production (Bauwens 2009). In contrast to the business world, some hacker- and activist communities view open production as having the potential to restructure how value is generated, and, as a consequence, to change economic structures and change society (Bauwens 2009). Between these two positions there are nuances of diverse understandings of open production practices. It may be about fostering citizens' participation and engagement in the public sector, or providing new opportunities for the cultural and arts sector, or generating new tools and modalities for education, or becoming a way to strengthen local communities and economies.

A landscape of open and collaborative cultures

To better understand the landscape of open and collaborative cultures, and how to enable such cultures, stimulate them, and act within them, let us look briefly at some intellectual antecedents and some societal developments that have contributed to the proliferation of open production practices.

Defining openness

The origin of open production practices as presented here can be located to the free software movement and to year 1983, which is when Richard Stallman launched the GNU project. (See Stallman 1984) In a manifesto he formulated for the project, Stallman set forth four freedoms associated with free software development: "the freedom to run the program," "the freedom to study how the program works, and change it," "the freedom to redistribute copies," and "the freedom to distribute copies of your modified version to others" (Free Software Foundation 2013, no paging). These principles have contributed significantly to the ethics of other projects and movements, including free and open culture and open access in education and science. By using the word 'free', Stallman wanted to emphasize the political implications of the project and how the point of departure was about developing software that could be available to everyone. Later, particularly after the development of the operating system Linux, the free-software community decided to use the word 'open' instead. This was a strategy to depoliticize and normalize free software, shifting the focus from political stands to how this form of software production could be more effective than traditional development methods (Benkler 2006).

The Open Definition project initiated by Open Knowledge Foundation defines openness in relation to content and data (Open Knowledge Foundation 2014). A work is defined to be open if it meets eleven requirements, of which the first three, as in Stallman's manifesto, are access, redistribution, and reuse. Similarly, the free-culture movement promotes the freedom to distribute, use, and reuse creative works. Lawrence Lessig (2004) coined and defined the term 'free culture', and various organizations (among them Freedom Defined, Students for Free Culture Organization, and Open Everything) have built upon this legacy and continued to define free and open cultural works. Creative Commons is probably the most prominent example of an organization advocating the sharing, use, and reuse of knowledge and cultural works through standardized permissive licenses and other legal tools. These licenses allow people to modify the default terms of copyrights they hold and give more freedoms (for example to share, distribute, and create derivative works) to others (Creative Commons 2014).

Recently, principles of openness have also reached fields that traditionally have been perceived as more closed. Among these fields are product design and manufacturing, in which discussions about open production are now emerging (van Abel et al. 2011; Roel 2012). Two main strands can be located in the contemporary practice and literature of open design and production: one focusing on open-ended collaborative design activity and practice, and the other producing open design documentation (e.g., blueprints). These strands address both how to develop the technical infrastructure for opening tangible production, such as licenses, open standards, and open tools, but also how to foster collaboration and open processes (van Abel et al. 2011). Thus, there is a connection between open production and PD—a connection related to the expertise in establishing and fostering processes of co-design that can be found within PD. Such expertise could be particularly valuable when it comes to dealing with issues and controversies that may emerge in collaborative and open design processes.

Open production practices are also presenting other challenges that require changes in production cultures and ways of operating. One question that arises is how to deal with technical issues of liability when it comes to complex products (Cruickshank and Atkinson 2013). For example, who ensures that open-source medical equipment meets safety standards? Other subjects of controversies are how to handle ethical and systemic questions having to do with labor and society organization, with empowerment, and with exploitation (Bauwens 2006, 2009).

Collaborative cultures and production practices

In social production, collaboration obviously plays a central role (Benkler 2006; Fischer 2011). In open production of software, the peer-to-peer model has emerged as a specific modality of collaboration in which participants are autonomous and can freely determine their behavior and linkages without the intermediary of an obligatory hub (Benkler 2006). Although peer-to-peer projects are most widely known in the areas of software development and the Internet, collaborative production is spreading rapidly in open culture and education, in hardware manufacturing, and in social movements such as Occupy Wall Street.

In social innovation, the idea of *collaborative services* has been developed (Jégou and Manzini 2008). Collaborative services can be described as new economic initiatives that, while economically sustainable, generate social value on a local level by binding together producers and consumers. Such initiatives can include such things as neighborhood kindergartens and farmers' markets. They are seen as having the potential to improve environmental and social sustainability by creating stronger bonds between economic activities and the local context.

More traditional forms of production also are being shaped by collaborative behaviors. *Collaborative consumption* accounts for emerging business models in traditional consumer markets where sharing and swapping are replacing consumption (Botsman and Rogers 2010)—for example, car-pooling and clothes-swapping services.

This diversity clearly demonstrates the spreading of collaborative production practices, and it shows that the open-production movement is diffusing into diverse sectors and assuming diverse connotations and aims. A central role in this development is played by open physical lab spaces, such as fab labs, hackerspaces, and makerspaces, where people can prototype and experiment with technology and production (Gershenfeld 2005; Hackerspaces 2013). These spaces, currently being established all over the world, support bottom-up local production initiatives by providing access to resources and the possibility of developing projects and learning by doing. In these spaces, people get access to tools and machines, and they develop skills and share knowledge and ideas in cumulative and collaborative processes.

Commons and ownership

Open production processes often rely on and generate *commons*, here understood as shared resources that are managed and governed through collective action (Ostrom 1990). How to organize access and handle resources is connected to the nature of the production process. Intangible processes are often constituted by open-access regimes in which individuals do not have "exclusive control over the use and disposition of any particular resource" (Benkler 2006, 61) and the shared materials and resources are available to all. Tangible processes, on the other hand, usually present a range of diverse possibilities, owing to the fact that materials, unlike information, get worn by use and the possibility of accessing them is limited by their physical characteristics.

To characterize the shift from producer-centered production to collaborative processes, the term *produsage* has sometimes been used, meaning "the collaborative and iterative content creation practices within many user-led environments as a hybrid and often inextricable combination of production and use" (Bruns 2007, no paging). According to Bruns, collaborative user-led content creation by online communities has four main characteristics: creation and production is community-based, participants have fluid roles in production, the content is constantly under development and the artifacts are unfinished, and the productions and the knowledge are community-owned common property (Bruns and Schmidt 2011; Bruns 2008).

Similarly, the founder of the Peer-to-Peer Foundation claims that, in comparison to corporate-driven production, the peer-to-peer systems have three novel modes: the mode of production (the use value is created through collaboration of people "who have access to distributed capital"), the mode of governance (the community is governed by itself, without corporate hierarchy), and the mode of distribution (property is common and freely accessible) (Bauwens 2006). Common to all these characterizations is that the information produced by a community forms a shared information commons that develops in a continuous social process of enriching, extending, and evaluating the shared resources (Bruns 2008).

Open tangible production and the role of the designer

Open production practices have now spread beyond the realm of the software world, and intangible production towards other domains. What happens when production processes and chains are opened up in relation to tangible artifacts? Is it possible to open tangible production? These questions are now widely discussed, particularly because of the proliferation of personal fabrication machines—smaller, cheaper versions of mass-production equipment (3D printers, laser cutting machines, CNC mills) that allow for small-scale industrial production (Lipson and Kurman 2010). Could these machines play the same role in opening tangible production processes that new technologies, social networks, and platforms have played for software and for intangible artifacts? Could the emergence of open physical lab spaces and prototyping platforms allow the creation of a non-proprietary and collaborative mode of production for tangible goods?

Many challenges arise when tangible production is opened with the aim of democratizing tangible processes of value production and making them more accessible. A direct translation of intangible production forms and paradigms doesn't seem to work very well. Thus, when moving from software to hardware, the opening of production ought to be understood and fostered differently (Powell 2012). First, open production practices in the tangible realm faces the constraints that the tangible nature of the artifacts themselves represent. Second, there are diverse communities of practices that are engaged in the opening of tangible production, including not only hardware developers, but also long-tail bricoleurs and artisans, production financed through public investments, open hardware for development, and industrial piracy (ibid.).

The modularity of open production, the shared ownership of process and outcome, and the fluid roles and modes of governance challenge the traditional role of the designer and the traditional design process and raise the question of how designers can operate in open production frameworks. When dealing with open tangible design and production, a designer has to create new methods and practices to include open and collaborative cultures in a tangible realm dominated by industrial design practices in which intellectual property rights are seen as crucial to the design and production process and in which a number of hindrances related to tangibility and scarcity of resources have to be faced. (See chapter 6.) In addition to these challenges other issues arise, some related to liability and roles and some to the future of production: What new responsibilities do designers face in relation to these transformations? How should technical issues of liability be dealt with when it comes to complex products (Cruickshank and Atkinson 2013)? How should ethical and systemic questions having to do with new forms of labor organization, empowerment, and/or exploitation be addressed (Bauwens 2006, 2009)?

The design research community has recently introduced the concept of *Open Design*. (van Abel et al. 2011; Roel 2012). Both academics and practitioners have attempted to tame this concept by aiming at describing the multi-faceted nature of the phenomenon (Avital 2011). Up to now it has been practice rather than theory that has driven openness in design. There is, however, a growing body of empirical research evaluating open design projects producing both intangible and tangible goods (Balka 2011). Examples of this are provided by the Fabriken, Illutron, and Arduino cases.

Co-constructing participation platforms for open collaborative production: Fabriken, Illutron, and Arduino

In chapters 6, 7, and 8, three stories about how design researchers and practitioners strive to run open design and production processes in collaborative cultures, and how they pursue the goals of empowerment, inclusiveness, and democratization of design and production processes inspired by PD and by FLOSS, are discussed. Those stories shed light on the strategies, opportunities, and challenges designers face when co-constructing open frameworks together with other stakeholders. Chapter 6 also describes the challenges that transferring practices and values from intangible open production practices to tangible production and into a physical realm present.

The first case is Fabriken, a makerspace in Malmö that has been jointly developed and run by a research center, a non-governmental organization, an interaction design company, and the users of the makerspace. Fabriken provides diverse possibilities of opening production: from tinkering with electrical circuits to sewing cloths, from fixing bikes to woodworking. By discussing practices and the way the space evolves, chapter 6 highlights problems and possibilities that arise in the course of moving from intangible forms of commons-based production to tangible ones.

The second case, Illutron, is presented in chapter 7. Illutron is a studio for experimentation in technology and art located on a barge in Copenhagen's harbor. It is a non-profit private initiative that was founded by a multidisciplinary group of people with backgrounds in various fields, including art and engineering. The chapter focuses on how a shared interest in exploring digital material became a common ground for collaboration, encouraged the formation of a community with shared values, and helped to keep the barge literally and figuratively afloat despite the absence of a formal organizational structure.

The subject of chapter 8 is Arduino, an open-source electronics prototyping platform based on flexible, easy-to-use hardware and software. Arduino was originally intended for artists, designers, hobbyists, and others interested in creating interactive objects or environments, but it has grown into a global online community. The chapter discusses how Arduino applies the concept of openness. After introducing the open-source hardware scene through a first-person narrative, it draws some conclusions about how the ideals behind the commons change when the everyday reality of a company with investors and clients, instead of concepts and users, must be faced.

As the cases of Fabriken, Illutron, and Arduino demonstrate, open platforms for collaborative production can take many forms: they can be formal infrastructures initiated by officials, established public venues maintained by communities, or ad hoc constellations created by random strangers driven by a shared urge or question.

Although the cases of Fabriken, Illutron, and Arduino involve the use of very different processes and tactics to empower, enable, and engage people, there are some similarities. They all strive toward an open and inclusive platform for participation that supports the flexible agency and multiple levels of participation. Various design-in-use activities are facilitated, from social practices and agreements to digital design and fabrication. Collaboration is recognized as an important asset in iterative and open-ended production. Through these cases, the authors discuss some of the challenges that arise in the course of opening tangible production, but they also put forward some of the core values and virtues of openness in design and production.

References

Avital, Michel. 2011. The Generative Bedrock of Open Design. In *Open Design Now: Why Design Cannot Remain Exclusive*, ed. B. van Abel, R. Klaassen, L. Evers, and P. Troxler. BIS.

Balka, Kerstin. 2011. *Open Source Product Development. The Meaning and Relevance of Openness*. Gabler.

Bauwens, Michel. 2006. The Political Economy of Peer Production. *Post-Autistic Economics Review* 37: 33–44.

Bauwens, Michel. 2009. Class and Capital in Peer Production. *Capital and Class* 33: 121–141.

Benkler, Yochai. 2006. *The Wealth of Networks*. Yale University Press.

Bjerknes, Gro, Pelle Ehn, and Morten Kyng, eds. 1983. *Computers and Democracy: A Scandinavian Challenge*. Avebury.

Björgvinsson, Erling, Pelle Ehn, and Per-Anders Hillgren. 2010. Participatory Design and Democratizing Innovation. Paper presented at Participatory Design Conference, Sydney.

Björgvinsson, Erling, Pelle Ehn, and Per-Anders Hillgren. 2012. Agonistic Participatory Design: Working with Marginalised Social Movements. *CoDesign* 8 (2–3): 127–144.

Botsman, Rachel, and Roo Rogers. 2010. *What's Mine Is Yours: The Rise of Collaborative Consumption*. HarperCollins.

Bruns, Axel. 2007. Produsage, generation C, and their effects on the democratic process. Paper presented at Media in Transition 5: Creativity, Ownershop, and Collaboration in the Digital Age, Boston.

Bruns, Axel. 2008. *Blogs, Wikipedia, Second Life, and Beyond: From Production to Produsage*. Peter Lang.

Bruns, Axel, and Jan Schmidt. 2011. Produsage: A Closer Look at Continuing Developments. *New Review of Hypermedia and Multimedia* 17 (1): 3–7.

Castells, Manuel. 1996. *The Rise of the Network Society*. Blackwell.

Chesbrough, Henry. 2003. *Open Innovation: The New Imperative for Creating and Profiting from Technology*. Harvard Business School Press. Creative Commons. 2014. (http://creativecommons.org).

Cruickshank, Leon, and Paul Atkinson. 2013. Closing In On Open Design: Comparing Casual and Critical Design Challenges. Paper presented at European Academy of Design Conference on Crafting the Future, Gothenburg.

Ehn, Pelle. 1988. *Work-Oriented Design of Computer Artifacts*. Arbetslivscentrum.

Fischer, Gerhard. 2011. Understanding, Fostering, and Supporting Cultures of Participation. *interactions* 18 (3): 42–53.

Free Software Foundation. 2013. The Free Software Definition (https://www.gnu.org/philosophy/free-sw.html).

Gerritzen, Mieke, and Geert Lovink. 2010. *Everyone Is a Designer in the Age of Social Media*. BIS.

Gregory, Judith. 2003. Scandinavian Approaches to Participatory Design. *International Journal of Engineering Education* 19 (1): 62–74.

Gershenfeld, Neil A. 2005. *Fab: The Coming Revolution on Your Desktop*. Basic Books.

Hackerspaces. 2013. "Hackerspaces" (http://hackerspaces.org).

Halse, Joachim, Eva Brandt, Brendon Clark, and Thomas Binder. 2010. *Rehearsing the Future*. Danish Design School Press.

Jenkins, Henry. 2006. *Convergence Culture: Where Old and New Media Collide*. New York University Press.

Kommonen, Kari-Hans, and Andrea Botero. 2013. Are the Users Driving, and How Open Is Open? Experiences from Living Lab and User Driven Innovation Projects. *Journal of Community Informatics* 9(3).

Lessig, Lawrence. 2004. *Free Culture: The Nature and Future of Creativity*. Penguin.

Lipson, Hod, and Melba Kurman. 2010. Factory@Home: The Emerging Economy of Personal Fabrication. White House Office of Science and Technology Policy.

Open Knowledge Foundation. 2014. "Open Definition" (http://opendefinition.org/).

Ostrom, Elinor. 1990. *Governing the Commons: The Evolution of Institutions for Collective Action*. Cambridge University Press.

Powell, Alison. 2012. Democratizing Production through Open Source Knowledge: From Open Software to Open Hardware. *Media, Culture & Society* 34 (6): 691–708.

Raymond, Eric S. 1999. A Brief History of Hackerdom. In *Open Sources: Voices from the Open Source Revolution*, ed. C. DiBona, S. Ockman, and M. Stone. O'Reilly.

Roel, Klaassen, ed. 2012. Special issue: Dutch Open. *Design Journal* 14 (4).

Schäfer, Mirko Tobias. 2011. *Bastard Culture! How User Participation Transforms Cultural Production.* Amsterdam University Press.

Stallman, Richard. 1984. The GNU Manifesto (http://www.gnu.org/gnu/manifesto.html).

Toffler, Alvin. 1980. *The Third Wave.* Bantam.

van Abel, Bas, Roel Klaassen, Lucas Evers, and Peter Troxler. 2011. *Open Design Now: Why Design Cannot Remain Exclusive.* BIS.

von Hippel, Eric. 2005. Democratizing Innovation. MIT Press.

Weber, Steven. 2004. *The Success of Open Source.* Harvard University Press.

6 While Waiting for the Third Industrial Revolution: Attempts at Commoning Production

Anna Seravalli

It is Thursday evening at STPLN, a makerspace located in an industrial building in Malmö. Davey is helping some newcomers with the milling machine. Chris and Frank are working on an old vending machine, trying to make it suitable for selling hardware boards. Someone else is mending a flat bike tire. In the textile corner, Luisa is teaching one of the hackers how to crochet. Quinn is in the kitchen, preparing food for tomorrow's catering. Some of the regulars are sitting on the sofa testing a robot they recently built. Jonathan is playing a cello he built from scrap material. In another room, a new group is experimenting with screen-printing.

The makerspace STPLN is a public workshop that provides access to machines and tools for production. Participants explore fabrication possibilities by sharing space, means, and sometimes knowledge and skills. The space is a platform for several activities, among them building robots, experimenting with new educational formats for sustainability, band rehearsals, and investigating how a café for families with small children could work. The facility is owned by the City of Malmö and is managed by an NGO. The activities are driven by citizens, small companies, groups of friends, and other NGOs.

STPLN, together with similar venues around the globe, is part of a growing network of what could be described as spaces for opening production. Through shared facilities, means of production, and knowledge, these spaces are providing citizens with the possibility to engage in production processes and to re-appropriate knowledge and practices having to do with making things. These open workshops may have different names and come in different formats (such as fab labs, hackerspaces, and makerspaces). What they have in common is the hope that they would be the venues from which the democratization of manufacturing (Mota 2011) could boost grassroots innovation (Gershenfeld 2005; Troxler 2010) that would lead to a "third industrial revolution" (Anderson 2012; Rifkin 2011; Troxler 2013). If textile companies—with steam engines—were the scene of the first industrial revolution, and automotive industries—with mass production and assembly lines—became the symbol for the second one, these spaces, with shared equipment and collaborative production processes driven by individuals outside traditional companies, may become the venue for the third one. Specifically,

Figure 6.1
Thursday evenings at Fabriken. Anna Seravalli (CC:BY-NC).

sharing means of production and knowledge about processes and collaboration seem to entail two possible scenarios. On one side they are looked upon as the seeds for the establishment of a new mode of production in which resources and means are treated as commons, allowing for individuals to collaborate and perform production outside traditional structures (through peer-to-peer relationships). Commons-based peer-to-peer production, which originated in the software field, is advocated as a more socially and environmentally sustainable way of performing production that could overcome the limits and problems of mass- and capitalist production (Carson 2010; P2P Foundation 2013). On the other hand, these practices could also be just the latest evolution of capitalist production (Bauwens 2006, 2009; Thrift 2006), with companies harvesting the commons and tapping into the creativity of open and collaborative processes.

By reflecting on the practices emerging in the everyday running of STPLN, and the way the space is organized, this chapter provides some insights into spaces for opening production by trying to enter the detail of commons-based practices, describing patterns and revealing some of the possibilities and the problems that may emerge when sharing and collaborating for making things.

Figure 6.2
Fixing bikes at the Bicycle Kitchen. Elisabet M. Nilsson (CC:BY-NC).

Welcome to STPLN!

The STPLN building is a former workers' diner in the center of what until the 1980s was one of the largest shipbuilding sites in Europe. The building, owned by the city of Malmö, is run by STPLN, an NGO that has a history of supporting grassroots cultural initiatives. The venue can be described as a space for opening production, since it enables individuals and small organizations to engage in diverse forms of making by sharing means, knowledge, and resources. Fabriken, the actual workshop, is located in the basement of the building and is equipped with a laser cutter and a CNC mill. The workshop has also some hand tools, a saw, a sander, and equipment for working with electronics.

The basement also houses a bicycle repair workshop (the Bicycle Kitchen), a textile corner (the Textile Department), a screen-printing workshop, and a library of cast-off materials (ReCreate) that organizes activities for children and adults to foster creativity and environmental awareness. On the ground floor there is a venue for concerts, a semi-professional kitchen, and a co-working facility (HUBn).

The idea of setting up a makerspace emerged in 2006 when STPLN bought a 3D printer and started to do some workshops with kids around the city. In 2010, with the involvement of the research center Medea, financial resources to begin designing and implementing the workshop became available. The agreement was that Medea would

Figure 6.3
The STPLN premises. Anna Seravalli (CC:BY-NC).

provide resources to buy some equipment, and would supply a design researcher (the author) who would work with Fabriken, while the NGO would take care of the general management of the space.

I was involved in the venue for nearly three years, taking part in setting up and running the space. During that time, I took on diverse roles and carried out diverse activities, including organizing the first co-design workshops, being actively involved in setting up some initiatives, collaborating with some of the projects hosted in the space, taking part in organizing and participating in events and other initiatives, and participating in the everyday life of the space itself. (For a more detailed account of how the space was set up and of the designer's role, see Seravalli 2013.)

This chapter wishes to articulate some insights in relation to spaces for opening production and the so-called third industrial revolution. It does so by reflecting on the experiences emerging from STPLN and Fabriken, looking at how it might be possible *to infrastructure* for production practices based on sharing and collaboration.

Toward the future?

The phenomenon of opening production has had a major effect on intangible, information-based forms of production. The success of FOSS (free and open source software), in terms of long-term sustainability and quality of production output, had a huge influence on the way in which the software sector operates (Benkler 2006). It massively introduced production practices based on shared resources, in which the processes are carried out by self-organized distributed communities not relying on market or managerial inputs to organize and perform production processes, that is, commons-based peer-to-peer production (Bauwens 2009).

A commons has been defined as a "pool of resources or facilities as well as property institutions that involve some aspects of joint ownership or access" (Ostrom et al. 2002, 18), where 'commons' can refer both to an intrinsic characteristic of the resource, in which case it is defined as a common-pool resource, or to a specific kind of management arrangement created by humans (commons as an institution) in which a specific resource is owned, managed, accessed, and used by a collective through the development of a system of shared rules and practices (Ostrom 1990). In commons-based peer-to-peer production, commons are of the second kind: a way of managing resources and outputs of the production processes (Benkler 2006). Specifically, in intangible processes, resources and outputs of production processes are usually made available to anyone through the Internet, according to an open-access model. Anybody can use them, but also can contribute to them and enhance them. Thus, they can be defined as open-access commons (Benkler 2013).

This mode of production is characterized by voluntary aggregations of individuals who are entangled in production processes in which resources and outputs are shared. In terms of organization, peer-to-peer processes are characterized by equipotentiality (Bauwens 2006), which means that there is no *a priori* selection of who gets to participate; processes are open to anybody, and skills and capacities are verified during production. This entails that organizational structures and hierarchies are merit-based and are modified according to the kind of production activities that need to be performed (ibid.).

Benkler (2006) defines commons-based peer-to-peer production as a form of social production, since its sustainability relies on social relations rather than on market or proprietary stands, and discusses how commons-based peer-to-peer production builds on individuals' intrinsic motivations of being part of a social entity and feeling related to other human beings. Being a form of social production means that, beside generating more or less tangible outputs, commons-based peer-to-peer production is also increasing participants' social capital, which consists of the connections between individuals and the norms of reciprocity and trustworthiness that arise from them (Putnam 1995). Moreover, human capital is often generated, since, by being involved in these processes, participants have the opportunity to develop skills and competencies (Gauntlett 2011).

If we look at the feasibility of intangible commons-based peer-to-peer production, two elements are central: the infrastructure (the Internet) and the means of production (personal computers). The Internet plays a central role in enabling commons-based intangible production processes because it lowers the costs of accessing, processing, and sharing information (the key resource in intangible production processes). Moreover, the distributed nature of the Internet eases participation, facilitating the spreading of production processes. The actual processes of production are carried out through a personal computer, which, like the Internet, allow multiple uses at the same time—for example, sending work e-mail messages, playing online games, chatting with a friend, and participating in commons-based peer-to-peer production. Thus, the cost of purchasing and maintaining a personal computer is spread across diverse uses, and this dramatically lowers the threshold of participation to commons-based production processes. The feasibility of commons-based peer-to-peer production in intangible forms is related to the fact that few resources are required to participate, since such processes can be performed through infrastructures and means of production that are acquired for and sustained through other uses. This is crucial to understanding the challenges of transferring commons-based peer-to-peer production to tangible processes. The FOSS movement has demonstrated the possibility of having commons-based production processes, but how this possibility could be transferred to other forms of production is still to be established. There are several scenarios for a commons-based provisional system (see, for example, Siefkes 2012; Helfrich 2013); some of them envisage a radical reorganization of society and of production systems. Meanwhile, commons-based peer-to-peer production may also end up being yet another transformation of production-as-usual. There have been only few successful instances in which, in establishing relationships with commercial players, open-source software projects have been able to develop ad hoc solutions to preserve the commons, avoiding allowing companies to tap into and free-ride the shared resources (Bauwens 2009; O'Mahony and Bechky 2008). Moreover, in open-source hardware, there have been a number of projects that, having thrived thanks to the contribution of a vast community, have patented and "closed" products once business possibilities have arisen. (See chapter 8.) Another issue relates to crowdsourcing initiatives in which corporate structures support users' peer-to-peer production and open up their innovation and production processes to users. Here no proper commons are generated, as ownership of and responsibility for production aren't shared. These initiatives have been celebrated as a way to support new forms of micro-entrepreneurship and self-entrepreneurship (Anderson 2010) and user-driven innovation (von Hippel 2005). However, they are also revealing another face of the so-called third industrial revolution, with companies outsourcing production tasks (but also risks) to the users (Bauwens 2009) and benefiting from free labor generated by crowdsourcing and by commons-based activities (Thrift 2006).

Figure 6.4
Collaborative production at Fabriken. Anna Seravalli (CC:BY-NC).

It isn't yet clear whether and in which terms the third industrial revolution is going to be a revolution, although it is already possible to see the emergence of some challenges associated with moving commons-based production from the intangible to the tangible realm and with infrastructures supporting collaboration and sharing in making things.

Going tangible: Beyond openness

The success of commons-based peer-to-peer production in information-based production processes, that is, production of intangible goods, has fostered the emergence of a number of open-source projects for the production of tangible goods and the articulation of a scenario for commons-based peer-to-peer production in the tangible realm (Siefkes 2012). As Bauwens pointed out (2009, 129), going tangible requires the creation of "mechanisms that combine the non-reciprocal peer production of designs for immaterial production with a separate system for physical production that relies on, cooperates and supports open design communities." In moving toward commons-based tangible production, beside the need to treat information and knowledge as open-access commons, there is also the need to develop an infrastructure in which tangible means of production and resources are treated as commons.

When it comes to sharing information about tangible production processes, there are several initiatives relying on the same mechanisms used in intangible commons-based peer-to-peer production. Proponents of open hardware and open design (van Abel et al. 2011) aim at creating and sharing files and knowledge about how artifacts work and how they can be manufactured, generating open-access commons very similar to the ones at play in FOSS. This approach seems particularly promising when it comes to production processes employing personal fabrication machines (such as 3D printers, laser-cutters, small-scale CNC mills). These machines are based on CAD-CAM systems, meaning that production processes are stirred through code and, therefore, entailing the possibility of treating atoms as bits (Anderson 2010). One of the most significant examples is the Open-Source Ecology project, which is developing open-source drawings, files, and instructions to create basic machinery for cultivation and construction.

A more challenging task is to treat tangible assets as commons, since machines and materials present the possibility that problems of rivalry and durability will emerge.

Rivalry and durability
Information and knowledge represent non-rivalrous goods, which means that they can be involved in diverse uses at the same time (Ostrom 1990). If a programmer uses a piece of code found on the Web for generating a program, she doesn't subtract the possibility that another individual will utilize the same piece of code at the same time in another production process. Knowledge and information are also durable goods, which means that they do not degrade by going through processes of production: a piece of code doesn't get worn by being used again and again, so in principle there is no cost of maintenance of the good itself. I write "in principle" because access to and provision of these goods demand an infrastructure that requires resources for its construction and maintenance. This clearly emerges in cases of intangible commons-based production in which access to code requires an Internet connection and working online platforms and repositories.

In shifting toward production processes in which tangibility has a prominent role, things get even more complex since tangible goods are rivalrous and present diverse degrees of durability (Ostrom 1990). For example, a 3D printer is a rivalrous good since it can only print one object at a time and, consequently, can be involved in only one production process at a time. As time passes, its components will wear out and eventually break down. Durability is even more critical if raw materials are considered: the plastic thread used by 3D printers can be used only once. In order for it to be re-used,

Figure 6.5
Rivalry at play in woodworking. Anna Seravalli (CC:BY-NC).

the previous printed objects have to be melted down and the filament has to be regenerated through a process that is costly in energy, time, and means. Moreover, every time a plastic is recycled, it loses some of its physical characteristics, and after a number of cycles it is useless.

Rivalry and durability, thus, represent a challenge to the establishment of commons-based peer-to-peer production. In working with information, it is necessary to find resources to maintain open-access commons, that is, to maintain the infrastructure and provide access to it. When it comes to tangible forms of production, beside the infrastructure challenge, there are also challenges about how to organize tangible commons assets, for example, by establishing practices for their maintenance, by finding resources to invest in these activities and, even, by introducing sanctioning mechanisms to avoid misusing of the commons and free-riding (Ostrom 1990, 1999). This implies that openness is not enough: there is a need to focus beyond the issue of access, also considering ownership, use, and maintenance of shared resources.

Infrastructures: Not only distributed but also scope-based

Another reflection that can be made about infrastructures "for going tangible" is related to the role that the Internet plays in ensuring the feasibility of intangible commons-based peer-to-peer production. Even if the Internet plays a fundamental role in collaborative and sharing practices, it often ends up being invisible. According to Star and Ruhleder (1995), this is a key characteristic of infrastructures, which become visible only when they break down. Internet invisibility seems to be amplified by the fact that, since the Net is enabling a number of diverse activities in diverse contexts (from sending emails for work to playing online with friends), its costs are spread broadly.

A major factor ensuring the sustainability of intangible commons-based peer-to-peer production is the fact that the Internet allows for so-called economies of scope. The costs of production can be written off either by reaching scale (that is, increasing the quantity of one type of production) or by increasing the scope (that is, using the same equipment for different purposes). Economies of scope look for possibilities of involving the same means of production in diverse processes, spreading the costs of acquiring and maintaining the equipment over a range of activities (Panzar and Willig 1981).

In discussing how to establish tangible commons-based peer-to-peer production, when it comes to infrastructures, the economies of scope pattern is often forgotten. Here, the discussion (and the examples) focus on how to replicate the distributed nature of the Internet through the creation of a network of physical spaces for opening production through which users could access shared technology and collaborate beyond location constraints (Gershenfeld 2005; Carson 2010). There is little discussion of the actual self-sustainability of these hubs, how to manage and maintain them as commons (Troxler 2013) and, to an extent, how economies of scopes, as supporting a variety of uses and holding diverse interests together, could play a role in the viability of tangible commons-based production.

Infrastructures for commons-based peer-to-peer production supporting tangible processes therefore have to face two challenges to maintain themselves over time. The first is to deal with rivalrous and non-durable commons. The second is related to how to establish economies of scope. The next section illustrates how these challenges require us to focus not so much on the technological aspects of the infrastructure as on how it is able to support practices and uses—that is, on infrastructuring.

Spaces for opening production: A matter of infrastructuring?

The first examples of physical spaces for opening production emerged in the 1970s, with Karl Hess' shared machines shops initiative. They were neighborhood-based workshops, in which people living in the surroundings could access tools and knowledge for making things and claim back production processes:

> The machine shop should have enough basic tools, both hand and power, to make the building of demonstration models or test facilities a practical and everyday activity. ... For inner-city residents the shared machine shop might be a sensible and practical doorway to the neglected world of productivity as well as being a base for community experimentation and demonstration. (Hess 2005, 96)

A similar underlying idea can be found in hackerspaces, community-operated physical places in which hackers meet and work on projects. In these spaces, tools and machines—as well as knowledge and skills—are usually shared between participants and treated as commons (Wikipedia 2011). Access to these spaces, however, usually remains restricted to so-called lead users, as emerges in the Illutron case (see chapter 7) and from an ongoing discussion inside the hacker community about the role of hackerspaces in enlarging access to the use of technology (Grenzfurthner and Schneider 2009).

A much more inclusive concept is that of the fab lab, which was developed by the Massachusetts Institute of Technology during the first mass diffusion of personal fabrication machines (Gershenfeld 2005). Fab labs build on the concept of hackerspaces as facilities for production based on shared knowledge and skills, but with a more formal structure, which make them more accessible. Fab labs have provided legitimacy and visibility to a counterculture niche phenomenon, transforming spaces in which knowledge and tools are shared for collective exploration of production processes into a network of platforms promoting the diffusion of the open and collaborative production in the tangible realm. According to the official MIT database, there were 80 fab labs in 2012 and 135 in 2013 (FabLab 2013); to these an undefined number of non-registered fab labs should be added.

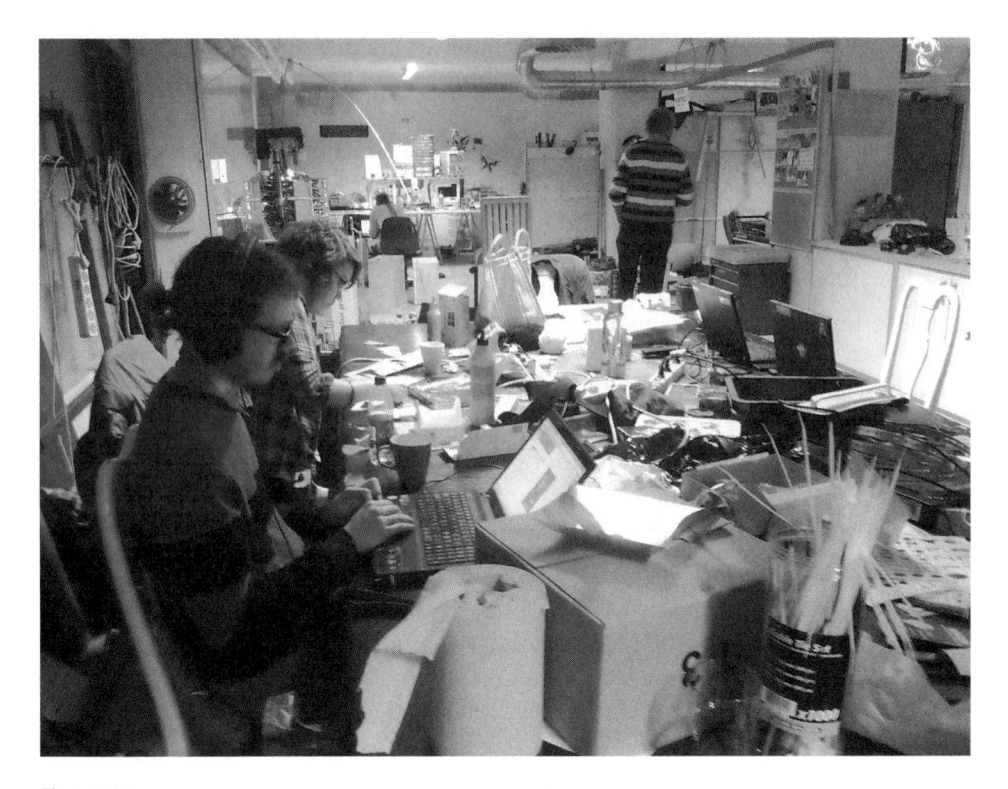

Figure 6.6
A contemporary shared machines workshop. Anna Seravalli (CC:BY-NC).

Fab labs have inspired the emergence of TechShops—commercial facilities where users, by paying a membership fee, gain access to advanced equipment for prototyping and small-scale manufacturing.

Another format is that of makerspaces. These do not have a specific definition, as Fab labs do, nor do they address specific communities, as hackerspaces do; they assume a variety of forms, usually trying to be more inclusive than hackerspaces by bringing together diverse forms of making and, consequently, diverse communities (Cavalcanti 2013). A very interesting example is the Artisan's Asylum in the United States focusing on craft production, offering access to professional equipment for small-scale production and organizing diverse kinds of courses.

In addition, a number of spaces for opening production are backed and financed by industry. Here, commons are seen as providing freedom of experimentation that eventually could lead to new ideas and products for the market (Benkler 2013).

Spaces for opening production are all characterized by the centrality of sharing (machines, knowledge, skills) and collaboration (between the participants), although what is shared and in what ways may differ according to their formats and aims, leading to diverse forms of commons-based production. Some such spaces are characterized by proper commons and peer-to-peer patterns, with users being directly involved in the managing and running of the hub. In others, an actor may be engaged in looking after the space and facilitating sharing and collaboration.

There are diverse expectations about these spaces. As has already been pointed out, they are looked upon as the premises that will support the development of commons-based peer-to-peer production (van Abel et al. 2011; Carson 2010). They are also considered incubators from which a new wave of small-scale production start-ups at the intersection between crafts and the so-called Internet of Things will develop (Anderson 2012) as a result of democratizing access to production technologies and fostering collaboration between diverse expertises. Aside from a few remarkable examples (Baichtal 2011), these expectations are often far from being met. A survey on fab labs concluded that they "were primarily offering infrastructures to students," that they "were relatively passive in reaching out to potential other users," and that they "had so far created a limited innovation ecosystem, which got used rather rarely" (Troxler 2010, 9). More recently fab labs have even been declared dead (Zijlstra 2013) because of their failures in developing meaningful relationships with local actors and in promoting the sharing of knowledge and information about production on a global scale.

These critical voices seem to point to another issue that needs to be considered when thinking about how to establish an infrastructure for commons-based peer-to-peer production in the tangible realm: that more than the technical aspects of the infrastructure should be considered. As Star and Ruhleder (1995) pointed out, an infrastructure is not a *what*; it is, rather, a *when*, since it becomes an infrastructure in relation to its ability of supporting a specific practice. Therefore, in trying to build an infrastructure, it is important to focus not only on the technological aspects but also on the uses, practices, and behaviors that it is able to support—that is, to think in terms of infrastructuring (Björgvinsson et al. 2010) rather than in terms of infrastructure. It is thus important to explore and understand to what extent spaces for opening production support or fail to support sharing and collaboration, what kinds of practices and behaviors emerge, who is participating, and what hindrances and challenges are present. The shift from infrastructure to infrastructuring can trigger a parallel shift from commons to commoning (Linebaugh 2009)—that is, a shift from understanding collective ownership institutions as a *what* to understanding them as a *when*, and from something that once implemented is given and defined in time to an ongoing process of negotiation between participants, both human and non-human, in which rules and relationships are redefined according to emerging contingencies. This shift emphasizes the evolutionary and context-related nature of commons and the fact that they are not just a matter of organizing ownership but also a matter of access to and use of a resource (Hess and Ostrom 2007), and how such organization necessarily emerges in

Figure 6.7
Commoning. Anna Seravalli (CC:BY-NC).

the interaction between the involved human and non-human actors. It also entails considering how rules, roles, and practices are at play in use, and how participation unfolds (Ostrom 1990, Ostrom 2011).

It is with a commoning perspective that the chapter now turns again to Fabriken and STPLN, looking at the practices, patterns, challenges, and possibilities emerging there, trying to unpack both how commons develop in time and how infrastructuring was carried out.

STPLN and Fabriken: Participants, practices, and rules in use

Fabriken is accessible when the STPLN premises are open, five days a week between 10 a.m. and 5 p.m., and this is when people can work autonomously on their projects. On Thursday evenings, Fabriken is open until late, and this is normally when diverse groups of participants are active in the space. Normally, between 10 and 30 people engage with the machines and equipment to work with electronics, and Thursday evenings is also when the members of the textile group, the Textile Department, meet to sew, stitch, knit, drink tea, and eat biscuits. Initially the Bicycle Kitchen was open on the very same evening, but since it was quite successful in attracting people a decision was made to move openings there to other days in order to keep the space from getting crowded. The screen-printing workshop operates mainly on Wednesday evenings; a group of volunteers, in addition to using the equipment for their own activities, organize courses and workshops for the public.

In Fabriken tools and machines are available to everybody, with the exception of the laser cutter and the CNC mill; their keys are placed in a "secret" drawer in a storage room. To be able to use them, one must come on a Thursday evening and learn from the more experienced participants. Learning and transfer of skills were, initially, not regulated through a formal system. The more experienced participants did not mind having to spend time to teach the few newcomers how the machines worked. As time went by, the number of new people coming to the space increased, and a need emerged to organize proper courses about the machines, as it was important to establish what people should be taught in order to don't ruin the equipment and to keep track of who attended the courses. The most experienced participants formally took on the tasks of education and machine maintenance. In exchange they were given a special status: beside social recognition, they were also involved in deciding what machines should be bought. However, later on, also this solution presented some problems, leading to the decision of hiring someone to take care of the space.

Diverse activities are taking place in Fabriken: repairing bikes, sewing clothes, experimenting with electronics, laser-cutting pieces for architecture models, and others. These activities are carried out by individuals or by small groups. Some are aimed at creating finished products, some at experimenting and playing around with tools, machines, and materials. Beside the private individuals who come to the space in their spare time, Fabriken has also been hosting two fashion-design ateliers and a catering company. The ateliers have been based in the Textile Department; one of them focuses on textile design in a broad sense and the other on "up-cycling" old garments. The catering company used for some time the kitchen for food workshops. These three initiatives are driven by people who have regular jobs and who, in their spare time, are trying to build professions out of their passions.

Fabriken attracts also long-term projects. One of them is ReCreate, which uses castoff materials from industrial production to build new things and to stimulate creativity and environmental awareness in children and adults. The driving force behind ReCreate is a former teacher who wanted to experiment with new ways to teach sustainability. She came to Fabriken looking for space and support for developing her idea. She began by collecting materials, prototyping formats, and holding workshops for adults and children. Moreover, she established a network in the space by getting to know the other projects and the people who gathered in the space on Thursday evenings. Some events in collaboration with the Bicycle Kitchen were organized, and also some workshops with Fabriken regular participants to explore new ways of using her materials. After some months, the former teacher got three years' worth of financing for developing her project.

Among the other participants in Fabriken are local hackers, programmers, and electronic musicians. The space is also frequently used by representatives of Malmö's cultural and art scene. A few students from the program in Interaction Design at Malmö University also hang around in the space. It is difficult to categorize the rest of the participants. All of them are interested in various forms of making and self-production. Most of them are well educated and have fairly well-paying jobs; however, there are also some unemployed people and some knowledge workers struggling to make a living. A few people on long-term sick leave come to the space almost every day, mainly for tinkering around and chatting, and three retirees (two engineers and a teacher) are regular visitors.

Figure 6.8
The Textile Department. Anna Seravalli (CC:BY-NC).

The ground floor of STPLN's premises is regularly used by small companies and freelancers working in Malmö's cultural and creative scene. The space also hosts short-term projects such as a café for families with small children, a tailor service for fixing clothes, and exhibitions of emerging local artists. These initiatives are driven by people who are looking for space and resources for testing activities and ideas and check if and how they might work before making large investments.

Production at Fabriken: Commons-based crafts and do-it-yourself activities

The production processes and the activities carried out at Fabriken can be defined as commons-based in the sense that they are carried out through sharing both facilities and the means of production. Generally, initiatives at Fabriken resemble craftsmanship (Sennet 2008) since activities are often about doing something concretely by developing a direct involvement with materials through working, often becoming an opportunity to learn and to acquire new skills. At the same time, activities are often characterized by mutual learning and collaboration, generating social connections and resembling the idea of "making is connecting" (Gauntlett 2011).

Fabriken activities are generating outputs of three kinds of value: (1) goods or services with use value, (2) human capital (that is, skills and competence), and (3) social capital (social connections and trust). Here use value is understood as the concrete way in which a thing meets human need, or its being functional in satisfying a specific need (Harvey 2010). In Fabriken, use value can address a private need, or it can be exchanged with others for money or for other values such as social recognition or friendship. Moreover, having access to machines and meeting skilled people contribute to the development of human capital: personal knowledge, competence, and attributes of each participant. Sharing of spaces, machines, and knowledge supports a do-it-together approach (Gauntlett 2011) by which new connections between participants are established, generating social capital that entails connections among individuals and the norms of reciprocity and trustworthiness that arise from them (Putnam 1995).

When it comes to the activities going on in the space it is possible to distinguish between do-it-yourself practices ((Shove et al. 2007; von Busch 2008) and craft practices (Greenhalgh 2002).

The "DIY movement" began in the middle of the twentieth century, promoted by manufacturers of hand tools who saw in amateurs a potential market (Shove et al. 2007). In the 1970s, DIY practices were embraced as a form of resistance against the industrial production system (Leadbeater and Miller 2004), starting from the assumption that everyone could build and repair things (Gauntlett 2011), as opposed to buying new things, and that such activities are rewarding not only in terms of saving and/or producing use value but also in terms of personal satisfaction and self-esteem (Shove et al. 2007). The idea of DIY as a critical practice was developed within punk subcultures, in which it was considered a way to reclaim music and information production through home-recorded music tapes and zines (home-made magazines) (Gauntlett 2011). Recently, DIY has also become a central practice in the sustainability discourse, since repairing and recycling are viewed as alternatives to mass consumption (ibid.). DIY as an approach to hack mass production and consumption (von Busch 2008) is also emerging in Fabriken; however, it is also possible to see the space as embedded in and heavily dependent on the current economic system, since most of the production is done as a leisure-time activity.

At the same time, some of the activities seem to have the potential to represent an alternative way of producing and acquiring things, and in that they more resemble crafts. Crafts aren't defined specifically, since they represent an assortment of genres that makes sense together for artistic, economic, and institutional reasons. They have no intrinsic cohesion, no *a priori* relationship that makes them a permanent peculiar or special gathering (Greenhalgh 2002). Crafts, though, present several distinct threads. This is evident in Fabriken, in which craft practices do not necessarily fall in the category of decorative arts, but they more generally include all the activities requiring "applied" forms of creativity in a broad sense, from embroidery to soldering circuits.

Nonetheless, crafts present some common traits, especially when it comes to quality, morality, and technology (Greenhalgh 2002). Whereas DIY focuses on the actual making as an appropriation of production processes and generation of human capital, the focus in crafts is more on making as a way to generate use value; therefore, crafts entail a distinctive notion of quality that brings together functionality, aesthetics, and skills.

Since the eighteenth century, with the rise of the Arts and Crafts movement based on the ideas of John Ruskin and William Morris, crafts have also been considered a more human way of organizing production processes in opposition to the alienation of industrial processes (Harvey 2010), bringing in the aspect of morality. This aspect is shared with DIY practices and the idea of production as a tool for self-expression (Gauntlett 2011). The technology aspect is also quite central. On several occasions crafts have been looked upon in opposition to technology as an expression of industrial society (Ruskin 1985). However, in Fabriken, crafts activities do actually rely on technologies as tools for improving quality, efficiency, and accessibility to practice.

DIY and crafts are not new inventions; these models of production have been around for a long time, and crafts represented a mainstream mode of production until the first two industrial revolutions. What is different in Fabriken, and at other spaces for opening production, is how DIY and crafts practices are performed through shared means of production and collaboration, which, sometimes, but not necessary, can lead to the generation of commons.

Figure 6.9
Setting up STPLN's common garden. Elisabet M. Nilsson (CC:BY-NC).

Trying to overcome scarcity of materials

A major difference between intangible commons-based peer-to-peer production and the activities at Fabriken is that in the latter materials and outputs are rarely treated as commons, largely because problems with durability and rivalry make it more difficult to share materials—once used, they aren't available for others, and, unlike information, they are difficult to produce. How to get hold of materials for production is a major challenge in spaces for opening production, since the possibility of gaining access to machines, equipment, and even knowledge doesn't generate anything if materials aren't available. Finding ways to gain access to materials has always been a main concern in Fabriken, and has led to the development of a number of strategies having to do with waste. Beside basic approaches such as disassembling electronic products in order to get parts and collecting old clothes that can then be remade or reused, more complex strategies have also been developed. The Bicycle Kitchen, for example, had an agreement with the company that handles waste in Malmö to get bikes that people no longer wanted. The company put a container dedicated to bicycles in one of its facilities in which citizens bring their garbage. Users bringing bicycles to that facility could then decide whether to throw them away or to donate them to the Bicycle Kitchen. Initially the same strategy was to be used to get other things for Fabriken, but that turned out to be too complicated. The practices in Fabriken were so diverse that many containers would have been needed. Moreover, some extra work would have been necessary to sort materials, since, for example, certain activities performed in the space do not require just wood in general; they require plywood, or boards, or other specific kinds of wood.

And even if we could get hold of the materials, we would not know where to store them. Recently the Bicycle Kitchen decided to stop its collaboration with the waste-management company because it was getting more bikes than it had space for.

An interesting opportunity seemed to arise when ReCreate entered the space, since, besides getting interesting materials, ReCreate was also sorting them out. A series of collaborative experiments ensued—for example, between ReCreate and the Textile Department in order to explore possible uses of a high-quality waterproof textile that ReCreate got from a sailmaking company. However, this was an exception rather than the rule. Most of the materials ReCreate gets are semi-finished products, already shaped and therefore not easy to reuse. Moreover, it is sometimes difficult to know the exact constituents of the things ReCreate collects, so it isn't easy to decide whether, for example, the laser cutter should be used on them.

Working with scrap and waste is a common practice in Fabriken to overcome material scarcity, although this approach is unable to fulfill the needs of most of the activities. Material scarcity makes it difficult to apply commons-based peer-to-peer production to tangible forms of production. Thus, there is a need to develop new strategies and tactics to acquire resources for tangible forms of social production.

Fabriken and STPLN as attempts at commoning

Despite the materials challenges, Fabriken has succeeded in attracting and supporting a range of production practices by lowering the barriers for performing DIY and crafts activities through shared means of production and collaboration. The machines and the space attract participants and activities, but treating them as commons has not always been easy. Commoning, it became apparent, is not just a matter of establishing shared ownership; it is also a matter of managing collective access to, use of, and maintenance of resources (Ostrom 1990). This implies that commoning is an ongoing activity that needs to continuously evolve and adapt to changes in the context (ibid.).

Since the opening of the space, the idea was to involve participants in its management and reward the most active participants with special status—for instance, keys to the space, social recognition, or the opportunity to be involved in deciding what equipment to purchase. This led to a model of managing the premises: the NGO takes care of the general functioning of the space, and the participants focus on specific tasks

Figure 6.10
ReCreate's workshop. Anna Seravalli (CC:BY-NC).

directly connected to their own interests. The hacker community is managing and taking care of the machines in Fabriken, a small group of designers is running the textile-printing workshop, and an old lady is in charge of the textile corner. An important role is also played by the founders of ReCreate and the Bicycle Kitchen, who besides running their own projects are often involved in the general management of the space.

The functioning of the space relies on both economic standing and social standing. The NGO people and those running ReCreate and the Bicycle Kitchen are salaried. The fabrication machines, the textile atelier, and the screen-printing workshop, however, are managed by volunteers who are rewarded mainly with social standing. They usually don't get involved in general organizational issues; instead they manage access to and functioning of specific features. These highly engaged participants seem to be more interested in specific and even quite complex activities (such as fixing the laser cutter) than in the general management of the space (which is, as said, mainly a task for the NGO people and the ones driving the in-house projects). However, not all the participants are actively engaged in the space. The layers and possibilities of participation range from simply having access to and using the shared resources to taking part in their maintenance.

The NGO as a partner in commoning

The NGO plays an important role in the complex interweaving of diverse modes of participation, overseeing the management of the premises, coordinating sharing and access, and providing financial resources for the purchase of machine parts and tools. Participants mainly contribute with time, skills, and some material resources (such as equipment and materials). The NGO can be seen as a kind of partner in the participants' production activities. Cosma Orsi (2009) used the notion of partner to describe the possible role of the state in a commons-based regime as a structure supporting and enabling citizens' initiatives. In STPLN, the NGO doesn't run or lead specific activities; rather, it provides support for the diverse projects and ensures the preservation of the commons by intervening in disputes having to do with the sharing of equipment, the space, and access to the premises.

Because the NGO is financed by the municipality of Malmö on the basis of how many activities and people it is able to mobilize, participants can exert power through their sheer presence (or, rather, absence). There is a mutual dependency between the participants and the NGO. The participants depend on the NGO for access to the space and for its basic management. The NGO is aware that without participants the premises are endangered. The NGO's role is particularly important because in Fabriken and STPLN a lot of the projects are short in duration and people easily move in and out of the space. While the NGO ensures the continuity of the commons, the participants in the space may change. The role of the NGO is ambivalent: it certainly enables commoning by facilitating sharing and collaborating between participants; on the other hand, it could also be said that the organization running STPLN hinders commoning by retaining a central role in the management of the space.

Challenges with transient commoning: Legitimate participants and non-participants

Commoning at Fabriken seems to run quite well, though there are occasional tensions related to how the NGO is distributing financial resources. Specifically, the non-durability of the resources in the space implies the need for constantly investing money to maintain and fix the machines. As said, the NGO has some financial resources that, however, are never enough to cover all the material needs of the initiatives in the space, thus, discontent between participants may emerge about how these resources are allocated.

Other challenges emerged as the number of participants grew. The increasing number of newcomers to Fabriken meant that the regulars had to spend more time providing education in how to use the machines, at the expenses of their own experiments and projects. Moreover, the regulars' increased effort could not be properly rewarded: beyond full and free access to the space and social recognition, there was nothing more that could be offered them. In addition, it is difficult for newcomers to understand and accept how Fabriken and STPLN work. The idea of a commons, in which all concerned take care of the space, seems difficult to grasp because people often look for "someone in charge." The trickiest issue has to do with the sporadic users. Being in a space day after day helps a person to be aware of the importance of cleaning up and putting tools back where they belong. The regulars often have to spend time cleaning up messes made by others, and they often find that tools or materials seem to have disappeared. Moreover, because the space hosts a number of short-term projects, some participants may become very engaged for a while and then disappear from the space.

The problems emerging in the Fabriken and STPLN can be partially explained in terms of Elinor Ostrom's general design principles[1] for sustainable commons (1990, 1999). Among regulars, sporadic users, and newcomers, there is an issue of fairness: newcomers and sporadic users get a proportionately bigger benefit for the effort they invest than the regulars. This suggests that there may be deficiencies in how the rules of use and access are communicated to newcomers. Moreover, Fabriken lacks a system for verifying and sanctioning misuse of the shared resources (Ostrom 1990, 1999)—a lack that raises the question of how to allow consistently for control over the common without investing too many resources when the number of participants gets too big for simple peer control.

Figure 6.11
Transient participation. Anna Seravalli (CC:BY-NC).

In Fabriken and STPLN there is clearly tension between embracing new participants, openness, and the intrinsic necessity for the commons to have defined boundaries (Ostrom 1990, 1999), specifically boundaries between legitimate participants and non-participants (Cox et al. 2010). However, it is important to note that Ostrom's principles are based on commons to which participants have a long-term commitment. As has already been pointed out, at STPLN participation is transient, which makes difficult to define a clear boundary between legitimate and non-legitimate participants. From this perspective, the role of the NGO as a partner appears to be fundamental in ensuring continuity to the commons, even though its way of operating could be improved (particularly in regard to informing newcomers and in regard to fairness).

A central challenge in spaces for opening production seems to be how to discourage free-riding and misuse by transient participants. It is also important to understand which approaches can be used to facilitate the inclusion of new participants in the commons, as doing so appears to be a fundamental step towards economies of scope.

Sustainability, scope, and located production

By attracting diverse practices, Fabriken and STPLN show how economies of scope can be at play in spaces for opening production. Economies of scope also figure in the financial sustainability of the entire premises. As has already been mentioned, most of the funding comes from the City of Malmö, which covers basic expenses such as electricity and heating. The municipality is also paying the salaries of the three people from the NGO. Other forms of financing come from the foundation subsidizing ReCreate and the Bicycle Kitchen and from the research center Medea, which invested in some of the machines and which pays the author's salary. Financial resources are also obtained by renting out the space for events or conferences. Some material resources are contributed by participants who share private machines and materials in the space.

However, sustainability is not just a matter of financial or material resources. Voluntary work—a great asset—is often repaid by social standing, but also in more tangible ways, such as the opportunity for the most engaged participants to hold parties and events in the space for no charge. From this perspective, STPLN is using economies of scope when it comes to rewarding participants' work.

The importance of participants' involvement in spaces for opening production is increasingly recognized—for example, a number of fab labs have implemented internal currency systems so that working hours can be exchanged for access to equipment or other privileges in a similar but more formal manner than is done in Fabriken. However, such a practice requires good calibration and continuous re-adaptation, as Fabriken's problem of participants' not being properly rewarded showed. The latter problem, in fact, led to a decision to hire someone to take care of the machines and of basic training, and to ask participants for a membership fee that could be paid either in money (which would be used to pay the technician's salary) or by working in the space.

In trying to work toward economies of scope, Fabriken and STPLN have made a major effort to focus on located production rather than local production. Instead of starting out from a defined set of machines and practices, STPLN has tried to adapt progressively to the practices emerging from and coming to the space and to see the space as supporting production practices that make sense in and work in the context of Malmö, rather than developing the space according to a more standardized format (for example, that of the fab lab).

Infrastructuring for co-ownership and multiple understandings

In setting up and running Fabriken and STPLN, a main concern has been how to develop meaningful relationships within the local context. The space has been built up starting from practices, rather than machines and technology. At the official opening, the premises were basically empty. Then, by engaging possible participants and hosting diverse initiatives, the premises were progressively equipped and developed.

In infrastructuring Fabriken, a number of diverse approaches have been taken. In the beginning, events were used to reach out to diverse audiences and to invite them to join the space. These events all had a similar loose format: people were invited to run their own activities. As time went by, we understood how these events worked well in attracting specific communities of makers, and that it was more difficult to create occasions to bring together diverse groups of participants. At the first Hackathon,[2] in February 2011, we assumed that it was enough to include a few craft workshops to reach crafters. Some people interested in crafts did show up, but the majority of participants were still hackers. We also saw how, in reaching out to a wider public, more structured events (with planned activities and workshops) worked better than loose formats, as people less skilled in making seemed not so comfortable with an open format.

Other ways of involving people have been to organize courses and workshops. These public and planned activities have been very useful in involving people who already knew the space but had not yet found an opportunity to enter it.

Another important aspect in the infrastructuring of Fabriken has been working with a long-term perspective to establish co-ownership over the space, and to support the coexistence of diverse activities and interests.

Organizing events and workshops and setting up small-scale experiments have been important ways of inviting people to participate, but to get them to stay it has been important to provide them with ownership of the facilities and to involve them in the running of the space. It has also been important to find a way to keep many different initiatives with divergent interests under the same roof. Instead of trying to come to a univocal and shared definition of what the premises are about, the approach has been

Figure 6.12
An afternoon workshop in the Textile Department. Anna Seravalli (CC:BY-NC).

to allow for diverse understandings of Fabriken and STPLN. We have encouraged participants to develop their own understandings of the space. This has been facilitated by the large size of the premises and by the opportunity to have diverse activities happening at the same time in diverse spaces, or in the same space at different times, so as to minimize the risk of friction. Allowing a multiplicity of understandings has been helpful in constructing co-ownership and working toward economies of scope; however, it may have played a negative role in matters of communication concerning rules and behavior.

New producers and old producers: Alliances in the margins?
The participants at Fabriken and STPLN, aside from their differences, can be described as "new producers": prosumers, amateurs, lead users, and, generally speaking, end users. There is a lack of more traditional producers such as artisans or small producers. Relationships with more traditional producers might help in gaining access to competences and to materials.

Through ReCreate, when looking for material suppliers, a number of contacts with small producers were made. The collaboration with them rarely went beyond getting production leftovers, but when it did, interesting alliances seemed to emerge, as it happened with Bertil and his small die-board workshop that produces molds for punching cardboard and other materials. ReCreate founder, Carin, got in contact with him, as we wanted to experiment with the possibilities of creating building blocks out from various kinds of plastic and cardboard foils that ReCreate got from a packaging company. These initial contacts developed in an ongoing collaboration between Bertil and ReCreate, which entails not only punching foils, but also skills exchange.

Meeting and working with Bertil helped me to understand the situation of local small producers, revealing how promising but also how difficult it could be to involve them in a space for opening production.

In his collaboration with ReCreate, Bertil is working for free. When Carin, the founder of ReCreate, tried to discuss paying for his work and the die-boards, he just smiled and pointed out how expensive developing a die-board is. However, Bertil, who is in his seventies and ready to retire, seems to appreciate the fact that his skills and knowledge can be applied in new areas and, somehow, be passed on. Bertil not only has knowledge of traditional techniques of die-cutting; he is also an expert on laser-cutting, which makes him, potentially, a great resource for Fabriken. Through Bertil it has also been possible to get in contact with a big supplier of plastic materials and looking for possibilities to get some materials from them. Moreover, working with Bertil has led to a better understanding of the situation of small producers around Malmö, which is quite discouraging. The die-board company has very few clients left, since, as Bertil once said, die-cutting, together with many other production activities, is now a Chinese business.

From this perspective, the third industrial revolution could also be about finding alliances that would enable new and old producers to exchange skills, knowledge, and material resources, but it could also be a way to support other practices defining new forms of local production. However, the collaboration with Bertil has been an exception. A number of attempts have been made to infrastructure with small producers in Fabriken, but none of them have succeeded. Once, for example, Fabriken hosted a workshop with a professional woodworker. When discussing the possibilities of collaborating with the space, he stated how the space could work well for teaching the basics of carving wood, but that he could never use it for his professional practice, since that would require the purchase of expensive machines that would be difficult to share because he would have to use them for long periods of time.

However, further exploration of how to infrastructure possible alliances between new and old producers may be worthwhile—collaborations between these two groups may turn out to be fruitful attempts at commoning production, as in the case of Carin and Bertil.

Conclusions

The experiences emerging from Fabriken and STPLN can be considered as examples of what it might mean (and take) to infrastructure and to common for tangible production practices based on sharing and collaboration. The insights coming from the Malmö makerspace reveal the challenges posed by commons with transient participation, as well as how working toward economies of scope demands a located and ongoing approach in exploring possible alliances and practices.

Fabriken and STPLN seem to play a role also in relation to what kind of forms the third industrial revolution may take, at least, in Malmö. Inspired by the practices and activities emerging in this makerspace, the city of Malmö has commissioned us (the researchers) to do a pre-study for another similar facility in another neighborhood, where unemployment and integration are burning issues. The aim of this pre-study is to explore how a makerspace, by supporting the development of human capital and social capital, could improve well-being and living conditions in this area. Another interesting development is related to the national agency that financed our (the researchers) participation to Fabriken and STPLN. The financing of Fabriken and the other two Living Labs (see chapters 3 and 11) was part of an EU structural funds program aiming for economic growth. During the running of the Living Labs, a number of discussions and tensions have emerged in relation to the fact that the Labs were not delivering enough jobs and companies, which were two of the main indicators of the program. However, it is interesting to notice, one year after the official ending of the project, how the national agency has granted funding for the establishment of a number of makerspaces around the country (Tillväxtverket 2014).

In this perspective, it seems possible to say that a located and explorative engagement with practices, people, and spaces could be a way, at least on a local scale, to influence forms and aims of the third industrial revolution.

Acknowledgments

This chapter is a result of ongoing and located commons-based reflections with Pelle Ehn, Richard Topgaard, Luisa Carbonelli, Carin Hernqvist, Caroline Lundholm, Oyuki Matsumoto, Ola Persson, Bertil Björk, David Cuartielles, and the people who have been and are producing and commoning at STPLN.

Notes

1. These principles are not be understood as design approaches for the establishment of successful commons. They represent recurring characteristics that have been found in successful commons. (See Hess and Ostrom 2007.)

2. The Hackathon is a format that emerged within hacker communities. Hackathons are 24–48-hour events in which participants gather to program and build things together.

References

Anderson, Chris. 2010. In the Next Industrial Revolution, Atoms Are the New Bits (http://www.wired.com/magazine/2010/01/ff_newrevolution/).

Anderson, Chris. 2012. *Makers: The New Industrial Revolution*. Crown Business.

Baichtal, John. 2011. *Hack This: 24 Incredible Hackerspace Projects from the DIY Movement*. QUE.

Bauwens, Michel. 2006. The Political Economy of Peer Production. Post-Autistic Economics Review 37 (3): 33–44.

Bauwens, Michel. 2009. Class and Capital in Peer Production. *Capital and Class* 33: 121–141.

Benkler, Yochai. 2006. *The Wealth of Networks*. Yale University Press.

Benkler, Yochai. 2013. Commons and Growth: The Essential Role of Open Commons in Market Economies. *University of Chicago Law Review* 80: 1499–1555.

Björgvinsson, Erling, Pelle Ehn, and Per-Anders Hillgren. 2010. Participatory design and democratizing innovation. In Proceedings of the 11th Biennial Participatory Design Conference, Sydney.

Carson, Kevin. 2010. *The Homebrew Industrial Revolution*. Book Surge.

Cavalcanti, Guy. 2013. Is it a Hackerspace, Makerspace, TechShop, or FabLab? (http://makezine.com/2013/05/22/the-difference-between-hackerspaces-makerspaces-techshops-and-fablabs/)

Cox, Michael, Gwen Arnold, and Tomás Sergio Villamayor. 2010. A Review of Design Principles for Community-Based Natural Resource Management. *Ecology and Society* 15 (4): 38.

FabLab. 2013. FabLabs list (http://fab.cba.mit.edu/about/labs/).

Gauntlett, David. 2011. *Making Is Connecting*. Polity.

Gershenfeld, Neil A. 2005. *Fab: The Coming Revolution on Your Desktop*. Basic Books.

Greenhalgh, Paul, ed. 2002. *The Persistence of Craft*. Rutgers University Press.

Grenzfurthner, Johannes, and Frank Apunkt Schneider. 2009. Hacking the Space (http://www.monochrom.at/english/2009/05/hacking-spaces-critical-acclaim-of-what.htm).

Harvey, David. 2010. *A Companion to Marx's* Capital. Verso.

Helfrich, Silke. 2013. Economics and Commons?! Towards s Commons-creating Peer Economy. Keynote speech at conference on Economics and the Common(s): From Seed Form to Core Paradigm, Berlin.

Hess, Charlotte, and Elinor Ostrom, eds. 2007. *Understanding Knowledge as a Commons: From Theory to Practice*. MIT Press.

Hess, Karl. 2005. *Community Technology*. Loompanics.

Leadbeater, Charles, and Paul Miller. 2004. *The Pro-Am Revolution*. Demos.

Linebaugh, Peter. 2009. *The Magna Carta Manifesto*. University of California Press.

Mota, Catarina. 2011. The Rise of Personal Fabrication. In Proceedings of the Eighth ACM Conference on Creativity and Cognition, Atlanta.

O'Mahony, S., and B. A. Bechky. 2008. Boundary Organizations: Enabling Collaboration among Unexpected Allies. *Administrative Science Quarterly* 53: 422–459.

Orsi, Cosma. 2009. Knowledge-Based Society, Peer Production and the Common Good. *Capital and Class* 33 (31): 31–51.

Ostrom, Elinor. 1990. *Governing the Commons*. Cambridge University Press.

Ostrom, Elinor, Dietz Thomas, Dolšak Nives, Stern C. Paul, Stonich Susan, and Weber U. Elke, eds. 2002. *The Drama of the Commons*. National Research Council.

Ostrom, Elinor. 1999. Design Principles and Threats to Sustainable Organizations That Manage Commons. Workshop in Political Theory and Policy Analysis, and the Center for the Study of Institutions, Population and Environmental Change, Indiana University.

Ostrom, Elinor. 2011. Background on the Institutional Analysis and Development Framework. *Policy Studies Journal* 39 (1): 7–27.

P2P Foundation. 2013. Peer Production (http://p2pfoundation.net/Peer_Production#Discussion_2:_Is_Peer_Production_Beyond_Capitalism.3F).

Panzar, C. John, and D. Robert Willig. 1981. The Economies of Scope. *American Economic Review* 71 (2): 268–272.

Putnam, Robert. 1995. Bowling Alone: America's Declining Social Capital. *Journal of Democracy* 6 (1): 65–78.

Rifkin, Jeremy. 2011. *The Third Industrial Revolution: How Lateral Power Is Transforming Energy, the Economy, and the World*. Palgrave Macmillan.

Ruskin, John. 1985. *Unto This Last and Other Writings*. Penguin.

Sennett, Richard. 2008. *The Craftsman*. Yale University Press.

Seravalli, Anna. 2013. Prototyping for Opening Production: From Designing for to Designing in the Making Together. Presented at European Academy of Design Conference on Crafting the Future, Gothenburg.

Shove, Elizabeth, Matthew Watson, and Martin Hand. 2007. *The Design of Everyday Life*. Berg.

Siefkes, Christian. 2012. Beyond Digital Plenty: Building Blocks for Physical Peer Production. *Journal of Peer Production* (http://peerproduction.net/issues/issue-1/invited-comments/beyond-digital-plenty/).

Star, Susan Leigh, and Karin Ruhleder. 1995. Steps toward an Ecology of Infrastructure: Design and Access for Large Information Spaces. *Information Systems Research* 7: 111–134.

Thrift, Nigel. 2006. Re-Inventing Invention: New Tendencies in Capitalist Commodification. Economy and Society 35 (2): 279–306.

Tillväxtverket. 2014. Pressmeddelande (http://www.tillvaxtverket.se/download/18.48a604441429 f3886202ca2/1387447430244/Bilaga+pressmeddelande_om+projekten.pdf).

Troxler, Peter. 2010. Commons-based Peer-Production of Physical Goods Is there Room for a Hybrid Innovation Ecology? Presented at Free Culture Research Conference, Berlin.

Troxler, Peter. 2013. Making the 3rd Industrial Revolution. The Struggle for Polycentric Structures and a New Peer-Production Commons in the Fab Lab Community. In *FabLabs: Of Machines, Makers and Inventors*, ed. J. Walter-Herrmann and C. Büching. Transcript.

van Abel, Bas, Luca Evers, Roel Klaassen, and Peter Troxler. 2011. *Open Design Now*. BIS.

von Busch, Otto. 2008. *Fashion(able): Hacktivism and engaged fashion design*. Art Monitor.

von Hippel, Erik. 2005. *Democratizing Innovation*. MIT Press.

Wikipedia. 2011. Hackerspace (http://en.wikipedia.org/wiki/Hackerspace).

Zijlstra, Ton. 2013. The Failings of FabLabs (http://fablab.nl/2013/09/29/the-failings-of-fablabs/).

7 Playing with Fire: Collaborating through Digital Sketching in a Creative Community

Mads Hobye

Figure 7.1, a photograph taken at the 2008 Roskilde Festival in Denmark, shows a huge flame exploding from the top of what looks like a cross between the Eiffel Tower and an old oil rig. Two hundred people—some playing big drums made out of water tanks, some cheering, some dancing around the tower—participated in the event. There was a loud uproar right until the explosion. Afterwards, there was silence until the noise returned and another explosion occurred. Each cycle lasted about 15 minutes, and the cycles repeated for five consecutive days. How this project and many others came to be requires us to look at a community experimenting with interactive installations as a way of sketching digitally on a rusty old barge in the South Harbor of Copenhagen. The community is called Illutron, a collaborative studio for interactive art installations.

As a co-founder and a core member of Illutron, I have been part of the day-to-day discussions and challenges building the community and maintaining it as a fertile environment for creative people. This has enabled me to get an intimate insight into how many small choices have formed the organization and the community around it. In this chapter I will outline some of the properties that, since 2007, have enabled Illutron to work as a collaborative community of people exploring digital materials.

Illutron was formed in 2007 by a group of people with a wide range of backgrounds: artists, designers, performers, programmers, electricians, musicians, and what might be referred to as "electronics wizards." The group started with the intention of creating an open platform for creative and artistic uses of technology. The ideal was that members should have the freedom to be driven by their own curiosity. You didn't have to justify yourself and your work; it was inherent in the culture that somehow, someday, your little experiment would find a greater role in an interactive art installation, in a gallery, or in playful contexts at festivals and events.

The Illutron collective purchased an old 800-square-meter barge to serve as its workspace. It soon became a lab filled with electronic components, steel, and old industrial robots that members had found in scrapyards. The scrap was taken apart, revived, and put into new interactive situations: a discarded score display from the Danish national football stadium became an interactive light wall, and an old diving pressure

Figure 7.1
Explosion Village. Schack Lindeman (CC:BY-NC).

tank became the buffer tank for an interactive fire cannon. All the experiments were explored by imagining and testing the possibilities they might have in a context of playful participants in the field.

After many installations, it has become apparent that the materials people bring to the space serve as starting points for collaborations forming the art installations, and forming the collective in itself. In this chapter, descriptions of how Illutron came to be and of the design process of three interactive art installations will serve as a basis for understanding some of the intertwined social, technical, and artistic processes that emerge in—and maintain—the community.

David Gauntlett (2011) argues for the potential of considering the creative process of *making* as a way to create communities that will unlock new innovative capacities. Later in this chapter, I will reflect on how Gauntlett's perspective can help us to understand the community of Illutron, on how the concrete examples can extend Gauntlett's theories with understandings of sketching in digital material, on the importance of frontrunners, on the need for a physical space, and on the qualities of a shared identity.

The case of Illutron: Finding an organizational form

To understand how Illutron has become a collaborative platform for a diverse group of people, I first need to introduce how the barge and the organizational values were formed. Furthermore, I need to elaborate on the role of digital material exploration as a facilitator for creative projects with as many as eighty stakeholders involved. This serves as the basis for relating to Gauntlett's model.

Illutron was formed by a group of people who had organized or participated in an annual event called Half Machine, a two-week event focusing on artistic experimentation between humans and technology using multiple expressive forms such as music, dance, robotic, and interactive installations. The event was inspired by Burning Man, a large annual event in Nevada that experimented with the freedom of self-expression by using recycled materials to create art pieces, art cars, and steampunk clothes.

The co-organizers of and participants in the Half Machine events talked about the potential of having a place to do the same thing all year round. We looked at multiple workshop spaces near Copenhagen, primarily closed factories. At the time, however, the economy was on an upturn and either the rental prices were unrealistically high

Figure 7.2
Illutron's barge. Mathias Vejerslev (CC:BY-NC).

or the owners would only give us a short-term lease because they were more interested in selling the property for urban renewal projects than leasing it out to us. One day, a person in the dispersed group noticed a rusty barge lying in a ferry dock. Five years earlier, the barge had been used to build the Great Belt Bridge; it hadn't been used since. It was in horrible shape, but the size and the price were right. Contrary to all odds he managed to get most important parts of the formalities organized. Specifically he managed to convince the bank to lend the money and a free mooring was granted by the Copenhagen harbor. This motivated others to go further with the project and form the studio. It became a standing joke that you had to move out onto the water to do something that was not driven by the market economy; not market-driven in the sense of not focusing on profit, but instead ones own creative curiosity with digital technology.

In the first year of its existence, the barge was called Half Machine, but it soon became clear that the idea of Half Machine was tied so closely to the yearly events that it was necessary to change the name. This enabled the newborn project to form its own principles and enabled new members to influence its direction. We created a manifesto to verbalize some of the motivations behind the organization:

Illutron is a space for adventures and experiments. Artistic and technological frontiers are challenged. Experiments can be based on intuition instead of reason. Creative thinking emerges from below, as long as a fertile creative environment is fostered, where small seeds can find nourishment and grow roots and flower.

Technological progress happens in dialog with the surrounding society and refers to both the past and the future. Our art is a joint creative process in a group, a dialog between the group members and with cultural undercurrents in society. Art involves the audience, they become actors in dialog with the work of art, with its story. We make the works of art and source code available under Creative Commons. We encourage others to expand on our work. (Hobye and Padfield 2009)

The main motivation behind the manifesto was to emphasize the importance of having a space where people could tinker collaboratively. We further acknowledged that we would get inspiration from society and that we hoped to give back to society by encouraging people to build upon our works and by releasing the concepts of the installations and the source codes under Creative Commons licenses.

Apart from the legal arrangements necessary to run a non-profit organization, we didn't make any formal rules. Instead, we looked for pragmatic ways of creating a collaborative culture for the barge. The primary decision-making body was an open meeting every Sunday. We gradually found a good compromise between talking and doing, and we respected the idea that a person who took initiative on a new interactive installation should have a major say in the actual aesthetical design choices of it. Officially, decisions are made by majority, but we have yet to take a vote on anything.

Illutron's biggest challenge was to motivate people to dare to change things and make decisions on behalf of the community. "The ones who take action decide" became a recurring saying in the community, both when people were wondering if they were allowed to make a drastic change on the barge and when newcomers wanted to understand what they were allowed to do. After a while, multiple small sayings appeared and it became obvious that they could be harvested and turned into an explicit set of values. This led to ten values that framed our previously tacit culture of collaboration. Here are four of them, as set forth by Hobye, Jensen, and Padfield (2011):

Support initiative

We strive towards an informal structure. Don't confuse this with non-leadership. The structure reveals itself through who takes responsibility, and who takes initiative. Make sure to look for the good intentions in people's initiatives and find ways to support or improve their process.

The person who acts upon something decides on it

We don't have time to decide everything together so if you take action and do something you also have the freedom and responsibility to decide on how it should be done. Responsibility in the sense that you should be aware of the common good of the community at the barge. Furthermore it is your responsibility to communicate your plans and actions to the rest of the community.

Sunday meeting is your chance to affect direction

Sunday meeting should be kept short and effective. Here bigger decisions can be heard in plenum and everyone who is a member has a vote. Decisions on the Sunday meeting should be treated with the uttermost respect.

Embrace newcomers

Every newcomer should feel welcome and feel that they can participate at some level. No old grumpy men—who know better and already tried it. So smile. This gives your brain endorphins, and makes for nicer pictures.

The values were a symbol of daring to lose control and letting people with initiative take the lead and decide what to do with the space. We e-mailed the values to everyone on the mailing list and presented it at one of the Sunday meetings, but the true communication was done by printing them and posting them on the inside of the rest-room door for people to read. We took the fact that visitors began to take better care of the space as evidence that people had read the values. This enabled people with diverse interests and skills to find the context in which they could participate. The barge became a place for 15–20 core members and about 1,100 people in an extended network.

As part of the organizational structure, we made a rule that every project that came into being because of Illutron should pay at least 10 percent of the revenue as a contribution to the barge. This, combined with a monthly membership fee from the core members, became the primary source of income for the barge. The monthly membership fee varied between 75 and 850 Danish Krone, depending on the member's economic resources and on his or her need to use the barge as a primary workspace.

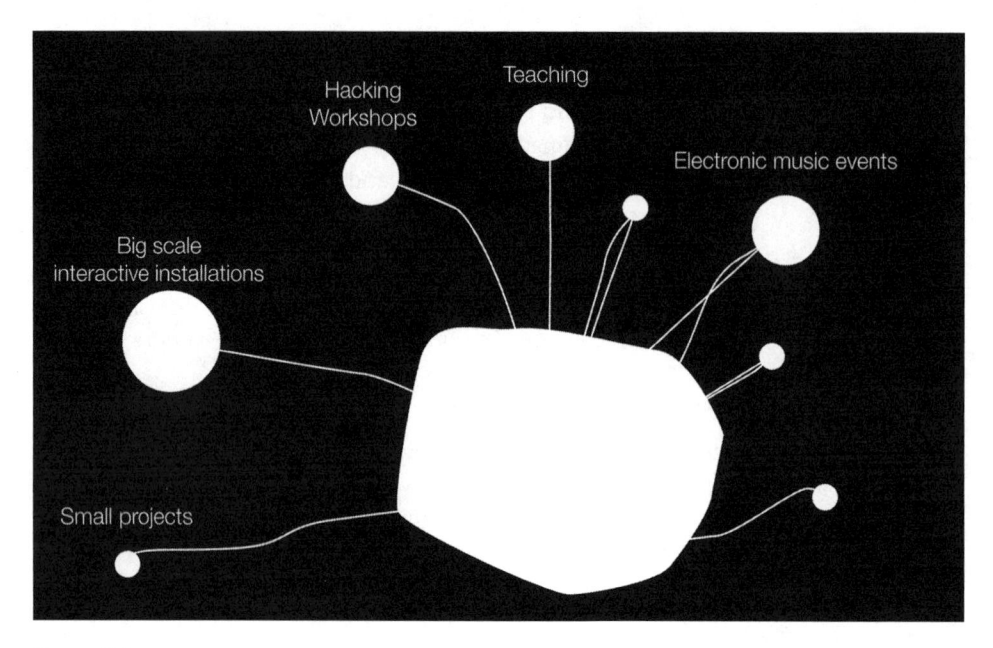

Figure 7.3
A hackerspace-like environment, but with an external mindset of creating for the broader public.

Also important when describing the intrinsic goals of the barge is what might be called "the external mindset." In contrast to a hackerspace, much of the work didn't happen for the sake of the technology itself but was embedded in a mindset oriented toward creating *for* and *with* participants in public events, such as festivals and exhibitions.

Although much emphasis has been put on Illutron's organizational structure, the true facilitator of collaboration was in the exploration of digital material. This became obvious after a couple of large projects that showed a direct correlation between how interesting a project was and how many people participated. People were willing to spend their holidays and spare time to get their hands dirty with rusty metal for the sake of creating an interactive art community.

Digital material exploration

There is no doubt that the organizational choices made have formed the community, but in hindsight the projects undertaken have played a major role in constituting the organizational framework. The projects became the conversation pieces that made it interesting to participate, and they enabled open-ended explorations with technologies.

In winter, when the water around the barge was frozen and we didn't have any concrete projects booked, only a few people would find time to visit and maintain the barge. As soon as spring came, more people began to work on projects. And after we started work on a larger project, such as an interactive installation, we soon had as many as 50 people working together. Since 2007, this has been the recurring rhythm of the barge. What factors are at work in this rhythm?

In the context of the barge, the term *digital material* is understood as a combination of electronic scrap material and embedded microcontroller platforms such as Arduino. The electronic scrap material could be old diode displays that once were used to show the score at a soccer stadium. The exploration in relationship to digital material is understood as the process of hacking (as in repurposing old technology for new things) and modifying those components into novel interactive designs. The original aesthetics of the recycled materials are used as inspiration for new forms of expressions. The embedded microcontroller platforms serve to extend the interactions of the scrap materials beyond their original possibilities—for example, to extend the diode displays with motion-detecting sensors that enable them to sense the presence of people in the surroundings and act accordingly. In this digital material exploration also lies a process

Figure 7.4
Diode displays set up in Copenhagen metro. Mathias Vejerslev (CC:BY-NC).

of moving the materials into new contexts, hence enabling new interpretations of their roles in the spaces—for example, using diode displays from a soccer stadium in an interactive piece in an art museum. It is a material exploration giving equal weight to both the digital and the physical properties of the material. In this sense it aligns itself to what Vallgårda and Sokoler (2010) call "composite materials"—that is, materials that have both digital and physical properties.

We found the old score displays from the national soccer stadium in 25 big old rusty boxes at the local scrapyard. At first they were unusable, but that rapidly changed when Illutron members began to figure out how they worked. Quite a few of the pixels didn't work at all, and those that did work could show only red, green, or yellow.

For the members, the score displays possessed potential for interactive installations with a certain "retro" aesthetic. Since the birth of Illutron in 2007, the diode displays, which together weigh more than a thousand kilograms, have been used in several installations—one at the Charlottenborg Museum of Art (in an interactive installation at the annual spring exhibition), one at the Roskilde Festival (in an interactive light

Figure 7.5
Medusae Nilfisk. Nicolas Padfield (CC:BY-NC).

tower five meters tall), one on the barge (as a VJ wall for parties), several on water (in moving light installations), and one at a Copenhagen Metro station (to visualize the trains going by).

We have lost count of how many people have worked with the displays, and in how many ways. Without the diode displays as a conversation starter, these projects and situations would not have happened. This is not a unique pattern but a recurring theme. Other artifacts, including industrial robots, gas cannons, and DMX controlled theater lighting could also be mentioned. The small experiments served as inspiration for bigger projects, as visualized in figure 7.5. In every case, the conversation began with messy explorations by a few people of how technology might be used in novel ways. In the subsections that follow, I will describe three projects that exemplify how digital material exploration is a source for collaboration and how each project inspires the next.

First story: From small light clouds to Medusae Nilfisk
The Floating Clouds installation at one of the early Half Machine events, in 2005, was an experiment in the aesthetic qualities of lights shining through fabric. Three balloons of white kite fabric were inflated by small computer cooling fans and would change color by means of three light bulbs inside (red, green, and blue). The balloons were quite passive.

Two years later, Roskilde Festival (a music festival with 100,000 participants) asked if we would be interested in making an installation for a usually badly lit area that many people walked through. It was basically a boring passage between two major stages.

We brainstormed about possible ideas, and "floating clouds" similar to those in the 2005 installation but much larger came to mind. Two old military parachutes were sewn together to form a sphere. Lights were added inside, and the sphere was inflated with antique Nilfisk vacuum cleaners (in reverse mode). Some members had begun to experiment with ways of igniting gas to create large interactive flame effects, and we thought of combining the two projects into one installation. Gas flames would be mounted on top to create fire explosions in the night. The Medusae Nilfisk project was born.

What in theory seemed to be a straightforward task quickly proved to be a constant battle with the materials. Each parachute had to be dipped in glue five times to make it sufficiently airtight. We had to find a way to control the fire cannon. We had to find a way to place the installation high enough that participants would not be able to destroy it. And participants had to be able to affect the light and set off the fire.

Seeing the installation with the lights, the fire, and the parachutes for the first time, we were pleased with the result and surprised by properties that we had not anticipated. The glue gave the parachutes a translucent texture. The metal frames that held the lights cast shadows on the parachutes, making them resemble super-sized Chinese lamps.

Figure 7.6
Night view of the Medusae Nilfisk installation. Schack Lindeman (CC:BY-NC).

For interactivity, we provided two poles that, when touched simultaneously, would set off the fire and change the colors of the lamps. We placed the poles so far apart that at least three people had to hold hands to connect them. At first, none of the participants seemed to understand what they were supposed to do with the poles. After an evening of explaining to random people that they would be able to set off the fire by holding hands, people started to explore it on their own. On the second day, the rumor had spread, and we observed an ongoing dialogue in which people would run around asking other people to hold their hands so they could see the fire. What we at first thought of as a failure in interaction proved to be a simple way of engaging people in playful interactions (Hobye, Padfield, and Löwgren 2013).

At first the Medusae Nilfisk project was mostly the work of four people, but slowly more and more people joined the project and helped out in various ways. We didn't plan this; it was a consequence of our needing help with various things. For example, we asked an engineer to help us get the touch-sensing poles to work. We had made a touch-sensing system that worked perfectly in the dry conditions of our workspace, but when we implemented it in the wet mud of the festival we could not read a signal. It seemed the signal went straight down into the ground instead of back into our measuring probe. With duct tape, hot glue, and components from a discarded circuit board, the engineer was able to get the system to detect if people had connected the two poles. It was like magic to us, and we all wanted to understand how he did it. Although he was not originally a member in the project, he ended up staying for a whole week, fixing things and playing with electronics.

Second story: From drum experiments to Explosion Village
In the fall of 2008, inspired by the playful interactions we had observed at Roskilde Festival, we began to experiment with percussive interfaces. We wondered how we could make an installation that allowed multiple festival participants to play music together. Answering this question would be a way of utilizing the energies of multiple participants interacting with an installation in real time.

In the first experiments, we used wooden boxes wired up with contact microphones. The sound from the wooden boxes was filtered through various sound effects to create interesting sound dynamics. The sound was analyzed and converted into light, so you could see your own drumming and a visualization of the overall activity (energy) in the installation. The experiment was rough—a bunch of people jumping on the boxes and drumming randomly. At certain times we sensed qualities that seemed likely to get a lot of people to create rhythms together. The project became quite enchanting, and we wanted to see what would happen if it was scaled up.

The next year, Roskilde Festival asked if we wanted to do an installation in an area larger than the one we had been given the year before. We proposed the interactive drumming installation combined with a huge gas cannon (The member of our group who had made the fire cannon for the Medusae Nilfisk installation said he would go to the festival again only if he could make the biggest fire cannon possible). Eventually we came up with the idea of the Explosion Village with multiple drum interfaces. When the participants had drummed for a certain time, a huge gas cannon in the middle of the site would fire.

Explosion Village was a much larger project than Medusae Nilfisk. Six groups worked on various parts of the installation. The musicians and the sound engineers explored different physical materials that would create interesting sounds when drummed on. The electricians and programmers built control systems that connected the drum interfaces to light effects and measured the activity so the explosion would go off at the right time. The people working with the gas cannon investigated ways of releasing a lot of gas while maintaining a safe and controlled situation. The groups were formed around key people within the community who took the lead on solving a specific problem within the larger project. There was a lot of interaction between members of different groups, especially when interesting experiments were underway. When the gas cannon was about to be fired for the first time, everyone worked on the preparations.

Figure 7.7
The initial experiment with drum interfaces. Mads Hobye (CC:BY-NC).

Besides people with assigned responsibilities, more and more people began to hang out and help. We had to ask the festival for tickets for sixty volunteers.

One of the most active individuals became the project's leader. This was never officially decided, but everyone knew that he was the one who could give status updates and could make sure that your part would fit into the whole picture, both technically and physically. His primary role was to think of all the things that had been overlooked—for example, making sure that we had containers for our gear at the festival and that there were people cooking so that we wouldn't starve while building the installation at the otherwise empty festival site.

Thousands of participants constantly played with the Explosion Village installation throughout the festival, drumming energetically while singing and dancing around the fire tower. Its success was dependent on people working behind the scenes, fixing broken lights and experimenting with different interaction patterns while people were playing. Musicians explored the possibilities of making people play together by playing along with them on various instruments, including electronic drum machines and a wooden double bass. It was an intense experience trying to play with the designed framework while 200 people were drumming like mad on big glowing water tanks. Through the code and the audio processing interfaces, we became co-players with rhythms created by the participants.

When the festival was over, we all were dirty and tired. We went home to get a week of rest. When we returned to the barge, the Illutron group had grown, mostly in its extended network, but we also had a few more core members.

Third story: From touch experiments to Pyrolandia

In 2010, we were asked to do an installation in the city of Roskilde at midwinter. Inspired by the experiment with the touch poles, we had discussed and experimented with ways of digitally sensing full-body touch-sensing. We now wanted to inspire an interaction that had more rich interaction properties than just a simple stimulus response of a gas cannon firing.

We wanted to make a more advanced fire cannon, partly because the rapid expansion of propane gas tends to freeze pipes, especially in the cold winter, and partly because we wanted to be able to control the size of the flame. We decided to use diesel this time.

The quest for understanding full-body touch-sensing led to multiple small experiments with circuit boards and programs designed to interpret when two bodies touched. We found that we were able to detect when one of three dancers got a hug from a participant by reading the capacitance of the individual dancer. When one dancer was connected to another body (a participant), the capacitance would change. For this to work each of the dancers had to wear a wire that was connected to the main circuitry. This became our first full-body touch-sensing installation. In Pyrolandia, the touch-sensing installation was incorporated in an aural and visual performance in which the amount of bodily connection (i.e., the change in capacitance) with the audience correlated to the amount of fire from the fire tower.

Connecting through digital sketching

Gauntlett's (2011) model of "making is connecting" sheds new light on processes such as the one that shaped Illutron and how digital material exploration became a central aspect of the community. On the other hand, experiences on the barge highlight some of the concrete nuances that Gauntlett seems to miss, thus enabling us to develop his theory further.

Gauntlett challenges the idea of creative processes as something that should be judged on their outcomes. He leaves behind, much in line with Dewey (2005), the institutionalized traditions of evaluating art as an end product and points out the inherent pleasure of the *making* in itself. The making, thus, becomes a creative process

Figure 7.8
The Pyrolandia installation, with a touch-reactive performer dancing in front of the flame effects.
Mathias Vejerslev (CC:BY-NC).

where the pleasure is first and foremost found in doing and building for your own satisfaction. To him, activities like small improvements to your home have satisfactory qualities in themselves.

Through making, people become participants rather than merely spectators or consumers. Further, you want to be recognized for what you do, not by being the first in the world to make something, but by sharing your skills and work in a community of interesting and interested peers. By sharing and making a mark, you become alive, connected and find a shared purpose, which Gauntlett (2011) argues is essential for human stability, happiness, and well-being. Hence, self-realization will not work if pursued in solitude. The source of happiness lies in everyday life collaboration as part of a community.

Gauntlett's arguments align well with the story of Illutron and how making has become a central aspect of its ecosystem. First and foremost, the barge was intended to be a space where people could create on their own terms and for the joy of creating itself. Second, the three stories recounted above exemplify how digital material exploration became a central aspect of sharing and collaborating within a dynamic group of people.

Gauntlett (2011) notes that sharing is a way of making in collaboration. He mentions the open-source software community and people sharing knitting patterns as examples of people building upon the work of others. In the case of Illutron, the digital material exploration has an inherently fluid structure. Parts and ideas from previous projects are reused and modified in new projects in a never-ending process. Projects are always open to new interpretations. This has been formulated in the manifesto by encouraging others to build upon our work, but also to consider the works as invitations for participants to use on their own terms in a collaboration with us.

In the case of Illutron, the digital material exploration can be considered as a form of sketching. By considering every project a sketch that hasn't found its final form, we make room for exploration and modification. Buxton (2007) introduces the concept of sketching user-experience as a way of enacting different interaction scenarios through easily moldable materials such as foam blocks and cardboard mockups. This enables the designer to quickly produce new sketches without the time-consuming work of programming and soldering functional prototypes, hence enabling the designer to have a short iteration cycle between ideas. Consider how collaboration unfolds through sketching in the context of Illutron.

At Illutron, people usually tinker with rapid prototyping tools that are technically more advanced than cardboard mockups, including embedded platforms (such as Arduino and Wiring) and creative programming languages (such as Processing, openFrameworks, and MaxMSP) that can be used to quickly prototype different interaction scenarios.

Illutron's sketching approach aligns with the concept of "sketching in 4D" (Kyffin et al. 2005) which underlines the need to move beyond screen-based interaction into a three-dimensional perspective, a spatial approach to sketching that requires a sensitivity to the forming of the materials itself. Kyffin et al. (ibid.) further argue for a fourth dimension: the temporal dimension. They exemplify this through a learning process in which students have to create prototypes via a set of technical steps. The individual steps in the process become a generative way of understanding the expressions of the design ideas and generating new ideas to elaborate on. To embrace evaluation and idea generation as a combined process, Kyffin et al. suggest, much in line with Buxton (2007), that one should start out with prototypes that are as "lo-fi" as is possible. With each iteration, a new layer of complexity is then added. Simply put, the students start out with simple sketches that they turn into mockups that can be acted out manually. In the final stage, they construct a working prototype with, for example, a programmed microcontroller, sensors, and actuators.

The key difference between the approach put forward by Kyffin et al. (2005) and the approach utilized on the barge lies in the sketching starting point and how the sketching evolves over time. Whereas the members of Illutron brainstorm (in a relatively disorganized way) about new projects, the initial sketching is actually done closer to what Kyffin et al. would consider a part of the final phases. To exemplify, the Illutron prototyping might start with a microcontroller (in our case an Arduino board), a first iteration that is considered an initial and crude mockup. This initial mockup serves to communicate an idea or to solve a core feature in the interaction, for example how to detect touch between two bodies or how to make large-scale fire effects in a controlled way.

There are two reasons for the members of Illutron having a more technically advanced starting point than Buxton's argument for lo-fi prototyping and the starting point used by Kyffin et al. First, it is a consequence of the rather high technical skill level present on the barge. It simply doesn't make sense to make a foam mockup and act out the interaction when one can just as easily wire up a servo to an Arduino board and see the actual working prototype from the beginning. This is also a consequence of the evolvement of general usability within microprocessor programming. In 2005, when Kyffin et al. argued for a fourth dimension (the temporal dimension in the form of real-time interactive properties), one had to be able to set up ones own chain of tools for one to be able to program a microcontroller (a task that required quite a bit of technical knowledge). Today, easily programmable microcontrollers, such as Arduino, set new standards in usability for cross-platform out-of-the-box programming interfaces. The second reason for Illutron's more technically advanced starting point is a consequence of the fact that most of the design within the community is rooted in technical challenges. For example, finding a way to detect body presence between two people works simultaneously as a technical challenge and a conceptual idea generator.

One could say that the Illutron sketching process is the reverse of the one proposed by Kyffin et al.—that Illutron sketching begins with the technical challenges of the sensors and the interaction and uses it as a skeleton around which to build the physical properties of the installation.

Using software development environments and embedded platforms for rapid prototyping in the early phases of design and development differs from using materials such as cardboard and styrofoam to make mockups. I argue that our technical starting point is given by the nature of the technicality of the materials and the engaging experiences we want to create. For example, in the case of the experiments with drumming, it would not have been possible to understand the interaction and the possible aural and visual feedback without experimenting with contact microphones and real-time analysis of the sounds. The interaction aesthetics (Petersen et al. 2004) we seek require an embodied (Dourish 2004) or somaesthetical (Shusterman 2008) exploration right from the early phases of the experimentation, something that cardboard mockups cannot facilitate. One can assess the potentials of the experience only by interacting with the working prototypes.

Thus, the sketching process at Illutron can be understood as a digital extension of Buxton's (2007) sketching user-experience and can be seen as a reversed version of the 4D sketching approach of Kyffin et al. (2005); all three of those approaches have similar agendas of gaining a craftsman-like way of exploring the digital materials. As a consequence of Illutron's digital/technical starting point, I argue that it should be considered digital sketching—a technique that resembles traditional sketching techniques, but with a focus on sketching in digital material (Hobye 2014). How this unfolds in the collaborative environment of Illutron depends on the factors described below.

In the lab vs. in the field

At Illutron, the immediate environment around the barge where the initial experiments are done can be considered the *lab*, and the larger context in which the installations are deployed can be considered the *field*. This is in line with the definition, proposed by Koskinen et al. (2011), according to which the lab is a decontextualized free space into which people bring things of interest for experimental studies, and where the field is a contextualized place where one studies how the designs are used, made sense of, and how they are talked about by audiences who become participants. Because Koskinen et al. study discrete cases, they do not elaborate on the transformation of the experiment when going from the lab to the field. In the three stories about Illutron projects recounted above, there is a natural inherent interplay between the lab and the field.

In the setting of the decontextualized lab of Illutron, exploration relies on enactment and the prediction of interaction, i.e., imagining how "real" participants will use it. Here, we do what Schön (1987) would call "knowing-in-action." Our tacit understandings of what works become the primary ground for choosing the way forward, understanding how participants have interacted in other projects, and reassessing how this relates to the current ideas. This is, as was mentioned above, a "messy" and open-ended process. Multiple experiments pull in different directions, and those experiments are mostly driven by questions such as "What if we can sense the distance between humans?" and "What is the perfect mixture between gas and air?" This results in workspaces filled with half-finished experiments. It becomes what Schön would call "reflection-in-action," a reflective process in which ideas materialize through collaborative kneading. The ideas and experiments become traveling conversations in which personal ownership is lost and it is often difficult to remember who came up with an idea first.

The decisions made through experiments and through enactments of interaction scenarios become our sketches to try out in the field. Although the experience of the crew enables us to predict some of the possible interaction scenarios, we still need to modify it to scenarios we had not anticipated. This becomes a running-in period during which parameters are tweaked to accommodate the actual interaction. Hence, the sketches serve as rudimentary frames to modulate live while participants interact with the installations in the field.

The field is an ongoing conversation with the participants through their interactions with the installations. Thus, it becomes a lab-in-practice where the initial ideas and designs imagined are bent and modulated to fit the context. There can be a multitude of interests, but a common underlining theme has been to inspire people to play with and explore the installations with one another.

The dialogue between the lab and the field characterized above are central to understand when we elaborate further on the collaborative group dynamics put forward by Gauntlett (2011), because it leads to an involuntary exclusion of members and a need for front-runners for the community to evolve.

Involuntary exclusion and the need for front-runners

In the examples presented above, multiple people working on a project together became a way of including new members into the core group. Gauntlett (2011) would consider this a process of communities forming through mutual creative interests. However, as much as this became a fruitful way of engaging new members, it also had its limitations. Specifically, the technical mindset of the community tended to lead to involuntary exclusion, and it depended rather heavily on front-runners.

The use of advanced technology and the advanced shaping of materials require that the designer have technical expertise. It has become apparent, through many projects, that the person designing an installation and the person building it are almost always the same.

The technical skills required to do digital sketching have led to involuntary exclusion. If you don't know how to work with the materials, you tend to become a visitor at the barge instead of a participant. In our experience, a few people became exceptions to this tendency because they had enough social skills and enough technical knowledge to have conversations about projects without actually building the projects. They found roles as project leaders or activists, helping with necessary but non-technical elements of the projects.

As a general rule of thumb, a person must have a set of (most often technical) skills to get involved in conversations about projects. It has not been uncommon to see members evolve over time and acquire multiple secondary skills by learning through collaboration with others. Now that Illutron has been active for several years, there is a general understanding of the individual members' primary and secondary skills—an understanding that comes in handy when new projects must be coordinated.

Since a larger project requires a period of preparation, negotiation of formal contracts, and conceptual presentation, Illutron is highly dependent on the front-runners to lead the way. The saying "Those who take initiative decide" is good for the front-runners, but it leaves little room for newcomers and activists who lack technical skills or sufficient knowledge of the working culture of the barge. They tend to be passive until someone with knowledge and greater experience takes the lead.

A shared space and a shared identity

Gauntlett (2011) mostly focuses on collaborations through unstructured online networks of people. Illutron, by contrast, has a more rigid physical and social structure, in which emergent collaborations occur. The barge is a physical workspace and a community with a shared identity. The physical workspace enables us to have much more hands-on collaboration than can be had in a virtual collaboration. Working on the same physical things together is different from tinkering with the same idea across the world. The latter could be described as a parallel virtual creative process that is useful for sharing and developing smaller projects (such as cooking recipes) and for working on software development. The former could be described as creative collaboration in a shared workspace. Our shared workspace has enabled us to create large-scale installations with as many as 80 people working on elements that are later combined in a greater whole. Furthermore, the physical space has enabled us to carry on traveling conversations about experiments. A small experimental prototype that one person made during the winter may lie on the floor for months until someone picks it up, builds upon it, and turns it into something great the next summer.

Besides the physical space, the identity of Illutron enables us to have a generous attitude toward ownership and crediting. People are able to share their ideas because they know that even if somebody else ends up using their idea or technology it will still be part of a project that will be branded under the shared identity. This enables us to focus on large-scale collaboration instead of small-scale self-realization.

In the beginning, we had many discussions about what titles and roles might be used when it came to defining people on websites and in projects. However, the shared creative processes made it practically impossible to figure out who should be credited for the ideas and the construction of the individual parts of projects. Two other questions were "What constitutes a work of art?" and "Who is the artist?" This led us to do two things. We decided to give equal credit to all those who were involved in a project, even if only remotely). You can see an example of this in the acknowledgments at the end of this chapter, where people are credited without any mention of their individual roles. In the manifesto, this is put as follows: "Credit all involved (including the tea person)." We also decided to consider everyone an artist:

Everyone is an artist hence nobody is an artist

Everybody pulls together to make art and everyone contributes to the art. Therefore the role of being "the" artist is non existing. (Hobye, Jensen, and Padfield 2011)

By considering everyone an artist, we leave behind the fine-arts institutions' need for classification and evaluation and instead focus on the qualities of the experiments and on interesting ideas people come up with under the identity of Illutron.

The individual ambitions of the members of Illutron differ from Gauntlett's descriptions of informal online communities. Online sharing communities have ambitions of recognition within their own circles. Compared to Gauntlett's perspective, Illutron also has an external focus. The creation of interactive art projects in public spaces attracts people with artistic or technical ambitions, something that could be an obstacle to free sharing of ideas and concepts within the organization. Through a shared identity, and by crediting everyone involved in projects without specific details on who did what, we defuse some of the inherent fear of sharing openly with other members. That gives a member the freedom to define his or her own contribution when describing the process to others inside or outside the community.

Conclusion

One of the objectives of this chapter was to add to Gauntlett's (2011) concept that "making is connecting" by describing and analyzing how Illutron works. Gauntlett's way of putting focus on the act of making together as an integrated part of connecting is true when it comes to the relationship between the fragile community on the barge and the digital material exploration that goes on there. Without our conversations about digital material we would not have had interesting projects, and without interesting projects we would not have been able to evolve the organization.

The main organizational question is how sustainable this rather informal model will be. Will the ecosystem slowly dry up, or will there always be new potential projects and new curious people? Since 2007, we have seen a slow change in the membership, "new" people learning from "old" people and some people moving on. Ideally, this would mean that in the future most of the founders have been exchanged, while some of the knowledge and experience is maintained and developed in a never-ending process.

Acknowledgments

Current members of Illutron (as of 2013): Mads Hobye, Vanessa Carpenter, Peter Madsen, Schack Lindemann, Nicolas Padfield, Bent Haugland, Daniel Brooks, Tobias Lukassen, Christian Liljedahl, Harald me. Viuff, Joachim Ante, Mona Jensen, Johan B. Lindegaard, Jonas Jongejan, Mathias Vejerslev, Dzl (Nicolaj Møbius), Simo Ekholm, Eva Kanstrup, Lin Routhe, Troels Just C, Benjamin Weber, Halfdan Hauch Jensen

Floating Clouds: Mads Hobye, Nynne Just Christoffersen, Nicolas Padfield

Medusae Nilfisk: Thomas Jørgensen, Nicolas Padfield, Mads Hobye and Schack Lindemann, Vibeke Hansen, Dzl (Nicolaj Møbius), Harald Viuff, Bo Boye

Score display hacking: Jacob Remin, Peter Boné, Kasper Pangbrun, Troels Christoffersen, Thomas Fabrik, Nicolas Padfield, Mads Hobye, Sonny Windstrup, Johan Bichel Lindegaard

Soundscape: Mads Hobye, Daniel Brynolf, Henrik Svarrer Larsen, Romy Kniewel, Khorsed Alam

Explosion village: Anders Olsen, Andreas Bennetzen, Annechien Seesink, Casper Øbro, Claus Jørgensen, Eva Kanstrup, Frederik Hilmer Jensen, Harald me Viuff, Helle Falk Jakobsen, Jakob Sindballe, Johannes Asker Andersen, Jonas Jongejan, Jun Philip Kamata, Karen Gamborg Knudsen, Kasper Rasmussen, Ki Elvira Roux Fuglsang, Mads Hobye, Marc Cedenius, Mathias Vejerslev, Morten Vendelboe, Nicolaj Møbius, Nicolas Padfield, Peter Madsen, Pia Nielsen, Vibeke Hansen, Rikke Rasmussen, Schack Lindemann, Simon Lausten Østergaard, Sofus Walbom Kring, Sonny Windstrup, Stig Eivind Vatne, Tanja Jørgensen, Thomas Fabian Eder, Thomas 'Fabrik' Jørgensen, Tobi Twang, Vanessa Carpenter, Roskilde Festival Volunteers

Pyrolandia: Christian Liljedahl, Nicolaj Møbius, Nicolas Padfield, Harald Viuff, Tobi Twang, Schack Lindemann, Brian Vandal, Sonny Windstrup, Mads Høbye, Mona Jensen, Rikke Rasmussen, Gemma Peramiquel Borjas, Emma-Cecilia Ajanki, Sophia Mage, Henry Tornow, Vanessa Carpenter, Johan Bichel Lindegaard, Lizette Bryrup, Max

Kim Tobiasen, Mathias Vejerslev, Lone Juul Dransfeldt Christensen, Christian Wang, Frederik Thaae

Photographers: Mathias Vejerslev, Schack Lindeman, Sonny Windstrup and Mads Hobye

References

Buxton, Bill. 2007. *Sketching User Experiences: Getting the Design Right and the Right Design*. Elsevier/ Morgan Kaufmann.

Dewey, John. 2005. *Art as Experience*. Penguin.

Dourish, Paul. 2004. *Where the Action Is: The Foundations of Embodied Interaction*. MIT Press.

Gauntlett, David. 2011. *Making Is Connecting: The Social Meaning of creativity, from DIY and Knitting to YouTube and Web 2.0*. Polity.

Hobye, Mads, Mona Jensen, and Nicolas Padfield. 2011. The Values of Illutron (updated version at http://illutron.dk/values/solo).

Hobye, Mads, and Nicolas Padfield. 2009. Manifesto 1.1 (updated version at http://illutron.dk/manifesto/solo).

Hobye, Mads. 2014. Designing for *Homo explorens*: Open Social Play in Performative Frames. PhD dissertation, Malmö University.

Hobye, Mads, Nicolas Padfield, and Jonas Löwgren. 2013. Designing Social Play through Interpersonal Touch: An Annotated Portfolio. Presented at Nordic Design Research Conference, Copenhagen and Malmö.

Koskinen, Ilpo, John Zimmerman, Thomas Binder, Johan Redström, and Stephan Wensveen. 2011. *Design Research through Practice: From the Lab, Field, and Showroom*. Morgan Kaufmann.

Kyffin, Steven, Loe Feijs, and Tom Djajadiningrat. 2005. Exploring Expression of Form, Action and Interaction. *Home-oriented Informatics and Telematics* 178: 171–192.

Petersen, Marianne Graves, Ole Sejer Iversen, Peter Gall Krogh, and Martin Ludvigsen. 2004. Aesthetic Interaction: A Pragmatist's Aesthetics of Interactive Systems. In Proceedings of the Fifth Conference on Designing Interactive Systems: Processes, Practices, Methods, and Techniques (doi:10.1145/1013115.1013153).

Schön, Donald A. 1987. *Educating the Reflective Practitioner*. Jossey-Bass.

Shusterman, Richard. 2008. *Body Consciousness: A Philosophy of Mindfulness and Somaesthetics*. Cambridge University Press.

Vallgårda, Anna, and Tomas Sokoler. 2010. A Material Strategy: Exploring the Material Properties of Computers. *International Journal of Design* 4 (3): 1–14.

8 How Deep Is Your Love? On Open-Source Hardware

David Cuartielles

This chapter looks at the history of open-source hardware design from the viewpoint of one of the creators of the Arduino project. Arduino is an open-source hardware platform that can be programmed from free IDE (Integrated Development Environment) software and comes with Creative Commons licensed documentation. According to many observers, it has changed how many people think about the way products can be licensed in order to reach the market.

Half academic experiment and half product, Arduino keeps on challenging business models around hardware as well as the fields touched by it, including educational tools and connected objects (the so-called Internet of Things).

Arduino grew from a five-man operation into a small multinational corporation with offices in Turin, Lugano, Malmö, Bangalore, and Taipei, and with representatives in San Francisco, New York, and Boston. It now employs 35 people dedicated to the creation of educational experiences in the world of electronics.

What the GNU[1] movement and its open-source counterpart[2] brought to the world of computation is a new type of thinking about how to share knowledge. The sharing happens thanks to the existence of legal frameworks that allow the creators to pass their work to others who can then build upon it. Arduino has used several different licensing models, mostly because it was one of the first projects to have a need to license physical objects and because when it was founded (in 2005) there was no proper licensing model for hardware.

This chapter is based on personal notes on events the author attended. It is written as the four acts of a love story (denial, white lies, open marriage, love) in which different non-fictional characters introduce the "drama of open hardware."

Everything starts at the Open Hardware Summit 2012 (OHS12) in New York, an event that gathered people from all around the world to discuss the state of openness of design tools such as 3D printers, microcontroller boards, and blueprints for workshop machinery.

Denial

Talk about the overall state of affairs, but still do not introduce the conflict, this is all about setting up the scene, who was there, what they were doing, what they were known for, how they relate to the others. ... No sex, strictly business, so leave gossip aside (even if that is the juicy part).
Cuartielles, notes

It is September 2012, and the second Open Hardware Summit is about to begin. There is a crowd of people willing to listen to their open-hardware heroes talk about their findings. The event had almost sold out before opening its doors, and I am not sure I will be able to get a ticket. Dave Mellis, my friend since we first met at Ivrea in 2005 and Arduino's co-founder, coordinated the peer-review committee for the event and surely had a ticket. This year, all I did was review a couple of submissions for talks, so I wasn't on the free-entrance list. I was far too busy throughout the summer writing a book about embedded electronics connected to phones, and forgot to purchase a ticket.

Luckily, on the way to Eyebeam, where the OHS was taking place, Dave and I met up with Bre Pettis. Bre, known for being one of the founders of the hackerspace NYC Resistor and of Makerbot, a 3D printing company, looks tired; he has had an exhausting week dealing with the launching of Makerbot's latest printer and software. He was featured on the cover of *Wired*—in the geek culture, equivalent to being on the cover of *Time*. As one of the event's sponsors, Bre's company has two free tickets, and his partner can't make it. Bre and I first met a couple of years ago, and probably have spoken four times since then. He offers me his other ticket.

One of the nice things about the OHS is that there is no VIP queue—everyone has to stand in the same queue to enter the event. I stand there with Dave and Bre, and see familiar faces all around. I see Ayah from littleBits and Mary, a former student of mine at CIID.[3] Michael from Arduino SF and Katia from Turin are already inside. I recognize some people from Dave's MIT crowd carrying heavy suitcases; they will demonstrate their new fablab tools, he says. Bre hands me his second badge and I enter Eyebeam.

It was five years ago that I first visited Eyebeam. I asked for permission to visit the space where the artists in residence developed their projects. H. C. Steiner, maintainer of PureData (Steiner et al. 2013) and my host in New York on that trip, was a resident there. It was through him that I got a quick introduction to the space and got to know some people there. One of them was Ayah Bdeir, then a recent MIT graduate interested in using microcontrollers in education and now an entrepreneur selling littleBits, a small electronics kit from which children can quickly build devices (Bdeir 2012). Her innovation is a Magsafe-like[4] connector for small circuits. Out of that simple idea, Ayah created a company that has been featured all over the media; her story has been told as an example of the "American Dream." Ayah was also behind the first OHS in 2010, which she initiated with Alicia Gibb, the current president of the Open Source Hardware Association.

I first got to know Alicia back in 2009, when she got in touch with the Arduino Team (this is how the core founders of the Arduino platform are known as a group) through e-mail. She was looking for some information about how people used the Arduino platform. Alicia was in the middle of writing her MSc in Theory, Criticism, and History of Art, Design and Architecture at Pratt Institute (Gibb 2010). That thesis was presented in 2010 in conjunction with an exhibition. Alicia teamed up with Ayah in promoting the Open Hardware Summit immediately after. It started as a meeting place for individuals, institutions, and companies to discuss openness in the creation of physical goods.

Alicia's thesis documented the state of the art of Arduino at many educational institutions. A tool created by us (the Arduino Team) to help our students to enter the world of embedded electronics had spread by word of mouth to most of the world's universities. I find some of the cases that Alicia mentioned in her thesis interesting. On page 53 there is a reference to DMDuino, an Arduino compatible board, produced by Professor Kim's students at Hongik University. This development happened in 2007, when I was teaching at another Korean design school. As a matter of fact, I gave a couple of talks for Professor Kim's students while I was living in Seoul, and one of those talks sparked the process of making that particular board.

Educational and recreational technologies took off in the 1980s. I am lucky to be among the first Spaniards who got access to computers back then. I don't recall Spain as having a lot of people who would build their own computers; however, there was a big interest in augmenting them and building circuits that would be controlled with early PCs.

As the PCs became more specialized and harder to access, the interest in "homebrew" electronics decreased. In the city of Zaragoza, where I come from, we jumped from having several small repair shops where it was possible to buy discrete electronic components to having only one. At that time, Zaragoza had three engineering schools—all of them offering courses in electrical engineering—with more than 6,000 students in all.

The small electronics stores probably were killed off by the arrival of the Internet and the engineers' early adoption of it for purchasing purposes, in conjunction with the arrival of cheaper consumer products that people tended to throw away rather than get them fixed. The electronics stores transformed into consumer electronics stores as the hobbyist engineers faded away.

When Arduino came along, there was no market for it. It was not intended for a market, either; it was intended to introduce design and art students to electronics in an easy way. We didn't anticipate its potential; we just wanted something cheap and useful to give an introduction to digital electronics. Those two characteristics were precisely what gave Arduino the reach it has today.

There was one person who anticipated the potential not just of Arduino, but of the maker community in general: Chris Anderson, then the main editor of *Wired*. The hacker movement had brought the concept of the more political hacklabs and that of the less political hackerspaces or makerspaces into popular culture. Those concepts somehow led Anderson to foresee that the maker community could eventually enter into a different category, and that makers were going to need tools and guidance. Anderson recognized that the maker movement had the potential to have an effect similar to that of the arrival of the PC in the 1980s.

Chris, a great speaker, is often invited to speak about innovation, technology, and other subjects. At OHS12, he gave a keynote address titled "Microeconomics for Makers: Business Models for the New Industrial Revolution" (Anderson 2012a).

OHS12 happened in September 2012, just a couple of days before the World Maker Faire in New York (WMFNY), an event arranged by *Make*, a magazine dedicated to the maker movement. The two previous editions of OSH took place on WMFNY's grounds, at the New York Hall of Science in Queens. However, the 2012 edition moved location in an attempt to detach the events from each other.

The September 2012 issue of *Wired* had a photo of Bre Pettis and, inside, an article on Makerbot—the 3D printer Bre and his team had developed—written by Chris Anderson himself (Anderson 2012b).

White Lies

this paragraph is about the illusion of open source, about people building things open for a while, long enough to get traction, and how they then discover that the market is a bitch and they want out, because it is hard to accept that things are the way they are and radical openness is tough. Not even Arduino is radically open

Cuartielles, notes

In the spring of 2007 I was an artist in residence at the Hangar in Barcelona. For three months I lived in a rental near the Hangar. I didn't manage to do any of the art works I had planned for the period. Arduino had become popular with artists by then, and I had to respond many requests for help and many invitations to give a talk or a course.

In a talk I gave at Dorkbot Barcelona, I made my standard presentation of the period: I spoke about the robot a Chinese student hacked using the first self-made Arduino in 2005, how the Involuntary Dance Machine project from Malmö emulated Stelarc's early works about body control at a fraction of the development time, how the boards changed to accommodate users' needs, and so on. At the end of the talk, a highly intoxicated young man approached me. At the time, I wasn't used to the idea of fandom. Why should anyone care about the things we do beyond the fact that they are useful? The young man asked a question that has followed me ever since: "How does it feel to be making something like this, something people look into? Don't you feel lonely when you are doing these things?"

That question happened to be extremely insightful. You might think that creating something like Arduino for a community of users is a pure participatory design (PD) process; that as part of an open-source community, you are doing everything to help your users; that they will be loyal to the brand you are building; that they will participate in the creative process—but in reality there have been situations and external influences that could have forced us to make decisions that would have compromised the basic ideology of our project.

This is the white lie of open source when it is brought into the mainstream. You cannot tell people that you will have to make design decisions in the end. Some of those might be really small ones: the distance between two connectors, the color of the silkscreen on a PCB,[5] the capacitors from this or that brand. Some others might be of great importance: the family of processors used to run the code, the way menus are structured on the UI, or the license for the design files. Eventually someone has to make these decisions, or else the conversations on the forum[6] will go on forever. The Arduino participation model operates from the point of view that it is impossible making 100 percent of the users happy.

Therefore, the concept of radical openness is just an illusion. There is no real democratic process in the making of many of the open-source projects anyway. You will find many projects where people have to take the role of benevolent dictators, as described by Eric Raymond in his essay "Homesteading the Noosphere" (Raymond 2000).

But there is yet another white lie, and this one goes deeper under the skin of the open-source movement. The fact is that open source is a trend. From bikes to computers, passing by utensils and patters for making clothes, there is an overwhelming amount of open projects showing up every week. People make open "stuff," sometimes out of good intentions, sometimes out of a willingness to gain recognition. "Open" is a buzzword, and many don't even understand the complexity behind the legal frameworks needed to make things open.

The One Laptop Per Child project (OLPC 2013) is trying to make an open-source computer running open-source software to provide access to open knowledge. OLPC's lobbyists[7] pitched the idea to whole countries and offered making millions of computers at a fraction of the money spent in books by the average kid. The hidden message behind this is that openness is good because of being cheap. People have a tendency to buy into this argument.

Where the second white lie resides is in thinking that open source is always making things cheaper. Take the maintenance of the software platform for a region as an example. There is the option to buy from a vendor like Microsoft or there is the option of hiring a local developer expert in the free Linux operating system to run the region's servers. In both cases there is an economic cost: either you pay for a pre-made system, or you pay for someone to tailor the software to your needs. The main difference is that a good open-source developer will write the code in such a way that it will be possible for other developers to reuse the code and maintain and enlarge the system.

The money needs to be spent anyway. The equation of cost needs to be analyzed every time; there is no magic formula.

Cost and openness, what matters the most? This is the issue here. If someone were giving us a machine to solve a task that was cheap enough, we would probably not think about making one ourselves. This is the basic principle of capitalism: we have learned to value our time, and we apply the simple equation of how much our time costs and what is the probability of successfully building something by ourselves. If the probability is low and the cost is high, we will never try. The price has to be right. Price seems to matter at least as much as openness.

Chris Anderson knows that openness is not really open but is trendy, and that openness doesn't necessarily make things cheaper. So he decided to step into the open-source hardware movement by exploiting one of the communities he had helped creating: DIY Drones. Chris created two different relevant communities on the side of his career as editor in chief of *Wired*: DIY Drones (Anderson 2008) and Geekdad (Anderson and Denmead 2013). At some point he decided to stick to DIY Drones, I guess because it was more rewarding both personally and economically.

Chris managed to grow a business around the idea of unmanned aerial vehicles and created the company 3D Robotics. On April 15, 2013, the company's website (Anderson and Munoz 2013) said "3D Robotics provides fully-autonomous aircraft and open-source UAV[8] technology that deliver professional performance at amazingly affordable prices." This clearly states both aspects I am trying to stress: cheap and open are elements of the present-day sales pitch. Many people think that because of being open and building on top of other projects, it has to be cheaper because it requires a smaller research-and-development effort.

3D Robotics sells all the parts needed to make a flying vehicle, but also sells fully assembled machines. The main component within 3D Robotics' UAVs is the so-called Ardupilot, an Arduino-compatible board that can run a variety of motors and can read data from onboard sensors needed for balancing and locating the flying vehicles it commands. It is the brain for all of their products. 3D Robotics is programmed using the software designed and maintained by Arduino. 3D Robotics maintains a special firmware for the Ardupilot boards, but doesn't need to be supporting the UI to program that firmware.

In 2012, I was invited to appear at a conference called Tijuana Innovadora (Cuartielles et al. 2012). I was to take part in a panel discussion with the main firmware maintainer for the Ardupilot, Jason Short. I didn't know then which was the relationship between Jason, Ardupilot, and Tijuana. The whole story wouldn't take long to unfold. Tijuana Innovadora is an initiative from a city benefactor trying to portray the city and the region around Tijuana as a reliable business hub. The trade agreements between the U.S. and the northern states of Mexico allow U.S. companies to manufacture for lower wages (as well as with lower manufacturing regulations) at factories located on Mexican ground. 3D Robotics is one of those. And the person responsible for 3D Robotics' *maquila*[9] is a young Mexican entrepreneur who tries to spread the open-source hardware culture among the local colleges. He suggested that Tijuana Innovadora 2012 have a panel on open-source hardware, where I spoke and where I met Jason.

At some point, we were invited to visit 3D Robotics' factory in Tijuana, which is where they manufacture the Ardupilot boards at a pace of 200 per week.[10] They are also assembling the full UAVs there, and serve them to the whole world via courier. It is a convenient location, as 3D Robotics has its headquarters in San Diego, California. All of these facts were clearly stated at 3D Robotics' website.

Yet again, I knew 3D Robotics was manufacturing in Mexico, not just because of the website. Just about a month earlier, while in New York visiting the OHS12, I happened to step outside the conference building to catch some air. I accidentally bumped into Chris Anderson and Ayah Bdeir, who were outside talking about their businesses. Ayah was worried about the quality of Chinese manufacturing. Chris was pitching Mexican professionalism and how much closer Mexico is to the United States than China. My only proof that that conversation happened is a picture I took of the three of us together (figure 8.1).

People tend to identify open source with "good will" and even with "ethical hacking." However, I find Eric Raymond's analysis much better:

Not until the Linux explosion of early 1993–1994 did pragmatism find a real power base. Although Linus Torvalds never made a point of opposing RMS [Richard Stallman], he set an example by looking benignly on the growth of a commercial Linux industry, by publicly endorsing the use of high-quality commercial software for specific tasks, and by gently deriding the more purist and fanatical elements in the culture.

A side effect of the rapid growth of Linux was the induction of a large number of new hackers for which Linux was their primary loyalty and the [Free Software Foundation]'s agenda primarily of historical interest. Though the newer wave of Linux hackers might describe the system as "the choice of a GNU generation," most tended to emulate Torvalds more than Stallman.

Increasingly it was the anticommercial purists who found themselves in a minority.

Open Source Hardware (OSH), the emergent field the Open Hardware Summit (OHS) is all about, unveiled the white lies to all of us in its 2012 edition. Chris Anderson's keynote speech was about how to run a business selling open-source technology. He introduced his vision of hybrid open-closed systems in order to keep the cloning of his company's original designs to a minimum. He found out what we—in the OSH business—had already discovered a long time ago: It is easy to clone our designs. The difference Chris was introducing was that it should not be possible to copy part of the designs, as he and his partner at 3D Robotics decided to make part of their designs closed to protect their IP.[11]

I wondered how much Chris had been influenced by the interview he had conducted with Bre Pettis just a couple of months before, the one that appeared in *Wired* just as OHS happened in New York. I bet that besides his personal experience dealing with IP protection, he had gained some understanding on how Bre and his partners had decided to run Makerbot Industries.

Figure 8.1
At OHS12: C. Anderson (left), D. Cuartielles (center), and A. Bdeir (right). 2012 David Cuartielles (CC:BY-NC).

Bre spoke later that same day at the conference in New York. His news was not just that Makerbot had released a new 3D printer and a new software to generate the GCode[12] for the printers; in addition, Makerbot, which had grown as an open-source business, was now going to close part of its IP. It capitalized on the contributions coming from hundreds of users and competitors that shared software, iterated the hardware and published their results online. Makerbot was highly regarded by a huge community of users and had among its original investors Adrian Bowyer, who according to Wikipedia (2013) had "spent twenty-two years as a lecturer then senior lecturer in the Mechanical Engineering Department at the University of Bath," had "retired from academic life in 2012," and had "invented the RepRap Project—an open-source self-replicating 3D printer."

I had given a talk at the Technical University of Denmark in 2011. Adrian and I had given a keynote presentation about open technologies titled "Creating wealth while giving it away" (Bowyer and Cuartielles 2011). It was then that I had heard from Adrian himself that he was an investor in Makerbot. After my initial surprise, I came to realize that this was an interesting situation. The creator of something as relevant as a self-replicating machine was an investor in a company that was capitalizing on his creation. I saw it as some sort of poetic justice.

Fast forward to 2012. Bre Pettis, giving his presentation at OHS12, was about to break into tears. He had had a tough week. Part of the Makerbot concept had gone closed-source. And now, at the open-source conference, everybody was expecting to hear Bre explain why Makerbot wouldn't release the blueprints to the mechanical construction of its latest printer and wouldn't release the source to the application to work with the 3D models and generate the GCode.

Bre's explanation was simple: they had invested a lot of time and money in creating their hardware and software, and they didn't want them to be cloned. This made a lot of people unhappy. Among other contributions to the open-source community, Makerbot Industries created Thingiverse (Makerbot 2013), an online repository of 3D shapes and designs for laser cutting, broadly used by Makerbot users but also by users of other 3D printing systems, mostly because there were no alternative free online services where to easily document their projects.

One of the Thingiverse users was a young Czech contributor to the RepRap project, Josef Prusa. His immediate response to Makerbot's new policies was to stop using the repository:

I'm leaving Thingiverse after seeing updated Terms of use thingiverse.com/legal, over next few days I will remove all my stuff. It will be downloadable on my website josefprusa.cz or reprap.org I prefer to be owner of my own designs:-)

We are not trolls, as Raldrich said.

The fact that the legal ramifications of MakerBot's TOS weren't discovered until today doesn't magically give them a free pass.

The fact that they don't intend (today) to exercise the rights they've granted themselves also doesn't magically give them a free pass. Companies change—take a look at their stance on Open Source Hardware." (Prusa 2012)

Josef is known as the maker of the most cloned open-source 3D printer, the so-called Prusa-Mendel model (Prusa 2013). In his "Occupy Thingiverse" statement, he invited unhappy Thingiverse users to make bad prints of cubes and upload them as a way to protest against Makerbot's policy shift. A cube is nothing but a three-dimensional shape that is used to check whether a 3D printer is properly calibrated. People within the printing community print many cubes to check if the printer can operate at a proper speed, if it responds to changes in the size of the prints, and so on.

One thing Josef quotes in his goodbye letter to Thingiverse is how the legal terms (Makerbot 2012) of the website weren't changed in September 2012, when Bre announced Makerbot's new designs, but were changed in February of that year. I have no proof of how these legal terms were before that, but it is clear that things had started to change for the users far before the big announcement. As a matter of fact, things might have been like that since the website was created years before, but people didn't realize until September that Makerbot kept the right to use the designs posted by users, at no cost, as long as they were hosted there. On top of that, they had the right to decide whether they could be there or not.

Consider the following quotation from the terms of service referenced by Makerbot (2012):

> You hereby represent and warrant that your User Content does not violate the Acceptable Use Policy (defined below). You may not state or imply that your User Content is in any way provided, sponsored or endorsed by Company [Makerbot Industries]. Because you alone are responsible for your User Content (and not Company), you may expose yourself to liability if, for example, your User Content violates the Acceptable Use Policy. Company is not obligated to backup any User Content and User Content may be deleted at anytime. You are solely responsible for creating backup copies of your User Content if you desire.

This is typical for a free-of-charge service; it amounts to "you can play in my playground as long as you follow my rules, whatever you do is your responsibility." A site like Thingiverse will, for example, avoid hosting pornographic pictures. On the other hand, this provoked an interesting reaction. Sites like Dongiverse showed up to cover a niche for 3D printing technologies: the sex market. At the time of writing, the official Dongiverse website seemed to be down. However, I found a reference to it in a blog dedicated to 3D printing:

> Almost all erotic gadgets have low-profiles on 3D model sharing sites. However, one website, launched three years ago, comes with an announcement—"to parody the awkward amount of suspiciously xxx objects uploaded daily to the popular 3D model warehouse Thingiverse." (3ders 2013)

A lot of people think this site is a joke. Dongiverse, a Thingiverse for dongs, has a very similar design as Thingiverse's old version. It is a site for sharing your designs (specially sex toys).

Thingiverse allows listing objects by collection. This allows checking whether there are objects tagged in a certain way. As the reference Rrix 2013 shows, it is possible to make a search, within Thingiverse's website, for the term 'dongiverse'. This search will list some objects that are specifically designed or can be perceived as sex toys. In other words, Makerbot might not be that strict in applying the policies they declare to be following in their terms of service.

But why the fuss then? Why does it matter that a company decides to close down its IP? In my opinion, Makerbot and 3D Robotics betrayed an image they built. They flirted with the open-source community and used it to build a customer base.

We had arrived at OHS12 believing in all the little white lies of open source. Within four hours, we heard Chris and Bre give up the idea of openness.

Arduino's designs are not radically open from a process viewpoint. When we made Arduino, we built upon years of accumulated experience in teaching electronics to beginners. We didn't sit down with users to create our first boards. We knew what needed to be done. The participatory design aspects of the creation had been done in the form of fieldwork by all of us. We decided back then that using expert knowledge about users, about technology, and about the relationship between users and technology should become our development method.

This became our design process: We go out in the field and try out a certain experiment with users. Most times, we come with a new type of board and a series of exercises for people to try. Once we get sure the design is not only functionally perfect, but also an interesting tool to use, we move into production. This means making thousands of boards to send to hundreds of distributors all over the world. Because we believe in the importance of sharing knowledge, Arduino releases the so-called reference designs (the hardware design files) to the boards under a Creative Commons license.

To have a radically open design process, we probably should start opening up during the conceptualization phase and not just when the final object is released. But in the same way that other entities decided to go for not opening their designs to their users for fear of being copied, we prefer to shortcut the IP problems by keeping things secret until the day they reach thousands of people at once.

Our designs will be cloned anyway, and we will have to enforce traditional IP protection (lawyers, cease-and-desist letters) for every new design we make. So why bother even trying to protect the IP in other ways? It is better to keep it open source for people to freely build upon it. As someone said, "you have to be ready to maintain open source," and we are ready to maintain our own reference designs, but not all the variations made by hundreds of people. That is a full-time job that we don't want.

Open as in open marriage until you turn into a yuppie

Arduino thinks about manufacturing in markets for their markets (the scale factor at low prices, a different paradigm in a changing global economy)

Arduino has users, not customers

Cuartielles, notes

Open is all about love and hate, about the lie that is kept for as long as possible until someone betrays the dream. What we have to ask our open-source idols is "How deep is your love (for openness)?"

It is easy to fall in love with the idea of people making something for the greater good, but how much of that is just a naive view of reality? How much are we living in denial, blind to the fact that things might work differently? Some lovers might show a face to you and lie, but most of the times you aren't ready to ask the right questions, mostly because you might not be willing to hear the truth.

Chris Anderson sent one of his journalists, Clive Thompson, to a small conference we attended at Potsdam University in 2008. The topic was the creation of Fritzing, a program that would allow people to jump from a prototype built on a breadboard to a PCB design that could be manufactured quickly (Fritzing 2013). Clive interviewed each member of the A-Team[13] and wrote his report (Thompson 2008) carefully.

I recall receiving an e-mail message from *Wired* cross-checking the facts of that interview several months later. *Wired* has long lead times—we were interviewed in Germany in June and the article came out in November. The publication of that article marked a "before" and an "after" in the history of Arduino.

The graph in figure 8.2 shows the number of people reaching the Arduino website, grouped by continent. To create that graph, I used all the historical data that had been stored in the Arduino.cc server between 2006 and 2011. What it shows is that Europe somehow got to know about Arduino thanks to the article in *Wired*. It is my understanding that all tech-related journalists in the world look at *Wired*, then write stories related to what they see there. In other words, Chris Anderson opened Europe to Arduino, even though we are a EU-centered entity in the first place.

Arduino, and articles like the one Chris Anderson commissioned in 2008 as editor of *Wired*, helped create the buzz around the OSH field, and once he saw an opportunity, he left everything and became an open-source entrepreneur. Sadly, at OHS12 he came to present his new approach to openness: closing things down.

When we all started this adventure of open-source hardware, there was a mantra we repeated many times: If they copy you, that means you are making something good. Chris didn't think that way any longer; he believed he needed something to differentiate his products from the ones from cloning factories around the world, and closing part of the design was his approach.

Bre, while on stage, introduced a similar idea. He spoke about how much Makerbot was being copied in China (he made explicit references to this aspect) and how the Makerbot partners felt they had to keep their IP protected by not sharing the source files with others.

Ayah, on the other hand, wasn't talking to Chris about copies when I met them outside the conference in New York. They were talking about quality in the manufacturing. Chris tried to convince her about how much more convenient the Mexicans were.

I have heard these words many times coming from different manufacturers and designers. Around the world, there are good manufacturers and bad ones, no matter where they come from. There are people who are ready to deliver on a tight schedule and with high quality, and there are people who aren't.

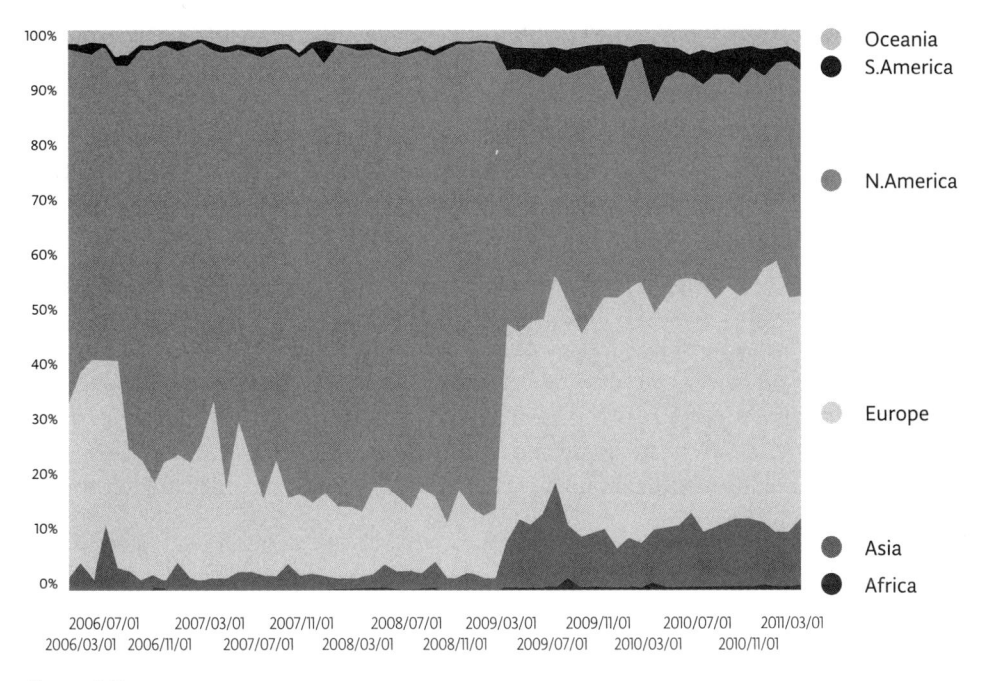

Figure 8.2
Users on the Arduino server by continent (percent, by month). David Cuartielles (CC:BY-NC).

I think that Ayah, in a very honorable way, was looking for a place to make things with the best relationship between quality and price, the same as Chris and the same as Bre. They figured out that to be able to keep that relationship, they had to stop people reproducing their designs and they had to build a narrative around it.

Since the open-source community is supposed to follow some ethical values, the narrative for OHS12 was "China is bad; we are being copied." But this wasn't news to us at Arduino—we have a person dedicated to hunt knock-offs from all over the world, and it is a fact that many of them come from China. However, we understood that protecting our brand image cost us the same if we were open source as if we weren't.

We invited people to replicate our boards. We asked only that they not call their designs Arduino and that they not use our logo. This was why we put the blueprints to our reference designs online at no cost and under Creative Commons licenses. If you wanted to, you could take our design, send it to a factory, and order 1,000 boards, and you wouldn't have to pay us anything.

Believe it or not, we still have to fight against counterfeiting. Today most of the Arduino boards are manufactured in Italy. About 43,000 units are produced per month.

That volume doesn't excuse going to China or Mexico to get things made. The expenses of keeping a team there to make sure our manufacturing requirements were met would make the boards too expensive.[14]

As an open-source project, we are ready to include modification proposals from our user community. This means we can never go into large-scale production, as that would imply not being able to modify the hardware design often. This is probably the biggest lesson we have learned so far about hardware: Don't increase production too much, because you want to be able to introduce modifications as you go. Therefore, the only way to keep prices low is to have a distributed factory structure, with manufacturing plants as close as possible to the potential users.

To spread the love, you need to be present in as many places as possible and you need to keep some balance between local and global production. I think that Arduino needs to grow in Asian, Latin American, and African markets at a local level, to be able of keeping the quality at a maximum and the price at a minimum adjusted to people's needs at different locations.

Love

seems to me this is one of those cycles, like it happened before. Those that participated in making the first personal computers in the early 80s were making an experiment in openness, until money came into play and Apple and Commodore showed up, then all the others followed. … It's like history repeating.

Cuartielles, notes

In 2005, at the Interaction Design Institute Ivrea, we had the vision that making a small prototyping platform aimed at designers would help them getting a better understanding of technology. We thought about our own interaction design students at Ivrea and at Malmö University and about their professional future. They should be able to talk to engineers about their ideation processes, build prototypes in record time, or create installations to display a concept to a certain audience.

We shared our views on what we thought would work, based on our life experiences as technology users and teaching others for several years. Putting the words into action was very natural, probably because of the empowerment one experiences when meeting like-minded people.

Arduino's growth has to be understood as part of an emergent interest in technology at a global level that circulates around the idea of co-creation throughout online knowledge exchange. There are multiple tools out there, but here are the ones I believe are interesting from a community-building point of view:

- PureData, an open-source tool for studying sound (Steiner et al. 2013)
- Processing, a tool for learning about animation (Reas and Fry 2013)

- the RepRap 3D printing movement (Bowyer et al. 2013)
- Arduino, the first successful open hardware project.

I have been involved with or in close contact with three of these (PureData, Processing, and Arduino). I see some similarities in them, but also some differences. When your goal is making the best (for education, society, the world), there isn't a pre-defined roadmap you can follow. To me, however, the process matters as much as the result. The debate and the inclusion of opinions during the making are very important. Keeping loyal to the dream, in this case openness, is also important.

If these four projects have something in common, it is the participation of users in the making, maintaining, and growth of the project's original idea into whatever it turns into. Both the do-it-yourself movement and its values are somehow a natural part of the current software and hardware culture.

The process of making prototyping boards has been like this since Motorola and Commodore introduced the first microcontrollers. The book *On the Edge* (Bagnall 2005) describes how Commodore, a company dedicated to the production of calculators, created the first single-board computer, called KIM-1, back in 1976. KIM-1 ran a processor priced at 25 U.S. dollars—only 10 percent as much as any of its competitors in the market. KIM-1 was a prototyping board that would allow engineers trying out the capabilities of the 6502 processor made by CMOS Technologies.

This board and its successors were the foundation of the first Apple computer, which was prototyped and built on Commodore technology. Since both Commodore and Apple computers had the same architecture, they could both run the same type of software. In this case, both would run Basic, created by Microsoft in the 1970s.

Despite the difference in the value of money between 1976 and 2005, we priced Arduino at a very similar level. This was a coincidence, as I doubt any of us knew anything about the initial value of Commodore's processor.

Besides the price, Arduino was similar to the KIM-1 prototyping platform in other ways. It is an open tool that can be used in building other systems. Those systems might even become competitors of the original platform, as Apple did. Arduino is the starting point for many competing projects, among them Maple (Leaflabs 2013), Freeduino (Freeduino 2012), Netduino (Netduino 2013), and Teensy (Badger 2013). Because we use open discussion tools, some of the developers of the other platforms have joined the discussion about the kind of features our system should include, as it will make it easier for them to build upon our system and to create new products.

What we see here is that before the idea of openness in software, there was an openness in hardware platforms. As the development kits are a business by themselves, there are companies that have no other choice but to make their IP available for others to use and build upon. In some cases (for example, that of Commodore, which had a hybrid model of tools and products) it resulted in the disappearance of a company; in other cases, a company was able to become much more successful.

For some reason, people like Chris and Bre don't realize that they are making the same mistakes that others made in the past. They are the Commodores of the 21st century. Let us be something else. Let us be open source.

Epilogue

A long time has passed since I began writing this chapter. I wanted to spark a discussion about the real value of openness. I hoped that my arguments would be heard by those I mentioned, and that there would be a chance to debate the steps they were taking before it was too late. However, the format of OHS12 didn't allow for discussion, and there was no time for questions directly after the presentations.

My initial idea was to persuade Bre and Chris that there was no reason to close the designs they were making, especially because they had built their business around open source and the idea of spending too many resources in protecting their IP instead of looking at the community needs and proposals to support their growth.

Almost ten months after I started writing, Chris went ahead with his plan of closing down some of the designs from 3D Robotics. He keeps on supporting his thesis of "hybrid business models" with open and closed parts put together.

Just a couple of days before I finished writing this, Makerbot was acquired by a traditional player in the 3D printing business called Stratasys (Denison 2013) in a transaction that involved 400 million U.S. dollars' worth of cash and stocks. In his article regarding the deal, D. C. Denison managed to get in touch with Adrian Bowyer, the creator of the RepRap project, who manifested his happiness for the deal, as he got a big return for his investment in the Makerbot company.

Business as usual, for everyone.

Notes

1. GNU is the name of a project initiated by Richard Stallman to create a completely free operating system. It was first announced in September 1983.

2. The two main views within the world of source-accessible code are free software and open-source software. The former was started by Richard Stallman and suggests that once a piece of code is licensed under the so-called GPL license, all the code produced using it will inherit that same license and will therefore have to be open. The latter embraces a more business-oriented viewpoint and allows people building "closed" applications on top of open blocks of code.

3. Copenhagen Institute for Interaction Design.

4. Magsafe is a brand registered by Apple Inc. and used to label the power connectors used in the most recent family of Macintosh computers. It uses magnets to get the connector to span to the computer in an easy way.

5. PCB stands for Printed Circuit Board. In more colloquial terms, it is how you would talk about a naked circuit before populating it with electronic components.

6. Arduino's main feedback system is an online forum. As of June 28, 2013, it had 140,000 registered users.

7. OLPC's founder, Nicholas Negroponte, was once the director of MIT's Media Lab. He used his fame and influence to pursue this mission. His initial goal—never attained—was to make an open-source computer for $100.

8. UAV stands for Unmanned Aerial Vehicle.

9. A *Maquila* is a factory located in northern Mexico and manufacturing mostly for the U.S. market.

10. I was told this by my guide at 3D Robotics' Tijuana factory. He also mentioned the intention of keeping their machinery running around the clock to triple the production capabilities at some point.

11. IP stands for *intellectual property*, a term people use to refer to the designs, inventions, processes, and services they create.

12. GCode is a markup language used to represent the movements of the head of a 3D printer or a CNC machine.

13. A-Team: the Arduino Team.

14. At the time of writing, Arduino was about to launch the Yun, the first official Arduino board designed and manufactured in China. The initial batch was to number 5,000.

References

3ders. 2013. Description of Dongiverse (http://www.3ders.org/articles/20130128-falling-cost-of-3d-printers-leads-to-rise-in-personalised-sex-toys.html).

Anderson, C. 2008. About page from the DIY Drones community: The DIY Drones Mission (aka The Five Rules) (http://diydrones.com/profiles/blog/show?id=705844:BlogPost:17789).

Anderson, C. 2012a. Microeconomics for Makers: Business Models for the New Industrial Revolution. Talk given at Open Source Hardware Summit, New York.

Anderson, Chris. 2012b. The New MakerBot Replicator Might Just Change Your World (http://www.wired.com/design/2012/09/how-makerbots-replicator2-will-launch-era-of-desktop-manufacturing/).

Anderson, C., and K. Denmead. 2013. Geekdad blog (http://geekdad.com/2013/03/the-geekdads-big-adventure/).

Anderson, C., and J. Munoz. 2013. 3D Robotics, UAV Technology (http://3drobotics.com/).

Badger, P. 2013. Teensy board (http://www.pjrc.com/teensy/index.html).

Bagnall, Brian. 2005. *On the Edge: The Spectacular Rise and Fall of Commodore.* Variant.

Bdeir, A. 2012. Website of littleBits (http://littlebits.cc).

Bowyer, A., et al. 2013. Website of RepRap project (http://reprap.org).

Bowyer, A., and D. Cuartielles. 2011. Creating wealth while giving it away (http://www.youtube.com/watch?v=2j84BDoNkt8).

Cuartielles, D., et al. 2012. Panelists at Tijuana Innovadora (http:// tijuanainnovadora.com).

Denison, D. C. 2013. Reactions to the MakerBot-Stratasys Deal (http://makezine.com/2013/06/20/reactions-to-the-makerbot-stratasys-deal/).

Freeduino. 2012. Freeduino board (http://freeduino.org/about.html).

Fritzing. 2013. http://fritzing.org/about/context/

Gibb, A. M. 2010. New Media Art, Design, and the Arduino Microcontroller: A Malleable Tool. MSc thesis, Pratt Institute.

Leaflabs. 2013. Maple Board (http://leaflabs.com/devices/maple/).

Makerbot. 2012. Thingiverse Legal Terms (http://www.thingiverse.com).

Makerbot. 2013. Thingiverse: A Repository of physical design (http://www.thingiverse.com).

Netduino. 2013. Netduino Board (http://netduino.com).

OLPC. 2013. One Laptop Per Child website (http://one.laptop.org).

OSHA. 2012. Open Source Hardware Summit 2012 (http://2012.oshwa.org/).

Prusa, J. 2012. Occupy Thingiverse (post on http://www.thingiverse.com).

Prusa, J. 2013. Prusa Mendel 2 3D printer on RepRap's website (http://reprap.org/wiki/Prusa_Mendel_(iteration_2)).

Raymond, E. S. 2000. Project Structures and Ownership (http://www.catb.org).

Reas, C., and B. Fry. 2013. Official website of Processing project (http://processing.org).

Rrix. 2013. Dongiverse—a Universe of Dongs (http://www.thingiverse.com/rrix/collections/dongiverse/page:1).

Steiner, Hans C., et al. 2013. Main website for PureData software (http://puredata.info).

Thompson, C. 2008. Build It. Share It. Profit. *Wired* 16 (11): 166–176.

Wikipedia. 2013. Adrian Bowyer (http://en.wikipedia.org/wiki/Adrian_Bowyer).

III Creative Class Struggles

9 Creative Class Struggles

Erling Björgvinsson and Pernilla Severson

The emerging of the labels *creative industries* and *creative class* is a policy-driven and powerful story of future-making that plays a big part as both the stage and the locality of the stories in this part of the book. The chapters in this part discuss creative workers, sometimes determined to belong to the creative class working in the creative industries. Specifically, they deal with designers, artists, prosumers, and researchers who together explore new ways of producing and engaging in cultural productions. Stories on creative industries, as future-making industries, are as multitudinous and diverse as they are embossed with ideology. Oakley (2009) argues that there is a relationship between innovation and creative industries, where innovation has taken over the role of creative industries as a policy discourse. Garnham (2005, 15) states that creative industries have always been about innovation, in which processes of cultural production unjustifiably are linked to economic development and ownership:

> This sustains the unjustified claim of the cultural sector as a key economic growth sector within the global economy and creates a coalition of disparate interests around the extension of intellectual property rights.

Stories on the creative industries go back to Theodor Adorno and Max Horkheimer's Marxist writings on the culture industry (2002). Their work was the starting point of a long historical struggle to articulate who should pay for the making of culture and what role it should play in society—a struggle that is still fervent, and that involves quite different perspectives on how the cultural industries should be financed and how cultural products should be made available and who should be given the opportunity to shape the future of the industry by having access to knowledgeable individuals and to funding for research and development.

In many cases, cultural productions, and the same goes for research and development within the cultural industries, come about through collaborations that cut across the public and the private, the state and the market, and state funds and private funding. Given that cultural productions cut across public and private spheres, how the balance between individual ownership and common good and the balance between cultural capital and economic capital should look is up for debate.

The people in the enterprises that figure in these chapters range from people being involved in cultural productions that are purely financed by private capital arguing that cultural enterprises should aim for economic growth, to those that argue for a mix of state and private financing of cultural production, to people that argue for the importance of social, cultural, economic, and ecological sustainability. Sustainable enterprises are not growth oriented, as more employees and higher turnover is not what guides their business. These enterprises do not fit the traditional definition of entrepreneurship and have therefore been overlooked by academic innovation research, innovation policy making, and innovation funding, as Fischer (2010) points out.

Given that cultural industries cut across the private and public, in relation to law, policy making, and funding, the various creative industries—film, music, literature, gaming, design—form numerous complex public spheres in which the political and governing (Barry 2001) are distributed rather than neatly contained within a national government and the official political sphere. And as the innovation discourse perhaps has replaced the creative industry discourse, what voices, alliances, and issues can affect and rearrange these public spheres into future practices is a governing issue, a political issue, and thus a democratic issue. As was stated earlier, different creative industries, creative classes, and enterprises face different challenges, have different expectations, and hold different ideas about the future. Therefore, value frictions pertaining to social, cultural, technical, and economic issues are embedded in democratic innovation. These frictions are articulated in these chapters by stories on actual future-making practices. Our hope is that our insights into opportunities and dilemmas facing these practices will influence the discussion on media development and contribute to a more democratic media development.

The chapters in this part of the book sketch some of the significant features of open innovation and participatory design through public co-productions carried out by researchers and actors operating within creative industries and the cultural sector in Malmö. They also present images, stories, and actions of future-making derived from a set of interviews with managers working in IT, design, and media companies in southern Sweden.

The making of creative industries and the creative class

In the making of creative industries, history starts with art (Hartley and Cunningham 2001). Here we retell the story of when creative and industries became *creative industries*, adding Swedish examples of the policy-driven development and taking a more critical approach. We do so to show how cultural production has increasingly become defined primarily as an industry, how it has become entangled in the innovation discourse, and to open up articulations of how these policy-driven discourses, at times, do not match the reality facing many individuals and enterprises operating within the creative industries. The creative industries are in fact engaged in a creative class struggle.

Strangely, as Hesmondhalgh and Baker (2011) point out, labor studies on creative production, despite how important the industry is considered to be, are meager. Hesmondhalgh and Baker note that neither the political economy of culture (PEC) perspective nor studies by political economists nor business and management studies nor cultural studies have focused extensively on labor. They define creative labor as a form of business in which the primary aim is to profit from "the activity of symbol-making" (ibid., 9), which consists of division of labor that produces distinctions and hierarchies within the creative labor force. The division of labor can crudely be divided into managers, professionals, and unskilled workers. Hesmondhalgh and Baker, referring to Wright (1997), argue that most cultural workers have high skills and low authority, whereas managers have high authority and high wages. The high wages buy their loyalty to the capitalist class. The managers, in turn, use wages as a loyalty-enhancing mechanism, and as a result only a few workers with sought-after talents get well paid.

The class concept is vital to Florida's arguments on the existence and importance of creative industries. Florida (2002, 8) defines the creative class as "a cluster of people who have common interests and tend to think, feel and behave similarly," where the similarities are determined by economic functions. Florida claims that we are entering a new class structure in which new class divisions are created between the creative class, the service class, the working class, and the agricultural class. A central attribute of members of the creative class is that they "add economic value through their creativity, creativity being the ability to create meaningful new forms" (Florida 2002, 68).

The creative class is a constructed concept. Florida argues that the class can be divided into two subgroups: the super-creative core and the creative professionals. "The super-creative core of this new class," he writes, "includes scientists and engineers, university professors, poets and novelists, artists, entertainers, actors, designers, and architects, as well as the 'thought leadership' of modern society: nonfiction writers, editors, cultural figures, think-tank researchers, analysts, and other opinion-makers" (Florida 2002, 34). The creative professionals, on the other hand, are found in as diverse areas as in management, legal, business, and financial occupations, and among health-care practitioners and people in high-end sales.

These groups' shared ideas and view on the world, what Florida calls their creative ethos, is a synthesis of bohemian values and a Protestant work ethic. According to Florida they are not aware that they belong to a class, and Florida's goal is to raise their class awareness.

Florida has been criticized for operating with a vague definition of class and for downplaying complexity and internal class struggles (Jeppesen 2004). His focus is primarily on how cities need cultural workers rather than on what cultural workers need, which is why his work has resonated better with politicians, policy makers, and branding consultants than with cultural workers. The underlying rhetoric of competitiveness also clashes with more commonality-oriented perspectives that argue for the value of all citizens; a perspective that is uneasy with pitting regions, cities, or people against one another.

Since the late 1990s, few terms have been more loaded with future hopes, or have at least been believed to point toward a new future for the Western world in a post-industrial era where manufacturing has for the most part moved to the eastern hemisphere, than the twin terms *creative industries* and *the creative class*. The terms have functioned as projections and rhetorical devices affecting government policies and research funding on European, national, regional, and municipal levels. As these terms have dealt with bright visionary futures, almost utopian in character—policy actions that have centered on the possibility of establishing new enterprises, economic growth and the branding of cities to attract hip, well-educated cultural workers— has become a battleground. One city after another has claimed to be uniquely creative. The terms have caused battles over what individuals and what groups are considered creative, and whether individual entrepreneurs or collectives are to be premiered. In the relationship between governmental funding, enterprise business logic, and the self-made cultural workers, the connection between capital and creativity becomes a question of *to what degree the creative practices should be industrious*?

The term *creative industries* is tightly linked to the notion of new forms of business. According to Cunningham (2002, 54), "'creative industries' … can claim to capture significant 'new economy' enterprise dynamics that such terms as 'the arts,' 'media' and 'cultural industries' do not." According to Flew (2002, 3), the concept of the creative industries grew out of a specific socio-political circumstance and, as is well known, was the construct of policy makers in Great Britain: "The formal origins of the concept of the creative industries can be found in the Blair Labour Government's establishment of a Creative Industries Task Force after its election in Britain in 1997, where the newly-created Department of Culture, Media and Sport (DCMS) set about mapping current activity in the creative industries, and identify policy measures that could promote their further development."

Closely linked to Blair's neoliberal venture into creative industries was Charles Leadbeater, who advised the British government on the knowledge-driven economy, the Internet, and the relationship between the two. Juxtaposing old and supposedly defunct organizational models found within big companies and universities with the more agile and inventive passionate self-organized Pro-Am consumers who have turned into professional amateur producers was central to Leadbeater and Miller's ways of arguing (Leadbeater and Miller 2004; Leadbeater 2004). Pro-Ams, they argued, are in closer touch with what needs to be developed and are therefore one step ahead of conventional producers.

Leadbeater and Miller further argued that governments needed to understand that creativity and innovation is not to be found in special people with special skills that meet in special places. Policy makers are mistaken when they think that they need more R&D parks since today large organizations that gather specialized skills are not needed in order to be inventive. Instead, policy makers needed to acknowledge the power of Pro-Ams and their way of organizing without organizations, which can intensify with the help of the Internet. Although Leadbeater acknowledges that innovation is cumulative and collaborative, something that some researchers of innovation—e.g., Bijker (1995)—would agree with, he still argues that big disruptions are possible and that they come from users and only rarely, if at all, from large organizations and mainstream markets.

Increasingly, the driving force of the economy, according to Leadbeater, is creativity, ingenuity, and imagination rather than raw materials, land, labor, and machinery, which were the central assets of the industrial age. Today, he claims, an increasing number of people make a living from their ideas and know-how or what he calls making a living from thin air (Leadbeater 1999). To foster innovative and inclusive thin-air creative practices, what needs to be acknowledged and foregrounded is the value of knowledge capital and social capital rather than such inhumane aspects as efficiency and increasing global corporate profit. This refocusing of values, in turn, demands organizational reorientation. A new breed of competitive creative communities are needed if one wants to survive in the global economy that are based on networks and spread-out ownership.

Although Leadbeater acknowledges that the thin-air economy is due to long-standing accumulation of knowledge within science and education, his juxtaposition of old and new ways of organizing was unfortunate. Other research shows that it doesn't hold true that small and agile necessarily means that one is more innovative. Big media corporations can foster innovative changes and productions as Hesmondhalgh and Baker (2011) point out. Size doesn't necessarily matter. Leadbeater also disregards Mode 2 (Gibbons et al. 1994; Stålbröst 2008) innovation initiatives, which have acknowledged the need to create bridges between research and societal practices. And, as McRobbie (2009) has argued, Leadbeater and others, with their neoliberal views, have idealized the creative entrepreneur as a way toward economic growth. This they have done at a time when cultural practices are increasingly expected to become entrepreneurial and take care of themselves leading to increased cultural individualization, competition, instability, and mobility; this at a time when societal structures supporting young up-and-coming creative talents have considerably diminished. It could even be argued that his arguments, although wanting to create a more modern and humane world of competitive communities, has contributed to individualization, instability, and mobility as policy makers and politicians have followed some of his advice.

Creative industries, democracy, and innovation

A discussion on democracy and innovation is to a large degree absent in research, in policy, and in the practices of creative industries. The exception is Eric von Hippel's book *Democratizing Innovation* (2005). Just as Leadbeater does, von Hippel acknowledges that the modes of production have to some degree changed, which has opened up for increased user-driven innovation. Innovation has become democratized, he claims, because information and the means of production—cheaper and more easily handled tools—have become more readily available leading to that more individuals can innovate. Innovation is thus defined as making discrete objects or products. Democracy is equated and delimited to having increased access to information and tools to make more products. And although von Hippel acknowledges users that are active creators, this rings true only to a small elite of lead users or domain experts who benefit from increased access to information and means of production—*lead users*, individuals who are ahead of the general market. To von Hippel democratization of innovation is therefore some sort of competitive elite market democracy. More recently this perspective has been problematized as focusing too much on lead users, ignoring the democratic responsibility of attending to the multitude of groups and perspectives that make up a democratic society (Björgvinsson, Ehn, and Hillgren 2010, 2012), and ignoring the responsibility of a democracy to attend to and take into account those marginalized by the majority rule. This alternative perspective argues that a more central issue pertaining to democratizing innovation is what groups are given access to *participating* in future-making, rather than solely the access to information and advanced means of production. In doing so, this perspective has built upon Mouffe's (1996) notion of agonistic controversies. It has aimed, through action-oriented research, at creating arenas in which different actors in society collaboratively explore future democratic media practices, rather than focusing on how products or services can be ahead of the market.

What groups are included and can get governmental funding is of particular relevance because research funding is an important innovation infrastructure device. EU's structural funds, which have partly financed the work discussed in this book, is an example of multilevel organizing of democracy where public and private actors collaborate horizontally across local, regional, national, and European levels to promote their interests (Erlingsson 1999). This is an organizational form that is not particularly transparent, open, or public, and which is heavily driven by lobbyism. It is an organizational form that some argue is a new form for democratic decision making, while others argue that semi-transparent lobbyism is anti-democratic. These regional funding strategies have also played some part in the spatial politics and the location and invigoration of creative hot spots.

The making of a creative class in Region Skåne and Malmö

Richard Florida's notion of the creative class has widely influenced politicians and city planners. His ideas have directly influenced political initiatives in southern Sweden, particularly in Malmö, for the last decade. Along similar lines as Leadbeater, Florida argued that we were witnessing substantial changes of values and ways of organizing. Cultural workers value rewarding work in which they can express themselves and their ideas and can learn and grow. They are driven by intrinsic motivation and peer recognition. They also value independent work that they can control and self-manage. These cultural workers do not look for safe jobs in which they can climb the corporate ladder; they look for tolerance, talent, technology, openness, and diversity. If cities are to become successful, they need to provide the three T's as the creative class, which is rising to power, generates economic growth. These cultural workers are, however, not interested in local traditional communities, but rather in communities that generate economic prosperity. Florida's main influence was making the connection between creativity, economic growth, and geographic concern, which to some degree fueled the spatial politics of growth. Current and future prosperity became a spatial competition, Malmö and other cities were working hard to brand themselves as creative and even measuring their talent, technology, and tolerance. According to one report (Mellander et al. 2010), 11 percent of Malmö's citizens were xenophobic, 14 percent were homophobic, 16 percent were unwilling to live next door to Muslims, and over 41 percent were unwilling to live next door to Romanis. Contrary to official rhetoric and frequent self-proclamations of tolerance, openness, and willingness to experiment, some cultural workers find these figures far from displaying high degree of tolerance, even though the figures are low when compared internationally.

Central to the revitalization of Malmö into a creative and knowledge-driven city, after some dormant years due to the shutdown of large industries, were large urban development projects and the establishment of Malmö University and Media Evolution. The revitalization strategy led to massive demographic changes. During the same time, Malmö also had substantial immigration, which is seldom acknowledged as having contributed to the revitalization.

The cluster formation Media Evolution creates mini-arenas for the creative sector and the creative industries. It has been a central organism of Malmö's "creative ecosystem," as defined by Florida (2002), according to whom a creative ecosystem "can include arts and culture, nightlife, the music scene, restaurants, artists and designers, innovators, entrepreneurs, affordable spaces, lively neighborhoods, spirituality, education, density, public spaces and third places" (ibid., 381). Media Evolution, framed as a cluster organization, has a clearly defined location, namely Media Evolution City, located in the Western Harbor district of Malmö. Although Media Evolution is in many ways an inclusive and open organization, it, like any organization, favors certain perspectives and actors. As was pointed out at Media Evolution's 2009 Annual General Members Meeting, none of the members of the steering board were from small media companies or non-governmental organizations. Members from such companies and organizations also felt that the membership rates, set according to number of employees, were too high and favored large enterprises. In the words of Florida (2002, 8), Media Evolution is "a cluster of people who have common interests and tend to think, feel and behave similarly", the similarities being determined mainly by economics.

Malmö University, established in 1998, was also central to the spatial politics of growth in Malmö. The university has been engaged in developing research and innovation strategies for how the private and public sectors and academia can conduct research and development on new media. Central to the research on media and design was the establishment of Medea Collaborative Media Initiative, which focuses on collaborative media and collaborative design research as it engages with society.

The design cases discussed in this part of the book were conducted through Malmö Living Lab the Stage. The purpose of Living Lab the Stage was to try out co-production models through the formation of various constellations of researchers and university students, cultural producers, and IT and media companies. These constellations have explored new forms of practices, expressions, services, and products through long-term engagements and iterative small-scale experiments in real-world contexts. This, in turn, has meant that the activities of the lab have been carried out in various locations in the city, but at times also connected to other places; each constellation and issue that has been researched generated its specific geography.

Over the years, the lab has worked with an arts and performance center and a media work center for visual artists and small publishers of literature and cultural magazines and some of their authors. It has also worked with small independent record companies and some of their artists, a hip-hop youth organization, and small up-and-coming independents filmmakers as well as with more established public and private media companies, newly established interaction design and industrial design bureaus, and more traditional IT companies.

Through the lab, cultural producers, artists, designers, media producers, and IT developers have negotiated as they envisioned the future together. One aspect of the work has been to create constructive and productive bridges for all the heterogeneous actors involved in addressing and envisioning the future, and to try to do so in a socially accountable way. The work carried out in the lab has given the researchers insights into how individuals and large and small companies organize their work and into how they relate to and act in relation to cultural capital, commerce, openness, co-production, democracy, and innovation.

The lab has found it important to open up participation to small content producers—not out of a belief that they are more innovative or agile, but rather on the basis of the

Creative Class Struggles

democratic ideals of participatory design. This has reconfigured how interaction design research and innovation are conducted, as it takes as its starting point the concerns currently facing these actors when challenging current infrastructures from the margins or, in the words of Suchman (2008, no paging), "disrupt[ing] particular arrangements," rather than imagining how the future could be ten years down the road.

The cultural sector, now often called the creative industries or the creative class, consists of various classes and public spheres that have distinct value systems and preconditions for producing and making a living. Physical, social, human, monetary, and creative capital are related to each other and are managed in different ways depending on what creative class the actors belong to. Bringing small and marginal enterprises and non-governmental organizations into the same story and future-making activities as more central powerful enterprises can at times lead to navigational difficulties, conflicts, and capsized collaborations. Two of the questions it raises are "Is collaboration between disparate creative classes desirable?" and "Do big issues need big companies?" At times, it is of value to collaborate with like-minded people. As one of the chapters in this part shows, infrastructures cannot change without powerful networks of people sharing the same values. Yet we can also see that aligning to different networks is important for different creative classes and enterprises within the creative industries. Collaborating and building bridges across organizational and professional borders is seldom easy. Problems quickly arise, some of them having to do with culture and capital.

Prominent themes

In this part of the book the creative class is analyzed through a set of collaborative design cases and through an interview study of creative industries managers. Internal class struggles and the complexity of the field of creative work are described and analyzed. The creative class is indeed a heterogeneous group with internal conflicts. Workers control the means of production because it is mental labor that is produced (Florida 2002), but the creative class still sells its labor in order to make a living. The shift from the feudal to the capitalist way of production focuses internal struggles on commodification rather than emancipation. Problems are discussed to clarify boundaries and what is taken for granted. There are dominating classes defending their position and justifying economic ideals of growth as the starting point for production. The agents see, judge, and act very differently depending on whether they are dominating or dominated. Depending on context and capital, there is a struggle between the super-creative core and the creative professionals. The creative professionals can be the hegemonic power.

The actors that we have interviewed and co-produced together with have in the interviews and during the co-production reasoned about the relationship between culture and capital and how they would like to and can position themselves. To gain cultural capital, one must disavow economic capital. Symbol production and symbol distinction, central aspects of cultural production, are always at play, though in different guises; as a product or event that is unique, as altruistic and autonomous creation with high level of integrity and quality, or as promoting craftsmanship and communality, or as embracing popularity and commerce. Creative workers, operating within the realm of culture and creative industries, inevitably face the challenge of where to position themselves on the industry-creative autonomy spectrum.

The tension between cultural commons and private property is particularly important. The relationship between private ownership of content or products and the common good is in no way settled, and it highlights democratic issues relating to cultural production. The actors in the chapters on co-production articulate tensions and challenge presuppositions about what is part of the cultural commons and what is private property. The interviewed managers' standard view is that cultural products and content is private property, where cultural commons is understood as being separated from the production being made and taken care of somewhere else. Democratic issues of cultural production are, if not dichotomized, marginalized or considered a non-issue by the creative industry class, and thus left to be taken care of by the cultural producers.

Another tension concerns what forms of collaborations are considered valuable and doable. The stories from design cases and interviews relating to open or closed innovation show that some people do not have the time to engage in collaborative research projects although they would want to engage in these kind of projects. Not only is open innovation time consuming; it also demands specific competences, which makes it difficult for some actors to become engaged in such innovation. They see participation in slow processes, which networked collaborations demand, as a form of luxury. Friction occurs when an actor can see the value of collaborating but is unable to engage in it. Friction also occurs in collaborative and networked research and development, but for the most part the various actors can tolerate it, as they gain from the collaboration even when they have to compromise some of their values.

Linked to the organization of work, and specifically to the matter of autonomy, is the issue of how to balance communality and individual autonomy. In critical theory, autonomy is described as a desirable political goal (Adorno 2004). Marshall (1996) points out how Adorno's notion of autonomy refers to liberty, and Marcuse (2001) how liberty is a mode of existence where true autonomy exists; an autonomy that allows people to practice altered consciousness, which allows them to break away from prevailing societal perceptions. McRobbie (2003) argues that the logic within creative industries is that the more autonomous you are, the more creative you can be—but that autonomy also comes with a price. This resonates with Hesmondhalgh and Baker's (2011) discussion of autonomy as a feature of good work. They argue that cultural workers lack managerial power and that friction between creative autonomy and commercial imperatives is a threat to creative autonomy. According to Habermas (1992), deliberative communication builds on political autonomy, which can be realized only in a joint enterprise in an intersubjective shared practice, not by a person pursuing his or her private interests. Habermas (ibid.) is therefore looking for forms of living together in which autonomy and dependency can truly enter into a non-antagonistic relation. In our studies this is articulated as the individual being able to be creatively autonomous and also having to withdraw from the structures of commercial imperatives. An enterprise can never defect from commercial imperatives, but an enterprise can commit to communality, supporting creative autonomy not only as an egoistic aspect but also as an opportunity to fulfill obligations to other people and the society at large. If we look into the professional lives of the actors in the interviews and in the co-producing practices, we can see that the relationship between autonomy and dependency is still antagonistic, and that the ability to control one's own production is sometimes decreased by collaboration and co-production.

We conclude this introductory chapter on class struggles within the creative industries by making prominent what it adds to earlier knowledge production: the locating of future-making. In the tense relationship of culture and capital, a prism of future-making reveals friction between industry and cultural production as how to approach future-making and newness, what we call *disengaged futures* or *engaged nows*. Cultural producers and the more industrious IT companies approach the future quite differently, but also show some similarities. One obvious similarity is that they both engage in practices of producing that which is *new* or at least considered new rather than mere imitation. However, how to approach the future differs considerably whether you belong to an IT and design company engaged in research and development or you are a cultural producer in relation to how far into the future the future tense stretches. Some international IT and design firms, often large ones, can engage in developing future scenarios and concepts, and at times prototypes that explore products and services that may be launched five to ten years later. Other IT and design companies do not have the opportunity to do R&D for potential products that may be launched years later. The logic of innovation they operate under is that they innovate and develop when their products or services need to be updated or have become obsolete. They are thus involuntarily entrepreneurs that innovate when trapped. Yet, a common approach to research and development within companies is to approach the future as disentangled from the now. Cultural producers, on the other hand, have little opportunity to engage in future scenarios or beta productions, as they operate under the logic of one production's leading to the next. They do this through rehearsing, which is their equivalent to prototyping and beta production. Nevertheless, the production that they are engaged in should aim at some form of distinction so that it can be recognized as new when presented. There are a few funding bodies that are geared toward cultural development, but such projects cannot simply produce *what if* scenarios or prototypes; they need to deliver and spread insights gained from the development of cultural practices or new forms of expression. As such, they are still focused on sharp productions rather than beta productions or prototypes. In some instances, getting these worlds to meet is challenging because they have considerably different approaches to the future and because their perspective and their modes of production are tremendously different when it comes to future-making. In addition, research conducted at a university in the intersection between media studies and interaction design has traditionally been closer aligned to IT and design firms that engage in research on what can potentially become realized five to ten years down the road. For the research conducted within the Living Lab the Stage, it has demanded considerable reorientation toward sharp productions since it has taken the needs of small cultural producers as its starting point. This reorientation has meant dealing with newness, even more insistently than before, through what Suchman (2008) calls local preoccupations where newness is produced through translation work in a given time and place, rather than as a universal quality produced through practices claiming to be operating at an empty frontier and disconnected from contextual entanglements of power, which often is the case with R&D conducted in research centers and larger organization.

The notion of innovation, in the form of a policy discourse, has had strong impact on creative labor. It has intensified the notion of industriousness in the term *creative industries*. In some quarters it is still viewed as a happy marriage with a bright future—for example, in the 2014 Creative Europe program run by the European Union, innovation is given high prominence. More and more, creative workers who have experienced the intensification of uncertainty, flexibility, and mobility have been raising their voices and demanding that cultural productions that cut across the public and private spheres need to become more democratic by loading the future with hopes not mainly made up of capital but also culture that slowly changes as it adds a new sediment to previous layers, reaching back and digging into older layers as it wanders into the future in an ongoing act of remediation.

References

Adorno, Theodor. 2004. *Aesthetic Theory*. Bloomsbury Academic.

Adorno, Theodor, and Max Horkheimer. 2002. *Dialectic of Enlightenment*. Stanford University Press.

Barry, Andrew. 2001. *Political Machines. Governing a Technological Society*. Athlone.

Bijker, Wiebe. 1995. *Of Bicycles, Bakelites, and Bulbs: Toward a Theory of Sociotechnical Change*. MIT Press.

Björgvinsson, Erling, Pelle Ehn, and Per-Anders Hillgren. 2010. Participatory Design and "Democratizing Innovation." In Proceedings of Eleventh Biennial Participatory Design Conference.

Björgvinsson, Erling, Pelle Ehn, and Per-Anders Hillgren. 2012. Agonistic Participatory Design: Working with Marginalized Social Movements. *CoDesign* 8 (2–3): 127–144.

Cunningham, Stuart. 2002. From cultural to creative industries: Theory, industry, and policy implications. *Media International Australia Incorporating Culture and Policy: Quarterly Journal of Media Research and Resources*: 54–65.

Erlingsson, Gissur Ó. 1999. *Ekonomi, demokrati och identitet i ett Europa under omvandling. En analys av ett forskningsområde*. Department of Political Science, Lunds Universitet.

Fischer, Josefine. 2010. The Other Entrepreneur: Alternative Approaches to Economics, Culture and How to Do Business. CIRCLE. University of Lund.

Flew, Terry. 2002. Beyond Ad Hocery: Defining Creative Industries. Paper presented at Second International Conference on Cultural Policy Research, Wellington, New Zealand.

Flew, Terry. 2011. Origins of Creative Industries Policy. In *The Creative Industries: Culture and Policy*. Sage.

Florida, Richard. 2002. *The Rise of The Creative Class*. Basic Books.

Garnham, Nicholas. 2005. From Cultural to Creative Industries: An Analysis of the Implications of the "Creative Industries" Approach to Arts and Media Policy Making in the United Kingdom. *International Journal of Cultural Policy* 11 (1): 15–29.

Gibbons, Michael, et al. 1994. *The New Production of Knowledge: The Dynamics of Science and Research in Societies*. Sage.

Habermas, Jürgen. 1992. *Autonomy and Solidarity*. Verso.

Hartley, John, and Stuart Cunningham. 2001. Creative Industries: From Blue Poles to Fat Pipes. In *The National Humanities and Social Sciences Summit: Position Papers*, ed. M. Gillies. Department of Education Science and Training, Canberra.

Hesmondhalgh, David, and Sarah Baker. 2011. Towards a Political Economy of Labour in the Media Industries. In *The Handbook of Political Economy of Communications*, ed. G. Murdock, H. Sousa, and J. Wasko. Wiley-Blackwell.

Jeppesen, Troels. 2004. The Creative Class Struggles. *Kontur* 10: 20–26.

Leadbeater, Charles. 1999. *Living on Thin Air: The New Economy*. Penguin.

Leadbeater, Charles. 2004. *Personalisation through Participation*. Demos.

Leadbeater, Charles. 2008. Charles Leadbeater: The Rise of the Amateur Professional (http://www.youtube.com/watch?v=W7raJeMpyM0).

Leadbeater, Charles, and Paul Miller. 2004. The Pro-Am Revolution: How Enthusiasts Are Changing Our Economy and Society (http://www.demos.co.uk/publications/proameconomy).

Marcuse, Herbert. 2001. *Towards a Critical Theory of Society: The Collected Papers of Herbert Marcuse, Volume Two*, ed. D. Kellner. Routledge.

Marshall, James D. 1996. *Michel Foucault: Personal Autonomy and Education*. Kluwer.

McRobbie, Angela. 2003. "Everyone Is Creative": Artists as Pioneers of the New Economy? (http://www.k3000.ch/becreative/texts/text_5.html).

McRobbie, Angela. 2009. Vi är alla kreativa. In *Kultur och politik*, ed. Y. Gislen et al. Fronesis.

Mellander, Charlotta, et al. 2010. Skånes kreativa kapacitet—Talang, tolerans och den kreativa klassen (http://www.skane.se/upload/Webbplatser/Strukturbild/H%C3%B6st%2010/skanes_kreativa_kapacitet_OK.pdf).

Mouffe, Chantal. 1996. Democracy, Power, and the "Political." In *Democracy and Difference*, ed. S. Benhabib. Princeton University Press.

Oakley, Kate. 2009. The Disappearing Arts: Creativity and Innovation after the Creative Industries. *International Journal of Cultural Policy* 15 (4): 403–413.

Stålbröst, A. 2008. Forming Future IT: The Living Lab Way of User Involvement. Doctoral thesis, Luleå University of Technology.

Suchman, Lucy. 2008. Striking Likenesses to Difference. Paper presented at annual meeting of Society for Social Studies of Science, Rotterdam.

Wright, E. O. 1997. *Class Counts: Comparative Studies in Class Analysis*. Cambridge University Press.

10   The Making of Cultural Commons: Nasty Old Film Distribution and Funding

Erling Björgvinsson

On October 10, 2009, the independently financed film *Nasty Old People* became the first Swedish feature film to be distributed for free under a Creative Commons license through the peer-to-peer file-sharing service The Pirate Bay. In conjunction with the release, a viral marketing strategy and donation campaign was launched. The launch, the campaign, and the donation came about because of a collaboration, enabled by the Living Lab the Stage, between the media production companies Tangram and Good, The Pirate Bay, and university researchers and students. Within five days, the film had been downloaded 14,000 times, translated by volunteers into thirteen languages, raised 5,000 euros, blogged about around the Western world, and a few weeks later was covered in traditional media channels. The exposure at The Pirate Bay and in the blogosphere, and a vivid social-media buzz, led to screenings at small theaters across Europe. A year later, Swedish public television (SVT) broadcast the film, which together with the donations paid the bank loan of 10,000 euros and saw the launch of the first Creative Commons Film Festival.

The collaboration between Tangram, Good, The Pirate Bay, and university researchers and students tried out new forms of distributed open innovation and new forms of participatory design. It tried out how collaboration across the knowledge domains of independent film production, the academic fields of media and communication studies and interaction design, media activists—or, according to some, media criminals: The Pirate Bay—and citizens could be carried out; fields that currently rarely engage in research together. The research thus tried out how innovation that cuts across academia and the public and private spheres can be conducted with partners that are seldom given the opportunity to participate in research and development. Swedish research funding to a large degree excludes partners that are economically small, as some of the biggest research and development funders in Sweden will fund only holding companies. This is a policy that is not particularly democratic as many companies within cultural industries are not holding companies and therefore cannot participate in state-funded research and development. The research also tried out what it means to conduct open innovation, as the constellation of partners grew along the way and

Figure 10.1
The doodle on The Pirate Bay announcing the release of *Nasty Old People*.

were not predetermined. Finally, it tried out how innovation, or future-making, can be conducted through experimentation in the public, rather than as design scenarios or temporary prototypical practices of future arrangements of people, cultural products, technologies, funding, and law. By trying out the distribution of *Nasty Old People* in public, it interweaved with larger social arenas—national and international—that pointed at how research and development, in particular within participatory design, can simultaneously engage in local development as well as larger social arenas, as the "object" or "issue" tried out is no longer only a boundary object (Star 1989) to be negotiated among known partners, but a contested issue on national and international arenas where various positions held by communities and organizations affect the perceptions and practices around the issue.

More important, the production, distribution, and marketing tried out a new—perhaps complementary—public model for the sharing and financing of film, which is tightly connected to forms of ownership. The distribution imagined and concretely suggested a new form for infrastructure for sharing of cultural products and knowledge in the form of cultural commons. The film went straight to the viewers, who were asked to donate if they could, rather than to distributors, cinemas and festivals—the traditional "bottlenecks" and gatekeepers of good taste and profiteers of cultural products. This challenged "business as usual" and the traditional order of releasing movies and charging for cultural products. It also challenged who is given the right to tell and spread stories via the art form of fiction film, a right that is tightly connected to film funding, as the production and distribution was to a large degree self-financed. Swedish films are typically funded through a mix of public funding allocated by the Swedish Film Institute and regional film funds, private financing, and citizens as they buy theater tickets. As such, Swedish film funding and distribution is a form of governing of a public sphere that cuts across public and private, the state and the market.

The release thus imagined and concretely suggested a different and complementary form for sharing and financing cultural products and a new form of a public sphere where film production and distribution practices are made accessible to more people, which leads to an increased diversity of "voices" in the making and debating of films, two issues central to democracy.

The collaboration raised several challenges in relation to participation and future-making interventions pertaining to film production.

First, the collaboration pointed at how the future-making activity is both inclusive and exclusive. The researchers have worked with small media actors and cultural producers within film, music, and literature. The small media actors are often excluded from research and development, as are the arts are in general. At the same time, the collaboration points at how the success was dependent on gathering resources quickly and at the right time. It also points at how the success was dependent on the combination of highly specialized know-how and access to exclusive networks within the media, the advanced tech-culture, and the cultural sphere. The transferability of the knowledge gained through the project to other marginal actors is thus minimal, as it cannot be "copied" if similar know-how and networks are out of reach.

Second, the collaboration raised questions about how cultural productions can and could be shared and financed in a small country belonging to a small language area. On the one hand, the actors behind the intervention argue for free and open access to culture that others can build upon, something that is difficult to convince current public and private funders to support. A niche activist audience, however, is willing to support such an initiative, as it challenges current distribution and financing infrastructures. The question it raises, however, is whether this is a sustainable funding model for small independent filmmakers, as raising large sums through crowd-funding is difficult and time consuming. It also points to the fact that such an intervention can be interpreted as supporting current neo-liberal tendencies of decreasing state funding of the arts and an increased demand for artists to become market-driven entrepreneurs who should fix their own funding and perhaps even their own audience to be granted state funding—an interpretation that is contrary to the team's intention to argue for cultural commons, which the current system of funding and distribution system finds problematic.

Infrastructuring, arena analysis, and commons

Living Lab the Stage has been engaged in experimenting with narrative forms and alternative ways of producing, distributing, financing and marketing film, literature, and music together with small independent companies and cultural workers in Malmö since 2009. The reasoning behind working primarily with small companies was that they are seldom included in exploring future possibilities and that they should be given the democratic opportunity to connect to research centers and participate in the imagining and exploring of alternative futures—an opportunity that should not be available only to large and well-established companies.

Building upon earlier participatory design research (Björgvinsson 2008; Björgvinsson et al. 2010, 2012), the lab has developed new infrastructuring processes as different partners form a temporary working constellation while exploring a particular issue and trying out future practices. Building upon Star and Bowker 2002 and Karasti et al. 2010, infrastructuring means the negotiation and sociomaterial configuration of how local needs can be adjusted and aligned to shared needs. Along similar lines, the lab has built upon Lucy Suchman's work (Suchman et al. 1998; Suchman 2002, 2008) that makes the case for seeing research and development as ongoing networks of relations, and as rearrangements of particular socio-technical arrangements, rather than as free-standing systems developed at some kind of imagined and decontextualized frontier. Here, it will be argued that open innovation and participatory design engaged in the development of new public spheres need, as Suchman (2002) suggests, to pay attention to how research and development connect to wider social systems, which I suggest can been done through arena analysis (Clarke 2005; Clarke and Star 2007). Arena analysis pays attention to communities and organizations and, I would add, to what Callon (1986) calls translations centers—or central networks—that many actors gather around and believe to be important to maintain and defend. In this case, the organizations and communities include the American Film Association, which through its lobbying affects international trade agreements and copyright laws (Lobato 2008), the Swedish Film Institute (SFI), large Swedish media companies and distributers, and The Pirate Bay. On a national level, SFI and media companies gather around the Swedish film agreement. On an international level, governments gather around trade agreements such as Trade Related Aspects of Intellectual Property Rights (TRIPS), General Agreements on Tariffs and Trade (GATT), and now through the World Trade Organization (WTO).

The notion of translation centers can be used both for analyzing current networks and for analyzing how new networks are constructed. As Callon (1986) points out, when actors face a new issue, try to define what the problem is and how it can be solved through an action program, and try to identify pertinent actors and their representatives, the actor who manages to become indispensible to the network becomes the main actor that all the other actors connect to and have to negotiate and work with. The main actor has managed, in other words, to become what Callon calls an "obligatory passage point" through which all other actors have to pass. All mediation between actors has to go through this obligatory point of passage, which makes the main actor a powerful translation center. The early stages of forming an actor network consist of what Callon calls problematization, interessement, enrollment, and mobilization. Problematization refers to the act of defining the problem and identifying the significant actors. Interessement refers to the stage at which actors are attracted to the problem and negotiations are made on how they should engage. Enrollment refers to the stage at which the actors agree to accept their assigned roles. Mobilization of allies refers to when actors actively support the action program, as the majority of the members in their constituencies support it. An action program can have several obligatory passage points. Local networks, by setting up spaces of negotiation that is channeled through obligatory points of passage, give them certain autonomy from global network actors.

Central to the notion of infrastructuring (Star and Bowker 2002; Karasti et al. 2010) is how overarching or shared needs across contexts can work together with local needs and circumstances. Although this is not stated explicitly, central to infrastructuring is that infrastructures come about through situated politics as agreements and stabilizations are negotiated and performed by the various partners gathering around a particular sociomaterial issue. This is a form of politics and governing that is closely related to Foucault's (1973, 1977; also see Barry 2001) expanded notion of the political and governing, which is more messy than the idealistic notion of governing often put forth in political science studies, as such distributed politics cut across various contexts; often mixing private and public spheres, the state and the market.

The relationship between local needs and global or shared needs, a central concern to proponents of infrastructuring, is also a central concern of advocates of commons, as they are concerned with common-pool resources or commons as property regimes and with how individual needs and rights and common good needs and rights can be balanced (Ostrom 1990; Hess and Ostrom 2003, 2007; Lessig 2001, 2004). Hess (2012, 25–26) has defined commons as a "cultural resource shared by a group where the resource is vulnerable to enclosure, overuse and social dilemmas," and she remarks that it is difficult to draw a clear line between commons and cultural commons, as many natural-resource commons "abound with cultural components." However, many cultural commons, which at times are spoken of as knowledge commons (Madison et al. 2010; Hyde 2010), seldom directly face the dilemma of overuse, which is central to natural-resource commons, as many cultural products, intellectual ideas, or organizations do not face the possibility that the resource might disappear through overuse. On the other hand, some cultural commons entangled in the digital face the specific problems of migration and archiving (Hess 2012), as new digital standards change quickly and demand resourceful heritage organizations.

As Hess and Ostrom (2007) have shown, common-pool resources, or shared resources, aren't necessarily connected to ownership or to property rights. Property rights, as Hess (2012) states, are just one of many kinds of rights. Other rights include management rights, access rights, exclusion rights, and extraction rights, which Creative Commons licenses address so as to expand and nuance the copyright law. Commons, as Hess (ibid.) states, can have various organizational forms, but are typically characterized by participatory engagement and are self-governing. Such self-governing and participatory forms of organizations can regulate their relations to the state and the market and are often independent of state governing. They demand "social capital, trust, and reciprocity", and they are vulnerable to "social dilemmas, such as non-compliance, free riding, lack of commitment, and so on" (ibid., 23).

The question of commons, particularly cultural commons and Creative Commons, is central to the case discussed here, which deals with how Swedish films can be owned, financed, accessed, and shared. However, approaches to infrastructuring could benefit by connecting to the debate and the practices concerned with commons. First of all, the commons debate has taken a relatively strong stand in relation to the question of how to balance local and global or shared needs. The notion of knowledge and information commons appeared in 1995 (Hess and Ostrom 2003), and the first books focusing on cultural commons were published in 2010 and 2012, namely *Common as Air* (Hyde 2010) and *Cultural Commons* (Bertacchini 2012). The attention to information, knowledge, and cultural commons came about because people building online resources saw problems related to commons emerge, such as free riding, congestion, "pollution," and conflict (Hess and Ostrom 2003). It also emerged, as Hess (2012) states, because of increased threats of enclosure and commodification of cultural resources, but also because networked technologies allowed for the formation of new types of communities. Simply put, an imbalance between private property and private resources and common good had to be addressed. Second, research on commons has clearly identified what characterizes what Hess (2012) calls "long-enduring commons." On the basis of extensive empirical research, Hess and Ostrom (2003) have identified the following set of features that characterize durable commons:

- Clearly defined boundaries should be in place.
- Rules in use are well matched to local needs and conditions.
- Individuals affected by these rules can usually participate in modifying the rules.
- The right of community members to devise their own rules is respected by external authorities.
- A system for self-monitoring members' behavior has been established.
- A graduated system of sanctions is available.
- Community members have access to low-cost conflict-resolution mechanisms.
- Nested enterprises—that is, appropriation, provision, monitoring and sanctioning, conflict resolution, and other governance activities—are organized in a nested structure with multiple layers of activities.

(See also Hess 2012.) Some of these characteristics resemble some of the issues addressed by the discourse on infrastructure, such as the need for local rules and clearly defined boundaries. However, these characteristics also point to the need, which has not been much addressed within the design-driven approach on infrastructuring, to device a set of explicit rules that can be modified and sanctions that can be carried out. Design-driven approaches to infrastructuring have emphasized exploring the development of new practices through enacting tacit rules. However, these approaches have perhaps not paid enough attention to the value and importance of explicit frameworks that contain explicit rules—such as those that are created by commons organizations—that guide how different stakeholders should collaborate and resolve conflicts.

Tangram

Common to all the cultural actors that the Living Lab the Stage has collaborated with is that they engage in cultural production mainly because they believe in the value, the power, and the social good of culture. (For a more in-depth analysis of how some of them reason, see Fischer 2010.) Although all of them hope to make a living out of their business, it is a secondary concern. Central to all of them is that they engage in meaningful work and that they can stand for and believe in what they produce.

Tangram, a small independent film production company run by Hanna Sköld, Andrea Kåberg, Vanja Sandell Billström, and Jennifer Malmqvist, is no exception. Like many other small independent film companies, it aims primarily to make films that it believes in and secondly to make a living from them.

Nasty Old People, directed and produced by Hanna Sköld, is a film about a nineteen-year-old neo-Nazi girl, named Mette, who works for a municipal home-help service. The theme of the film is the clash between disdain and caring. We follow how Mette and the senior citizens change and manage to come to terms with their shortcomings and become more caring and less disdaining individuals.

The film was largely a do-it-yourself (DIY) production. Hanna Sköld applied for a Rookie stipend, which was funded by SFI, SVT, and Film i Väst and geared toward young directors. However, because Hanna wasn't associated with an established producer, she wasn't qualified for the grant. To make the film, she took out a 10,000-euro bank loan and persuaded actors and a production crew to participate for free. Good helped out with the post-production, and with a small grant from Film i Skåne Hanna was able to complete the film. The production is, as such, a good example that it is possible to make feature films without large funding, thanks in part to cheaper and more accessible production gear, if one has the time, the contacts, and the willingness of a large group of people to work for free.

The collaboration with Tangram happened because the lab had worked with the production company Good on several projects between 2007 and 2009. This long-term collaboration meant that we had good knowledge of each other's competences and that we shared some common values and trust. When Helene Granqvist, CEO of Good, heard that Hanna needed help with the post-production, she decided to help her out—offering her a place at Good and helped her to get some financing from Film i Skåne and SFI. However, because the film was made outside the official system, gaining access to traditional distribution channels was difficult. And there was no budget for distributing and marketing the film, a problem that Tangram shares with many DIY filmmakers.

The main function of film festivals and theater screenings is promotion and marketing, as the main revenue comes from rental and (more recently) through online subscription streaming services. Because only a fraction of the films made are shown at festivals and theaters, these venues function as "bottlenecks," or quality controls, which gives the distributors considerable power. Film funders, some of whom also are distributors, thus ensure that films they have funded are screened at festivals and in theaters. Films made outside the official funding system, except those made by well-established film producers who fund their own films and have a guaranteed large audience, do not have access to these distribution channels. The rhetoric that is used is that these channels are quality controls or a form of editorial work that guarantees that only the best films reach the viewers.

At a sneak preview of *Nasty Old People* in Malmö, Richard Topgaard, a Living Lab the Stage co-worker, talked to Hanna Sköld and suggested that we could help her with distribution. On short notice, the author of this chapter connected the case to an interaction design course in which the students were to collaborate with the Living Lab the Stage. The students, who worked on the project for five weeks, came up with various distribution strategies. One idea was to recruit volunteers around the world to premiere the film in their homes, at senior citizen care centers, and in small theaters. Hanna and the students decided to opt for online distribution through the file-sharing site The Pirate Bay, and thus to bypass the traditional practice of releasing films.[1] Thus *Nasty Old People* became the first Swedish full-length feature film to be released on a peer-to-peer file-sharing site under a Creative Commons license. This was a public experiment suggesting a complementary distribution and funding model that believed in free access to culture. The experiment was made possible by a long-term engagement with Good and a quickly formed constellation of partners that included Tangram, The Pirate Bay, and university researchers and students and later expanded to include numerous offline and online collaborators from San Francisco to Kiev.

Distributing and marketing *Nasty Old People*: Exclusive inclusion

According to influential thinkers on creativity and innovation, Tangram and Good should be optimal creative innovators that should be greatly valued by the municipality of Malmö (Florida 2002). Insofar as these companies are close to what Leadbeater and Miller (2004) call "Pro-Ams," they should be highly innovative, and if we accept Eric von Hippel's (2005) argument that innovation has become more democratic as a result of greater access to information, tools, and technological infrastructures, they should be more agile and more open to collaboration and sharing of competences and resources than traditional innovation clusters that gather experts under the same roof. What if the distribution and financing of *Nasty Old People* was an excellent example of these arguments? How did the process affect and transform the collaborators? How democratic can it be said to be? The account of the experiment that follows will show that these claims are partially true. The collaborators are small and agile, but also big and powerful, as is evident in the impact The Pirate Bay has had on the international media landscape. Tangram is valued by some public institutions, but faces constant difficulties of finding funding. Access to technologies and information is central, but so is the access to networks and skills.

The distribution and marketing of *Nasty Old People* started with uploading a torrent file on The Pirate Bay, which lowered the distribution cost to zero and handed over the distribution to the users. How successful the distribution would become depended, consequently, on users' willingness to "seed" the film (that is, to making your copy of the movie available for others to download through a peer-to-peer file-sharing network) and spread the word. After less than a week, 14,000 copies of the film had been distributed, equaling 12,550.5 gigabytes, a bandwidth that a single distributer would have to pay hundreds if not thousands of dollars to transfer.

To give the release official status, *Nasty Old People* was registered on the Internet Movie Database, an entry on Wikipedia was posted, a trailer was put on YouTube, and a premiere screening and release party was arranged by Luffarbion at Kontrapunkt, an offline event in Malmö emphasizing the importance of coming together and communal belonging.

To gain exposure, the team contacted The Pirate Bay and convinced them to exchange the "doodle"—the image of a pirate ship normally meeting the users of the site—on The Pirate Bay's front page, which would considerably increase the exposure of the film.[2] Placing a torrent file on The Pirate Bay without the front-page "doodle" would have meant simply placing a link to a file among millions of other pointers, and in order to find it people would have had to know what to search for.

The Pirate Bay was difficult to get hold of, since none of the people behind it had public telephone numbers or e-mail addresses. At the time, the mass media were on their trail because The Pirate Bay was facing legal charges and because sale of the site was being discussed. We were able to get in contact with one of them through the microblogging site Twitter, as one member of our team knew the Twitter username of a person who might have information on whom to contact.

The Pirate Bay agreed to put a doodle on their front page because it resonated with their values. The doodle was central to the success of the distribution of the film, as the ups and downs in the number of page views of the *Nasty Old People* Blog clearly showed.[3]

To gain additional exposure, we sent press releases to traditional media channels and contacted people we knew who worked for some of Sweden's larger newspapers. We also contacted prominent bloggers, among them Unni Drougge (a famous Swedish author and an acquaintance of Hanna Sköld) and Mathias Klang (who is engaged in Creative Commons Sweden and who has a considerable following on social media channels and access to an influential international network). Klang, in turn, contacted the influential journalist, activist, and author Cory Doctorow, who writes for the well-visited website Boingboing.net. After Doctorow's post about *Nasty Old People* appeared on Boingboing, we observed a considerable increase in the numbers of posts in the blogosphere and in online fanzines in the Western world. The amount of exposure hinged on good contacts, cunning use of social media, and a fair amount of luck.

In anticipation of user engagement, a blog had been created so that donations could be made through PayPal. Hanna regularly posted updates on the progress of distribution and donation, so as to be in close contact with the audience and create an as transparent process as possible. A Facebook page was created that enabled the audience to send messages to Tangram and to ask questions of Hanna and the team. The Facebook page was "liked" by 1,500 people, and a dialogue with the team went on for several weeks. Hanna alone was in e-mail contact with about 130 people, something that she appreciated but sometimes found overwhelming.

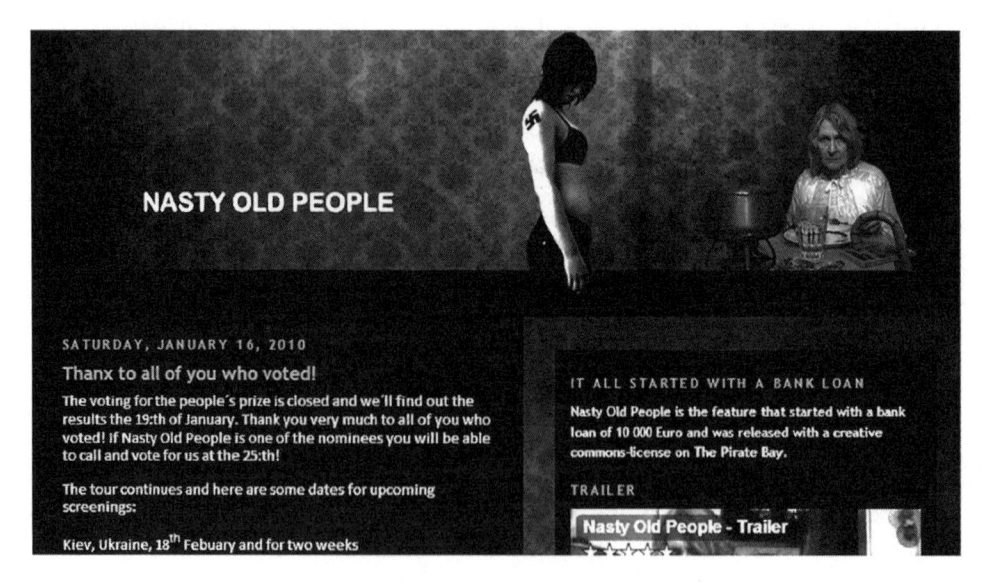

Figure 10.2
A screenshot from the *Nasty Old People* blog.

The above account illustrates how alternative distribution and financing of a movie demands specialized knowledge on how to intertwine social, technical, and economic systems and practices, including knowledge of how various social media platforms work (both technically and socially), of how various online financing systems work and can be set up, and of how to encourage and motivate the audience to donate. Most filmmakers do not have such knowledge, and buying competence in these specialties is too expensive for a small independent film company. In 2009 (when the campaign for *Nasty Old People* was conducted) most filmmakers and production companies wouldn't have known how to create a torrent file or how to seed a film via a peer-to-peer file-sharing network, and most would have had only limited knowledge of the online practices that were considered for *Nasty Old People* and those that were used.

The account also shows how important it was to be able to connect to strong networks in the high-tech world and in the cultural world of bloggers and journalists who share similar values and interests. Without gaining access to The Pirate Bay's front page (which has millions of visitors per week), and without the blog post written by Cory Doctorow, the distribution and financing of the film probably would have been quite meager. Being displayed on the front page of The Pirate Bay, and being given exposure on the online new-media website Boingboing were, thus, essential to the success of the release. In other words, a small and unknown actor needs to associate and adjust itself to important media outlets.

The same goes for niche products, such as avant-garde literature, sold in large online stores such as Amazon. Chris Anderson (2007) has hailed how the Internet makes it possible for niche products to become more accessible through online distribution. He also points out how these products are a considerable source of income for large online stores such as Amazon through what he calls the long-tail effect. But from the perspective of small media companies, such as Tangram, if they were to sell their products on such sites with the aim of reaching a large customer base, it would demand having access to digital windows with high exposure, i.e., many visitors. This is because an online database doesn't reveal much of its content. It is therefore hard to stumble upon less-known titles, and you need to know what you are looking for, as the search field is blank which creates a narrow field of vision. The storefronts, where certain products are highlighted, are for the most part reserved for large companies that are able to pay for the exposure. On The Pirate Bay you cannot buy front-page ads, and without an ad your product becomes a needle in a haystack. The only way to get front-page exposure at the time of the release was to have enough cultural or social capital, and since 2012 one has had to acquire that by going through the Promo Bay application process. Gaining online exposure on The Pirate Bay is therefore, just as on commercial sites, reserved for a few strong actors having either a lot of cultural capital or a lot of money.

The campaign for *Nasty Old People* was based on access to "free" student and research labor and on the film company's ability to devote unpaid time to it.[4] The students worked on the project full-time for six weeks, and each of the researchers devoted about 40 percent of his or her time to teaching the students and facilitating and documenting the project together with students and Tangram; this included coming up with various concepts, producing visuals, and launching websites and services. Tangram spent considerable amounts of time "living on thin air," especially when it came to running the campaign itself, which at times became labor intensive for Tangram because of extensive dialogue with the audience. From a strictly economic perspective, the work put into the campaign exceeded the money raised.

Our tracking of the downloading and media exposure shows how short-lived the media attention was. The window of exposure was limited to four high-exposure days. The downloading peaked at 14,000 copies on the fourth day and thereafter slowly rose to 25,000 copies during the next weeks. The media exposure was concentrated to three days. It started with Sofia Mirjamsdotter's—Mymlan's—post on Aftonbladet's blog on October 8, 2009. On October 10, when Klang and thereafter Doctorow had written about the release, between twenty and thirty posts—articles and blog posts—were written per day. Geographically, the media attention was concentrated in Europe and to some degree the United States. No posts south of Italy or east of Turkey were detected. Traditional media covered the story only when the media attention in the blogosphere and in online fanzines was over. *Sydsvenskan*, southern Sweden's largest newspaper, was the first newspaper to cover it (on October 23). News articles published in traditional media had no noticeable effect on the number of downloads or the number of visits to the *Nasty Old People* blog. Online niche media channels, at least when it came to the topic of a free film and free culture, had greater exposure and audience engagement impact than traditional media channels. Two reasonable assumptions are that readers of online niche media sources are more likely to have activist leanings toward the topic in question than readers of more traditional news sources and that traditional news media rarely hyperlink to blogs and torrent pages and thus do not provide their readers with call-to-action triggers.

The success of the campaign depended to a not-insignificant extent on the ability to gather the right resources, the knowledge, skills, networks of people, and technologies at the right time and have them perform well in a loosely connected and distributed manner. The stages of problematization, interessement, enrollment, and mobilization went quite smoothly. The researchers/teachers, on short notice, added the project to a university course. The people at The Pirate Bay, also on short notice, were willing to give active support to the project and gave us access to their vast network, even though they were facing legal charges and frequent attacks on their servers and were negotiating a sale. Tangram quickly decided to run the alternative distribution strategy. Collaborating with The Pirate Bay meant accepting that The Pirate Bay had become the main network actor and therefore an obligatory point of passage for major translations, which redefined Tangram considerably as they became allies with a piracy organization.

The alliance with The Pirate Bay—an obligatory point of passage—could be considered controversial by the Swedish Film Institute and Swedish film companies and distributors, which in the so-called Film Agreement clearly states their intention to work against illegal downloading and piracy, and Hanna Sköld was potentially risking her career as a director hoping to operating within the traditional film system. Teaming up with The Pirate Bay considerably altered the meaning of the film *Nasty Old People*, the director, and Tangram. Instead of being a cultural product that was to be protected as a commodity, the film advocated not only that cultural products should be accessible to all for free, but also that the people behind The Pirate Bay were spreaders and educators of culture, not criminals. Simultaneously, the film bypassed the traditional translation center made up by the Swedish Film Institute and their partners that co-finance the Swedish Film Agreement, whereof some of the partners own the current film distribution infrastructure—comprised of theaters, video rentals, and online streaming services in Sweden.

Although we did not know if neither traditional nor more experimental online media channels would catch on, when they did, the speed of it was not surprising as that is a common characteristic of online social media. The novelty of the distribution and funding strategy was also a resource played upon. As Kerrigan (2009) points out, "calling cards" can be an effective way to become recognized and receive attention. But being first would not necessarily have meant much if it had not been for a strong alignment of humans, media, and technical actors; a driven and communicative director, a DIY film, university resources, The Pirate Bay and The Pirate Bay doodle, Doctorow and Boingboing, PayPal, and the audience.[5] Gathering the right resources meant drawing upon existing networks that shared common values and trust, but also effectively inserting or aligning us (that is, Tangram and the university actors) with a new powerful obligatory point of passage and translation center in the form of The Pirate Bay and their actor networks. What allowed this temporary but effective infrastructure to develop was a shared value system that enabled the actors to gather around the boundary object, which in this case was a free Creative Commons film.

Many would agree that the release tried out a new and innovative way of distributing and funding film and suggested an alternative view of the value of cultural products. But what were the politics of participation, and how democratic? The collaboration came about primarily through personal contacts and through networking.[6] The Living Lab the Stage, making use of earlier research and development conducted with Good, connected to Tangram, which together with the researchers teamed up with The Pirate Bay and with various media and tech people, and finally made the experiment public and debatable. This initial phase of "connecting" was therefore highly exclusive and not particularly accessible to other film companies—a feature it shares with most state-funded or regionally funded research and development projects. This is not particularly democratic if you don't consider lobbying to be a new viable form for conducting democracy. (See chapter 9.) However, given that many EU research and development funds, exemplified by the research and development accounted for here, are considered to be democratizing arenas (Erlingsson 1999), the lab took the stance to work with partners typically excluded from research and development. The reasoning behind this stance was that a central aspect of democracy is not only to cater to the majority rule, but also to pay attention to those in minority and at times ignored by those in power. When the release was made public, participation and discussion were welcomed. However, the discussion it generated was one-sided, coming primarily from people who had positive attitudes toward open, shareable, and free culture. Those controlling the current film financing and distribution in Sweden remained silent, perhaps because they didn't want to enter the debate, as that would acknowledge that there was an issue to be debated. The release, thus, was highly political, as it wanted to address who gets to tell stories, in what way stories are made accessible and to whom, and how they can be reworked.

A commons battle: Creative commons, remixing, and funding

The close relationship between innovation and copyright, which the release of *Nasty Old People* challenged, is well documented (Frow 2000; Vaidhyanathan 2001). The battle over the last two decades has been largely about how to protect creative work and how it can be cited, reworked, and monetized, which in turn relates to and affects how it is financed. The copyright law, as Lobato (2008, 2012) argues, came about to ensure that cultural producers would be rewarded for their work and to foster future innovation. Copyright has become so entrenched in the Western culture that it for a long time was considered as "a common-sense way of protecting the rights of cultural producers" (Lobato 2008, 17). However, as Lobato argues, "copyright is also a historically and culturally specific ideology, one founded upon modernist notions of innovation and deeply embedded in capitalist thought and practice" (ibid.). The common sense of copyright has more recently been questioned in the struggle for redefining how we approach the future in innovative ways.

The release of *Nasty Old People* was seen in this light by the journalist Sofia Mirjamsdotter (2009), who presented it as forward-thinking and modern. In the same post, she contrasts *Nasty Old People* to the new Swedish film commission report: "Yesterday, the new film commission report was presented, which was done by Mats Svegfors. He suggests, among other things, higher taxes on cinema tickets. Another suggestion is that the state takes over the film politics. It really does not feel like 2009, more like 1939, or something like that" (author's translation).

The release, clearly, cannot be analyzed in isolation. The intervention challenged current film distribution and funding practices by trying out new forms for distribution and funding. As such, it connects to national and international debates and sociomaterial struggles relating to film distribution and funding; a debate and struggle that has to a large degree centered around copyright and piracy in relation to networked technologies. This demands what Clarke (2005) calls "social worlds/arena analysis," or what Clarke and Star (2007) call "infrastructure arena mapping"—that is, an analysis that focuses on the main discursive perspectives as well as on how meso-level human and nonhuman stakeholders (communities and organizations) act. The aim of such an analysis is to identify commitments and how the actors (be they communities or organizations) frame and interpret the issue.

The Swedish funding and distribution infrastructure

Since the early 2000s, Sweden has seen the emergence of The Pirate Bay, the largest file-sharing service on the Internet, which has taken a critical stance toward how cultural products and knowledge is locked down, monetized, and controlled by largely big corporate interests. On the other hand, Swedish film financing and distribution—which is one of many important public spheres in Sweden that cut across public and private funding—has during the last decade adamantly wanted to protect copyrighted material and fight piracy and ensure that the existing distribution infrastructure is protected.

The Swedish Film Institute's objective, on behalf of the Swedish government, is to "support the production and development of valuable Swedish film; to support the distribution and screening of films of value in various viewing formats across the whole of Sweden; to preserve and develop the Swedish film heritage and make it accessible; [and] to collaborate internationally and strengthen the export and screening of Swedish film abroad" (Svenska Filminstitutet 2012, 4). Swedish films, produced within a small language area, are highly dependent on state financing and rarely break even (Statskontoret 2013). SFI's yearly production budget for films is only about 23 million euros, 51 percent of which is tax-based funding from SFI, regional film funds, and Swedish public television. The film producers, through their own investments, fund 19 percent. The remaining 30 percent comes from private media companies and to the largest degree from theater ticket sales paid by Swedish cinemagoers. Since 2007, the media group Bonnier controls SF, a company that owns 95 percent of all theaters in Sweden and is, according to the Swedish Film Agreement, obliged—just as all theater owners are—to pay 10 percent of proceeds from ticket sales of Swedish and foreign movies to SFI. Accordingly, the funding and the distribution of film in Sweden are tightly connected, as they cut across public and private funders. Only the distributors (more precisely, one distributor—SF) make sizeable profit through ticket sales, which raises the issue whether state funds should support private profiting of cultural products by supporting actors that considerably limit the access to these largely state-funded products.

The two latest Swedish Film Agreements (Svenska Filminstitutet 2006, Svenska Filminstitutet 2013) state that the partners, besides the SFI objectives listed above, should increase the number of visits to theaters and should support the work against illegal viewing of Swedish film, on which SFI spends 900,000 euros per year.[7] It is interesting that these film agreements were negotiated without the representation of Swedish directors. Two statutes that address accessibility connect to governmental guidelines, which demand that SFI should make a wide assortment of films available in a variety of media outlets to as big and as diverse audience as is possible in the whole of Sweden (Statskontoret 2013). The government-commissioned inquiry carried out by Statskontoret states, however, that SFI to a small degree has worked on making films broadly available and has focused mainly on theater distribution (ibid.). This at a time when the average Swede sees two films per year in the theater, while 78 out of 80 films are seen in other media outlets. (On average, Sweden has 15 million theater visits per year, which can be compared to the 1950s when visits to the cinema amounted to 80 million per year) (ibid.). Also, as Bonnier is a privately held commercial company, it understandably prioritizes theater screenings of productions that it has funded (Hirschfeldt 2012). Furthermore, outside Stockholm, Gothenburg, and Malmö, the number of titles available is small and mainly consists of U.S. blockbusters. The Film Agreement partners—the state, SFI, regional film centers, theater owners, and film production companies—therefore can be said to work for upholding the current infrastructure for funding and distributing film. The Film Agreement also doesn't pay much attention to, or cater to, the fact that the consumption of film—which has increased—has changed as viewers more frequently choose other media outlets than theaters, at times illegal media outlets as viable legal alternatives have not been available.[8]

Film distribution, as the above account shows, is not a mere technical infrastructure but rather a complex interweaving of socio-technical-economical arrangements that are culturally and geographically specific. But, although they are geographically specific, the local is entangled in the global networks in a complex way, as Lobato argues (2008, 2012). Another word for socio-technical arrangements is infrastructure, which are ongoing negotiation processes between various local circumstances and more overarching needs of defining common socio-technical standards and conducts (Star and Bowker 2002; Star and Ruhleder 1996). Infrastructure is not a given stable entity, and considerable work is needed to uphold infrastructures. If an infrastructure stabilizes over an extended period of time, it often becomes a "frozen discourse," naturalized, invisible, and normative. When it breaks down, or when cracks appear, it becomes visible. That an infrastructure needs constant maintenance work to be upheld means that one can step into these infrastructures and reconfigure and influence them to some degree. This is, however, not easy to do, although Star (1991) argues that a renewal is possible in the margins or by those marginalized by prevailing infrastructures. The notion of infrastructures and socio-technical arrangements helps to make visible how distribution and financing of film stretches across state institutions, markets, private artistic ambitions and norms, and technical aspects. These spheres are highly entangled and cannot be separated, which is in line with Barry's (2001) notion of technological zones. The distribution of *Nasty Old People* created, temporarily, a new infrastructure through new alliances and alignments of actors that had not worked together before.

Arena analysis of piracy and the qualities of Creative Commons

Lobato (2008) effectively summarizes some of the main perspectives on an international arena on the topic of piracy and how it relates to copyright, shared knowledge, and future possibilities. His "arena analysis" points at how great the divide is between how culture should be shared and how various organizations and communities "meet" and perform around the topic. Furthermore, he suggests that the debate needs to move from focusing on whose *properties* we want to support to focusing on whose *future* we want to support.

The "piracy as theft" perspective, put forth by strong trade associations such as the Motion Picture Association of America, aims to protect large Hollywood-based film studios' special interests even though it is unclear whether there is a strong link between file sharing and a loss of revenue. The opposite perspective, "piracy as free enterprise," argues for liberating and even doing away with copyright. According to proponents of the "piracy as free enterprise" perspective, it would supposedly increase creativity and economic development (Kinsella 2008; Choate 2005; Paradise 1999). This extreme laissez-faire position mainly frames the debate in relation to a market-driven logic where piracy is not considered a problem. The "piracy as free speech" perspective, promoted by Lessig (2001, 2004), the Creative Commons movement, and Libertarians, argues that a balance between private interests and commons is needed. For proponents of the "piracy as free speech" perspective, it is essential to check big business monopolies. According to Lobato (2008, 2012), this perspective is strongly Western, mainly supports and benefits the Western creative class, and is admired by an academic elite that fetishizes the cut-and-paste remix culture. The "piracy as resistance" perspective, which is closely linked to the Copyleft movement, builds on Marxist labor perspectives that point at how media productions are created by a large body of workers, but only a few workers gain economically from the labor. From this perspective, file sharing—as Lobato (2008, 2012) states—becomes a political agenda where the aim is to work against this division of labor. Many proponents of this perspective are, not surprisingly, against market-driven media productions. The "piracy as access" perspective, which has grown out of postcolonial, legal, and developmental studies, is interested mainly in the power of dissemination of knowledge and culture, rather than in the ethics of property. We need, Lobato (2008, 2012) argues, to refocus the debate to whose future we want to support instead of whose property needs protection. The main concern of the "piracy as access" perspective is how information and knowledge production can be made accessible to those disempowered, so that they can uphold their activities and their work, which today demands engaging in piracy as many copyrighted products are too expensive to purchase. (See, for example, Philip 2005 or Sundaram 2001.) The loss of revenue due to piracy, Lobato (2008, 2012) argues, is often highly exaggerated, as piracy is often a form of what Davis (2003) calls "cockroach capitalism" that operates in markets which the media institutions have found uninteresting, where pirated materials are the only options available. Piracy, he argues, can therefore be seen as "routes to knowledge, development and citizenship," rather than primarily as "deviant behavior" (Lobato 2008, 16). Tangram, not surprisingly, views piracy as free speech, as resistance, and as access, while the film agreement views it as theft.

Hanna Sköld, the director of *Nasty Old People*, was at first indecisive whether she should release the film under a Creative Commons license, mainly because she felt that it was her work and that it should not be opened up for others to rework. Creative Commons was developed as an alternative to intellectual-property licenses because

Figure 10.3
The premiere of *Nasty Old People* in Kiev.

the copyright law was considered to have become too restrictive and mainly benefitting large media companies. This licensing scheme thus aims to create a better balance between (on the one hand) private ownership and rights and (on the other hand) the common good and cultural heritage.[9]

"It of course felt strange for me to let anyone remix the film," Hanna Sköld stated in a newspaper interview (Arbsjö 2009, author's translation). In the end, however, she decided to release it under a Creative Commons Attribution-NonCommercial-Share-Alike (CC:BY-NC-SA) license, which meant that the film may be copied, distributed, and shown as long as the author is credited, the use is not commercial, and derivative works are licensed in the same manner as the original. Hanna motivated her decision with the following statement posted on the *Nasty Old People* blog (nastyoldpeople.org 2010):

To us it's important with free art and culture, and if all features are made by big corporations and funded by the same institutes all over the world, the culture is no longer free. Then the stories that reflect and create the societies we live in will come from just a few sources, perspective on the world will be excluded, and there will be voices around the world that will never be heard.

This is why we started the shooting with just our passion to tell the story and a bank loan of 10 000 euros, to cover the most basic expenses. We worked together for hundreds of hours of non-paid work and despite lack of money and equipment we managed to finish the shooting of *Nasty Old People* on 32 days over a period of nine months.

With no money you need something else: Creativity, nights, lots and lots of tape and many very kind people. Most of the scenes in the feature are shot in the homes of the team and the actors.

In a later interview, she stated:

To me, it's a principle: the less ownership you demand the more you can do together and the better it becomes. If the film can live on and be used for other expression it is super good." (Arbsjö 2009, author's translation)

When interviewed by *Helsingborgs Dagblad*, she stated:

At first, I was in doubt. I wanted the film to be as we wanted it, but when the first remix that others had done came, I felt 'God, this is really exciting.'" (Bergdahl 2009, author's translation).

These motivations resonate with arguments put forth by creative producers using Creative Commons licenses. Andrea Hemetsberger (2003), as Rachel Cobcroft (2010) notes, has identified "publicity," "legal certainty," "reciprocity," "public good," and "co-creation" as the main incentives for using the licenses. "Publicity" and "legal certainty" point at how the license allows creators to distribute their work freely without making fans engage in illegal activity. At the same time, they can maintain creative integrity and legal control, which is trustworthy, transparent, and cheap, as no expensive lawyers are needed. And, as Hanna says, she wants the film to spread as much as possible and not be locked down by strict copyright laws and agreements between artists, companies, and institutions, but at the same time she has expressed how she wants to maintain certain creative and financial control over the material. Many artists feel that Creative Commons gives them greater control over their work than other legal agreements.

"Reciprocity" builds on the expectation that contributing to the commons will benefit the creators economically, socially, and culturally. Hanna Sköld has, on several occasions, expressed how an open and giving attitude is rewarding, as people give back. The *Nasty Old People* release also shows how the fans were willing to help distribute and market the film, subtitle it into various languages, and arrange home screenings. Fans actively engaged in the distribution not only by seeding the film but also in helping to spread the word, which at times met unexpected resistance. For example, Facebook blocked links posted on Facebook leading to the *Nasty Old People* torrent file on The Pirate Bay, apparently assuming that any link to The Pirate Bay equaled a link to illegal copyrighted material. Fans, however, gave each other tips on how this could be circumvented so that the news about the release could be spread on Facebook. One of the translators of subtitles stated that he thought his contribution was worth more than donating a small sum of money. The social gain was thus considerable for the *Nasty Old People* team.

The release also provided additional social and cultural capital. Tangram gained many followers, became well known in Sweden and in parts of Europe, and has been invited to show the film in small theaters from Kiev to Los Angeles. Hanna Sköld has been invited to talk about "alternative film distribution" at seminars and conferences (including the Barcelona Creative Commons Film Festival, which was started as a result of the release of *Nasty Old People*). The concept of the Creative Commons Film Festival, itself licensed as NonCommercial-ShareAlike, has since spread to South America and Africa. In 2013, the first Scandinavian Creative Commons Film Festival was held. Interestingly, the festivals also aim at establishing a new way for directors and producers to distribute their films directly to independent theaters and the audience.

The notion of "co-creation" concerns making works available for others to build upon through remixing and mashups. The remix and mashup culture commonly questions, as is well known, the position that a work can be viewed as belonging to one person; it believes that cultural expressions always build upon and appropriate others' work. Hanna Sköld, as stated earlier, was at first reluctant to let others build upon her work. Her initial reluctance turned, however, into positive excitement as she saw the first remix posted to YouTube.

"Reciprocity" and "co-creation" show that the audience is willing to help and contribute to the media production if there is a sense of belonging, if there is a shared concern, and if a shared value system is in place. The sense of belonging and the shared concern can vary depending on whether the perspective is that of "free culture," that of "independent cinema," or that of "alternative stories." A common ideal sought after, however, is connection. Being in a close relationship—perhaps even an intimate relationship—with the creative team is valued. This is a relation that goes beyond mere consumption and includes, in various degrees, creative engagement. However, intimacy is hard to scale up, as it asks for a one-to-one relationship, which is hard to maintain if there are more than a few relationships.

The "public good" perspective concerns making publicly funded research and cultural productions, as well as state-funded institutional documents, more open and accessible. To work for "public good" may be tricky for purely state-funded institutions, but it is considerably trickier for actors who have to operate in a mixed economy of state and private funding. The *Nasty Old People* team's fight for Creative Commons and the common good has met with considerable resistance in Sweden and Europe. Finding a balance between private property, capital, and commons remains a challenge; it raises fundamental questions about how independent actors can operate outside the system, about the current infrastructure of film funding, about how the relationship between private funding and state funding can be configured, and about how independent initiatives are to be understood given the current state of cultural politics and policy in Sweden.

Crowd-funding in relation to broadened financing and Swedish cultural politics

Film financing is tightly connected to copyright and distribution, and thus to ideological and political perspectives that concern creative autonomy, audience relations, and the politics and policies of cultural funding. For some time it has been debated whether Sweden should open up for widened cultural financing. Fundamental to that debate is the relationship between culture and commerce. Swedish film is considered both culture (since it receives public funding) and as an industry (since it is expected to survive on the market even though only one tenth of Swedish films break even). Broadened financing is thus already a central part of Swedish film production. However, very few films get funding from other public and private sources if they have not received funding from SFI.

Karlsson (2010) describes how those who favor broadened funding believe that the state should not have the sole influence on what culture should be funded, an ideological argument favored by right-wing parties that want to break the hegemonic power of the state. Very few, if any, of these proponents believe it is realistic with a completely neo-liberal market-driven culture, Karlsson (ibid.) argues, even though they may argue for broadened financing and increased entrepreneurial ways of working. Karlsson also points out that the cost for culture constantly increases while the tax base decreases. From a state financial perspective, broadened financing is therefore a necessity. Karlsson (ibid.) also discusses how broadened funding can be favorable for cultural workers. Having the opportunity to turn to different funders when one funding source turns a project down makes cultural workers less vulnerable and may ensure diversity and more artistic freedom. He describes, for example, how cultural workers can turn to regional or state funds when municipal funds fail, or vice versa. Karlsson thus favors broadened funding. He cites Sven-Eric Liedman's remark that "a work practice that is always dependent on economic support from the outside (even donations) survives best if it has more than one master." (ibid., 70, author's translation). However, getting film funding in Sweden is for the most part highly centralized, and hinges on the judgment of two film consultants at SFI, since other financers are reluctant to fund projects that have not received the blessing of SFI. In an international perspective, as Karlsson states, the cultural politics of the Swedish government is unusually strong, as tax-deductible donations are not possible and private independent foundations are few. As Karlsson points out, the only example of larger independent cultural foundation was Framtidens kultur, which started in 1994. In 2011 it was turned into Kulturbryggan by the right-wing government whereby the government demanded that independent cultural institutions and workers needed to match Kulturbryggan's funding with private funding.

The need to act outside established systems has a long tradition, and do-it-yourself and independent scenes have existed for decades for the arts in general and films in particular. Today, DIY actors and non-governmental organizations can fund their projects through online crowd-funding sites or by setting up their own donating campaigns (as the *Nasty Old People* team did when governmental and regional film funds were out of reach). It isn't easy—especially for un-established and unknown actors—to act outside the state funding system and finance film productions through donations or crowd-funding. Two additional questions are whether such funding strategies spur the Swedish government toward a more individualized entrepreneurial and liberal cultural funding policy and whether financing through donations or crowd-funding is a viable option for small cultural producers.

Before the launching of *Nasty Old People* on The Pirate Bay, the group discussed various financing strategies and which values should be promoted. For example, should there be non-monetary forms of donation, in order to enable participation for those who can't donate money? The idea of accepting other forms of donations was inspired by the Canadian musician Jane Siberry, who had experimented with online financing even before Radiohead's famous 2007 experiment in which one could purchase the album *In Rainbows* by paying however much one wanted to pay. Siberry's "pay-what-you-can" policy showed that buyers were willing to pay more for songs than the iTunes Store charged. When buying her songs, one could see the average price that the customers were willing to pay, which created transparency and made the customers aware of what her fans were willing to pay or how they valued her music. For a while she even encouraged people who felt that they could not pay at all to pay by "doing a good deed," more specifically to send a postcard to a loved one that they had not been in contact with for some time. It is difficult to say if this was a genuine gesture or if she wanted to point at what small amounts she was asking for: the price of a stamp.

Donations, as Vasiliev (2011) argues, means that the audience or consumer sets the price instead of the market. Donations can also be made to support the creators (which can be a form of activism, the product or experience being seen in relation to a political and cultural context that the donator wants to influence). Donation, according to Cox (2010), is often tied to an underdog position and seen as authentic. Cox also argues that film, music, and other forms of cultural productions should be viewed as public goods, and that the cultural industry should be financed through various mechanisms controlled by the public sector.

In the end, the *Nasty Old People* team decided to go for monetary-only donations and to accept them through the *Nasty Old People* blog. A decision to use PayPal as the payment service was made after several other options were considered. The biggest disadvantage of using PayPal was the business model, which is expensive if only small amounts of money are contributed. Another problem was that PayPal sets its own currency rates, which were to PayPal's favor if the donation was in another currency than the account you donated to.

About 250 people, out of the approximately 35,000 who downloaded the film, donated a total of approximately 5,000 euros. Another 5,000 euros came from SVT, which broadcast the film as part of their series on new independent filmmakers; that made it possible to pay back the bank loan in full.

The ratio between downloaders and donators may seem poor, but it fits well with participatory trends on the Internet. It is commonly known that only about 1 percent of users of a particular site or community are actively engaged, about 10 percent are moderately engaged, and the rest are passive onlookers, also called lurkers. This goes for most forms of online engagement, whether money is involved or not. Running the campaign was quite time consuming, since it was necessary to build up trust and to be in constant dialogue with the audience. Getting the whole loan funded through donation would have required getting considerably more people to download the film, which would have required an even larger campaign.

A distribution and financing campaign such as that for *Nasty Old People*, however, cannot be measured from a monetary perspective. The campaign builds up a considerable network, a potential future audience, reputation, and cultural capital, at least within certain subcultures. The members of the audience, at least some of whom share common values, such as free culture, not only donate money but also become ambassadors and even team members as they help to spread the film, provide new subtitles, and arrange theater screenings in their home countries. Nevertheless, the distribution and the financing of a film needs to address what it means for a small independent filmmaker to operate outside the established system, specifically in relation to access to media outlets and in relation to broadened and independent funding.

When it comes to media outlets, I have previously argued how important it was for the distribution of *Nasty Old People* that it got a front-page exposure at The Pirate Bay.

However, getting such an exposure on the Web is more easily said than done. The Web has its own bottlenecks and media consumption practices. There are indications that Chris Anderson's (2007) "Long Tail," which some believed to be the savior for small niche products, doesn't seem to hold true. The Long Tail, as is now well known, was an argument that the range of offerings of niche products would increase due to the Internet, as more consumers can find niche products. Chris Anderson's study focused on the distributors, not the small producers who drown in the large media landscape. This means that small independent production companies need to create their own promotion and sales windows lest they drown in the media noise. Customers need to know what they are searching for, which today demands that one keeps updated and actively search for niche sites that cover niche topics. Today, in a time of what Gourville and Soman (2005) call "overchoice," there are so many products that we find it difficult to navigate among them. Furthermore, we are social creatures, and we consume media to be able to share and talk about the experience. This makes us want to see the same films and read the same books as the people around us.

Vasiliev (2011), referring to McPhee (1963), points out that there is a big difference between "light consumers" and "heavy consumers." Light consumers consume mainly popular products and prefer these even when they are exposed to more niche products. Heavy consumers consume both popular and niche products, but prefer the later. The Internet is therefore, not surprisingly, dominated by a few "hit" products. Large companies can buy good placements at important distribution and sales windows such as Amazon and Google. Old economically strong bottlenecks are thus replaced by new, large, and economically strong media-company bottlenecks.

For Tangram, broadened financing in the form of crowd-funding was necessary since state and regional funding were not within reach. Crowd-funding, which has gained ground particularly in the U.S. but also in Sweden, raises interesting questions related to the relationship between state funding and private funding. Many crowd-funding platforms, such as the U.S.-based Kickstarter and the Swedish Funded by Me, are privately run businesses that make money from those who use their services. More important for the discussion here, Sweden has seen the emergence of public crowd-funding initiatives. Crowdculture, one such initiative, allocates public funding if the "cultural entrepreneurs" manage to gather a crowd and reach the amount of crowd money they have asked for. In a similar fashion, Kulturbryggan, a state-run funding body geared toward independent creative groups and individuals, demands private co-funding. For every euro contributed, the independent cultural workers need to obtain one euro from private funders—something that many of them find time consuming and difficult because they are not as attractive as larger, more mainstream cultural institutions and because cultural funding is not tax-deductible. In its former incarnation as Framtidens Kultur, which Karlsson (2010) welcomed as widened form for cultural financing, Kulturbryggan was an independent foundation not governed by the state. Kulturbryggan's demand for private co-funding shows that it isn't independent from political steering and that its aim may not be to broaden the funding possibilities further but rather to push cultural workers in a more entrepreneurial direction so that the state can get more culture for less funding. Kulturbryggan, it should be noted, has presented Tangram as a good example of what Kulturbryggan wants to promote and has funded parts of Tangram's next production, *Granny's Dancing on the Table*. Is this a sign that the politicians wish to decrease the state's funding of culture? Do they wish to hand over more responsibility to the creative entrepreneurs, and to see cultural products adjusted to audiences' expectations? In other words, if consumers or private funders aren't willing to support a project, should the state fund it? Does this imply that our "successful" experiment risked pushing cultural productions toward even more entrepreneurial activities that increasingly become dependent on opaque corporate bottlenecks, driven by market populism and private funding interest, rather than state-funded bottlenecks that are supposed to ensure democratic plurality?

Granny's Dancing on the Table and ongoing infrastructuring

Because Living Lab the Stage functioned as a "future-making" environment with an open-ended structure, rather than as a project-based research project with predefined goals, the lab was able to collaborate with Tangram and Good on *Granny's Dancing on the Table*, a film project that explored how current modes of production can allow the filmic media to expand and include gaming and become more transparent and open to vernacular storytelling without losing the enchantment and aura of the silver screen. How this could be done was highly unclear at the start of the project. (For example, should the gaming elements push toward role playing, or toward more traditional online gaming?) Owing to this lack of clarity, a range of concepts were sketched, tried, and scrapped. Furthermore, it was unclear how participatory storytelling could be combined with the director's creative vision.

The ambition of opening up and expanding the filmic medium meant that new competences needed to be connected to the team. The lab contacted Ozma Game Design, a firm that had developed traditional games as well as more participatory gaming experiences. It also commissioned Kore Film and Transmedia to develop characters and the initial plot for the "transmedia" world that became partially included in the story world put together by the extended *Granny's Dancing on the Table* team. This expansion created some confusion about roles, responsibilities, and creative autonomy.

Experiments in opening up the production process have included inviting followers to participate in scriptwriting. Through the film's Facebook page, people were asked to contribute anecdotes and their thoughts on three topics addressed in the film. More ambitiously, the team designated August 21, 2011, a celebratory Granny Day—a day dedicated to bring forth, in a commemorative gesture, multitudinous vernacular stories

Figure 10.4
Still from the *Granny's Dancing on the Table* feature film pilot.

about grandmothers, stories that had not been acknowledged or been considered worthy to be included in public memory practices. Through vernacular storytelling workshops and online participation, people from all over the world contributed stories about grandmothers. These stories were also made public through street art and media guerilla tactics by posting them in the streets of Malmö. Later in 2011 the Serbian city of Novi Sad held a Granny Day activity, and on August 21, 2012 the Swedish team arranged its second Granny Day, which included an exhibition at Malmö's Form and Design Center. These events, where audiences have engaged in active creation, has influenced the script and film production. Hanna Sköld, for example, has used some of the Granny stories when shaping the Granny character in the film.

The financing of the project has included considerable pitching and project application work, with both hits and misses, as is common in the film industry. The successes have included being awarded the 2010 ARTE Pixel Pitch Award, which besides the recognition included 6,000 British pounds in prize money. In 2011, *Granny's Dancing on the Table* received 60,000 euros from Kulturbryggan and 20,000 euros from Kulturkontakt Nord to develop "Art Pieces," a production that explored how to develop

Figure 10.5
Granny Day.

participatory artistic processes that engage the audience in the development of, for example, the film music, the set design, and the clay animations that are one of the aesthetic expressions used in the film. Getting funding for exploring how participatory audience engagement can be creatively put into play has been fairly easy, and is where the production team has expanded the most. Getting funding for the feature film and the game has been more difficult, because the competition for film money is fierce, because there is hardly any national or European funding for transmedia productions, and because the gaming concepts developed have been heavily character-driven and story-driven (something that game funders tend to shun). And financers have found it difficult to accept the demand that the film be released under Creative Commons and released in parallel online and in theaters. Nonetheless, the producers were able to get several co-funders on board. SFI was at first quite receptive to the script and the pilot, but suddenly withdrew from engagement. What was behind the sudden change is far from clear, but it is not far fetched to guess that SFI and other film funders found it difficult to team up with a film company that had sided with The Pirate Bay.

During the spring of 2012, the difficulty of finding funding led the team, in an act of frustration, to launch a Kickstarter campaign that was simultaneously promoted at The Pirate Bay's Promo Bay. The campaign raised 50,000 U.S. dollars, which meant that the first shootings of the film could be made. That campaign had many similarities to the first one, as it built on good contacts and clever viral marketing and once again showed that online outreach played an important role, whereas exposure in traditional media, such a newspapers, had no impact at all. When it comes to the funding of the film, the team has had to operate, as with the *Nasty Old People*, as DIY filmmakers that aren't able to enter the official funding system, at least not yet. This implies that engaging in cultural commons film production doesn't go well with the current mix of state and private funding that dictates how films are produced and distributed in Sweden.

Conclusion

Collaboration on *Nasty Old People* and *Granny's Dancing on the Table* has provided opportunities to try out, and to some degree challenge, current models of film distribution and to explore new expanded forms of filmic storytelling. These activities have, in turn, given insights into the practicalities and politics of future-making activities related to Swedish film production, in particular how such activities relate to infrastructuring, democratization, cultural commons, and funding.

The collaboration described and analyzed above points at how an open-ended and ongoing infrastructuring approach to collaborative explorations of future-making practices opens up for ways of working that are different in form from the classical research and development project. Open-ended infrastructuring allows for partner constellations to grow as issues become defined. It also shows how the form enables both quick-footed organizing and longer-term engagements in which issues, roles, and interventions take longer to define, as there is a tolerance for drifting and trying out various ideas and identities as the actors have gained insight into each other's constituencies, skills, and accountabilities.

The collaboration furthermore shows that there is a close connection between the ways of organizing activities and interventions and the emergence of a new distribution infrastructure—and distribution practices—for film, as a new film distribution and financing infrastructure may grow out of the network constellation through the work of the Creative Commons Film Festival and The Promo Bay. The collaboration points toward the closeness between a particular issue and socio-technical networks. Infrastructure is never solely technical; it is a lived practice in which techniques of access and control and social relations are fostered and kept at bay.

Given that infrastructuring are socio-technical processes and techniques involving agreements, alignments, and distribution of power, designers and researchers with democratic ambitions need to consider how democratic ideals can be promoted. Whereas von Hippel (2005) argues that innovation has been democratized because citizens have greater access to tools and information, I argue that access to knowledgeable and skilled networks of people is more essential. Thus, if innovation is to become truly democratic, a diversity of citizens should be given the opportunity to connect with skilled and knowledgeable people. The reason that Living Lab the Stage started to collaborate with Tangram and Good was based on the democratic ideal that those often excluded from the making of futures should be given the opportunity to influence how aspects of Swedish film's future could look like. At the same time, I point at how the constellation of partners builds on established connections, and how it was successful and agile because it operated, at least to begin with, as a closed, highly skilled, and exclusive network. On the other hand, the number of participating actors exploded as the project went public, which led to unforeseen actions such as the launch of the Creative Commons Film Festival and the establishing of The Promo Bay.

Working for cultural commons within the current financing and distribution culture appears to be difficult. One reason is that the discussion around commons is locked down in a discourse focused on the producer-consumer battle, rather than a discourse on whose future we want to promote. Taking the step for cultural workers to work for cultural commons is not just a question of access and commerce, but also relates to how willing cultural workers are to ease on their "moral" rights so that other cultural workers can build upon their work. For Hanna Sköld, it was not—at first—evident that *Nasty Old People* should be released under a Creative Commons license, with the attribute share-alike, as that meant giving up the control over the artistic creation and the team's professional integrity. Opening up a production so that others can build upon it can, as we have seen, be highly rewarding. There are, of course, instances where share-alike is not applicable; for example can it be problematic when it comes to sensitive and controversial documentaries, as they could be reworked into propaganda by regimes and radical groups. However, the main obstacle for Tangram has been to convince financers of the value of a cultural commons practice, which is not necessarily embedded in the Creative Commons licenses, by making Hanna's next film freely accessible on the Web. The film "industry," it seems, favors enclosure and commodification over access and re-workable knowledge.

In a more speculative manner, the issue is raised whether the *Nasty Old People* and *Granny's Dancing on the Table* projects risk becoming "good" examples of how cultural workers, if they are willing to be entrepreneurial, can largely manage on their own, with reduced or no state funding. Current funding and distribution infrastructures that mix state funding and the private market have their bottlenecks. However, I argue that if the current infrastructure were to become even more private and commercial then cultural workers might have to operate within an infrastructure that would have other forms of bottlenecks and would be even less transparent, less democratic, and less likely to work for the diversity of cultural expression.

Discussion

Lobato (2008, 2012) argues that there is a need to refocus the debate on copyright, which has been too narrow. He suggests that it needs to focus on whose future we want to support, rather than on how products can be increasingly locked down and protected in a producer-consumer battle, as we have seen with stricter copyright laws, increased fines and various attempts with Digital Rights Management. Within co-design and participatory design, there is a similar discussion on where the focus of design should be: Is the designer to focus primarily on developing new tools or rather new mediated practices? As I have argued before (Björgvinsson 2008), participatory design from the beginning (Ehn and Sjögren 1991) saw design primarily as a broad open-ended activity of exploring and opening up for new practices rather than more narrow tool-centric and system-centric approaches common within IT research at the time. Suchman et al. (1998) argued for viewing design as the making of emergent practices through "occasioned technology design and use" that accountably reconfigures current practices and their constituencies. The starting point of the activities carried out by the members of the *Nasty Old People* and *Granny's Dancing on the Table* team was current concerns that explored changed future practices, rather than specific tools or mediated forms. They saw the making of futures as cultural processes where the new is approached, as Suchman (2008) describes, by disrupting particular and historically and culturally located socio-technical arrangements.

The collaboration was also made possible by the lab's ability to engage in co-production open-endedly and through an ongoing process of infrastructuring. The lab's funding was not dedicated to specific predefined projects; rather, the lab was given the opportunity to approach the future—whom to work with, what issues to address, and how—in a more explorative manner. This meant that new collaborations and new partner constellations could be established according to what issues where being addressed, and more quickly than if the lab had had to apply for funding for specific projects. The lab had thus a greater space of autonomy to direct the inquiry than many research projects are given these days. This has given the lab and its collaborators the opportunity to go from one case to another more smoothly than if the interventions had been based on a traditional project format with pre-defined budgets, deliverables, and schedules.

Building understanding and trust across practices, institutions, and people through long-term engagement has been central to this form of work. This perspective builds on Suchman's notion of co-development as an ongoing "networks of working relations—including both contests and alliances" (2002, 92), rather than being delimited to project phases with the aim of creating free-standing systems. Understanding each other's constituencies and accountabilities takes considerable time, even though it can at times be quick-footed (as happened with *Nasty Old People*). The long-term engagement was, however, important as the team started working on *Granny's Dancing on the Table*, as the constellation of collaborators expanded, and as the issues addressed were more unknown—namely to open up the creative film-making process and expand the filmic medium to include gaming and participatory storytelling. Without funding that allowed for certain autonomy, the work accounted for here would not have been possible.

The work on *Nasty Old People* and *Granny's Dancing on the Table* also shows that infrastructuring is not inherently democratic. This doesn't mean that designers and researchers with democratic ambitions should not engage in infrastructuring activities. Rather, it suggests that design and media researchers engaged in action-oriented research on future possibilities and future practices should carefully consider what actors are given the opportunity to participate in the making of futures. This is essential, as access to tools means very little if it is not paired with access to skilled and knowledgeable people and organizations. It also means that those engaged in affecting current infrastructures, or making new infrastructures, should consider how they can do so in a democratic way rather than solely catering to special interests. Making infrastructuring more entrepreneurial and market-driven, I suggest, will most likely not make it more democratic or open for diversity. The market, consisting of private actors and corporations, doesn't have to be as transparent as governmental institutions. Neither are corporations expected to pay attention to diversity and minority issues, nor can the civil society vote on their policies or company politics.

The work on *Nasty Old People* and *Granny's Dancing on the Table* also raises the question of how to organize explorations into futures. Should all actors affected by the issues be on board from the start? The work discussed here suggests that it is not fully possible to know what actors would be involved. An experiment that fifteen years ago would have been a local, regional, or national concern now connects to global networks of actors and people, making it impossible to predict what actors to include. Thus, the enrollment of actors happened on the go. However, on a more critical note, we need to ask ourselves if, early on, we should have aimed to enroll more established actors—such as SFI—in the process, or at least started a more active and organized dialogue with them.

The making of infrastructure on the go seems to imply that it is difficult to know and control how activities can be reinterpreted and used for purposes that differ from initial intentions. For example, I raised the question whether the work carried out with *Nasty Old People* and *Granny's Dancing on the Table* has been reinterpreted to be an exemplary case of more entrepreneurial and market-driven cultural politics. Further, have *Nasty Old People* and *Granny's Dancing on the Table*, as boundary objects, been too plastic and not enough immutable across boundaries? Can an object be negatively mutable in an all too fiery and fluid world? If so, does this mean that Tangram, as a small film company, is too weak an actor to confront the established system? Does this, in turn, mean that the *Nasty Old People* and *Granny's Dancing on the Table* team should connect with non-governmental organizations that work for promoting cultural commons?

The distribution of *Nasty Old People* and the financing of it and *Granny's Dancing on the Table* were singular productions. These productions, and in particular the distribution of *Nasty Old People*, had considerable impact, as they led to international engagement and to the launching of the Creative Commons Film Festival. However, for a more fundamental rebalancing of how cultural products are made and made accessible, one production after another—although important—will not suffice. Laws will have to be changed, or alternative licenses (such as Creative Commons licenses) will have to become more widely spread, and durable organizations capable of countering the strong lobbying and singular view on piracy and the monopoly of cultural funding and access will have to be established. The attributes of durable commons identified by Hess and Ostrom (2003) seem to fit the Creative Commons organization, although cultural producers point out that they have no way of monitoring whether their licenses are respected, and that they don't know of any sanctioning systems that can determine whether a license has been breached, nor do they have access to inexpensive ways to resolve a conflict. The Creative Commons Film Festival, as it is nested within a Creative Commons licensing regime, has some of the attributes of durable commons. However, becoming a durable commons organization for distribution and archiving, which includes migrating films to new formats and platforms, requires stable resources. Basing such an organization entirely on free labor leads to precarious work and a precarious organization. The Creative Commons Film Festival has worked hard to build up its reputation as a respectful organization. It has done so by ensuring that they are covered by established news channels and that the festival is arranged in collaboration with established museums and arts and performance centers. The problem it faces as a commons organization is that, like any commons, it needs to be politically autonomous. Durability is particularly tricky for cultural commons organizations because they do not have natural resources they can cultivate. Getting funding from the SFI, or from some other governmental body, or from MEDIA Antenna (a European audiovisual program) probably isn't a viable option, as it would risk political filtering. Also, in view of how SFI and the European Union have favored stricter copyright laws, it isn't particularly plausible that they would be willing to support such an initiative. Many directors and producers would welcome broadened financing for film production in Sweden, which today is to a large degree based on a mono-funding structure, which in turn makes the film career for many directors and producers highly precarious. However, given the cultural political climate, it again is not plausible that the state would fund a commons film organization with complete political autonomy, and no political filtering, especially since it would have little interest in market-driven film production. Thus, it is likely that a cultural commons organization will have to concentrate mainly on do-it-yourself productions.

The notion of the marginal, the importance of actors operating outside established systems, and the importance of in-between practices are common tropes in the innovation discourse. But whether a practice is marginal depends on from where those engaged in the discourse situate themselves and where they speak from. In the case of *Nasty Old People*, it can be argued that Tangram is a marginal actor that has been admitted only marginally into the established film system in Sweden. Those engaged in cultural commons, as well as those engaged in alternative distribution formats that bypass the established order, are not as powerful as the anti-piracy agenda and the distribution infrastructure controlled by the hegemonic actors within the film industry. From another perspective, it can be argued that those engaged in cultural commons are powerfully networked and agile actors that have some impact on both the national level and the European level, as evidenced by the fact that The Pirate Bay still plays an important role in the international media landscape and the fact that the Creative Commons Film Festival is gaining increased international momentum.

The actors that have engaged in collaboration on *Nasty Old People* and *Granny's Dancing on the Table* have, because of the collaboration, changed considerably. New networks have been established, leading to access to new competences and infrastructures. For the film and gaming companies, new ways of telling stories and engaging with audiences and new ways of sharing creative work have been opened up. For the researchers, it has meant approaching the future starting from current issues and facing practices entangled in specific socio-technical arrangements. And, when doing so, the researchers have been engaged in an activist way when rearranging, at least temporarily, not only local arrangements but also arrangements that operate on the national and transnational levels. What implications this has for the methods and the credibility of research will require further analysis. At least, it seems to imply that approaching the future can be done through local preoccupation with exploring and trying out new practices, rather than decontextualized R&D operating at an imagined empty frontier (Suchman 2008). The collaborative exploration in new practices also seems to imply that such old structures as the university and new "agile" actors can fruitfully work together, and that making something new doesn't inevitably mean that the old has to be wiped out.

Acknowledgments

This contribution would not have seen the day of light without the work carried out by Richard Topgaard, my colleague, the interaction design bachelor students Nathalie Anteskog, Marie Ehrndal, Marie Lindblom, Christoffer Teves, and Christian Vilstrup as well as Hanna Sköld, Andrea Kåberg from Tangram film, Helene Granqvist from Good World AB, Karin Ryding, and Bobbi Sand from Ozma Game Design, Anna Nevander from Kore Film and Transmedia, The Pirate Bay, seeders, donators, subtitle translators, and many others.

Notes

1. Several alternative distribution and financing initiatives have been launched internationally the last five years; distribution strategies that challenge the traditional order of exposure windows, which traditionally have been festivals, followed by theater releases, followed by DVD releases, to thereafter be shown on television. More recently releasing a title on DVD and online simultaneously has become more common. Michael Moore released *Slacker Uprising* in 2004 for free for Americans and Canadians—if they registered their e-mail addresses. Wayne Wang launched *The Princess of Nebraska* the same year on YouTube's Screening Room with the aim of maximizing viewers rather than venues; it was later sold on DVD. It thus bypassed theaters, traditionally considered one of the most important distribution and promotion windows. Sites that offer a mix of free streaming and pay-per view have become more frequent over the last five years. These sites, such as Voddler in Sweden, are partly financed by advertisements. In 2010, Voddler premiered the Swedish film *Insane*. We have for some time had file sharing on the Internet. Like *Slacker Uprising* and *The Princess of Nebraska*, *Nasty Old People* challenged the order of exposure and did so by teaming up with The Pirate Bay rather than commercial actors and by arguing for the sharing of cultural products with the help of Creative Commons. A different but related trend is place-intensifying screenings. Among big commercial productions, special-effects films that can only be experienced in the theaters have become more common. Such place-intensifying strategies play upon the aura of exclusivity. For smaller niche films, such as documentaries, viewing clubs have also become more popular. Such initiatives emphasize the collective, communicative, and discursive aspects of cultural productions and are closely tied to Rasmus Fleischer's (2009) notion of the post-digital.

2. Similar promotion had been conducted before on a few occasions at The Pirate Bay. To promote the release of the album *En hi-5 och en falafel*, the Swedish artist Timbuktu released the single "Tack för kaffet" on The Pirate Bay with an accompanying doodle.

3. We do not have exact data from the traffic from The Pirate Bay, since they did not save any such data. According to The Pirate Bay's press secretary, such data is not stored, since it can be used as evidence during a court proceeding.

4. The students were not expected to participate in running a sharp project, but did so freely.

5. Certain non-human actors played important roles. As was argued earlier, having no doodle would have made for a weaker alignment.

6. The lab was open to any cultural actor and to IT and design companies in the region, and was constantly meeting new regional actors.

7. The partners are the Swedish government, Sveriges Biografägareförbund, Folket Hus och Parker, Riksföreningen Våra Gårdar, Sveriges Filmuthyrningsförening, u.p.a., Film och TV-producenterna i Sverige och Nätverket för Regionala Filmproduktionscenter, Sveriges Television (SVT), Television AB, TV4 AB, Modern Times Group MTG AB, SBS TV AB och C, and More Entertainment AB.

8. As of 2013, Svensk Filmindustri (SF) makes some titles available through the streaming service Netflix.

9. Creative Commons was adjusted and translated to Swedish law by Mathias Klang and Karl Jonsson at the University of Gothenburg and was released in 2005.

References

Anderson, Chris. 2007. *The Longer Long Tail: How Endless Choice Is Creating Unlimited Demand.* Random House.

Arbsjö, Karin. 2009. Intervju Hanna Sköld. Betala bara om du gillar vad du ser. *Sydsvenskan*, October 23.

Barry, Andrew. 2001. *Political Machines: Governing a Technological Society.* Athlone.

Bergdahl, Gunnar. 2009. I Lillhongas Fotspår. *Helsingborgs Dagblad*, November 27 (http://hd.se/kultur/2009/11/27/i-lillhongas-fotspar/).

Bertacchini, Enrico Eraldo, ed. 2012. *Cultural Commons: A New Perspective on the Production and Evolution of Cultures.* Elgar.

Björgvinsson, Erling. 2008. Open-Ended Participatory Design as Prototypical Practice. *CoDesign* 4 (2): 85–99.

Björgvinsson, Erling, Pelle Ehn, and Per-Anders Hillgren. 2010. Participatory Design and "Democratizing Innovation." In Proceedings of Eleventh Biennial Participatory Design Conference.

Björgvinsson, Erling, Pelle Ehn, and Per-Anders Hillgren. 2012. Agonistic Participatory Design: Working with Marginalised Social Movements. *CoDesign* 8, no. 2–3: 127–144.

Callon, Michael. 1986. Some Elements of a Sociology of Translation: Domestication of the Scallops and the Fishermen of St Brieuc Bay. In *Power, Action and Belief*, ed. J. Law. Routledge & Kegan Paul.

Choate, Pat. 2005. *Hot Property: The Stealing of Ideas in an Age of Globalization*. Knopf.

Clarke, Adele. 2005. *Situational Analysis: Grounded Theory After the Postmodern Turn*. Sage.

Clarke, Adele E., and Star, Susan L. 2007. The Social World Framework: A Theory/Method Package. In *The Handbook of Science and Technology Studies*, ed. E. Hackett et al. MIT Press.

Cobcroft, Rachel. 2010. The State of the Commons: Case studies 2010. *PLATFORM* special edition (December): 14–63.

Cox, Joe. 2010. Q&A: Why Money Doesn't Motivate File-Sharers (http://www.pcpro.co.uk/news/interviews/363418/q-a-why-money-doesnt-motivate-file-sharers/2).

Davis, Darrel William. 2003. Compact Generation: VCD Markets in Asia. *Historical Journal of Film, Radio and Television* 23 (2): 165–176.

Ehn, P., and D. Sjögren. 1991. From System Description to Script for Action. In *Design at Work: Cooperative Design of Computer Systems*, ed. J. Greenbaum and M. Kyng. Erlbaum.

Erlingsson, Gissur Ó. 1999. Ekonomi, demokrati och identitet i ett Europa under omvandling. Department of Political Science, University of Lund.

Fischer, Josefine. 2010. The Other Entrepreneur: Alternative Approaches to Economics, Culture and How to Do Business. CIRCLE. University of Lund.

Fleischer, Rasmus. 2009. *Det Postdigitala Manifestet*. Ink.

Florida, Richard. 2002. *The Rise of The Creative Class*. Basic Books.

Foucault, M. 1973. *The Birth of the Clinic*. Tavistock.

Foucault, M. 1977. *Discipline and Punish: The Birth of the Prison*. Penguin.

Frow, John. 2000. Public Domain and the New World Order in Knowledge. *Social Semiotics* 10 (2): 173–185.

Gourville, John T., and Dilip Soman. 2005. Overchoice and Assortment Type: When and Why Variety Backfires. *Marketing Science* 24 (3): 382–395.

Hemetsberger, A. 2003. When Consumers Produce on the Internet: The Relationship between Cognitive-affective, Socially-based, and Behavioral Involvement of Prosumers (http://opensource.mit.edu/papers/hemetsberger1.pdf).

Hess, Charlotte. 2012. Constructing a New Research Agenda for Cultural Commons. In *Cultural Commons. A New Perspective on the Production and Evolution of Cultures*, ed. E. Bertacchini, G. Bravo, M. Marrelli, and W. Santagata. Elgar.

Hess, Charlotte, and Elinor Ostrom. 2003. Ideas, Artifacts, and Facilities: Information as a Common-Pool Resource. *Law and Contemporary Problems* 66 (winter-spring): 111–146.

Hess, Charlotte, and Elinor Ostrom. 2007. Introduction: An Overview of the Knowledge Commons. In *Understanding Knowledge as Commons*, ed. C. Hess and E. Ostrom. MIT Press.

Hirschfeldt, Måns. 2012. Monopol! Kino om vem som bestämmer vad du får se på bio (http://sverigesradio.se/sida/avsnitt/45584?programid=3051).

Hyde, Lewis. 2010. *Common as Air: Revolution, Art and Ownership*. Farrar, Straus & Giroux.

Karlsson, David. 2010. *En kulturutredning: pengar, konst och politik*. David Karlsson och Glänta Produktion.

Karasti, Helen, Karen S. Baker and Florence Millerand. 2010. Infrastructure Time: Long-Term Matters in Collaborative Development. *Computer Supported Cooperative Work* 19: 377–405.

Kerrigan, Finola. 2009. *Film Marketing*. Butterworth-Heinemann.

Kinsella, Stephan N. 2008. *Against Intellectual Property*. Auburn. Ludwig von Mises Institute.

Leadbeater, Charles, and Paul Miller. 2004. *The Pro-Am Revolution: How Enthusiasts Are Changing Our Economy and Society*. Demos.

Lessig, Lawrence. 2001. *The Future of Ideas: The Fate of the Commons in a Connected World*. Random House.

Lessig, Lawrence. 2004. *Free Culture: The Nature and Future of Creativity*. Penguin.

Lobato, Ramon. 2008. The Six Faces of Piracy: Global Media Distribution from Below. In *The Business of Entertainment*, volume 1: *Movies*, ed. R. C. Sickels. Greenwood.

Lobato, Ramon. 2012. *Shadow Economies of Cinema: Mapping Informal Film Distribution*. British Film Institute.

Madison, M. J., B. M Frischmann, and K. J Strandburg. 2010. Constructing Commons in the Cultural Environment. *Cornell Law Review* 95: 657–709.

McPhee, William. 1963. *Formal Theories of Mass Behavior*. Free Press of Glencoe.

Mirjamsdotter, Sofia. 2009. Nasty Old People (http://bloggar.aftonbladet.se/1/2009/10/nasty-old-people/).

Ostrom, Elinor. 1990. *Governing the Commons: The Evolution of Institutions for Collective Action*. Cambridge University Press.

Paradise, Paul. 1999. *Trademark Counterftiting, Product Piracy, and the Billion Dollar Threat to the U.S. Economy*. Quorum Books.

Philip, Kavita. 2005. What Is a Technological Author? The Pirate Function and Intellectual Property. *Postcolonial Studies* 8 (2): 199–218.

Star, Susan Leigh. 1989. The Structure of Ill-Structured Solutions: Heterogeneous Problem-Solving, Boundary Objects and Distributed Artificial Intelligence. In *Distributed Artificial Intelligence 2*, ed. L Gasser and M. Huhns. Morgan Kaufman.

Star, Susan Leigh. 1991. Power, Technology and the Phenomenology of Conventions: On Being Allergic to onions. In *A Sociology of Monsters: Essays on Power, Technology and Domination*, ed. J. Law. Routledge.

Star, Susan Leigh, and Geoffrey C. Bowker. 2002. How to Infrastructure. In *The Handbook of New Media: Social Shaping and Consequences of ICTs*, ed. L. Lievrouw and S. Livingstone. Sage.

Star, Susan L., and Karen Ruhleder. 1996. Steps toward an Ecology of infrastructure. Design and Access for Large Information Spaces. *Information Systems Research* 7 (1): 111–134.

Statskontoret. 2013. *Scener ur et Filminstitut*. Statskontoret, Stockholm.

Suchman, Lucy. 2002. Located accountabilities in technology production. *Scandinavian Journal of Information Systems* 14 (2): 91–105.

Suchman, Lucy. 2008. Striking Likenesses to Difference. Paper presented at annual meeting of Society for Social Studies of Science, Rotterdam.

Suchman, L., R. Trigg, and J. Blomberg. 1998. Working Artifacts: Ethnomethods of the Prototype. Paper presented at annual meeting of American Sociological Association, San Francisco.

Sundaram, Ravi. 2001. Recycling Modernity: Pirate Electronic Cultures in India. In *Sarai Reader 1: The Public Domain*. Sarai/CSDS.

Svenska Filminstitutet. 2006. *2006 års filmavtal*. 2006 (http://www.sfi.se/sv/om-svenska-filminstitutet/Verksamheten/Filmavtalet/).

Svenska Filminstitutet. 2012. *Filmåret i siffror 2012*.

Svenska Filminstitutet. 2013. *2013 års filmavtal* (http://www.sfi.se/sv/om-svenska-filminstitutet/Verksamheten/Filmavtalet/).

Vaidhyanathan, Siva. 2001. *Copyrights and Copywrongs: The Rise of Intellectual Property and How It Threatens Creativity*. New York University Press.

Vasiliev, Sergey. 2011. *Den legala kostnadsfria distributionen av långfilmer*. Lunds Universitet.

von Hippel, E. 2005. *Democratizing Innovation*. MIT Press.

Webpages

http://www.facebook.com/nastyoldpeople
http://www.facebook.com/grannysdancing
http://nastyoldpeople.blogspot.com/
http://thepiratebay.org/torrent/5117424/Nasty.Old.People.2009.XviD

11 Collaborative Design and Grassroots Journalism: Public Controversies and Controversial Publics

Erling Björgvinsson

Many hoped that the advent of networked media would lead to the democratization of media. Media being central to democratic practices, there was also hope that more democratized media, in turn, would nurture civic engagement that would lead to more distributed and democratic decision making. Now that we have lived with networked media for some time, belief in the democratic potential of networked media has diminished. New media public spheres quickly develop their own hierarchies, and small elites control the debates. The impact of these new practices and public spheres on the larger media landscape is often meager and easily ignored, effectively attacked, or subsumed by larger media forces. Yet even though the new practices and public spheres face internal and external difficulties, many still believe in their importance.

The two design cases analyzed in this chapter involved public experiments in which new forms and practices of mobile-media broadcasting were co-developed to support grassroots journalism. The cases thus deal with the making of new media public spheres that build on civic engagement. They explore more decentralized media practices and civic political engagement conducted outside the official political system and outside and at the periphery of the established media landscape. The first case involved an arts and performance center,[1] cultural workers, an IT company, and university researchers; it explored how the arts and performance center could become a grassroots producer of critical media broadcast dealing with cultural and societal issues. The second case involved public service radio and TV broadcasters, a small media company, a grassroots hip-hop organization, and university researchers; it explored how a small grassroots broadcaster could adjoin, albeit at the periphery, a mass-media production by large public radio and television broadcasters. The cases will be analyzed from a co-design and innovation perspective. The focus is thus on how broadcast formats and civic media practices and public spheres were co-developed and what happened during the broadcasts.

The concepts of open innovation, co-design, prosumers, user-generated content, and a read-write culture have become widely accepted in business and in academia. These terms suggest an erosion of older distinctions such as those between the professional and the amateur, between the designer and the user, and between mass media and grassroots media. It suggests the collapse, or at least the blurring, of established institutional and professional boundaries. Whether these boundaries are more blurred now than they were twenty or thirty years ago can be debated, but during the last two decades these tendencies, which previously existed only at the margins, have become prominent in business, innovation, and academic discourses. The aim of this chapter is to shed light on what these changes may imply.

Specifically, what will be addressed is how roles and responsibilities are negotiated and distributed across competences and practices as new forms of publics are explored. Here "publics" is defined, as by Foucault (1973, 1977) and by Barry (2001), as an expanded form of governing and the political in which governing of public concerns generates multiple terrains made by particular actor networks that blur traditional distinctions between public and private and between the state and the market. For example, Barry (2001) points out that requiring seat belts in automobiles is a regulatory practice that cuts across state law, car manufacturing, and citizens' behavior. In the cases discussed here, the experiments are made possible by both public (national, regional, and municipal) and private funding. Similar to Barry's seat-belt example, broadcast technologies and broadcast and copyright laws cut across international and national laws, as well as the rules set up by the collaborating partners. This chapter focuses on how the initial issue is negotiated, defined, and redefined as organizations, people, and technologies are enrolled and made to perform. Thus, how knowledge and power intertwine and affect what spaces for negotiation are made possible, what possibilities are closed down, and how the users challenge these decisions are central issues—issues that have to do with distributed decision making, with infrastructuring, and with the everyday politics of public spheres. Another central issue is how different perspectives on innovation (future-making) are negotiated—for example, how the various partners imagine the future, how willing the partners are to imagine themselves as something else or someone else, and how willing they are to become the other as they imagine and try out future media practices and future forms of communication. The chapter also addresses how these distributed processes produce particular working relations and divisions of labor. The assumption is that the design process should be seen as prototypical exploration of future possibilities and practices (Björgvinsson 2008). Thus, the chapter addresses the question "What are the futures of such production and what do they say about division of work and responsibilities, about the politics of work, as future possibilities are imagined?" Finally, the chapter discusses what happens when research experiments enter various public spheres full of conflicting heterogeneous perspectives that are constantly becoming and constantly intersecting.

Open innovation, co-design, infrastructuring, and democratic innovation

A central assumption made by proponents of open innovation and co-design is that no partner alone has all the knowledge needed to develop new products, services, or experiences. Working across institutional and professional borders is thus necessary. How open innovation and co-design should be done and for what reasons is, however, debated. Chesbrough (2003) has studied how enterprises have come to rely increasingly on external ideas when innovating, rather than only on internally generated ideas. By combining internal and external ideas, enterprises are able to evaluate ideas on the basis of their commercial viability. The paradigmatic change from internal and closed innovation to open innovation, Chesbrough argues, is due in part to an increase in the mobility of labor. Surowiecki (2004), Howe (2008), and Brabham (2008) have argued for the harnessing of "the wisdom of the crowds" through so-called crowd-sourcing, while Petersen (2008) has argued that crowd-sourcing is a way for companies to piggyback on users and gain access to free labor. Etzkowitz and Leydsdorff (2001) have argued for the value of so-called Triple Helix incubators where universities, industry, and the public sphere intersect and engage in innovation processes. Proponents of "living labs" have criticized such traditional innovation milieus and incubators for being too closed and too far from the market and for stifling the innovation potential of Triple Helix incubators (CoreLabs 2006; Stålbröst 2008). Various "living lab" initiatives have therefore argued for situating innovation in real-world environments where user-driven innovation is carried out as research organizations, companies, public institutions, and the civic society develop new products and services together with end users (CoreLabs 2006; Stålbröst 2008). Leadbeater (1999, 2008), Leadbeater and Miller (2004), and von Hippel (2005) have argued that entrepreneurial individuals and groups residing outside more formal innovation structures are more innovative, agile, and open to collaborating and sharing competences and resources. To Leadbeater (1999), these entrepreneurs largely "live on thin air"—that is, make their living by producing ideas and realizing them through their know-how. Some critics point out that "living on thin air" is often not done by choice and is a highly insecure form of work (Born 2000); others point to the uneasy relationship between small independent actors and large corporations, noting that large corporations tend to court and seize products and competences generated by smaller companies (Wark 2006). The cultural anthropologist and feminist scholar Angela McRobbie (2009) has pointed out how Charles Leadbeater and others with allegedly neoliberal views idealize creative practices as a source of economic growth at a time when cultural practices are increasingly expected to become entrepreneurial and to be self-supported rather than funded by government grants (which has led to increased individualization, competition, instability, and mobility), when societal structures supporting young creative talent have diminished considerably, resulting in fewer small start-ups and the quick turnaround of young creative talents in multinational corporations, as McRobbie states, and when "convergence" mainly means that multinational enterprises become bigger and bigger as they acquire smaller companies. The relationship between large and small actors is therefore an uneasy one. Wark (2006) argues that the "vectoralist class," which controls, owns, and monetizes flows of intellectual property, persistently courts the "hacker class," which refines information into affective and desirable products. That big media corporations acknowledge the value and the power of independent culture, cultural resistance, and grassroots media is well known in the field of critical media studies. Enzensberger (2001), for example, pointed out how powerful enterprises aim to trap less powerful forces—media activists and grassroots media—so as to appropriate their verve. Open innovation across institutions of varying sizes is thus not always an easy match.

Research that demands extensive collaboration across professional and institutional boundaries is not only multi-sited, but also multicultural. Various institutional cultures—with distinct values and norms—need to learn how they differ and how they can collaborate. Distributed innovation, as one might call it, therefore demands that differences be acknowledged and that people with conflicting views and practices settle on what to agree upon and what to disagree upon. This means resolving conflicts on a paradigmatic level—for example, what is considered new and what the focus should be—as well as resolving how resources and competences should be organized, distributed, and shared. Of fundamental importance to such research and development projects—as Pedersen (2007) argues, building upon work by Callon (1986)—is paying attention to how the initial object of design is constructed: Is it, for example, a discrete new marketable object, or is it new ways of thinking and behaving? It is important to consider how the participants should work together, how the issues to be looked into are initially defined, and how interests, enrollments, and mobilizations of allies are carried through, as well as how moldable and open to controversy the objects to be tried out are. Unless discontinuities between contexts are resolved, collaboration will be difficult.

Resolving discontinuities between local contexts and global needs has been defined by Star and Ruhleder (1996) as the making of infrastructure, and by actor-network researchers (Latour 1999a,b, 2005a; Law 1991) as the gradual coming-together and stabilization of actor networks and black-boxing of the negotiations—or, in Latour's (2005b) words, the Things—or socio-material political assemblies—where "matters of concern" have been addressed and resolved. These perspectives acknowledge that design and innovation is, as Suchman (2002) writes, a collective interweaving of people, artifacts, and processes. This view, as Suchman notes, stands in stark contrast to views—popular in the fields of design and IT development—of innovation as the making of discrete objects and as networks of devices, rather than as networks of relations. Even though both Star (1996) and actor-network researchers emphasize that a stabilization of the actor network or infrastructure is needed, they also note that actor networks are constantly performed and are in constant "becoming" or evolving. Hence, it is more correct to speak, as Karasti et al. (2010) do, of infrastructuring as well as actor networking. Upholding relations, consequently, demands ongoing negotiations.

Latour (1999b) humorously suggested that actor-network theory could be renamed "actant-rhizome ontology," and Law and Mol (2000) pointed out that some networks are more like fire and fluid spaces, as they are simultaneously stable and unstable as they diverge and change. In view of this, "intersecting rhizomes" (Deleuze 1980; Deleuze and Guattari 1984) is a more useful term than "infrastructuring." It suggests that various networks or infrastructuring processes are less homogeneous, as they have various roots rather than one root or truth, and it suggests that certain rhizomes intersect—and thereby affect one another—but aren't necessarily aiming for stability across contexts. This is particular true when infrastructuring processes enter public spheres.

The question of democracy in relation to innovation hasn't been addressed much within the innovation discourse. However, von Hippel (2005) claims that innovation has become more democratic as access to information and to advanced production tools has become more available, enabling lead users to innovate. If that is the case, lead users can play a role in competitive elite markets (an argument that is contested in chapter 10 of this book).

Infrastructuring, or actor networking, says little about how power could or should be distributed. In fact, early actor-network research was criticized for being apolitical and for focusing too much on large and powerful actors. Star (1991) argued that actor-network theory did not take into account who benefits and who is marginalized when socio-material relations are made durable, and that we could benefit from looking at the margins where actors struggle to redefine pre-existing categories. Deleuze (1980) and Deleuze and Guattari (1984) suggested, along similar lines, that we should aim at "performing the other"—for example, being a woman, or being marginal—if we want to create new societal orders that go beyond the dualistic thinking so prevalent within Western societies.

Building upon work by Star, a few researchers, including the author of this chapter, have aimed at intertwining the notion of infrastructuring and actor networking with the Scandinavian tradition of Participatory Design. Participatory Design is a perspective that early on emphasized the political aspects of design (Ehn 1988), arguing that all partners affected by design—including those typically marginalized (e.g., blue-collar workers)—should participate in the shaping of how the tools and practices are to be combined. More recently, as Participatory Design no longer solely is engaged in design for workplaces and has entered design in and for public spheres, some proponents of Participatory Design (Björgvinsson et al. 2012b; Ehn 2008) have viewed distributed design work as a balancing act between infrastructuring (which aims at resolving conflicts across contexts) and socio-material debates, or what Latour calls "Things" (which are socio-material political assemblies). The newer Participatory Design perspective thus acknowledges, in line with Mouffe's (2000) notion of agonism, that design should not aim solely at resolving conflicts and reaching consensus, but should acknowledge that disagreement and conflicting perspectives are fundamental features of a democratic practice. Thus, how access to and sharing of knowledge can be supported, as well as how knowledge is controlled (who gets to speak, who gets to influence what is being developed, what is inscribed into the socio-technical arrangements), is central to various co-design initiatives, particularly Participatory Design initiatives.

Live mobile video reporting from a city festival

Each of the two design cases analyzed in this chapter involved public experiments in which new forms of mobile-media broadcasting formats were developed to support grassroots journalism. The first case, described here, involved an IT company, an arts and performance center, seven cultural workers, and a number of researchers from the university. This constellation of partners conducted a one-week experiment during the annual Malmö City Festival. Seven cultural workers broadcast live videos that viewers could interact with through the Web and their mobile phones. The Malmö City Festival features free concerts by international, national, and local performers. It also has art, design, film, and theater shows. In the center of the city, food stands serve foods from all parts of the world. The experiment happened because all of the partners saw that they could gain knowledge of new forms of broadcasting, increased public exposure, and the development and testing of new mobile phone audience-interaction features for live video broadcasts.

Co-design as the reproduction of established knowledge and power relations
The idea of setting up an alternative broadcast space originated at the arts and performance center. Members of the staff wanted to explore how a cultural center could be engaged in producing grassroots radio or television in which current events were dealt with from artistic and critical perspectives, with high aesthetic quality and with social relevance. According to them, traditional Swedish broadcasters ignored important subcultural expressions and perspectives. They were interested in what it could mean to a cultural center to be an independent media publisher. The IT company, which wished to be an anonymous partner in the experiment, was interested in exploring the use of mobile interfaces to enable viewers to be in direct dialogue with the broadcasters during live broadcasts, a feature that fitted well into their design portfolio and that was of interest to their customers. It was important to them that the video broadcast would be live and personalized. They argued that news today is instant and becomes obsolete quickly and that viewers want to be able to select and personalize what they consume and be in direct contact with the broadcasters. A broadcaster, they argued, must be

Collaborative Design and Grassroots Journalism

first with the news or else it will lose viewers. The IT company made a non-negotiable demand: it would participate only if the video broadcast from the festival were broadcast live. The researchers were interested in studying how such a collaborative design and media experiment could be staged and what new broadcast forms could be developed, and in working with the IT company to develop new mobile-video interfaces. The cultural workers' interests were not clearly stated at the beginning. They joined in the experiment mainly because they found it interesting and thought it might provide them with new insights and new contacts and because they were supporters of the arts and performance center.

The staff of the arts and performance center did the initial framing. In their view, the Swedish media lacked diversity, didn't cover Swedish subcultural activities adequately, and didn't have a subcultural view of popular culture and current events. For the arts and performance center the speed of broadcasting was not important, which it was to the IT company as they saw a new form of broadcasting emerge. Both the arts and performance center and the researchers thought that live broadcasting might be too demanding on the cultural workers, that it would compromise the quality of the content, and that the video quality of the broadcasts would be too low. (At the time, live mobile-video streaming yielded blurred and pixelated images and metallic sound.) The IT company, however, was able to reframe the problem and enroll and mobilize both the arts and performance center and the researchers to adopt its agenda. This shift came about partly because the IT company made its demand a prerequisite and partly because the arts and performance center would not be able to broadcast without the assistance from the IT company and the researchers. For the researchers, who could have set up a less technologically advanced broadcast solution, the participation of the IT company was essential from a funding point of view. The grant funding the researchers' salaries explicitly stated that prototypes for new media production were to be developed in collaboration with companies and it was therefore important that the collaboration did not collapse. The cultural workers were not on board at this stage and therefore couldn't affect the framing of the problem. Thus, the partner with advanced knowledge of mobile media, which also controlled the technical infrastructure and was economically the strongest partner, was able to fundamentally shift the direction of the collaboration and, consequently, making it more difficult for the arts and performance center to produce well-planned artistic and visually pleasing broadcasts.[2]

Although the arts and performance center's initial framing had been redefined, the center still had a considerable opportunity to influence the experiment—for example, who would be recruited to report, how they would report, what the broadcast would be titled, and how to shape the media outlets on the Web and in their festival café tent. The editorial strategy of the head of the arts and performance center was to recruit seven prominent figures from the local cultural scene to work *pro bono* and give them free rein in covering the festival.

The seven cultural workers—henceforth referred to as "the bloggers"—were Roger, the artistic director of The Chamber, a controversial theater company; Nouri, a leader of the grassroots hip-hop organization Elementz of the Street; Rebecka, a journalist for the biggest newspaper in southern Sweden; Julia, an actor and a filmmaker; Frida, a "club arranger" (that is, a person who arranges for bands to play in nightclubs) and the The Diva Duo (Maria and Elin), an art-and-design duo. The bloggers had no experience with live video broadcasting, and only one of them was a trained journalist. A dedicated webpage named Bloggen (meaning The Blog) was designed and programmed, and the video clips were also put on YouTube for later viewing. During the live broadcasts, viewers could communicate with the bloggers via text messages. A café tent, located at one of the central areas of the festival, was given a graphical profile clearly associated with the cultural center, and was where festival visitors could watch the broadcasts projected on a large screen. Both the webpage and the café clearly indicated the arts and performance center as the publisher.

In six days, the bloggers broadcast nearly 200 two-to-three-minute video clips. As the experiment unfolded, it yielded considerable insights into central qualities and problems of the new broadcast format as well as new design solutions—for example, that the live audience feedback was engaging to the reporters, but that texting was too slow and emotion icons would work better. Also, that the broadcasters needed visual feedback of the status of the live screen on their phones, and that the broadcasters could announce to each other a few minutes before going live that they planned to do so. It also revealed that the bloggers felt constrained by and tried to redefine and reposition themselves in relation to inscriptions—or socio-material decisions—made by the IT company, the arts and performance center, and the researchers before they came on board. Decisions such as that they were expected to do live broadcasts, that the broadcast was personalized by enabling the viewers to subscribe to individual broadcasters, that it was named Bloggen, which also signaled that their broadcast was personal, as well as their working terms. The experiment pointed out how infrastructuring, or agreement across contexts, is not only technological inscriptions, but how the technological constraints intertwine with division of labor and working conditions, the branding (the visual aesthetics and naming of the project), the bloggers' construction of a broadcast persona, so as not to confuse their role as festival broadcasters with other professional commitments and their private identity, and the audience's perception of the broadcast.

The construction of media personas and broadcasting tactics as features of infrastructuring

Infrastructuring, the aligning of inscribed norms and values across contexts, as Star and Bowker (2002) and Karasti et al. (2010) point out, involves socio-material negotiations in which ideas and material fuse into particular configurations. Whether we name them infrastructuring or actor networks is perhaps less important than the observation that they come about through the fusion of relations that are constantly in motion, that are constantly becoming, as Karasti et al. (2010), Suchman (2002), Deleuze (1980), and Deleuze and Guattari (1984) emphasize. As will become clear, infrastructuring at the intersection between the academic and professional fields of interaction design and media and communication studies is not simply a matter of what is often delimited to the material inscriptions in technical protocols and interactive interfaces, but includes the configuration of the broadcasters in relation to established inscriptions, other roles and obligations that they hold, and in relation to their fellow broadcasters. This in turn points toward why it is difficult to draw clear borders between design and use, and designer and user. In relation to innovation, and research and development, it points to the importance of co-developing the social and technical, rather than delimiting questions that concern content, identity, and roles to the later phases of development.

The bloggers, as was previously stated, had not been members of the team during the concept-development phase and the building of the prototype. This meant that the technical infrastructure and the framing, naming, and visual expression of the project were already in place when they joined. They were therefore bound by considerable constraints, which in turn meant that they needed to invest significant time thinking through, struggling with and working around these constraints as well as configure their relations to each other, as well as define and position their role as "bloggers" in relation to their professional and private identity and roles. Although not traditionally acknowledged as design work, their struggle with the inscriptions—naming and categorizations—demanded considerable "designerly" work. Categorizations and selection is thus not only a question of interface design or technical inscriptions, but also includes positioning-strategies in relation to what roles and identities are taken by the broadcasters.

The expression "video bloggers" suggested that the broadcasts were the bloggers' personal perspectives on the festival. Today, blogging consists of various genres (Sarrimo 2012). However, during the heyday of video blogging, or vlogging, of which Steve Garfield is considered to be one of the instigators (Ressner 2004; Wikipedia 2013), video blogs were thought of mainly as personal visual essays (Sydell 2005). The link between video blogging and direct cinema, personal cinema, and the cinema verité of the 1960s is made apparent by the work of Jonas Mekas, who in the 1960s made personal documentary films and who later embraced video blogging.

Most of the bloggers gave considerable thought to what role and position they should take on, a role that was neither their personal nor their professional selves. It was also important to them that the media personas chosen not resemble one another. The journalist Rebecka, who writes mostly on cultural issues, often with ethnic and gender perspectives, only once did a traditional journalistic broadcast. Instead, many of her broadcasts were artsy short films as well as snapshots of everyday "poetic" activities that had nothing to do with the festival. This made her video blogging distinct from her professional journalistic work, while not venturing into a private blogging style. Roger, who had recently been a subject of heated debate in the Swedish media because of his controversial theater pieces, decided to take on what he called a "folklig Svensson" persona—that is, an ordinary-Swede persona. Frida, although not a journalist, took on a traditional journalistic role aiming at more factual and contextualized reporting. Maria and Elin reported as The Diva Duo, wearing hip-hop-oriented outfits and acting with overwrought gusto and often with slapstick humor. Nouri was the only one of the bloggers who pretty much was himself, the grassroots hip-hop educationalist. Julia, who made rather personal visual essays, was the only one who refused to broadcast live; she saved her black-and-white films on a mobile phone and uploaded them later.

The bloggers did not intend to give personal reports of the sort typically associated with private blogs, yet there was a tendency by the audience to view their reports as personal reflections. This was because the inscriptions to some degree overpowered the bloggers' reconfigurations. The organizational arrangements—that they mainly blogged on their own—and the constraints of mobile media, which favored extreme close-ups, since the bloggers acted both as cameraman and bloggers, signaled a personalized media space. That the audience could subscribe to a particular blogger suggested, furthermore, that the viewer could enter a more personal relational media space instead of a more shared collective space. The naming of the project as Bloggen, and perhaps the newness of blogging (which was then still perceived by many to belong to private and even confessional essays) to some degree overpowered the bloggers intentions, as the reading or reception of the broadcasts is perceived as personal, even narcissistic. Even though they did not fully succeed in relation to their audience to completely reconfigure the inscriptions in place, their aim to reconfigure it shows how the bloggers saw their participation not as an isolated instance, but that their participation in the experiment and the reporting connected to wider social systems, in particular to their public roles and responsibilities within their professional domains. For them, it was important to pay attention to the symbolic or cultural significance of their broadcasts, which demanded that they spend considerable time thinking through how they would present themselves and what the "tones" of the broadcasts should be; a form of work that is often made invisible, marginalized and comes often too late in the developmental phase of design research projects, perhaps because it is highly performative and ephemeral, and because of the lack of knowledge and the importance of these issues by IT developers and designers.

Rhizomatic intersection and spatial reconfigurations through erasure
Infrastructuring, as we have seen, involves power struggles around what is to be inscribed into the sociomaterial mediascape. Previously, it has been briefly touched

upon how needs are silenced, for example the need to have a say on the broadcast quality, which was erased in favor of live broadcasting. It has also been briefly touched upon how the mise-en-scène, how the mobile interaction, the close-up recording and the design of the website shaped the experiment. It has furthermore briefly been discussed how selection, for example the selection of bloggers, is a central feature of infrastructuring. In relation to this, it is worth noting that many of the bloggers in turn relied heavily on their own cultural networks when deciding what to cover. It has also briefly been pointed out how infrastructuring connects to wider social systems, for example the bloggers professional identity, as they are public figures.

What is to be emphasized here is that the mise-en-scène also includes spatial reconfigurations through erasure conducted by cropping, as well as by overlayering. Within film and photography, these are often used and are well-known features, but are perhaps less addressed in design discussion on infrastructuring. Another central feature of infrastructuring is that it is continuously in becoming and changing, for example by connecting to other infrastructures.

That particular infrastructuring processes perpetually connects to other infrastructuring processes, as well as includes silencing through cropping and overlayering, became evident during a broadcast done simultaneously by local newspaper *Sydsvenskan* and the hip-hop blogger Nouri, at the time working for Elementz of the Street. *Sydsvenskan* had asked Elementz of the Street if *Sydsvenskan*'s youth section, *Postis,* could broadcast a poetry reading and a poetry prize ceremony outside Elementz of the Street's festival tent. Elementz's tent was chosen despite the fact that—or perhaps because—*Sydsvenskan*'s new online youth community venture Nellad had a festival tent, which was for the most part empty, close to Elementz of the Street. At the same time, Elementz of the Street's tent was crowded with teenagers attending activities run by teenagers for teenagers. (The online youth community Nellad flopped and closed down a few months later.) That *Postis* used Elementz of the Street's tent made sense since they needed a mise-en-scène of teenagers. It did not matter that the Elementz of the Street teenagers weren't *Postis* readers and weren't participating in the poetry competition. In line with *Sydsvenskan*'s need for a backdrop of energetic teenagers, not Elementz of the Street as such, the *Sydsvenskan* photographer arranged the camera in such a way that Elementz of the Street's logos were cropped out of the frame, while clearly displaying *Sydsvenskan*'s mobile *Postis* banner. (It is, of course, difficult to confirm that this was the explicit intention, but it appears to be so; every camera angle avoids the Elementz of the Street logos, which were all over their tent.) This appropriation created an exclusive *Sydsvenskan* mediascape that effectively and pristinely erased Elementz of the Street from the mise-en-scène.

Nouri's live coverage of the *Postis* broadcast also involves erasure as he, for the most part, displayed the poetry reading as a backdrop to his broadcast, explicitly overwriting or erasing *Postis*' poetry broadcast. He begins his coverage by explaining that Elementz of the Street is being visited by a *Postis* journalist, who is there to read poems, and that he will show the crew filming the event. He ends the introduction with a brief glimpse of the poetry reading and a joke. After remarking "Here is the camera crew, they wanted to do a story on me, but unfortunately that is not happening," he turns his camera toward the camera crew. After panning the camera over the area, he asks some visitors if they have written any of the poems (the answer is "No"), which leads into a discussion of teenage poems. Next he moves away from the poetry reading and starts talking to two girls in the vicinity trying out foil fencing. He then returns to the woman reading poetry and says "I am not sure, from my mouth," whereupon he starts beatboxing "Ajaw ajaw, bam bam, boom, chick ... " and drowns out and thus silences the *Postis* broadcast.

In the broadcast, which is layered on top of another broadcast, Nouri is critical of the *Postis* broadcast several times. When he jokingly states that they had planned to interview him, he points out that Elementz of the Street's activities, which he thinks deserves coverage, are ignored. When he starts beatboxing, he is further commenting that hip-hop is street poetry that is not acknowledged by *Postis* and that it is far from the self-centered existential teenage poems being read. Just as *Sydsvenskan* silences and erases the presence of Elementz of the Street by consistently cropping Elementz of the Street's banners no matter what camera angle is used, Nouri silences *Sydsvenskan*'s poetry reading by layering his voice over their broadcast. The viewer gets only a fragmented view of it and a general feeling that Nouri is bored by the event as he jumps from one thing to another, moving farther away from the *Postis* event. Thus, while *Sydsvenskan* erases Elementz of the Street's presence quietly through cropping and excluding Elementz of the Street logos, leaving no trace of it visible to the viewer, Nouri explicitly puts his act of silencing and erasure on display.

Distributed innovation across professional borders in real-life settings consequently and continuously evolves, connects, and intersects in unpredictable ways. Infrastructuring mediascapes rhizomatically connect to other mediascapes and therefore are volatile and need to again and again engage in new problematization, interessement, and enrollment (Callon 1986; Pedersen 2007). What intersection of time and place will occur is, however, impossible to predict. The case also shows the uneasy relationship between professional media and grassroots media, although they are able in different ways to gain knowledge and "products" from the collaboration. The professional media companies, be it the IT company or *Sydsvenskan*, through their power and importance, are able to get what they need by engaging in a quasi-problematization, interessement, and enrollment process, as it is valuable for an organization such as Elementz of the Street to be on good terms with them. *Sydsvenskan*, however, is not able to mobilize Elementz of the Street as their allies, as they do not become active participants and supporters of the broadcast. Instead the enrollment results in a media battle, which *Sydsvenskan* is unaware of and which doesn't lead to a constructive public dispute.

The struggle is thus one-sided, and the grassroots mediascape and the professional mediascape are like two mirrors placed back to back, one of them (the professional mediascape) without any transparency and one of them (the grassroots mediascape) quasi-transparent, allowing the professional mediascape to appear in the background.

Reproducing labor politics
Just as the design decisions reproduced existing power relations in which the IT company had the most to say about the design direction, the arts and performance center and the researchers less, and the bloggers the least, the experiment also reproduced existing working relations and labor politics. Members of the IT company's staff would work on the experiment only as part of their paid work. However, the bulk of the work hours carried out by the IT company was done by a student who worked long days as it was part of her exam project. The time put in by the staff of the arts and performance center staff and by the researchers was paid for, although the researchers needed to put in a lot of extra hours so as to ensure that the experiment would not collapse; helping out both the student at the IT company and the cultural center, and functioning as a middleman between the two. The bloggers, who represented the project's image and risked their standing the most, were the only people that were expected to participate for free, as neither the cultural center nor the research project had a budget for their participation. Thus, the experiment reproduced a form of labor common within the cultural sector.

Before the festival, several of the bloggers commented on the work burden that the broadcast would entail and the fact that the work was *pro bono*. Frida demanded a salary, or at least a free mobile phone. When the cultural center turned down her demands a day before the opening of the festival, she stated that she would not participate, but later the same day she reconsidered. Rebecka and Nouri were both concerned that the task would be too demanding, insofar as they would simultaneously be working full time. Rebecka stated that her participation would entail a lot of thinking and planning in addition to the reporting. Four days into the festival, she ended her participation after consulting with her chief editor, as it occupied her thoughts too much and infringed on her regular work. During the festival, Nouri was frustrated by the need to alternate between reporting and running activities in the Elementz of the Street tent.

Although all of the participants adjusted to the cultural center's *pro bono* demand, many of the bloggers used the broadcasting opportunity to make public their frustration with the city's cultural funding policies. Frida did a broadcast in which she stated that she opposed the festival and suggested that it would be better if the city used the money to subsidize local initiatives that arrange cultural events throughout the year (an argument also made by many of the small commercial music venues and festival arrangers, as it makes it difficult for them to book popular acts during the fall or to arrange commercial music festivals in Malmö) (Oscarsson 2010). Roger, in one of his broadcasts, tried to force the leader of a local band to reveal how little the band was paid to play at the festival, so as to expose how—according to him—the city exploits local musicians.

Frida's demand for a salary clearly shows how our experiment presupposed that cultural workers will work for free. Several of the bloggers also pointed out that their commitment to the experiment would double their workloads, as they already had other commitments, which, as McRobbie (2009) has shown, has become the expected way of living for many cultural workers. The means of production is even more problematic in the light of Thrift's (2006) argument that many businesses today have blurred the distinction between prototyping and release of products. It is worth noting that in the case being discussed here the cultural workers were well established and weren't hunting for jobs; they participated because they considered the cultural center an important alternative cultural venue. However, the experiment still shows that issues such as workload and financing are central aspects of infrastructuring, and that cultural workers are more often expected to work *pro bono* than are people in other professions. It also points to the uneasy relationship between grassroots media and large media companies. The cultural center and the IT company had quite different views on what constituted a valuable media practice, and Elementz of the Street and *Sydsvenskan* erased each other. The "new" thus turned out to be quite familiar, just wearing slightly different shoes as it strolled into the future.

The Musikhjälpen experiment

Innovation across contexts—be it open innovation or various co-design approaches—have arranged and described collaborations between various partners as structured and planned processes in the sense that what partners, what issues, and how to organize the design process, is to some extent planned in advance. The outcome of a collaboration, however, is not known in advance and is open-ended. Brandt (2001) sketches how co-design processes can alternate between field observations and collaborative design workshops, and later on between contextual design interventions and collaborative design workshops. For Binder (2007), the lab is a temporary suspension from everyday activities at work as the partners need a "what if" space in which future possibilities are explored and decisions are delayed through a defined research program. My fellow researchers and I (Björgvinsson, Ehn, and Hillgren 2012b) have argued for mixing "what if" spaces with real-life experiments. We have also argued for a more radically open-ended approach in which even what partners are involved and where and when the design activities happen are defined along the way.

In 2006, Malmö University researchers started what would become a long-term engagement with Elementz of the Street, an organization the researchers got to know because it held monthly events at the cultural center. Elementz of the Street is a grassroots hip-hop youth organization that has strong ties to *folkbildning* (popular education) and to *folkrörelse* (Söderman 2013; Sernhede and Söderman 2013), traditions that are in line with the education tradition of DuBois (1973/2001) and Dewey (1916/1999). Many of Elementz of the Street's members are children or grandchildren of immigrants, and the organization's philosophy is that multi-ethnic encounters should happen through cultural activities. Societal inclusion is addressed indirectly through rap, dance, and graffiti, rather than being explicitly on the agenda. Elementz of the Street also emphasizes active engagement, be it in the urban environment or in the Swedish media landscape. The activities of Elementz of the Street's members often counter negative images projected by mass medias.

The collaboration with Elementz of the Street started without pre-defined ideas of what to focus on in relation to new media practices, or what constellations of partners would be formed. It has led to several research and development projects and experiments in which representatives of Elementz of the Street worked with the researchers and various partners on new forms of local media distribution, experimental remix interfaces, urban games (Björgvinsson et al. 2012a), and grassroots journalism.

Musikhjälpen and the partners' agendas

In connection with a fundraising campaign called Musikhjälpen (Music Aid), a week-long street-journalism experiment was carried out in which Elementz of the Street collaborated with the researchers, with the media company Paradise Production, and with Swedish public television and radio broadcasters (SVT and SR). The collaboration, which was initiated by Paradise Production, came about just a month before the launching of the Musikhjälpen campaign.

The experiment shows how uneasy the relationship between grassroots media and larger media companies and public institutions is. It also shows that the various partners' constituencies have internal conflicts and are not as homogeneous as they often are portrayed to be, and how volatile and "constantly becoming" infrastructuring processes are when they are carried out in public settings. Furthermore, it reiterates how selection, constraints, exclusion, and branding are central to infrastructuring and how design decisions—which are also about selection, constraints, exclusion, and branding—corresponds in many ways to categorizations and selection of who participates in the design and development phases of the cases.

The purpose of the Musikhjälpen campaign was to raise awareness and money for humanitarian projects. In Malmö's main square, three radio hosts were locked in a glass cage, without solid food, for six days. The campaign was broadcast on radio and television around the clock. Its theme was "Människor på flykt," meaning "refugees." Listeners could request songs and could donate money to a bank account or leave cash near the glass cage. The aim was to attract people younger than those a traditional fundraising gala would attract.

SVT and SR broadcast from the glass cage, but also from the streets of Malmö. They outsourced to Paradise Production the task of organizing events to be put on by humanitarian and grassroots organizations in a marquee tent near the glass cage. Paradise Production's tasks were to draw people to the square, to raise awareness of refugee issues, and to make visible grassroots initiatives in Malmö. The activities were to create a closer connection between the broadcasters, non-governmental organizations engaged in refugee and immigrant issues, and the audience; a connection that the fenced-in glass cage achieved poorly. Paradise Production was hired because it had proposed not only to house arrangements by humanitarian and grassroots organizations, but also to engage Elementz of the Street in street journalism together with Malmö University researchers.

The partners in this constellation had quite different representatives, constituencies, accountabilities, and protocols. Elementz of the Street was represented by its leader during the early part of the design process. Its constituency consisted of teenagers engaged in rapping, music production, and dancing. Elementz of the Street was accountable to its members, to the municipality of Malmö, and to the general public when broadcasting during the experiment. The protocols guiding Elementz of the Street during the experiment were that it should promote meetings across cultures through cultural activities, give voice to those not heard in the public sphere, and keep its activities informal. Paradise Production was represented by its CEO; its constituency included both the temporary employees engaged in Musikhjälpen and its permanent employees. Paradise Production, as a media production company, was accountable to its employees, to SVT and SR, to film funders, and to the society, as it aims to engage in productions that make a societal difference. Its guiding protocol was to make profitable or at least break-even productions. Nouri, the leader of Elementz of the Street, reluctantly accepted a double role, as he represented not only Elementz of the Street but also himself as an artist and a public debater. His constituency consisted of his family, and he was accountable to his audience and to other artists. Nouri's protocols were to make a living through socially engaged music and public debating and to become part of the established media and music landscape in Sweden. SVT and SR were represented by the producer of Musikhjälpen; their constituency consisted of their employees and the citizens of Sweden. Their protocol was to provide public service productions from the whole of Sweden, in this case from Malmö, and broadcast media that took into account the diversity of the Swedish population. Malmö University was represented by three researchers; their constituency consisted of fellow researchers at their university, and they were accountable to their national and international research communities and to their funders. Their protocols were to see to it that their research and development activities would benefit all involved (especially those with few resources), to maintain good relations with their partners, and to explore and develop media practices, products, services, interaction design perspectives, and methods through real-life prototyping.

With this arrangement, Paradise Production saw the potential to make the fundraising campaign genuinely street-based, and to promote Elementz of the Street and Nouri. Giving Nouri more broadcast experience was important because Paradise Production, together with the researchers, had worked hard on pitching a television program idea to SVT, with a prospect of success if Nouri acquired more media experience. SVT found the campaign concept presented by Paradise Production attractive, and the researchers were enrolled and aligned to Paradise Production's problematization and interessement (although they found many aspects of the fundraising campaign problematic) and helped in the setting up of a mobile broadcasting facility. The mobile-video broadcasts by Elementz of the Street and Nouri were published online under their own domain name, but were hyperlinked to and from the official campaign website run by SVT and SR. Having Elementz of the Street's broadcasts published on the official website would have been problematic for both parties since that would have made SVT and SR the legal publisher of the broadcast, which would have entailed that SVT and SR would have to exercise more control over what would be broadcast.

Constituencies often consist of people with conflicting views, a fact that became apparent when designing the Elementz of the Street website. The double agenda of promoting both Elementz of the Street and Nouri caused a discussion among the researchers, Nouri, and Paradise Production about the choice of a domain name and the structure and visual identity of the website. Three alternatives were discussed at meetings held at Paradise Production and at the university—meetings to which the Elementz of the Street youngsters had not been invited. One proposal was to have one domain name for Nouri and another for Elementz of the Street, since they had somewhat different audiences and purposes. An alternative proposal was that Elementz of the Street and Nouri should share a domain name but have separate webpages. Yet another alternative was to have Elementz of the Street and Nouri broadcast under the same domain name and on the same webpage. The third solution was adopted, and the website was launched as nouritv.se with the heading Nouri-Kåren (Nouri Brigade) and with the subheading Elementz of the Street. This solution considerably diminished Elementz of the Street's role in the broadcast while foregrounding Nouri. Thus, the broadcast officially became primarily a vehicle to promote Nouri, so as to potentially increase the chance of selling the previously mentioned television program idea to SVT. At first the researchers and Nouri opposed this solution because it breached accountabilities and protocols upheld by both the researchers and Elementz of the Street. It also mixed Nouri's different roles and responsibilities as the leader of Elementz of the Street and his own artistic career, a mix he was uncomfortable with.

Several of the constituencies had internal conflicts but ended up aligning to a design decision that focused more on future possibilities, in this case a new SVT production, than on the immediate experiment. This points at how small actors—a small media company, grassroots media, and the researchers—align the direction of their work so as to enable a future enrollment of SVT, a large and resourceful actor, into their problematization and interessement. Thus SVT's previous statement that Nouri needed to gain more media experience had a direct impact on the design direction of the experiment. SVT, although not present, figured indirectly from a distance as a powerful actor in problematization, interessement, and enrollment.

During the six days of Musikhjälpen, Nouri and eight street journalists affiliated with Elementz of the Street broadcast 120 reports from the streets of Malmö. The broadcasts included interviews with teenagers, rapping, dancing, parlor performances, and an exclusive interview with Petter, one of Sweden's best-known hip-hop artists. All video clips were streamed live on nouritv.se, and the best clips were published on Elementz of the Street's YouTube channel.

Many Elementz of the Street members stated that it was interesting and enriching to participate in the fundraising campaign as street journalists and believed that the broadcasts made them more publicly visible. Some members also stated that during breaks between classes they would go to YouTube to watch some of their own video clips, and that the clips made them proud of what Elementz of the Street had accomplished. Many of them also said that they had learned to become more skilled reporters. At the same time, they tended to judge their broadcasts as substandard in comparison with professional mainstream broadcasts.

Infrastructuring as fleeting rhizomatic collisions of imaginaries

The real-life context of the experiment led to a volatile infrastructuring process in which unexpected disturbances in the district of Rosengård forced Elementz of the Street and Nouri to deal with conflicts both within Elementz of the Street and with the municipality. Simultaneously, Nouri battled the mass media's imaginaries of the turmoil, the stereotypic image of Malmö, and immigrants in Sweden in general. Again, this points at how infrastructuring is constantly becoming as it connects to other infrastructuring processes and, in the words of Appadurai (1996), are made up of negotiations between "sites of agency" and "globally defined fields of possibilities" that, in turn, are made up of imaginaries consisting of ethnoscapes, mediascapes, technoscapes, financescapes, and ideoscapes. These imaginaries affect our perception of the world, and thus they have to be counted as social facts. This again points at how infrastructuring and design decisions play central roles in the making of these imaginaries.

Two days into the Musikhjälpen campaign, Rosengård—Malmö's most infamous district—was in turmoil. For several nights in a row, a small group of young people set fire to rental trailers at a gas station and trash containers. The conflict began when a mosque was closed down; however, any explanation of it must mention the long-term frustration and dissatisfaction in the district, where an extremely high percentage of adults were unemployed, sub-standard housing conditions were regularly reported in the media, and there was a long history of conflict between the police and young immigrants.

The conflict in Rosengård directly affected the street-journalism experiment. That summer, Elementz of the Street had been given a building to use for street-dance classes and weekly street-journalism meetings, and a recording studio was under construction. During the Rosengård turmoil, the municipality of Malmö began to pressure Nouri to speed up the construction of the studio, threatening to revoke permission for Elementz of the Street to use the building. Suddenly, the municipality felt that Elementz of the Street had too few activities going on in Rosengård. It did not matter that dance classes were held there and that quite a few youngsters were involved in the street-journalism project. Given how the mediascape mainly portrayed the turmoil as an ethnic problem rather than as a socioeconomic issue, it catered to the mainstream imaginaries of ethnoscapes and ideoscapes of a Malmö. Imaginaries that saw immigration as the cause of the problem. It was important for the municipality to be able to show that it supported constructive youth activities in Rosengård.

To someone not aware of the street-journalism activities, which did not take place there except for the weekly meetings, and because the dance classes happened only a few times per week, the building and thus Elementz of the Street's activities appeared to be dormant. The dominating mediascapes, ethnoscapes, and ideoscapes thus forced Elementz of the Street to temporarily redirect its energies and activities to the building and to mass media. Because Elementz of the Street, and in particular Nouri, were under pressure, Nouri asked the researchers to transport some recently purchased studio equipment to the building. Hastily, Elementz of the Street set up a basic recording studio and scheduled an interview with *Sydnytt*, a regional TV news program, at the building at a time when it was full of activity, so as to show an alternative image of Rosengård, to satisfy the municipality, and to minimize the risk of losing the building. Shortly thereafter, Nouri appeared on several morning television programs and made efforts to counter the image of Rosengård that was being presented by the mainstream media.

The conflicts in Rosengård contributed to the tensions within Elementz of the Street's constituency and showed how those tensions were related to larger forces. Some Elementz of the Street members who lived in Rosengård saw in the Musikhjälpen campaign an opportunity to give their version of the turmoil in the district and perhaps to counter the dominating mediascapes and ideoscapes—an opportunity they missed out on, because the mobile phones used for reporting were collected after each broadcasting session. When they contacted one of the researchers to see if they could get the phones, access to the area had been closed off by the police. These youngsters were not in conflict with the street-journalism experiment or with Elementz of the Street. Nevertheless, a few youngsters from the Rosengård section who weren't participating in the street-journalism experiment used the conflict to criticize Elementz of the Street's engagement in Rosengård, thinking they might be able to use the conflict to take over leadership of Elementz of the Street and run the activities in the building as employees of the municipality (as one of the dissatisfied members had been promised).

According to Nouri, the municipality had not wanted to support the Elementz of the Street leaders by employing them, even though they had ran successful summer activities in Rosengård that had attracted a lot more youngsters than those arranged by the municipality. In fact, a common strategy of the municipality, according to Nouri, was to recruit engaged grassroots individuals rather than to help the grassroots organizations uphold their activities and maintain their independence.

The conflict within Elementz of the Street was exacerbated by another powerful force: mass media. Elementz of the Street's dissatisfied faction in Rosengård demanded a meeting with Nouri. At that meeting they expressed their frustration with Elementz of the Street's supposed lack of activities in the building, and they expressed suspicion that Nouri had become more interested in promoting his own career than in taking care of Elementz of the Street. Unfounded rumors circulated that Nouri had made quite a bit of money from his engagement in Musikhjälpen. The faction demanded that nouritv.se be shut down, but agreed that the videos on the Elementz of the Street YouTube channel could remain there. The main broadcasting website was shut down, and Nouri reduced his direct involvement in Rosengård. These disagreements did not end the collaboration between Elementz of the Street and the researchers, however. Later, for example, that constellation worked together on developing broadcast formats for Elementz of the Street's local talent competition *Jalla Upp På Scen (Jalla On Stage)*, a talent competition whose main purpose was to enable youngsters from different neighborhoods to meet one another in a constructive way.

The imaginaries produced by the faction saw the mediascapes Nouri was involved in solely as self-promotion and a means of entrance into professional mediascapes and lucrative financescapes. The faction's assessment that the Musikhjälpen broadcasts had been framed partially as promoting Nouri was correct, but that framing increased in importance and shaped the faction's interpretation of what Elementz of the Street's broadcast signified when the mass media began to cover the turmoil.

The accounts presented above point at the uneasy relationship between grassroots initiatives and more powerful actors (the municipality, specific mass-media companies, the mass media at large). These actors, both directly and indirectly, affected the space of possibilities and the design decisions, and they contributed to the conflicts that arose as the experiment unfolded. At times, professional media exercised indirect or implicit power on the smaller and less resourceful actors in this experiment. For instance, although decisions about website design and branding were made without demands from SVT and SR, those powerful media networks exercised their power as they became part of the Elementz of the Street's and the researchers' imaginaries and future plans. Established professional media organizations strongly influence the agenda through their sheer existence; they don't have to express their wishes explicitly, since they are such an important media hub, or in Callon's (1986) terminology an important translation center, which smaller actors feel required to assemble around. These powerful media networks are present at a distance and influence the problematization processes, as when small local networks feel forced to funnel their views and activities into a united stance so that it aligns with the requirements set up by the translation center and passes through what Callon (1986) calls the obligatory points of passages.

Even though powerful media organizations exercise power, that doesn't mean that marginal and less powerful actors are to be seen as disempowered wretches or victims. More marginal actors often show considerable agency and decision-making power and are also accountable for their decisions—to their constituencies—and the conflicts these decisions generate. This account also points at how those who are being decided over simultaneously decide and exercise similar power over others less empowered, such as the Elementz of the Street youngsters.

Just as in the previous case, the Musikhjälpen street-journalism experiment points at how branding through the naming of Internet domain names, logos, and the structuring of websites is a central part of the infrastructuring of media practices. The categorization, selection, and exclusion directly correspond with selections and exclusions of participation in the design and development process. The Elementz of the Street teenagers were, for example, not included in important decisions such as the naming and structure of the online broadcast space. Thus, their marginalization from the design process was evident in the end result and contributed to the conflicts that surfaced. The design researchers disagreed on the naming and structuring, but none of them questioned the absence of youth representatives. They had paid too little attention to the initial organization and decision-making arrangement of the design process, such as who should be included and how much power each participant should be given.

More powerfully than the Bloggen experiment, the street-journalism experiment shows how unpredictable and volatile real-life public infrastructuring processes are. None of the participants could have known in advance that the design and media experiment would be directly involved in, and interweave with, wider social systems and imaginaries, other infrastructuring processes, or rhizomes. With the aim of exploring a new relational media space in which public professional media and grassroots media cooperated, exploring uncharted territories in the Swedish mediascape, those territories quickly became reterritorialized by more powerful forces. The reterritorialization by mass media and large media companies changed the meaning of the street-journalism experiment considerably. The work of selecting, categorizing, branding, and naming was not optimal and could possibly have created conflicts later on. The importance of this work, however, increased and became more loaded, in the form of fiercer media-, finance-, and ideoscape imaginaries, when it interweaved with mass-media spaces, municipal politics, and real-world conflicts. Curiously, the media actors—although forcefully affecting the experiment—were not aware of their impact as their power was channeled through and embodied in the reasoning, debates, and actions carried out by the municipality, the dissatisfied faction within Elementz of the Street, Paradise Production, Nouri, and the researchers.

The Musikhjälpen case also shows how two of the constituencies are not homogeneous, but rather consist of conflicting views. Negotiations are thus not only carried out between different partners, but also within each constituency. The case also shows how "living lab" activities, which are highly distributed in time and space, are simultaneously inclusive and exclusive, as participation in meetings is regulated so as to simplify and speed up decision-making processes. These design processes, thus, may resemble lobbying and fleeting rhizomatic collisions more than they resemble public democratic decision-making processes.

Discussion

Some of the significant features emerging from the collaborative experiments are that probing into future mobile-media practices through an ongoing and open-ended infrastructuring process—where diverse partners negotiate and collaboratively experiment—yield valuable outcomes in the form of new temporary working relations, which at times led to later collaborations as well as insights into new forms of media practices. It must be noted that all of the partners were willing to chart unknown territories and participate in new collaborations; however, those that have most fundamentally been willing to imagine and explore themselves as something else—or as someone else—have been the small partners. The arts and performance center and Elementz of the Street imagined themselves as small media houses that could play a role in the Swedish media landscape, which was a profoundly new role for them. Similarly, the researchers imagined and tried out a new research role as they explored how media and communication studies and interaction design could connect, as well as how research and development could be conducted in the public sphere. SVT, SR, and the IT company placed their engagement at the margins of their businesses. That said, all the partners have gained new insights, whether through mobile-video audience-interaction prototypes, through prototypical media practices, or through new methods of co-designing in the public. That some partners take larger leaps into the future than others is not a problem. What is interesting to note is that those who take the largest leap into an uncharted future are the partners not typically associated with innovation.

Co-design and open-innovation research into new media and interaction design demand that we consider the grounds and preconditions for problematization, interessement, and enrollment that such research builds upon and what these negotiation processes do to the various partners involved (Pedersen 2007; Ehn 2008). Inherent in co-design and in open-innovation infrastructuring processes are conflicts of interessement as various partners negotiate and align their disparate interests and agendas. In the cases described above, the initial problematization, interessement, and enrollment were done by the small actors (the arts and performance center and Elementz of the Street) in collaboration with Paradise Production, the IT company, and the researchers. However, as they enrolled and courted larger partners, their initial idea was fundamentally redefined, as they needed to realign to the newcomers' agendas. In the collaboration between the arts and performance center, the IT company, and the university researchers, the IT company had the strongest impact on what type of media infrastructure was to be developed and tried, as people working for that company had more knowledge about and more skill in working with new media than any of the other participants. At times this impact was indirect, as in the case of Musikhjälpen, where SVT and SR implicitly influenced the decisions made. The bloggers, who were enrolled late in the process, had the least negotiation power and could therefore to a limited degree affect the framing of the experiment and how it should materialize, which indicates that one way of regulating decision making has to do with when stakeholders and constituencies are enrolled. However, the order of enrollment is less important than the size and power of the various constituencies. More powerful partners can thus more forcefully define what is to be inquired into and enroll the smaller partners in their problematization and interessement, and thus reterritorialize the deterritorialization aimed for by the small actors, even though the more powerful partners have not defined the initial problematization.

The negotiations, which were dispersed in time and space, consisted of various forms of performing sociomaterial politics within public spheres as broadcast forms were developed. Initial negotiations were typically carried out through meetings at which one or two representatives of each constituency—typically, decision makers—were present. Who should have decision-making power was never discussed. The taken-for-granted norm was that it was the leader from each constituency, with the exception of the researchers who had no clear leader. Nevertheless, issues negotiated were seldom brought back to be debated by their respective constituencies. The underlying assumption was that each representative would represent his or her assumed homogeneous constituency. However, as the cases show, the constituencies were far from homogeneous, and the lack of grounding decisions within a constituency can at times lead to conflicts further down the road. A central reason for conducting the negotiations in such a manner was that bringing back an issue to each constituency would considerably slow down the design process and possibly bring it to a standstill. Furthermore, certain constituencies, such as the video bloggers and the grassroots journalists, were not brought into the decision-making process until very late. One reason for this was that they worked *pro bono*, but two other reasons were that it made the decision-making process easier and that their perspective wasn't acknowledged as important.

Infrastructuring negotiations at the intersection of the fields of media and communication studies and interaction design include the following:

the technical network—in this case, how the streaming and interaction with the audience was enabled through the configuration of software and servers

the framing of the broadcast—that is, who the broadcaster is and the perspective taken on the broadcast

the textual and visual naming, expressed through the graphical user interface and the naming of the broadcast and the Web address

how the reporting is organized—for example, whether it is distributed or happening in one particular place, and whether the reporting is done by one individual or by a team

the construction of media personas by the reporter, the tones chosen for the broadcasts, and the framing of scenes—what is cut out, put in the background, foregrounded, and so on.

Certain of these features, such as the naming and graphical look, are more definitive than others. Other features, such as the framing of the scenes, can be done more on the spur of the moment. Framing is a powerful "tool," as it can drastically reconfigure the meaning of a broadcast.

When experiments enter the public sphere as socio-material assemblies or Things, it is difficult to predict what shapes and forms of representation and participation they will generate. At times, what happens is neither infrastructuring nor Things, but intersecting rhizomes that affect each other, though not leading to consensus or agreement across contexts. The terms infrastructuring and Things are no longer useful to describe what happens. The two cases discussed in this chapter show that mass media can intersect with municipal organizations or with grassroots politics without knowing that they were doing so. Bombardment by mass media is done from a distance. Much less precise than drone attacks, it is more like cluster bombing that hits unknown targets that can't properly enter into negotiations with the media. In turn, the mass media generate disciplinary relations, as for example when Elementz of the Street is forced by the municipality to speed up the building of the recording studio. The mediascapes thus have direct repercussions for urban politics. In other instances, the mediascapes generate a Thing, as happened when the different factions of Elementz of the Street negotiated how to publish the street-journalism broadcasts. In yet other instances, there are shadow battles, as happened when *Sydsvenskan* and Elementz of the Street erased each other's mediascapes. The variations of political types that intersecting rhizomes can generate are probably endless. Here, I have argued for how cases have generated political types that include direct negotiations within a particular constituency, and direct and indirect disciplining, as happened with Elementz of the Street and the municipality and with the mass media and Elementz of the Street's grassroots journalism.

Co-design processes of new media practices that are in the public sphere are inevitably more volatile than co-design processes in less sharp settings as they interweave or intersect to a larger degree with other social systems, networks, rhizomes, alliances, and counter forces. As networks or rhizomes constantly become, interweave and intersect, their meaning changes. What from the start was thought of as a culture-based critical perspective on media—the arts and performance center's motive behind Bloggen—was redefined as speedy and interactive news, which is in line with the dominating logic within design firms and many mass-media companies where being first is paramount; what was planned as an alternative and separate media space intersected with mass media and power demonstration through erasure. What was planned as grassroots journalism was partially turned into promotion of a TV persona to increase the chances of a future TV production. And, as it intersected with mass media's coverage of the turmoil in Rosengård, it turned into a power battle within Elementz of the Street. Designing as infrastructuring is therefore challenging, and it also seems to be impossible to design *for* infrastructuring in the public, as it is impossible to regulate how various infrastructuring processes will intersect, as matters of concern quickly change.

As the academic discipline and the practice of interaction design move closer to the domain of media and what is typically categorized as content, they also move away from producing objects to producing experiences and events. Traditionally, design has been concerned with developing objects that can generate multiple marketable objects, whereas content producers are more concerned with selling one experience after another—even though music and films can obviously be mass produced and sold in physical forms or in various online formats. Content, at least up to now, has a shorter life span than design objects, although the life span of design objects is constantly shortened. What counts as infrastructuring processes have become more fluid and temporary, which to some degree has blurred the border between research and development and use. This is in line with Thrift's (2006) argument that prototyping has become a central aspect of an economy in which many companies push beta products that blur the border between research and development and the market.

Also significant in the cases discussed in this chapter was the uneasy (though somewhat productive) relationship between large media actors and grassroots media actors. The IT company argued for the speed of production and the importance of liveness, while the arts and performance center argued for quality and media criticism. The collaboration has shown how cultural workers, who produce the content, symbolically and meritocratically risk the most: their reputation is at stake as they engage in the broadcasts. At the same time they are expected to contribute for free, which suggests that producers and their content—as infrastructuring material—has less value than more technical material. Both the arts and performance center and other cultural producers have expressed how the researchers and companies do not risk anything, and that, whatever way the inquiry goes, it will yield research results while they could have hurt their reputation if the outcome has been poor.

Genuine co-creative and long-term engagement needs to be nuanced. Our joint inquiries show that such vast collaborative processes cannot consist of long-term engagements with every partner and every individual that becomes involved. The duration and the depth of engagement must vary. However, the joint inquiries discussed here clearly show that both the research and the collaborative experiments would have gained considerably by engaging in negotiations with the content producers early on. Both of the experiments discussed above clearly failed in this regard, partly because of conflicting agendas but partly because of poor planning and the speed of production.

We need to consider whether open innovation and co-design that involves partners from academia and the private and public sectors is productive or counterproductive, especially for less powerful actors. As we engage in future-making through infrastructuring and deterritorialization, we need to critically ask ourselves if we have unintentionally created an optimized relational space that quickens reterritorialization by more powerful rhizomes that aim for fluid spaces and fast-flowing capital, which was not the aim of the researchers. We also need to ask ourselves when innovation and research and development across contexts lead to network romanticism that pushes the need for accountable intersections of networks to the margins, as well as fencing off certain infrastructures or rhizomes to maintain autonomy through slower and more accountable processes of approaching the future. Because infrastructuring is not inherently democratic and takes on various guises, accountable practicing of the politics of infrastructuring needs to be constantly attended to.

Notes

1. All names have been anonymized with the exceptions of Malmö, Rosengård, SR, SVT, and Sydsvenskan.

2. The arts and performance center, which initiated the process, had stated that it would host the broadcast on their newly redesigned website to be launched a few days before the festival and the public broadcast at its festival café. The IT company and the researchers would be responsible for developing the mobile interface and the streaming from the mobile phones. The researchers would help the arts and performance center to screen the broadcast in the tent. They, it turned out, did not know that they needed to have a media server on their site to stream the mobile broadcasts, which they did not have, and could therefore not host the broadcasts. The IT company agreed to fix a streaming server, but would not do the website design and stated that it could not host the media server, as its servers were heavily firewalled. The researchers functioned as middlemen and were able to quickly arrange for the media server to be placed at the university and for a former student to be hired to design the broadcast webpage. These infrastructuring activities, which were mainly technical in character, were easily solved, as the IT company and the researchers had the network relations to resort to with the right combination of competence and the resources to temporarily recruit a former student to design the broadcast page.

References

Appadurai, Arjun. 1996. *Modernity at Large: Cultural Dimensions of Globalization*. University of Minnesota Press.

Barry, Andrew. 2001. *Political Machines: Governing a Technological Society*. Athlone.

Binder, Thomas. 2007. Why Design Labs? *Design Inquiries 2007* (www.nordes.org).

Björgvinsson, Erling. 2008. Open-Ended Participatory Design as Prototypical Practice. *CoDesign* 4 (2): 85–99.

Björgvinsson, Erling, Pelle Ehn, and Per-Anders Hillgren. 2012a. Design Things and Design Thinking: Contemporary Participatory Design Challenges. *Design Issues* 28 (3): 101–116.

Björgvinsson, Erling, Pelle Ehn, and Per-Anders Hillgren. 2012b. Agonistic Participatory Design: Working with Marginalized Social Movements. *CoDesign* 8 (2–3): 127–144.

Born, G. 2000. Inside Television: Television Research and the Sociology of Culture. *Screen* 41 (4): 68–96.

Brabham, Daren C. 2008. Crowdsourcing as a Model for Problem Solving: An Introduction and Cases. *Convergence* 14: 75–90.

Brandt, Eva. 2001. Event-Driven Product Development: Collaboration and Learning. Department of Manufacturing Engineering and Management, Technical University of Denmark.

Callon, M. 1986. Some Elements of a Sociology of Translation: Domestication of the Scallops and the Fishermen of St Brieuc Bay. In *Power, Action and Belief*, ed. J. Law. Routledge & Kegan Paul.

Chesbrough, H. 2003. *Open Innovation: The New Imperative for Creating and Profiting from Technology*. Harvard Business School Press.

CoreLabs. 2006. CoreLabs (http://www.ami-communities.net/wiki/CORELABS).

Deleuze, Gilles. 1980. *A Thousand Plateaus: Capitalism and schizophrenia*. Athlone.

Deleuze, Gilles, and Felix Guattari. 1984. *Anti-Oedipus: Capitalism and schizophrenia*. Athlone.

Dewey, John. [1916] 1999. *Demokrati och utbildning*. Daidalos.

DuBois, W. E. B. [1973] 2001. *The Education of Black People*. Monthly Review Press.

Ehn, Pelle. 1988. *Work-Oriented Design of Computer Artifacts*. Almqvist and Wiksell.

Ehn, Pelle. 2008. Participation in Design Things. In Proceedings of the Tenth Anniversary Conference on Participatory Design, Indiana University.

Enzensberger, Hans Magnus. 1970. Constituents of a Theory of the Media. In *Raids and Reconstructions*. Pluto.

Etzkowitz, H., and L. Leydesdorff, eds. 2001. *Universities and the Global Knowledge Economy*. Continuum.

Foucault, M. 1973. *The Birth of the Clinic*. Tavistock.

Foucault, M. 1977. *Discipline and Punish: The Birth of the Prison*. Penguin.

Howe, Jeff. 2008. *Crowdsourcing: How the Power of the Crowd Is Driving the Future of Business*. Crown Business.

Karasti, Helen, Karen S. Baker, and Florence Millerand. 2010. Infrastructure Time: Long-Term Matters in Collaborative Development. *Computer Supported Cooperative Work* 19: 377–405.

Latour, Bruno. 1999a. *Pandora's Hope: Essays on the Reality of Science Studies*. Harvard University Press.

Latour, Bruno. 1999b. Technology Is Society Made Durable. In *A Sociology of Monsters: Essays on Power, Technology and Domination*, ed. J. Law. Routledge.

Latour, Bruno. 2005a. *Reassembling the Social: An Introduction to Actor-Network-Theory*. Oxford University Press.

Latour, Bruno. 2005b. From Realpolitik to Dingpolitik or How to Make Things Public. In *Making Things Public: Atmospheres of Democracy*, ed. Bruno Latour and Peter Weibel. MIT Press.

Law, John, ed. 1991. *A Sociology of Monsters: Essays on Power, Technology and Domination*. Routledge.

Law, John, and Ann-Marie Mol. 2000. Situating Technoscience: An Inquiry into Spatialities. Centre for Science Studies, Lancaster University.

Leadbeater, Charles. 1999. *Living on Thin Air: The New Economy*. Penguin.

Leadbeater, Charles. 2008. Charles Leadbeater: The Rise of the amateur professional (http://www.youtube.com/watch?v=W7raJeMpyM0).

Leadbeater, Charles, and Paul Miller. 2004. *The Pro-Am Revolution: How Enthusiasts Are Changing Our Economy and Society*. DEMOS.

McRobbie, Angela. 2009. Vi är alla kreativa. In *Kultur och politik*, ed. Y. Gislen et al. Fronesis.

Mouffe, Chantal. 2000. *The Democratic Paradox*. Verso.

Oscarsson, Mattias. 2010. Poliskostnad kan flytta festivaler (http://www.sydsvenskan.se/kultur--nojen/poliskostnad-kan-flytta-festivaler/).

Pedersen, Jens. 2007. Protocols of Research and Design. PhD thesis, Copenhagen IT University.

Petersen, Sören Mörk. 2008. Loser Generated Content: From Participation to Exploitation. *First Monday* 13 (3) (http://firstmonday.org/article/view/2141/1948).

Ressner, Jeffrey. 2004. See Me, Blog Me. *Time*, April 11.

Sarrimo, Cristine. 2012. *Jagets scen—självframställning i olika medier*. Makadam.

Sernhede, Ove, and Johan Söderman. 2013. Kur mot kravaller (Sydsvenskan.se/kultur—nojen/kultur-mot kravaller/).

Söderman, Johan. 2013. The Formation of "Hip-Hop Academicus": How American Scholars Talk about the Academisation of Hip-Hop. *British Journal of Music Education* 30 (3): 369–381.

Stålbröst, A. 2008. Forming Future IT: The Living Lab Way of User Involvement. Doctoral thesis, Luleå University of Technology.

Star, Susan Leigh. 1991. Power, Technology and the Phenomenology of Conventions: On Being Allergic to Onions. In *A Sociology of Monsters: Essays on Power, Technology and Domination*, ed. J. Law. Routledge.

Star, Susan Leigh, and Geoffrey C. Bowker. 2002. How to Infrastructure. In *The Handbook of New Media*, ed. L. Lievrouw and S. Livingstone. Sage.

Star, Susan Leigh, and Karen Ruhleder. 1996. Steps toward an Ecology of Infrastructure: Design and Access for Large Information Spaces. *Information Systems Research* 7 (1): 111–134.

Suchman, Lucy. 2002. Located Accountabilities in Technology Production. *Scandinavian Journal of Information Systems* 14 (2): 91–105.

Surowiecki, J. 2004. *The Wisdom of Crowds*. Anchor.

Sydell, Laura. 2005. Digital Life, NPR Weekend Edition, August 5 (http://www.npr.org/player/v2/mediaPlayer.html?action=1&t=1&islist=false&id=4787757&m=4787766).

Thrift, Nigel. 2006. Re-Inventing Invention: New Tendencies in Capitalist Commodification. *Economy and Society* 35 (2): 279–306.

von Hippel, E. 2005. *Democratizing Innovation*. MIT Press.

Wark, McKenzie. 2006. Information Wants to Be Free (But Is Everywhere in Chains). *Cultural Studies* 20, no. 2–3: 165–183.

Wikipedia. 2013. Steve Garfield (http://en.wikipedia.org/wiki/Steve_Garfield).

12 Stories on Future-Making in Everyday Practices from Managers in the Creative Industries

Pernilla Severson

Stories can rehearse and stabilise particular futures, and in so doing make others absent.
Watts 2008, 188

In many ways this book is a reaction to Eric von Hippel's assertions that democratic innovation enables users to develop "exactly what they want, rather than relying on manufacturers to act as their (often very imperfect) agents" and that users can "benefit from innovations developed and freely shared by others" (2005, 11). Most of the chapters in the present book respond to this view of innovation with stories of design experiments in which marginalized groups in society participated in alternative kinds of design and innovation. The "Scandinavian collective designer" is the ideal type to ignite and lead an alternative future-making: making other futures possible and present.

This chapter, however, is an interweaving of stories and theories exploring meaning-making and sense-making of innovation and collaboration in everyday practices among managers on different levels in the creative industries entities labeled as IT, design, and media companies. The interviewed managers[1] are storytellers who interpret the world they experience and sometimes tell stories about how the world should be. Innovation is approached as something integrated in everyday practices, rather than in special and clearly demarcated situations.

Stories are not mirrors of the past. Instead they are what Riessman (2003, 708) describes as refracting the past and in that are valuable to research because of the interpretive aspects from storytellers that exist in such a refraction: "The 'truths' of narrative accounts are not in their faithful representations of a past world, but in the shifting connections they forge among past, present, and future. They offer storytellers a way to re-imagine lives (as narratives do for nations, organisations, ethnic/racial and other groups forming collective identities)." In this chapter you will encounter theory-infused themed selections from arguments based in performed stories in the interviews with regard to everyday practices for creative class people involved in future-making as managers. At the end of the chapter, these stories are applied more broadly by commenting on how they are relevant to this book's main themes.

Stories on innovation

The stories on innovation from the more industrious sphere of creative industries are centered on the notion that the future is connected with the past and the present (Watts 2008). When the fourteen managers are re-telling of the ordinary of innovation, it has therefore meant flashbacking approached as one of those "constitutive moments in the reproduction of familiar modes of identification and action within particular locales and imaginaries" (Suchman 2008, 3) and "how future making requires the simultaneous making of relevant histories as a practice intimately enfolded into acts of invention" (ibid., 9).

In these stories on innovation, key events in everyday practices consist of stating resistance to talking about an ordinary day. Nobody wants to be or do *ordinary* or *same* as managers in the creative industries. To express and emphasize change and creativity, one has to disassociate oneself from ordinary in the meaning of sameness:

Well, you can't describe an ordinary day, that's impossible. However, I can boil together what could be a representative day. Because we live in an unprecedented time of change, it also means that one day is very mixed between incredible operational activities one minute and in-depth strategic thinking next hour. (Francis)

In flashbacking an ordinary day, a sort of situated ordinariness occurs that guide future-making. It influences what alternative futures are perceived as possible. It also articulates how innovation is always part of, or made part of, an everyday with routines and things that usually occur. An ordinary day is circling around the issue of ontological safety linked to ongoing change and with different strategies to deal with uncertainties. The situated ordinariness becomes achieving a goal rather than certain activities—for example "setting the brand," as manager Cam says.

To deal with changes by not only accepting them but also welcoming them is part of the job of managing future-making within the creative industries. Leadbeater (2002) make a case that an important part of innovation is that it is inherently uncertain and that innovation is made possible to make use of by being open to uncertainty. Latour (2005) makes an argument on uncertainty that there are five sources of uncertainties for what the social is made up of. Both Leadbeater and Latour are embracing uncertainty, but they differ in their views of what insight and action on uncertainties can and should mean. Whereas Leadbeater is arguing for uncertainties as foundation for making innovation, Latour is arguing for uncertainties as base for making a revelation about what the social is made up of. In the stories from the interviewed managers, dealing with change has made possible future-making as both innovating and revealing. Uncertainties are to be managed, but first what they are made up of has to be revealed.

Another story line on innovation concerns that being a manager usually involves being sometimes located in and sometimes dislocated from the workplace. Some of the interviewees tell stories about their importance in the company as something that is not always a good thing. It is important to be important for getting things done, but not to be the one standing in the way of people wanting to do things:

It will be difficult to do things unless I'm on track, and that's a bit of a problem. (Mika)

Agency then is ascribed to people and the connecting of managers to others. For Leadbeater (2002) this would imply lacking practitioner autonomy, not maximizing operational diversity. For Latour (2005) this would be revealing the perception of connection of things, of being social: social actors in the interviews map their own social context, a context highlighting the value of being in action, and in connection and signaling "without connection, no action." At the same time these are stories about a sense of belonging, where identity is primarily linked to the company and collaborating with the ones inside the company.

A connected story on innovation, uncertainties, and action relates to the fact that among the managers what is true and/or most important is not valued. Instead these uncertainties probe a relationship to what can be described as catalyst for perceived authentic relevance: the things that make you want to do things and whatever works in a special setting, situation, or location. Jamie argues that the actual truth is not as important as the way to take what makes you want to do things and then you try it. All managers tell the story of that an opinion is better than no opinion and in somewhat way this is based in a story that there are no answers for really complex issues. Nike is involving user innovation as one part of getting an opinion: "There we have some thoughts and ideas to invite them more in the creation. We have done it a few times. … It is better to get an opinion than no opinion at all." Francis reduces uncertainty by acknowledging it and at the same time to decide on some sort of picture of the future: "No one has the answer to this question, but we must seek the answers to them, we must act on the basis of some sort of picture of the future." Linked to the issue of practitioner autonomy, this self-governing act demands a context where people have the same sort of picture of the future, and where the managers' role is to align and bridge the picturing of the future.

Claims for facts exist for future-making nevertheless concerning different aspects, sometimes creating clear principles for do's and don'ts. Here the growth of technological uptake is a powerful agent in the stories. For Eddy, no complexity exists; the future is knowable and reachable because of the development of the mobile phone market and Eddy's experience in that area: "I'm terribly knowledgeable about the market, of the mobile phone market. I do not think you can argue that mobile phones are not growing. One can argue who is growing and not and how the technology infrastructure will look like. … It's pretty clear that it will happen." This echoes Suchman's (2008, 2) remark that "the techno frontier of cyberspace is imagined to be indefinitely extensible."

Other managers touch upon complexity, and some state very clearly that navigating in complex processes for the organization puts demands to solve things in the flow of things to be able to deal with the timing issue. In business as usual and in talk about everyday practices, dealing with uncertainties means managing space (being present) and time (at the right time), and in this timing for future-making you can either change your plans as you go along, or making it fit to the present:

The key is to get a flow from concept to function out there, live. ... That's how the whole company's thinking. ... It does not always end how you have imagined it, even during a day. That's why it's a bit we are acting under this principle—because it is impossible to plan. ... There may be new insights; ideas that have emerged that make us change focus. (Nike)

For Cam dealing with uncertainties and timing is rather discussing how the pressing need for "now" and "sooner" is present in development/innovation. In a conversation about change, Cam talks of "a battle of time." Cam also touches upon timing of raising awareness in the organization and of the future, by showing the uncertainty and at the same time making people being comfortable with that uncertainty. Cam brings forward that a lot of business development has been "too far into the future."

For Mika there is an experience of innovating too late and therefore a changed temporal attitude of doing future-making now: "When do you start to innovate, or, when do you start creating new business development, product development? You do this, when the old one starts to fail—you do not do it in good times." This can be contrasted with Eli's story of the future as something way into the future: "Future issues are seldom so urgent that they need to be solved in seconds. ... And then we have of course the bigger issues for the future. ... they're not subject to any five-minute discussions." A sense of urgency is crucial to stories of change or innovation, and it is linked to economic aspects: to survive as a company you need a viable business model.

Beside flashbacks of daily future-making there are stories from the past among the managers. Making sense of future-making comes from experiences from the past and attitudes toward what will and can happen and perceptions of power that influence future-making. Looking back creates inner confidence, especially if you set your mind on remembering and learning from history. An aspect of this is efforts to manage future-making by history. Francis sketches during the interview, visualizing historical time lines and different key driving forces influencing the company. The sketch on the whiteboard eventually becomes a map of how to manage the future. Overall, Francis is excited about all the changes: "What you and I are talking about is very interesting." Billie tells a story of meaning-making and says "It has become quite clear what possibilities there are." Experience creates security about what future-making is possible. Billie says things like "We could probably not, at least not me, fully articulate what this change would mean, for example, in 2001." Back then the future was attached with strong negative emotions, in Billie's words that it was a "stupid fucking future."

For Cam, flashbacking is a way to navigate through history in a comprehensive way and to go back to the "origin." Cam declares that one "must create a memory" and that one must learn from mistakes. Cam goes on to say that documentation is important: "Apply it to more areas and we will remember it." This indicates a strong perception of getting documentation of what happened and why, as part of the job as manager within the creative industries: managing future-making also includes managing history-making.

Local aspects are important in the stories, but global aspects are also present. According to Mika, "the media industry is no longer agenda setting in its own sector as much as before." Changes in the world, on a global level, is adding complexity when one's own business is changing and when power relations change between businesses. Dealing with these external factors is an internal matter, articulated by Cam as "Our biggest competitor is ourselves.". In this line of thinking, the organization's mental frames of how to approach and create the future in relation to the changes in the world is spoken in metaphors of a battle; a competition. Managing future-making means managing how changes are perceived and infuse agency in how to handle the future.

Stories on collaboration

The managers' stories of the everyday making of innovation include accounts of collaborating with people in various ways. In these stories of collaborating with people, collaborating with users are not made very present in the way von Hippel argues that democratic innovation can and should happen. Leadbeater and Miller (2004) claim that creativity and innovation are found in the power of self-organizing Pro-Ams (professional amateurs), supercharged by the Internet. The stories from managers within the creative industries rather portray the people one is collaborating with as professionals and where these professionals are to be found and made contact with in networks. And in these professional networks the industrial logic prevails as norm. Being a manager is belonging to the creative professionals, managing the super-creative core, where the creatives are attributed according to added economic value. The manager's role is to align creative autonomy with industrial logic. Collaboration is made best with sharing the creative ethos and its economic connotations. Involving oneself in collaboration with others not sharing this creative ethos means bringing forward an articulation of an internal class struggle.

For managers an individualistic mode of working is not possible. Collaboration is based on hierarchical power and/or linking of competences. Key activities for the storytellers as managers are organizing people and making people comfortable. Collaboration is addressed as essential. Francis says "We are totally smoked if we do not cooperate." When asked about collaboration, René uses the metaphor of an ecosystem to illustrate a change from doing everything yourself to doing things together:

We notice that our industry is changing. Previously it was very ... one should do everything oneself. But now it's a lot of talking about these ecosystems. And it's not just talk that one is talking about an ecosystem, but what is happening is that it is very important that you are in a context, in a region actually. I find that very interesting.

Here collaboration is made meaningful as being something linked to certain actors, competences, and values in a region. The story of clusters and their value to regions is made present.

The main focus in stories on collaborating for innovation is the *managing of the creatives in the company*, and in the *contact-making and collaborating with customers* (sometimes mentioned as partners). Collaborating with *academia* for future-making together is present by me making it a question demanding an answer, and then academic collaboration is linked to the customer-partner relationship.

Stories on the managers collaborating with the *creatives* highlight the interplay including different human aspects that is demanded: the creativity aspect, emotive aspects, and the process and goal of improving things that ease the relationship. The closest and most important collaboration that the managers are involved in is the relationship with the creatives within the workplace. When asked what is most rewarding about the work, Mika answers "I usually say that what is the best with this job, it's the people." For Jamie it is the people linked to a creative process: "Design discussions are always fun. It is a combination of unleashed creativity ... and the opposite, must decide what to do." For Mika, "the hard part is not coming up with stuff; the hard part is to organize them, create opportunities and viability in—to carry out projects is absolutely the hardest." When asked about what is the most challenging thing to deal with in general in work, Alex says "to make people work along together, the interplay between people" and adds the tricky question of balancing work and life: "How do you do when you try to make life and work work for a guy who really only wants to be on parental leave?" Making people comfortable in this process is key and concerns many different things:

We can go through it on the board there, then we follow up: what has been done and not done? ... It can be anything from that it's cold ... or the coffee tastes bad. It can be very small improvements that make people feel better. ... At the same time it may be to question the way we work, or purely technical stuff. ... That's the kind of things we're trying to sift out. (Nike)

An interesting part of collaboration for innovation for managers in creative industries is relating to and working with *higher management*, whose failure to understand digital development can be problematic for a manager:

It's very, very old thinking and structures. ... In management, there are people who actually do not have any clue of what digital is. ... I've sat in meetings where I was asked. ... Can you change in a blog post after you have published it? I mean, seriously! I think it would be like if you were in the car industry and so you sat in a meeting with the management team and it's someone there who asked—that automatic transmission, what is that thing? (Gill)

Another significant collaboration that the managers are involved in is the relationship with the customers. For Kim, collaborating is a part of the company-customer relationship: "Without close cooperation with our customers, we have no assignments: it is that simple!" Robyn answers the question about what is hardest to deal with this way: "When it is difficult to have a constructive dialogue with the customer, it is, well, ... to handle, what you feel as a person, as a human." One characteristic of collaboration with customers is the meeting, which involves aligning and bridging in a communicative setting. There are different expectations of what a meeting can lead to, and the norm for managers is to avoid involvement in meetings that do not lead to future-making in the sense of creating viability of the company. In the interviews, meetings were spoken of as a way of life, a responsibility, and a possibility. For Cam, meetings are linked to a professional role in which "visibility is enormously important" and you must "practice what you preach." For Kim, meeting people is a big part of what work consists of: "computer, meetings, telephone, or traveling to meetings." Some meetings are planned; others are unplanned. For René, planned meetings with customers are particularly important:

We give, actually, an offer at the meeting, where we say what we could do for you. Then the goal is also to have the right decision makers there with the customer, so that we more or less can lock the transaction at the meeting so that there will be no postponement.

All the managers valorize meetings as opportunities for innovation and collaboration. Jamie says that you never know what the next meeting can result in, but that meeting people almost always yields something: "It really works!" For Mika, meetings with the outside world are crucial for "being in the eye of the storm." Meetings usually are assessed for their business value. Here the valorization of connecting becomes visible, and the good meetings are the ones thought like to contribute to a company's viability.

"It's also an issue of time," says Mika. He/she continues:

I participate in really a lot of meetings. There, somewhere, if I realize that this meeting will not result in anything—even if I become smarter somewhere of it. ... My company will not be much happier for it if I do not make a turnover somewhere. Then I think there is a profit in the meeting anyway, it is not like that, there is a huge profit, but we're really in a situation where we need to find new business. (Mika)

Meet with people simply in order to chat can also be seen as valuable—if it is in the workplace. "I set aside time just to chat," says Toni, who adds that small talk may involve emotions: "The feeling, how it feels, purely spontaneous."

In the stories on collaboration for innovation where otherness is involved, it is spoken of as collaborating with some "others" is easier than with other "others". Gill comments that he/she finds it relatively easy to work with a certain company because "They understand what we are doing." Academia's part in this is in the stories linked to the possibilities of method, financing, and credibility. Collaborating with academia is spoken of as a marginal activity, where one's participation is not always paid for and is also associated with hesitations because of academia's tradition of supporting non-commercial ideal. Cam wants to create a "method" as a possible common ground, achieving understanding and competence between both theorists and practitioners. For Kim, "the research that we are interested to engage in is close to commercialization." Financing influences collaboration with academia for innovation, where the research approach is desirable also because of its credibility:

> Going forward with this EU money is something that is becoming increasingly important for companies. ... This will take you automatically to cooperate more with the academic world. Then it's good to have an academic world because you need the research approach to the whole, a company never does research. You do not get the credibility by just being... Sometimes you want to have a study you can go back to. (René).

For Kim, hesitation concerns an experience of academic collaboration as something not always paid for and Kim also states that this kind of collaboration is and should only be a small part of what a company does: "At best, we have the cost of such projects. It is not something you can build a business on." Kim says that funding is mostly "guided a lot to universities to pay their salaries." Kim speaks of the European Union as a "hassle factor" with "a mammoth job to work with accounting." Managers say that they are working for free in research projects. The discourse is usually the other way around, that companies exploit academic research as free labor, not that companies are being exploited in research projects with academia. This is a contrast to what other researchers point to (see, for example, Weber 2004). For Eli, collaboration with academia sometimes holds disappointment: "We experienced that one often on a politically symbolic level was interested in cooperation and change, but not when it came to the crunch." Yet another disinclination concerns a perception that academia is supporting non-commercial ideals (which for other managers are seen as the raison d'être of universities) such as striving to enhance the development of open-source software. When asked whether he/she wants to add anything about collaboration with academia, Toni says:

> I do not see that commercial cannot be artistic or not indie. I can see a bit as we. ... First and foremost for me as a manager. I want it to go well. I want us to feel good and produce good stuff. But then in the long run, it remains artistically even though it is commercial. Then you do not have to get rich of it. But show me the indie guy who does not like to get paid for just being able to sit and. ...

In the making of creative industries, history starts with art (Hartley and Cunningham 2001). But here art becomes the classic friction between art and commerce. The relationship between capital and creativity becomes a tension to what degree the creative practices should be industrious. The stories from the managers embody this.

Applying these stories more broadly

The ability of managers in the creative industries to exert hegemonic power in future-making should not be overlooked or underestimated. They can and do routinize future-making according to experiences, perceptions, and ideals. Days are not the same, but they aren't too different either. The drawback of the firmness of situated ordinariness is that not all uncertainties are revealed, just some—especially the ones you can deal with. Technology and economy are perceived as hard facts that set the frameworks for what futures are possible to make. Perceived authentic relevance is also created, insofar as future-making is seen as primarily something happening within the company and managers, not co-workers or users, are seen as catalysts for innovation. Managers fit new collaborations into earlier experiences and perceptions, reproducing a commodified collaboration as primary goal. The rationale for collaboration is that it is to make the future knowable and possible to create according to one's needs. In future-making, common goods are downplayed in relation to business logic, because managers choose what uncertainties and/or complexities to accept and because managers decide what is counted as memory, as method, as useful, and as difficult.

The valorization of future-making and the valorization of collaboration show traces of iteration (Suchman 2008). In the managers' stories, business and profit always come first, where creativity, innovation, and design from users and/or researchers constantly is an issue of if one can afford that collaboration. Connections and collaborations are commodified in an industrial perspective. This doesn't mean that the stories from the manager's only are limited to being narrations from a marketization perspective. Stories can be about things being hard, fun, rewarding, and not always based on aiming for profit. But decisions on actions on how to create futures for the company can never be solely based on this, whether it being looking for pleasure and/or more or less linked to democratic hopes. In the stories from managers in the creative industries democratic aspects are so marginalized that they are virtually invisible. The creative class struggle becomes a separation of the private and public where managerial work represents supervising that this boundary is maintained.

Note

1. In all, 14 people at ten companies were interviewed. Most of the companies were located in Malmö, but some were in Karlshamn and some were in Karlskrona. The companies were in various IT, design, or media-oriented sectors, and were connected to the cluster initiative Media Evolution. The individuals interviewed were managers on different levels. The interviews were based on 1–2 hours of conversations structured around the themes of everyday activities at work, the future, challenges, and collaboration.

References

Hartley, John, and Stuart Cunningham. 2001. Creative Industries: From Blue Poles to Fat Pipes. In *The National Humanities and Social Sciences Summit: Position Papers*, ed. M. Gillies. Department of Education Science and Training, Canberra.

Latour, Bruno. 2005. *Reassembling the Social: An Introduction to Actor-Network-Theory*. Oxford University Press.

Leadbeater, Charles. 2002. *Innovate from Within: An Open Letter to the New Cabinet Secretary*. Demos.

Leadbeater, Charles, and Paul Miller. 2004. *The Pro-Am Revolution: How Enthusiasts Are Changing our Economy and Society*. Demos.

Riessman, Catherine Kohler. 2003. Narrative Analysis. In *The Sage Encyclopedia of Social Science Research Methods*, ed. M. Lewis-Beck, A. Bryman, and T. Liao. Sage.

Suchman, Lucy. 2008. Striking Likenesses to Difference. Paper presented at annual meeting of Society for Social Studies of Science, Rotterdam.

von Hippel, Eric. 2005. *Democratizing Innovation*. MIT Press.

Watts, Laura. 2008. The Future Is Boring: Stories from the Landscapes of the Mobile Telecoms Industry. *Twenty-First Century Society* 3: 187–198.

Weber, Steven. 2004. *The Success of Open Source*. Harvard University Press.

IV Emerging Publics

13 Emerging Publics: Totem-Poling the 'We's and 'Me's of Citizen Participation

Per Linde

Almost a century ago, a debate on the relation between new emerging technologies and the constitution of publics took place between Walter Lippmann and John Dewey. Marres (2005) states that at the time it was often assumed that complexities related to new technology for communication, as well as transport and manufacturing, were a threat to the democratic society. The remedy, many thought, would be to simplify. Although Lippmann and Dewey debated from different perspectives, they both argued that strange, unfamiliar, and entangled objects are the conditions for public engagement and for public affairs to arise, rather than a threat. A concern or an issue that can be resolved by experts, institutions, or a social community doesn't become a public affair. In other words, issues that are too complex for a community to resolve bring *a public* into being. Although the Lippmann-Dewey debate took place almost a century ago, it still seems relevant.

The processes and places for innovation are often characterized by ubiquitous speed; unbounding collective intelligence in the service of societal and technological development is an act of fast, rational, and efficient production. In this production, places and agoras can be exemplified by artifacts such as meeting rooms, online or offline forums, conferences, and voting machines. These artifacts are considered tools for "coming together," but it is often a coming together that has the goal of increasing the speed of production. Virilio (1986, 5) describes the city as a "human dwelling place penetrated by channels of rapid communication." But when the pace is slowed, we can recognize that places, as well as objects, are more than mere tools. They have a role in the collective, quite similar to their human counterparts, and the doings of the collective constitute what we call "the public." Those publics, because they are numerous and diverse, are *emerging* rather than specified in constitutions, blueprints, or construction plans. And sometimes we must permit those publics to be slow-paced. We must also recognize that they are often ephemeral, highly situated, and entangled in complex ways.

An older example of public artifacts is the totem pole. Slowly carving a totem pole from a cedar tree was a tedious and slow process. Contrary to popular belief, totem poles were not meant for worship. Their meanings were as varied as the cultures that produced them. Neither were they monumental in the sense of permanence; most often they were left to rot once erected. But they were carriers of meaning within local communities, and they were public artifacts.

The chapters in this part of the book will address different aspects of how the "totem poles" of collective future-making are constructed as public places. This doesn't imply the geographical meaning of place as being superior. The act of "becoming public" is also processes and tactics. Both objects and places participate in the act of "becoming public." For example, shouldn't we recognize the SIM card in a mobile phone as one of the communicating actors in a phone call? Means for "becoming public," such as designed objects and places, are also highly *appropriated* by people other than those who often are mentioned as "originators." The act of appropriation is perhaps the most important aspect of the emergence of publics, especially if we want to address behavioral changes toward more sustainable lifestyles. This calls for also accepting slowness in ways that differ from the traditional notion of innovation in product development and business development. However, we do not see the emerging publics, here elaborated and recounted, as oppositional to design, service, and product development. On the contrary, we find them to be strong candidates for producing good and sound things, elaborating mutual joint futures, and, in cases, also good business opportunities for product development. The way people appropriate technologies has long been a focus for understanding future use of the developed technologies. Open innovation models in which "the public" is represented are no longer new. Many stories stress how gaining insight to the everyday creativity of the public might be crucial for successful innovation. The concept of open source, exemplified by the development of the operating system Linux, is but one such story. How Short Message Service (SMS) was implemented as a marginal feature is another example; no one anticipated that it would be a foundationally new way of communicating, with large social, societal, and cultural effects. From the point of view of innovation, the notion of public participation is now widely accepted. The concept of public participation is a central theme of this book. It is reflected differently in each chapter, but the relation to different socio-material practices and issues of spatiality binds the chapters together. All the authors attempt to instantiate actual geographical places as innovation platforms and to frame problems at the hyper-local scale, mobilizing local residents to innovate solutions.

The notion of *practices* is important, since all the chapters in this part address different ways of *making* spaces public. The *makings* and the *doings* of these publics are performed differently in each case. In all cases, however, we can observe how networks of actors are emerging. These networks are being constituted by complex and dynamically changing relations of people, artifacts, spaces, and activities. The networks get stabilized before again being re-configured in rhythm to the doings that constitute their very essence. As spaces, they need not only to be produced but also to be re-produced, and they are enacted as different sets of artifacts. Normative values affect the flow of participation.

As has already been said, participatory culture has its place in a chain of innovation, and that has implications for the market economy. But, of course, participation in public spaces also has implications for our understanding of the democratic public. It is often taken for granted, quite spontaneously, that a strong relation between publicness (as in being *visible to all*) and democracy is inherent, almost like a natural relationship. But in view of how political instability and the ever-changing nature of public acts get entangled with a variety of sometimes competing other public acts, the "bond" between publicness and democracy may not be so straightforward. New media practices and ICT development have created multi-layered territorializations in which different communities populate the same ground and engage with the same issues from different perspectives. The ways in which issues of concern become public matters are becoming more and more complex, and the border between public and private gets more and more blurred everyday as a result of the increasing use of social media.

The authors of the chapters in this part do not aspire to give an overarching analytical account of this complex discourse. Rather, we aim to give concrete accounts, more at the level of storytelling, of various public practices. Some short reflections on the concept of the public as put forth by Jürgen Habermas and a commentator on his work on publics and structural transformation might shed some light on the reference to totem poles and to 'we's and 'me's.

In his 1962 book *The Structural Transformation of the Public Sphere*, Habermas describes the public sphere as a space between the private and the authoritarian state. This space is neither private nor individual. It is also a "non-representational" sphere, not governed by governments, kings, or presidents. Public debate takes place in face-to-face meetings between citizens. Strong socio-material aspects, where the material settings affect social relations, are also at play. Habermas mentions coffee houses and Tischgesellschaften (table societies). One of the chapters in this part of the present volume (chapter 15) mentions a sewing circle, adding a maker's perspective to the "talked" debate. For Habermas, an overall inclusiveness characterizes the public sphere; it is open for everyone, which is an idea that also has been subject of criticism since specific positions, such as gender, ethnic origin, and social status still were criteria for inclusion or exclusion. It has been observed that the relationships between multiple publics are conflictual. Issues of governance with regard to participation certainly can be applied. That a public be open for everyone all of the time seems to be an unreachable ideal. To be fair to Habermas, it must be said that he observed that the claim to open access was never fully realized. However, distinguishing a space that is neither private nor governed by official institutions still provides a good framework in which to reflect on the notion of the public.

The lack of completeness in Habermas' thoughts can be observed and debated. Nancy Fraser (1990) challenges some of the assumptions underlying Habermas' notion of the public sphere. First, she addresses how open access to the public sphere relied upon a bracketing of indifferences in social status, a bracketing that was really not efficient since the public sphere indeed was governed by protocols which themselves were correlating markers of social inequality. Thus, a public sphere cannot be a zero-degree culture. Even more important, inclusiveness should also deal with decreasing social inequality, and should not pretend that it doesn't matter. Second, Fraser questions the possibility of a single, homogeneous public sphere. She argues that a multiplicity of publics serves better to advance democracy. In line with the idea of parallel discourses, Fraser argues, we should focus not only on internal public communication but also on inter-public interactions. An interesting example of pluralistic use of technological tools for publicness, such as smartphones, can be found in the story of Bambuser (chapter 16). Participants in a demonstration broadcast the events with their mobile phones, while simultaneously being documented by the police using the very same application. Another example is *Threads*, the sewing-circle project discussed in chapter 15; it illustrates how, even within the same framing, the networks change as the *Threads* exhibition travels from one place to another. Third, Fraser stresses a complex relation between private and public interests in debates. There are no clear boundaries between private matters and what will constitute common affairs; it cannot be foreseen or decided at beforehand. A democratic, public space must ensure that there are opportunities for minorities to convince others that what in the past counted as private actually should be a concern for the public; as an example, Fraser notes that domestic violence was once considered a private affair. Interest groups, and *self*-interest, cannot be ruled out from the public; the entanglement of the private and the public is a complex mesh. Addressing the tension between the shared common and at times hidden private motivates trying to enroll both the 'we's and the 'me's of public participation, cutting across the distinction between public and private. Finally, Fraser questions the sharp distinction between society and state. If the gap between public debate and decision-making mechanisms remains, what will then be the effects of a good public debate? In contrast, Fraser puts forth the idea that the public includes both strong publics (as in decision makers) and weaker publics (which should not be constrained to mere opinion forming).

Chantal Mouffe is another scholar who has sought to find other ways to think of democracy than the liberal one. She writes about the drawbacks of the universality that, for example, Habermas and Richard Rorty put forward: the liberal framework forecloses the antagonistic dimension of coexistence. Mouffe writes that Habermas and Rorty want to "retain the vision of a consensus that would not imply any form of exclusion and the availability of some form of realization of universality" (Mouffe 2005, 88). "This," Mouffe continues, "is why, no more than the Habermasian discourse-theoretical approach, can Rorty's pragmatism provide an adequate framework for a pluralist democratic politics."

Mouffe herself argues for an agonistic, non-consensus-seeking democracy. While antagonism is a we/they relation in which the two sides are enemies who do not share any common ground, agonism is a we/they relation in which the conflicting parties recognize the legitimacy of their opponents, although acknowledging that there is no rational solution to their conflict. They are adversaries, not enemies. This means that while in conflict they see themselves as belonging to the same political association, as sharing a common symbolic space within which the conflict takes place (Mouffe 2005). Mouffe means that the way to live in a pluralistic democracy is to bring issues and concerns into a political sphere, not a moral one.

Judith Butler's (2011) account of street politics uses the mass demonstrations that occurred that year in Cairo's Tahrir Square—with movements between the square, side streets, and back alleys—to contest the distinction between political and moral and the distinction between public and private. Butler argues that public space is not public in itself, or because it is planned to be so; publicness has to emerge through action, and the material conditions for political actions matter. Every act needs some kind of material support, which in turn means that the material support is part of the action, as well as that which the struggle is about. In other words, it matters that it is a public square that is being occupied. It matters because it becomes a way of securing the material conditions that are needed to perform in public, such as the square having a certain size, being accessible for many and do not have locked gates etc., and this is also what the struggle is about. It becomes a way of negotiating the public character of our material environment.

Public spheres do not necessarily have to achieve permanent status. If we reflect on the totem pole metaphor, we can say that totem poles are not monumental but they are rather included in the complex ecology of everyday things, mundane doings as well as institutional practices, and not with the presumption of permanence. They emerge and vaporize. They have a socio-material foundation, thus constructing spaces for social interaction, meaning that they are not foremost abstracted in principles and legislation, but in concrete doings, beyond mere talk. A common misunderstanding of totem poles is that they are foremost religious icons. It is true that they express relations with Native American spirituality, but as a metaphor joining the chapters in this part, a stronger interpretation is to see them not as containers of original culture but as part of a narrative that tells us about a long history of cultural relationships—both colonialism and the history of settlement—as well as the reaction against it: a Native American response made for a specific representational practice. That is also the case with the three chapters in this part. They are not stories from a specific point-of-view only, but the stories are integrated in a complex mesh of relationships, and it is the very entanglement that is put forth as characteristic of the idea of emerging publics.

On a conceptual level, two interrelated things bind the chapters in this part of the book together. First, we have the notion of *appropriation* and the accompanying aspect of social shaping of technology. In chapters 14 and 16, the design of empowering technologies is described, but it is stressed how the technologies must be appropriated in use. That they must be appropriated implies that without the social shaping of them—and the user-generated content necessary for making them meaningful—they are really nothing. The technologies themselves are simply empty placeholders, and it is the creative "colonialization" of them that make them players in the "collective creation of values" described in chapters 14 and 16. They, thus, represent how the participatory function of media is necessary for an understanding of present-day media ecologies. Second, the concept of *boundary infrastructuring* might be used as a common denominator for the three chapters. Earlier in this introduction, the possibility of a single homogeneous public sphere is heavily questioned. On the contrary, it is argued here that a multiplicity of publics actually better advances democracy. This implies that the often-sought consensus of opinions in debates is not what is strived for. Instead, what matters is to find commonalities strong enough to support the formation of publics but weak enough to permit different publics to appropriate them differently. One such concept, put forth by Star and Griesemer (1989, 297), is that of boundary objects:

> Boundary objects are those objects that both inhabit several communities of practice and satisfy the informal requirements of each of them. Boundary objects are thus both plastic enough to adapt to local needs and constraints of the several parties employing them, yet robust enough to maintain a common identity across sites. They are weakly structured in common use and become strongly structured in individual-site use.

Boundary objects are similar to boundary infrastructuring, but the latter can be understood as a process of providing a common ground for diverse stakeholders who at times have different agendas. This can be applied to the technological design of artifacts, which plays a major role in the chapters in this part, but it goes beyond the border constituted by material objects. It can also include the building of relationships and the shaping of communities through collective actions, as described in chapter 15. The re-configuration discussed in chapter 15 relates back to the concept of appropriation. It can be said that several of the technological artifacts described in this part of the book originate from technologies for monitoring and control, but as they are contextualized here—not least in the case of Bambuser—they rather try to re-direct the power of consumer- and monitoring technologies.

Chapter 14 explores the setting up of digital flows in the city of Malmö through the use of wireless media distribution in public spaces, and how mobile gaming can be used for storytelling about the mundane places that have potential for being transformed into a kind of urban publics. With a focus on urban youths, the chapter addresses the role of devices in urban place-making and the relationship between places and the everyday practices of urban youth and highlights the complex entanglement of relations, between citizens and other actors, that are characteristic for emerging publics in cities. Stories are provided from two different design experiments, each constructed of a series of events, where rather simple technologies have been used as sketching tools for how new-media applications can be used for temporarily appropriating public spaces. The first experiment involves the use of BluePromo (what could be described as a technology probe for distributing self-produced digital media via Bluetooth) by a grassroots youth movement in various urban places. Some specific qualities of the probe are discussed, as is the importance of performing public experiments. The second case, Urblove, makes use of a mobile gaming platform for storytelling about mundane local places. The discussion of Urblove focuses on what kinds of places were chosen and their meaning to the young people involved. Through the emerging design, associated both with the co-creation process and with the potential of the product/game engine, possible controversies in the use of urban spaces are put forth as they are used differently by actors with diverging agendas. These public experiments, in which different youth groups try out prototypes, bring forth narratives and stories of alternative use of urban spaces.

The subject of chapter 15 is a mobile sewing circle in which messages received by means of SMS (Short Message Service) were embroidered by hand or by an embroidery machine with bespoke software. While many stories in this book argue for design as a driving force in emerging publics, they do so from different perspectives. Most of the time, design prompts us to think about the products that are made. This chapter, however, explores how processes of making can constitute ground for co-articulations of issues from a multiplicity of perspectives. Here, the active building of new relationships can be seen as an example of how a strong boundary infrastructuring process makes it possible for a collective, not knowing each other in advance, to become materially implicated in a variety of potential issues. The invitation to embroider text messages is not a definition of a problem in itself, but rather an articulation of an area of curiosity, which can be framed as curiosity concerning ways of living with technologies. The account deals with how new relationships emerge through *making* (that is, being in close relation to digital and physical materials, as well as being close to other human beings). The chapter suggests that it is important to extend the network of connections to humans and non-humans that are not in the immediate realm, be it geographical or temporal.

Chapter 16 shares the story of the development and use of a highly relevant tool for democratic interventions in emerging publics: the Bambuser mobile-phone application, which is democratizing the live video broadcast. The Bambuser application enables streaming of live video, at almost no cost. It was used extensively at demonstrations and protests in Egypt and Tunisia during the so-called Arab Spring. The redirecting of what originally were intended as consumer- and monitoring technologies is very obvious in this chapter. Surveillance is turned into *sousveillance*—the monitoring of events by citizens rather than authorities. The chapter recounts both the design of Bambuser and interesting examples of its use. It highlights how much of the research on digital divides has been focused on access, while little attention has been given to inequality in the ability to use and fully comprehend the nature of the technology. In line with this, the chapter argues that the digital divide should be seen as, first of all, a social problem in which the technological aspect is highly integrated, and that Bambuser provides opportunities to significantly alter the structure of public spheres and bring marginalized groups of citizens closer to a deliberative state of forming public opinion. A central argument is how the use of technology could, and should, be seen as support for citizens in reflecting on their own awareness of what citizenship mean, rather than simply being a tool for political change.

References

Butler, Judith. 2011. Bodies in Alliance and the Politics of the Streets (http://eipcp.net/transversal/1011/butler/en).

Fraser, Nancy. 1990. Rethinking the Public Sphere: A Contribution to the Critique of Actually Existing Democracy. *Social Text* 25/26: 56–80.

Habermas, Jürgen. 1962. *The Structural Transformation of the Public Sphere: An Inquiry into a Category of Bourgeois Society*. Polity.

Marres, Nortje. 2005. Issues Spark a Public into Being: A Key But Often Forgotten Point of the Lippman-Dewey Debate. In *Making Things Public: Atmospheres of Democracy*, ed. B. Latour and P. Weibel. MIT Press.

Mouffe, Chantal. 2005. *On the Political*. Routledge.

Star, Susan Leigh, and James R. Griesemer. 1989. Institutional Ecology, "Translations" and Boundary Objects: Amateurs and Professionals in Berkeley's Museum of Vertebrate Zoology, 1907–39. *Social Studies of Science* 19 (3): 387–420.

Virilio, Paul. 1986. *Speed and Politics: An Essay on Dromology*. Semiotext(e).

14 Performing the City: Exploring the Bandwidth of Urban Place-Making through New-Media Tactics

Per Linde and Karin Book

Discourses on political participation, urban studies, innovation, and ICT development are becoming more and more entangled. Although social and cultural studies have recognized the importance of material entities in organizing and performing civic engagement for quite some time (see, for example, Marres 2011), we can also observe how the notion of *publics* is gaining more and more influence in the fields of design and technological development (see, for example, Le Dantec 2012). Within the context of urbanity, much falls into the realm of "smart cities," but the notion of "smart" is contested. We have heard about the number of people with Internet access, the number of devices talking to each other, and the potential revenue achievable for future service providers over and over again. It is not surprising that a transaction-based business rhetoric prevails, but we can also observe how the potential of networked communities, online or offline, is becoming an increasingly important factor in debating the concept of "smart cities." Halpern (2005), for example, understands the combination of ICTs and networked communities as a form of social capital, and his take on smartness, which is shared by many others, stresses the potential of local interaction:

… ICT networks may have great potential to boost local social capital, provided they are geographically "intelligent," that is, are smart enough to connect you directly to your neighbors; are built around natural communities; and facilitate the collective knowledge. (ibid., 509–510).

This takes us one step beyond a mere technology-centered perspective. Furthermore, we can, together with Marres (2011), claim that participation is located in everyday material practices and that these are connected with other modalities of action, such as innovation or democratization. In this respect, material participation challenges the long-prevalent assumption that "the notion that participation can in principle be contained in a singular space of political or moral engagement (i.e. a public debate forum)" (ibid., 514). Participation in publics "takes place." Whereas spaces might be stumbled upon, places are produced and constructed, and today such spatial practices are diverse and intersecting in cities. When different people and organizations develop their own spatial practices, the same urban space will be subject to diverging and at times conflicting agendas for how the space can be used. In this chapter, we will address how participatory devices are part of this place-making and what relation places have to the everyday practices of urban youth. After reflecting on the concept of smart cities, we will highlight the complex entanglement of relations that are characteristic of emerging new publics in cities. We will provide stories from two different design experiments in which rather simple technological prototypes have been used as means for collaboratively sketching how new-media applications can be used for temporarily appropriating public spaces. In the first experiment, a grassroots youth movement used BluePromo—a technology probe for distributing self-produced media via Bluetooth—at various urban places. Some specific qualities of the probe will be discussed, as will the importance of performing public experiments. In the second experiment, Urblove, a mobile gaming platform was used by some young people for storytelling about mundane local places in their neighborhoods. A focus for this case is to describe what kind of places that were chosen for the games produced and the meaning the places provide for the youths. Both cases can be conceptualized as "design things." Through the emerging design, associating both to the co-creation process and the potential of the product/game engine, possible controversies in the use of urban space are put forth. Not the least does the public experiments, where prototypes are tried out by different youth groups, bring forth narratives and storytelling of alternative use of urban space.

The impact that ubiquitous wireless network technologies and mobile phones have on our experience of the modern cityscape has been a driving force in many research projects in recent years. It seems safe to claim that such technologies are no longer considered to be neutral layers in urban living, but are rather an integrated part of the materialities of architecture and urban planning, in the social dimensions of city life, and in emerging cultural frameworks. Arguably, we have reached a point at which digital designs may be regarded as elements of our everyday construction of place in the urban setting. Castells (2007, 171) has described these aspects of city spaces as a "space of flows," addressing how the materialization of social interaction is performed also with and through combinations of networked telecommunication technologies and new media. These spaces can be said to be hybrid spaces, being influenced both by their physical manifestation and the digital content accessible, and to bring forth the fundamental question of how meaning can emerge in the interplay between people, artifacts, and place. From this perspective, what we refer to as *new-media tactics* can also be a way of temporarily appropriating places within the city space for a variety of different groups, at times questioning hierarchical structures of ownership of public spaces.

Emergence and temporality are coming more and more into focus as the building of fixed and inflexible large-scale infrastructures has resulted in many costly failures, but also because democratic sharing of public spaces calls for other strategies. Citing the "master builder" Robert Moses, Eric Paulos (2008, xxiv) writes "When you operate in an overbuilt metropolis, you have to hack your way with a meat ax." But those meat axes are no longer the only way to go. Instead, Paulos points to how "today's urban informatics effect change at the other end of the spectrum." "Instead of rewriting space with a few large-scale strokes," he continues, "they allow us to re-engineer an infinite number of small-scale relationships."

In this re-engineering of small-scale relationships, new publics will arise, and they will overlap with processes and "things" of design. The use of quotation marks around "things" is deliberate. The etymology of the word, originating from the Nordic pre-Christian culture, can be traced back to the meaning of an assembly, which was decided on beforehand to take place at a certain time and at a certain place to deal with certain "matters of concern" to a specific community. In the book *Design Things*, we suggest that we revisit and partly revert to the etymological history of things (A. Telier 2011). A major challenge for design today has to do with what is being designed: it is not just an object or a product, but also a thing—that is, a socio-material assembly that deals with matters of concern—in the original meaning of the word. Things are, thus, not only the results of understanding human relations and then developing a product addressing the relations such as in user-centered design. Rather, they are performed by socio-material "collectives of humans and non-humans," including both designed artifacts and the places where they are used. At the same time, a designed artifact is potentially a thing made public, since once it is delivered to its users it becomes a matter of concern to them with its new possibilities of interaction.

Consequently, in emerging publics, there is a complex entanglement taking place between citizens, public spaces, and things. Furthermore, if objects are seen as an effect of an array of relations, it follows that they do not exist in themselves; they are, rather, performed and emerging. They are also spatial, in that they establish the necessary conditions for creating and transforming space, which is also not given or fixed but, rather, performed. According to Bruno Latour (2004), we are accustomed to smooth and risk-free objects that are characterized by having clear boundaries with a well-defined essence, in which the producer becomes invisible when, for example, a product is released. In contrast, Latour puts forth the concept of tangled objects, or risky attachments, with no clear boundaries to the environment and where the producers are part of the definition. "Mad cow disease" and contaminated blood may be two examples of such tangled, complex, hard to manage objects. They are subject to constant translation and re-definition and are not detached from the consequences they trigger. In many cases, the triggered consequences take the form of revealed issues and controversies in relation to how public spaces are planned and used.

Carl DiSalvo elaborates another reference to Latour, developed in co-operation with Weibel, while considering their question "How things are made public?"—a question that addresses how complex situations of present-day society are made visible in a way that permits people to take actions on the situations at hand. DiSalvo (2009) complements that question with another one: "How are publics made with things?" What he aims at is how the processes and products of design might contribute to the formation and construction of publics, and thus also how a relationship might arise between design and collective action. His tentative answer on the relationship is that "projection" (as in representing possible alternative futures by creating scenarios) and "tracing" (as in revealing the origin of an issue) are valuable and designerly methods of constructing publics around issues. Both "projection" and "tracing" can be performed through participative and public design experiments. Relating to the design cases analyzed in this chapter, they can take on the form of questions such as "What if the local community could decide what media content can be accessed on the city buses?" and "Why is this neighborhood planned without regard to where youths could hang out?" For other actors, the questions could be posed differently, because that is the nature of issues and publics: several publics can be formed around the same issue, and the people belonging to the same community will have different takes on similar controversies. This says something about the emerging character of publics, which is also hinted at in chapter 13's mention of totem poles; they are not fixed or eternal entities, but are emerging. Furthermore, the cases mentioned here highlight other aspects of design as a socially motivated practice. They both invite marginalized groups (immigrant youths, skateboarding girls) to participate. Design is also seen as "design of tool kits" for participation in non-commercialized contexts, even though designs that most of the times are used within a commercialized context are applied in attempts to re-direct the power of consumer technologies (and thus indirectly to re-politicize consumer citizenship).

It is from this perspective we shall interpret the title "Performing the city" and the concepts of urban place-making and new-media tactics. Whereas strategies are planned from above, with strong power hierarchies inherent in the planning, tactics have a bottom-up character, supporting citizens in experiencing and living in the city in the way they want to (de Certeau 1984). If a public is formed from a heterogeneity of perspectives and actors, how can we designers act in a way that supports them in populating the same public spaces despite their different agendas and desires? How can we support them in appropriating these spaces in ways that may be completely different from the intention of the original "master planners"? How might the re-engineering of small-scale relationships, hinted at here, take place?

De-Euclidiating space: the BluePromo case

Fundamental to our design experiments is how the "everyday man" can, either temporarily or long-term, appropriate public urban spaces, which traditionally are designed for a specific purpose and are governed by official policies on how the space should be used. This appropriation can only partially be imagined mentally. A stronger approach would be to regard the temporal appropriation as an act of performance. We therefore would like to conceptualize the "performance" of space as an innovation practice in constructing emerging publics. From this perspective, as well as from the perspective of interaction design that has been a driving force in the projects, it becomes necessary to address the use of public urban spaces as something lived and experienced and something that through the potential of the design experiments can be re-experienced as possible and different futures. It must be possible to rehearse alternatives of spatial use. In recent years we have seen a huge variety of design projects dealing with combinations of geographical coordinates, mobile phones, and digital media, most often under the umbrella of mobile computing or locative media applications. In many cases, however, and perhaps because of the fact that augmented maps provide such a strong potential, space is often related to the more abstract idea of maps. What is needed is a perspective that treats space not as mathematical coordinates, as in Euclidian geometry, but as social and lived spaces that empowers emerging publics to try out alternative use of those spaces.

One such perspective is the concept of *place-centric computing*, which argues for a place-centric perspective on digital designs in which digital technology is regarded as an element of the ongoing social construction of place (Messeter 2009). Place-centric computing may be described as a class of digital designs in which functions, as well as the information these functions provide, are inherently grounded in place-specific

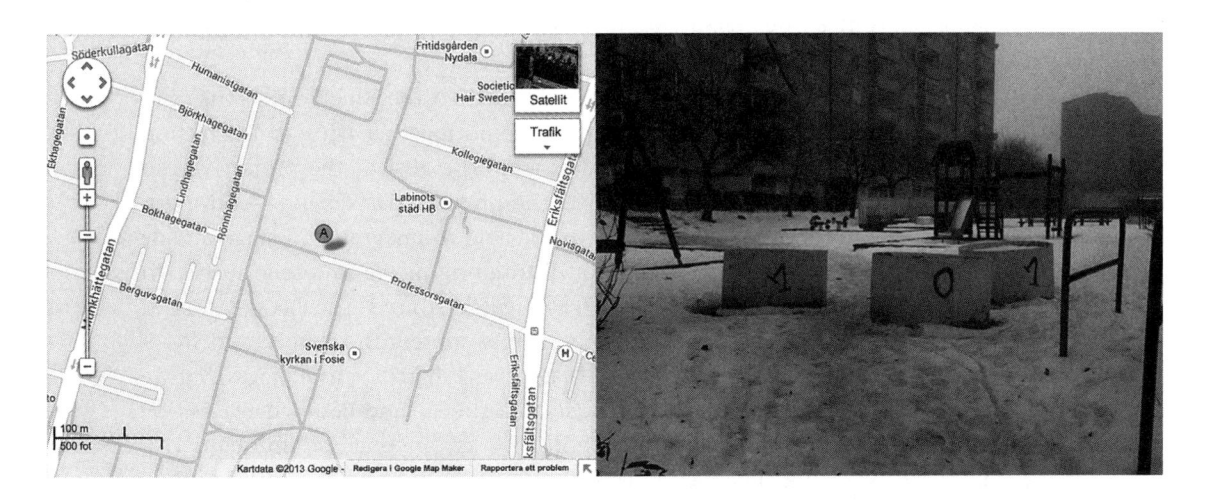

Figure 14.1
Right: The 101 yard (Per Linde, CC:BY-NC), which is not easily represented on the map shown at left (map data copyright 2013 Google).

social and cultural practices, and account for the structuring conditions of place construction—social and cultural as well as material.

Such a perspective stands in contrast to the general anytime-anywhere perspective of commercial mobile services, as well as much of the current research in location-aware systems and location-based services, where usually generic functions serve users with place-specific content. The perspective of place-centric computing partially overlaps with the growing discipline of urban informatics (Foth 2009), which considers the present-day city to be a dense ecology of impersonal social interactions occurring within recognizably public places, thus looking upon the urban environment as an appealing design resource. A shift in perspective is advocated, replacing the emphasis on urban form with an emphasis on urban *experience*. In particular, this chapter takes inspiration from Paulos' notion of participatory urbanism, which "promotes new styles and methods for individual citizens to become proactive in their involvement with their city, neighborhood, and urban self-reflexivity" (2008, 420).

Consequently, one challenge for us designers becomes to stage a design process in which we can, together with users, explore the new possibilities of integrating digital media services and content with the city landscape, and shape place-centric interactions for city dwellers, commuters, and visitors. Envisioning these place-centric interactions, arguably, requires live experiments in real-world settings with design representations that evoke experiences beyond everyday commercial mobile applications. Therefore, it is important to develop design formats robust enough to be used in live experiments, but sufficiently open to re-interpretation to allow a constructive dialogue between users and designers.

With these directions as a starting point, we launched the BluePromo project to explore place-centric interactions in the city of Malmö together with an interaction design company and a grassroots youth movement. The goal of the project was to set up a participatory process that would spur the project's participants—end users, designers, and technology developers alike—to be able to imagine and stage a wide array of use situations and service models for distributing media in public spaces. In urban planning, public space is often regarded as "neutral ground" such as squares and parks, or as public or semi-public institutions such as museums, schools, and shopping malls. Reviewing the literature reveals a bias toward shared central places, but we wanted to include backyards, public toilets, isolated streets, and deserted places. We avoided general conceptions of city population such as "anyone" or "museum visitors," just as we avoided general activities such as "leisure time in the park." Rather, we chose to cooperate with the grassroots youth movement RGRA (Rörelsen Gatans Röst och Ansikte, meaning "voice and face of the street movement"). RGRA is formally run as a nonprofit organization, but is in reality a rather loosely structured organization with several subgroups. Thus, the organization could be characterized as consisting of "clans" or "tribes" rather than as an organized community. Its members are youths between 12 and 20 years of age, many of them born in Sweden but with parents born in non-European countries. What unites them is a shared interest in hip-hop culture. Since many of the members are producing music themselves, even though they don't have contracts with record companies, alternative ways of distributing media are highly interesting to them. Many already do so, using MySpace and similar online platforms. Their consumption of music is highly mobile, but the old "boom box" is mostly replaced by the mobile phone.

In one of the first workshops, the youngsters came up with the idea "What if we had a radio tower of our own?" A first experiment was performed on city buses. Hip-hop songs that had been produced in one of the neighborhoods that the bus went through were distributed to passengers. In the discourse around place and space, many places have been disregarded as being too transient for having any significance for human life. The anthropologist Marc Augé, for example, talks about "non-places," such as highways, hotels, or supermarkets (1995). Many consider public transport to be such a non-place.

In our view, the notion of non-places is not necessarily true in the case of RGRA. The youngsters spend a significant amount of time each day on the city buses, and the buses are not just anonymous vehicles for transport. You get to know the drivers and your fellow passengers. You sit down in specific seats, if available, and the routes taken become part of the complexity of rhythms that shape the patterns of movement in the cityscape. The bus ride is, as such, a place for possible inhabitation, even though it has a highly temporary character. The hip-hop artist Rap-Tor articulated that very theme

Figure 14.2
Left: The BluePromo box. Right: Snapshots from the experiment on the bus. Per Linde (CC:BY-NC).

in a song titled "On the Bus." The experiment was quite successful and was enjoyed by the producers, the passengers, and the bus company.

To highlight issues of "ownership" of the bus as a public space, and to spur the creation of a wide set of use situations, the bus company was invited to participate in the project. At the start, the bus company insisted that it "owned" all advertising space on the bus, including wireless channels of distribution, while RGRA maintained that anyone going on the bus could distribute music to other travellers on the bus, using a wireless service. Despite initial hopes on cooperation between conflicting interests, the focus of the project became how RGRA could use the opportunities provided by the device—a Bluetooth box—developed in the project. It became obvious to them that the specific device was just one of many possible instances where their mobile phones could be used for augmenting public participation at specific events and at certain places.

After the experiment on the bus, we tried out a variety of places and settings where RGRA used the Bluetooth box to set up temporary streams of digital media, thus appropriating places within the city for shorter time periods. In doing so, the media enriched the youth's feelings of being in control of the events set up, as well as the visitors' experience of RGRA as the organizer and sender of the media.

Even though the content primarily has been self-produced music, other content such as jingles for their radio station or pictures of hip-hop artists within RGRA has been used. While alternative music distribution, beyond records and online accessibility, were the starting point of the project, an explorative learning process commenced. What emerged was a tactical thinking within the community, where it was continuously experimented with how these place-specific media streams could be used as a tactic for appropriating urban places for a short while.

In terms of design products, the Bluetooth box was developed within the project and has been used in a variety of settings. But even more important, from the perspective of emerging publics and possibilities to "perform the city," a learning process started together with RGRA on how they could benefit from mobile wireless technologies while appropriating urban places. Their growing attention to how to benefit from such technologies started a long-term process, in which we (in 2014) are still involved.

In another example of the use of Bluetooth technology for creating an overall experience of a place rather than of a "system," we, together with RGRA and the interaction design company Do-Fi, worked on "The Parliament of the Suburbs," an event aimed at increasing participation in democratic processes among youths in suburbs. While the box was used to push a jingle for RGRA's then new radio channel, several other wireless installations were present for other purposes. For example, you could send a text message to a display located on a stage where a debate between youths, politicians, and representatives from the police was taking place. Other examples of Bluetooth-based services were the BlueWall, where you could push images from a mobile phone to a public

Figure 14.3
Narrowcasting "taking place." Per Linde (CC:BY-NC).

display, and BlukeBox, which made it possible to push a song from a mobile phone to the playlist of a public jukebox. The variety of wireless devices created opportunities for participation at the event and encouraged use of mobile media, as part of experiencing the place. Just as important, it provides means for grasping the mechanisms and the possibilities for the flow of push and pull of digital media through wireless technologies. Equally important is that such events provide a learning situation where it becomes possible to grasp and understand the mechanisms and the possibilities for the flow of digital media through wireless technologies. This can then be the topic of discussion and re-design in workshops, but, most important, it supports the youth's ability to actually appropriate the technology beyond the scope of the singular device.

Here, it is interesting to address an observation in our experiments that adds to the discussion on the so-called physical-digital divide. It came to our attention that for the user it becomes more and more complex to understand what is digital and what is not. For example, it is hard to perceive invisible phenomena, such as Internet connectivity, as belonging to a specific device.

For developers, a focus on constant connectivity of the smartphone as a discrete device is understandable, but entering into a network of humans and other devices, the perception of what is connected to what gets blurred for the human user. When connectivity is mediated by other devices, such as a Bluetooth pushing device or an SMS-engine connected to a gaming platform, the user achieves a portion of the connectivity, and in most cases that is good enough. Having the functionality working in a wanted way is enough. You don't have to worry about the Internet as a matter of device capability as long as results of actions are satisfying. The focus is more on the phone as just another element in the networked ecology of humans, places, and technology and the relations that entangle them all. There is no longer a distinction between what is digital and what is not. This is also stressed by Ragano (2002), who recounts how Japanese i-mode developers avoided presenting e-services as "Internet things" and instead presented bundles of phone features as if they were material things.

Furthermore, these hybrid spaces are characterized by yet another layer, that of the social:

> A hybrid space, thus, is a conceptual space created by the merging of borders between physical and digital spaces, because of the use of mobile technologies as social devices. Nevertheless, a hybrid space is not constructed by technology. It is built by the connection of mobility and communication and materialized by social networks. (de Souza e Silva 2006, 265)

These social networks can be either present or absent, either known or unknown, because what arises is that places are constructed of a variety of different contexts, which no longer are inaccessible. Instead, the meaning of places can be addressed in terms of the potential for absorbing the many folded connections and relationships. Thus, it is worthwhile to stress both the spatiality and the multiplicity of connections in these networks in order to understand how meaning emerge in interaction with hybrid spaces:

> Networks are spatial structures, and what guides their existence is the large number of connections embedded in them. A hybrid space is also a networked space, constituted by a mobile network of people and nomadic technologies that operate in noncontiguous physical spaces. (ibid., 272).

What takes place is a kind of re-contextualization. Places are made aware of, and accessible for, each other, and people are drawn into their respective "world of places" (Wikström 2009).

From the perspective of emerging publics, the instantiated learning process among all stakeholders has been important. But, as designers, we also learned to work with the qualities of simplicity and "underdetermination" while putting technological prototypes into play. It is indisputable that the extremely extended functionality of mobile devices increases complexity, and in many cases the computational material is hidden. Johan Redström (2008) comments on how the perspectives on form and material are in conflict with each other to the extent that they create a boundary that tangible interaction design cannot pass. This is, of course, even more so in the case of multi-functional devices such as mobile phones. Redström argues that the shift from carburetors to fuel injection in motor vehicles "offers far less D.I.Y. (do-it-yourself) opportunities for the more mechanically oriented" (ibid., 123). While this creates a complexity in interfaces, there is also another side of the coin, namely the tendency to design even further complex bodies of functionality. Chang et al. (2007) describe a phenomenon, common among students, that they call "featuritis": a tendency to emphasize the number or the novelty of features over usability. They recognize that this tendency is prevalent not only among students but also among design professionals. This can become an even more potential hazard when we approach the field of user-driven innovation, where users' potential to learn about possibilities and constraints in design materials is crucial for their ability to appropriate technology. Ron Wakkary (2009, 16) writes about the concept of the everyday designer, and how underdetermination (as opposed to multi-complex and overdetermined design) creates a space for people to "perform themselves through the use of the technology." Wakkary suggests two design goals: "simplicity" (designing artifacts to be simple and to have the potential to be combined with other artifacts to better support unique and complex needs) and "undirected affordances" (that is, trying *not* to leverage specific affordances to perform tasks, instead trying to be open for more diverse use and interpretation). The goal of simplicity resonates well with Fitzmaurice and Buxton (1997, 47), who state that "the ultimate benefit may be to have a collection of strong specific devices creating a strong general system." Imagining aspects of combinations and bricolage, instead of thinking "one device with complex functionality," was the goal for the BluePromo project. Here we have not dwelt much on the design as such; rather, we have argued for how the "underdesign" of the probe and the public participatory experiments both figured in a collaborative "rehearsing of the future" (Halse et al. 2010).

In our project, we did not start out from the design-as-problem-solving perspective. Rather, we aspired to set up a design space that took "possibilities for change" as a starting point, rather than try to solve existing problems within a specific practice. That required exploring what such a transformation could mean, not only for designers and developers but also for user groups such as RGRA. If the design is aiming at radical transformation rather than incremental improvement of an existing practice, the object of study, of course, disappears, but the design also limits the user's understanding of what can be achieved with the design.

Action science, which for many designers seems more relevant than the traditional philosophy of science, seeks knowledge that serves action. It is argued that knowledge is developed with not only general knowledge in mind, but also with the human in mind. The discipline also tries to facilitate learning about change from within practice. The knowledge achieved should be relevant also for forming purposes, just as much as achieving purposes already formed. In doing this, forming of purposes, the actor also enacts values. As new technologies and thus new ways of performing practice are introduced, we should, while trying out the technologies, reflect on the context in where they are used. Is the current way of working or doing things really appropriate? Answering the question "What shall I do?" gives rise to formulating an intentionality that might be congruent with the existing practice, or it might express a deviation from the current norm of practice (Argyris et al. 1985).

Argyris et al. (ibid., 237) claim that action science "must devise some process (1) that will allow participants to make explicit the data they select and the meanings they impose and (2) that will enable them to negotiate the differences in meaning that arise so that they might reach agreement." Foundational for a practice is that it concerns both an established and specific context of doings and also the common understanding which permeates the doing in sometimes tacit ways and thus makes it possible. It is both activity and the reflection necessary for understanding it. This is a knowledge that must be understood socially. It is produced, but it is also re-produced, since it includes traces of previous practice.

The arguments above also point in the direction of another definition of hybridity. In cultural studies, 'hybridity' refers to fluid and performative subjectivity that resists the rigidity of any fixed and static categories of identity, such as gender, race, and nationality (Kwan 2004). In performative acts, a public presentation of the self takes place, but strong forces of ideology also are at play. Butler (1997) highlights political aspects of performativity in addressing how often conventions, at times tacit and taken for granted, also are enacted, for example, in terms of gender issues. But at the same time, as conventions have the potential of being strengthened and unconsciously affirmed, deliberation and boundary breaking become possible. Since performative acts relate to conventional power, the very conventions themselves can be reiterated and re-lived, which opens up possibilities for appropriation and for alternative (often unauthorized) use. As an example, Butler (ibid., 147) cites Rosa Parks: "When Rosa Parks sat in the front of the bus, she had no prior right to do so guaranteed by any … conventions of the South. And yet, in laying claim to the right for which she had no prior authorization, she endowed a certain authority on the act, and began the insurrectionary process of overthrowing those established codes of legitimacy."

In "performing" the city and the technologies accessible there (now exchanging the more traditional "moving through" or "using" as in describing a city in terms of its functional components), an ongoing exploration of the liminal aspects of a city is unfolded. Victor Turner (1988) articulates the concept of liminality in his work on anthropology and performance. Liminality can be described as a passage and a "no man's land" between the known and the potential. Typically, the concept can be referred to a transitional space or state of identity, as in initiation rites in which an individual passes from childhood to adulthood or as when a public space is temporarily turned into a site for a carnival. Fragmentation, estrangement, and hybridization are all qualities put into play in liminal acts. On the learning of metapatterns, Turner (1998, 103) writes that "metapatterns are akin to what some call 'frames[,]' the metaphorical borders within which the facts of experience can be viewed, reflected upon and evaluated," and that "they are liminal, in the sense that they are suspensions of quotidian reality, occupying privileged spaces where people are allowed to think about how they think, about the terms in which they conduct their thinking, or how they feel about how they feel in everyday life" (Turner 1988, 102).

Notions of metapatterns and liminality have several implications for "city-based" development of mobile technologies, which is, we argue, strongly related to the emergence of new publics. First, the focus may shift from the final product and the decontextualized computable artifact to the qualities that make them open to citizens' participation "before use," in open and public experimentation with prototypes during design time, and their potential for appropriation and configurability "during use." This has been addressed in the discussion of the BluePromo project. Second, analysis can move "away from totalizing explanations or representations and towards decentralized performativity, which 'forces one to consider the space that would otherwise simply be glossed over as void'" (Galloway 2004, 398, quoting Joost van Loon). These spaces are, thus, not voids. Quite the contrary, that is where much of everyday life takes place, and theses spaces are the in-betweens where social innovation might occur.

Storytelling neighborhoods: The Urblove project

Working with RGRA enabled us to study an informal group's patterns of movement and its strategies for appropriating urban places. We have continued the cooperation with RGRA in several other projects, of which one addresses the notion of mobile urban gaming. In present-day urban life, we can observe a tension between habitual patterns of movement and possible expansions of such movements. An observation on urban living is how many youth groups move primarily within the same blocks they are living in. This is especially true in many suburbs dominated by immigrants, which at times also are being marginalized by media, with social isolation as a result. As major Swedish cities are becoming increasingly segregated, how designers can support urban exploration beyond the "home turf" is an important question. One exciting prospect is to let inhabitants of a neighborhood create "game routes" within the neighborhood—routes to be experienced by others playing the game, thus inviting to a more true perception of the places and cultures within different city districts. With this ambition, the Urblove project sought to explore the possibilities of a service that combines urban exploring and mobile gaming with the possibilities inherent in participatory cultures and the potential of user-created content. The project was carried out in cooperation with the gaming company Ozma, with RGRA, with two school classes, and with a group of girl skateboarders. Two goals of the project were to develop a platform for mobile games and to develop a number of specific game route examples. Other goals, from the perspective of emerging publics and public space, were to study youths' urban spatial practices and to achieve an understanding of their relationship to different local places and how their means for temporary appropriation of those places could change through use of new media. What places did the youths choose for the games, and how could that be interpreted?

Urblove takes concrete urban places as its starting point for developing and playing games. We set up participatory processes where youths took on the on the role of co-designers. Using an SMS engine complemented with a Web platform, the youth groups created "routes" for playing and crafted narratives that take players through local neighborhoods or more central parts of the city. The game "stories" are presented in fragments and sent to the players via text messages. Each message contains a part of the story and a puzzle to be solved in order to obtain the next part of the story. The riddles, which can only be answered by being at a specific place, are answered through sending a text message, and new riddles are sent, resulting in the narrative unfolding piece by piece along with the players moving through a dedicated area in the city. The game engine calculates points to the teams playing in relation to the amount of right answers and the time spent on the game. The games also draw upon the capabilities of mobile phones to produce and consume new digital media formats, and use of a phone's camera is often a central component of a game. Cheap-to-use technologies, such as SMS, make the games easily accessible.

Just as in the BluePromo case, the notion of the public experiments was a driving force for all actors in the project, which demanded lots of engagement and cross-community communication. Engaging with known places in new ways provided means for recognizing the places as having meaning and for being further invested with value through the games. Throughout the project, cross-community communication helped participants to invite others to play the games. For example, RGRA created games that the girl skateboarders were invited to play. While the skateboarders were in a part of Malmö they had never visited before, they were exposed to people in that neighborhood. The girls then produced their own games and invited RGRA youths to play. Skateboarders from other parts of Sweden were invited to play during a big skateboarding event.

For outsiders exploring the appropriation of urban public spaces, understanding the everyday spatial practices of local communities is a challenge. In an article about urban exploring, Pinder (2005, 391) cites an interview in which an urban exploring project is described as "about trying to find what's marvelous, life-affirming, or at least exciting about seemingly mundane places."

Three different groups of young people were invited to create routes and play the game: (1) a group of young men from RGRA (age 15–20) living or at least being connected to the area of Hermodsdal, (2) a group of young female skateboarders in their twenties, and (3) two school classes in secondary schools located in different areas (the inner city area Rörsjöstaden and the low-status area Rosengård). The focus here will be on Hermodsdal and the skating games.

The Game Routes in Hermodsdal

The first group to create a game route and a story connected to it was made up of young men in Hermodsdal. The area is considered to be quite low in status. It has about 3,000 inhabitants and consists of multi-family houses. To outsiders, the area is—through mass media—primarily known for criminality, violence, and vandalism. When going to Hermodsdal to observe the group developing games, we thought about possible strategies for selecting places/spots. Two strategies were identified: either the boys would select nice (as in interesting, beautiful, or otherwise attractive) spots in order to show that Hermodsdal is better than its reputation, or they would use the area's reputation to create fear, excitement, and perhaps even respect. The first strategy could be referred to as a place-marketing way of selecting spots—a positive image production. The second could be referred to as a way of strengthening the conceptions and perceptions of the place—a negative image production.

The boys were divided into two groups. Both groups selected similar and in most cases identical places/spots:

the 101 yard ("everyone knows this yard")
a small grocery shop
the place and clock in front of a larger grocery shop
the underground passageway under the road separating Hermodsdal from Gullviksborg
the sign at the entrance of Gullviksborg
a bus stop
the sign outside the police station
the statue in the school yard
a flagpole
a free-standing church bell

These places are by no means extraordinary or exciting. They are neither intimidating nor nice and attractive. Why didn't the participants select more interesting places?

Figure 14.4
An everyday view in Hermodsdal. Karin Book (CC:BY-NC).

One probable reason is that these are the most common and well-known places in the everyday lives of the people living in the area.

As Crang (1998) points out, it is common to define oneself through a place. The place is not just geographical hardware but is also loaded with meaning. It reflects the people living there, but it could just as well be a reflection of preconceived notions and stereotypes of the place and its inhabitants. Seen from this perspective, the youngsters in Hermodsdal do not have an illusion of something more than the very everyday and basic. Their choices probably just reflect the sense of place by the inhabitants, or the preconceived sense of place. It might just be that they see meaning in those places that an outside observer cannot see. It might even be a provocative act to choose such mundane places in order to get a reaction, but in this case there were no signs of a hidden message.

Lefebvre (1991) developed a conceptual framework for describing how spaces are produced, perceived, and used. In order to use that conceptual framework to discuss the chosen places in Hermodsdal, we will simplify it.

Lefebvre's so-called spatial triad contains three levels, or types, of spaces:

Spatial practice or *perceived space* refers to the observable practices of space.
Representations of space or *conceived space* refers to a conceptual space. The simplest way of exemplifying representations of space is by means of maps and diagrams. Also, a more complex view of this type of space has been presented; conceived space, as the concept indicates, is about how space is pictured or reproduced by certain individuals or groups. The received representation tends to be that of experts—for instance, planners, architects, and urban researchers. Also, media could probably be added to the list of those producing recognized representations of space. To sum up, conceived space is a dominating conception, and connected discourse, about what a certain space is and how it should be interpreted on the basis of power, ideology, and knowledge.
Representational space is the *lived space* in the ordinary life of the residents and users. The lived space is, of course, based on the spatial practice, but also on symbols, images, and experiences by the users. The lived experiences developed in space are results of a dialectic relationship between spatial practice and the representations of space, or, as Zhang (2006, 221) puts it, "the third term of lived space is balanced carefully between the two poles of conceived space (purely idealism) and perceived space (pure materialism)." A material space is given social meaning.

When going to low-status areas such as Hermodsdal and Rosengård, outside visitors often have a certain conception about the areas and the places within them—conceptions based on the expert and media discourse on these low-status areas, which were developed during the 1960s and the 1970s. The common notions based on this discourse are mainly negative and almost threatening. As was noted above, the boys in Hermodsdal selected ordinary places when creating their game routes, and what we as observers perceive is purely the material, spatial practices. The places seem ordinary and, to an outsider, without social meaning. To the young people who selected the places, however, they were important and loaded with meaning, both in a practical way and in a social way. For the residents, the places constitute representational, lived space. The bus stop is not just a bus stop; it is an important meeting place where information is exchanged and relations are developed. The tunnel is not just a tunnel for cyclists and pedestrians; it is a symbol of the connection—but also the division—of two neighborhoods. When a teacher at one of the schools involved in the project complained that the youngsters had selected boring places, she, like us and other adults involved in the project, expressed her perception of what a nice, interesting, or exciting place is—a perception based on a superior discourse.

How representations of and discourses on space are produced, and by whom, probably are undergoing changes in the era of modern communication technologies. Now, it is not only people with power and the "right type" of knowledge and networks who have the opportunity to decide how a space should be represented and interpreted; others also have the opportunity to do so. Thus, two or more parallel representations of the same place/space can be produced in different forums and groups—one of them official and dominant among those with official power and valued knowledge, one or more unofficial. The unofficial representation could be the same as the lived space, but not necessarily. As it is produced in the intersection between the physical space and the communication technologies used, it could also be considered a hybrid space (de Souza e Silva 2006). Today, representations of space aren't just about the tension and interplay between physical and social space, as Lefebvre wrote; they are also about the digital space. The technologies make it possible to create individual representations of space—for instance, personalized maps highlighting an individual's favorite spots.

The Game Routes of the Skateboard Games
One day a group of female skateboarders gathered to create routes for Urblove games for other skateboarders. Among skateboarders, the places used for skating are referred to as spots. The spots occurring in the games were the following:

the hump in an inner-city park called Rörsjöparken ("unknown among skaters," according to one of them)
the parking garage underneath the Triangeln shopping center (described by one skateboarder as a "well-known, exciting spot where skating is actually not allowed")
Steppen, an illegally or spontaneously built skatepark, located at an old industrial site, which after the official skate parks is Malmö's best-known and most extensive skateboarding facility
a smaller illegally or spontaneously built skatepark along a bike lane between a railway and an industrial site
the humps in a public playground
an indoor skatepark called Bryggeriet

The selected spots thus included officially built skateparks, unofficially built skateparks or spots, and facilities built for other purposes but usable for skateboarding.

When we asked the skateboarders about the selection of spots, two reasons were prominent. One was externally oriented: to display Malmö as a skate city by emphasizing less well known spots and those not officially established. It was for this reason that the internationally recognized Stapelbäddsparken and the skatepark in Sibbarp were left out. The other reason was more internal-oriented: the spots had social importance for the skateboarders, who associated them with social activities—meeting with other skateboarders, barbecues, and so on.

When the skateboarders talked about their game routes, they gave them special names, such as "The humps" and "Steppen." Borden (2001, 50) notes that the naming of skate spots seems to be important in "providing a consensus label by which skaters could refer to locations." However, the labeling could also be about keeping spots hidden from people not included in the skateboarding community. The skateboarders know the names; others often don't. However, the proliferation of social media has made it harder to keep a spot hidden—pictures and film clips of the spots are widely available.

Among skateboarders, where one skates seems to be as important as the skating itself. One of the female skateboarders taking part in the game commented that "skating around to look for spots is the foundation of skating." Borden (2001, 47) argues that places have always been important in skateboarding: "The spatial tactics associated with skateboarding were … initially those of reconnaissance, roving the city to identify new spaces for skateboarding." Another of the female skateboarders said "a spot that is too challenging or not at all challenging could still be a place where I spend time because it is a cool place to be, rather than a good skating experience." Social

Figure 14.5
Left: The Steppen skatepark. Right: an illegally or spontaneously built skatepark along a bicycle path. Karin Book (CC:BY-NC).

media help skateboarders to find spots, but some of the cachet of a spot depends on its uniqueness. Thus, in one sense social media are important tools for skateboarders, but in another sense they are quite the opposite.

Different kinds of skateboarders seem to have different relations to space. Borden (2001) notes that street-skating is more based on everyday activities and spaces and could be said to be a part of the urban fabric and movements, whereas more spectacular and extreme forms of skating are done at purpose-built facilities and in special events. The skate spots of the Urblove games follow the logic of street-skating. One of the most interesting aspects of the skaters' (or more specifically the street-skaters') relation to the urban space is that they give space a new meaning and a new scope of use. According to Borden (2001, 187), skateboarders "implicitly realize the importance of the streets and neglected architecture as a place to act." As Lefebvre (1991) and Lieberg (1992) note, border areas between residential areas are used in identity processes. Some skateboarders tend to skate at abandoned and derelict places and urban structures; Malmö's Steppen is an obvious example of that. Modernist urban structures, which have found to be inappropriate for a vibrant urban life, sometimes are brought alive by skateboarders.

On the subject of time and space in relation to skateboarding, Borden (2001, 198) comments that skaters "construct a different temporal rhythm by staying longer in an urban plaza as others hurry through." Skaters also use places (for instance, a commuter bus station, a plaza in a business district, or the parking garage used in in the Urblove games) at times when few others use them, such as nights and Sundays.

One of the skateboarders involved in the Urblove project described her favorite skate spot in her home town. A spontaneously developed, self-organized skate park at an empty industrial site, it is located in a hidden place, which is well-known among skateboarders but fairly unknown among others, though information about it has been spread by means of blogs, Facebook, YouTube, and the local newspaper. The place is a bit messy and rough, but according to the skateboarder that is good—it sends the message "This is our place; keep out." Until recently, skateboarders used the site illegally. They were threatened with ejection by the owner of the property, but after discussions with city officials and the owner the skateboarders were allowed to use the site for the time being. That skate park, like several others that have been mentioned, could be considered as a hybrid space developed at the intersection of physical space, digital space, and social networks.

In connection with Borden's discussion of the importance of abandoned and shabby places, it may be fruitful to mention a number of concepts pointing at similar phenomena. Högdahl (2003) uses the term *creative loopholes* to suggest that these places inspire creativity. Cupers and Miessen (2002) talk of *spaces of uncertainty* and *margins*. De Sola Moralés (1995) refers to *terrain vague*, and Jarnäng (2010) to *undefined spaces*. These concepts pertain to left-over spaces, or interspaces, that have lost their former functions and have been invaded by new groups and uses. As was briefly mentioned above, old industrial sites, abandoned railyards, parking spaces, and derelict parts of a residential area may fit into this category. New users may imprint a space and redefine it. Therefore, *redefined space* is probably a more suitable term than *undefined space*, insofar as the space is defined though perhaps not in an official way.

According to Jarnäng (2010), an undefined spaces (or what we prefer to call a redefined space) may be useful as an alternative public space; may provide opportunities for self-organization, creativity, and spontaneity; may be suitable for temporal and flexible activities; may have an identity-building function; and may have a narrative function.

If we go back to the conceptual triad developed by Lefebvre (1991), the concept of undefined or redefined places, or places of uncertainty for that matter, are undefined or refined or uncertain in relation to something else, namely the official view of the function of the place. This view could be deduced in official planning documents or maps (straightforward representations of places) or is a common understanding—a dominating discourse—of how a certain place or space should be defined and used. There are few places in our Swedish cities without a planned function, which in turn give few opportunities to spontaneous, flexible, and identity-developing activities, without going against proper or even allowed behavior. Moreover, there are few places without commercial powers behind them. Commercialism is a powerful force in the development of urban discourses and public spaces. In this context, the redefinition of places into alternative public spaces by skateboarders is important in the creation of identities and symbols of their own. The redefined spaces are definitely lived spaces for the skateboarders, who, according to Borden (2001, 219), "undertake a discontinuous edit of architecture and urban space, recomposing their own city from different places, locations, urban elements, routes and times."

Lieberg (1992) uses a study of activities and spaces of teenagers in a residential area in a medium-size Swedish town to divide the youngsters into three groups: the home-oriented, the organization-oriented, and the friends-oriented. This division is similar to the one used by Hermansson (1988): the parent-oriented, the *Umwelt*-oriented, and the friends-oriented. If we use these divisions in regard to the two groups of young people in the Urblove project, the young boys in Hermodsdal are friends-oriented and the girl skateboarders are *Umwelt*-oriented. According to Lieberg and Hermansson, the friends-oriented youngsters spend a lot of their time in their neighborhood, socializing with friends in public spaces or in the local youth recreation center. In contrast with the *Umwelt*-oriented youngsters, they do not participate in organized activities. Lieberg refers to Alberto Mellucci's concept "nomads of the present" to describe these youngsters as living in the present, engaging in what is happening right at the moment. Life revolves around the friends (or the "gang") and certain meeting places in the neighborhood. Lieberg describes it as an informal, non-organized rationality. They develop a certain sense of place at the neighborhood level.

Inspired by Pinder (2005) we thought about the aim and use of different spots in the Urblove project. What is the player expected to do at the spot? Is the expected doing about the place, or the activity? One might pass by in a fairly passive way, one might see something, or (a bit stronger) one might observe something. One might use the place for a given or a not-given activity, or experience the place, or think about it, or change it in some way. Here we can see a difference between the games in the residential areas and the skating games. Whereas in the Hermodsdal games the places were seen as places to pass by quite passively or to observe only briefly, in the skateboarders' games the use of the selected spots was more active, including not only observing but also using and experiencing. The skate spots and the communication around them, not only in the Urblove games but also generally, have a clear performative ingredient. However, the lack of activity and performative content in the games in Hermodsdal doesn't necessarily mean that the places are without content and not used for activities. As was noted above, the places have social meaning and content that are not reflected in the games, at least not to an outsider's eye. Perhaps this is attributable to a lack of competence to communicate the meaning and the use of places, or perhaps the meaning is taken for granted.

'We's, 'me's, journeymen, and mastership

Social media, mobile technologies, and games such as those in the Urblove project have great potential to communicate messages about places. The sense and the meaning of a place are locally embedded and not always obvious to outsiders. Therefore, the perspective of insiders is important in analyzing, understanding, and developing the city. However, it is also an important tool for helping insiders, such as users and residents, to reflect on the places of everyday life and to bring content and meaning to life. On the basis of the Urblove experience, we can say that reflecting on places and communicating about them require practice, courage, and probably pride. The skateboarders were used to do so and by doing so they are proactive and provide examples on how urban space can be re-defined or re-contextualized. For the young men in Hermodsdal, to communicate about their places and neighborhood, as in the Urblove case, is a new experience. The means for doing so, if developed and practiced, have a great potential in the process of re-contextualizing the mundane city and discovering the liminality. A higher degree of self-reflexivity has to take place in order to call it participatory urbanism, but it is a first step.

This is not to say that self-reflexivity doesn't take place. It does, but it is a highly enacted and performed reflexivity. For the participants in the project it would've been beneficial to allocate more time discussing and analyzing the possible social effects, both of the technologies themselves and the here described place-making. Long-term interactions between researchers and local initiatives are needed in order to support collaborative sense-making and reflection. Full engagement in design must be complemented by distancing from the experiments and technical issues in order to jointly address the underlying issues and societal challenges that emerge through the activities. The design researcher should be capable of taking on such a role, and communities such as RGRA have certainly shown themselves worthy of the task. We can observe how their engagement in co-design open up opportunities for a new understanding and interpretation of the spatial differences and the local effects in the city, seen through the experiences and desires of the local citizens, leading to new forms of empowerment for those citizens. The latter, in return, enables the citizens to build up the social capital and the capacity necessary to become co-creators and co-producers of new and innovative services, but even more important in raising questions such as "Who gets to use public spaces?" and "How can values be enacted in public spaces?" To an extent, the alternative use of ordinary consumer technologies strives at re-politicizing citizen consumership. It also affords ways of acting upon those issues, and the "empowering tool kit" aspect is an important one. Youths in RGRA are already quite skilled and creative in using mobile and social media, and taking part in innovation increases their tinkering skills even further. If not yet masters, they can surely be seen as journeymen with high potential for crafting public spaces through distributing mobile media. An example is

Figure 14.6
Old and new artisans: rope-making and urban place-making (left: public domain; right: Per Linde, CC:BY-NC).

how they appropriated the idea of the BluePromo box and spontaneously integrated it into the Urblove project. Another example comes from a later experiment with a "public boom box" in a skatepark. RGRA members immediately searched for flaws in the prototype of shared music selection. In only a few minutes, they discovered that constantly "disliking", which could be done by "like" or "dislike" buttons, an item in a playlist moved it down in the list, making their own choices move up. This also hints at a governance aspect we want to address in further research: In engaging with emerging publics, who gets to participate and who is excluded?

Nancy Fraser (2011), in commenting on Habermas' notion of publics, addressed how open access to the public sphere rested upon a bracketing of indifferences in social status—a bracketing that was not efficient, since the public sphere was governed by protocols which themselves were correlating markers of social inequality. In our experiments, we have focused on marginalized groups and non-commercial contexts that don't hide social inequality.

Also questioned by Fraser was the possibility of a single homogeneous public sphere. Both Urblove and BluePromo contest the idea of a homogeneous use of public spaces, and the parallel place-making creates new alignments and nodes and overlapping places.

Another unexplored issue is the blurring of private and public. In our experiments we have deliberately worked towards supporting collaborative issue formation, and elaborating challenges in local urban life, as an integral part of co-design activities. Yet it is important not to enforce agendas and to support individual exploration of possibilities and self-expression in less politicized formats. In the picture reproduced here as figure 14.7, a girl is trying out a "public expression" tool—an installation that permits a person to take a photo inside a photo booth and compose a 140-character message to accompany it. The photo and the message are then displayed, in large format, on a screen near the installation. People passing by can then comment on them, and the comments are layered on top of the displayed image and text. (The girl shown in the photo reproduced here simply wrote "This is me.")

It is fair to say that the research described in this chapter still has numerous white spots that must be addressed in future work. One example is the governance problematic hinted at previously. From the point of governance, a lot of the research, including the here presented work, has not yet been successful in integrating decision makers and local initiatives in the same public. The "weaker" publics (grassroots organizations and NGOs) are in many ways still constrained to mere opinion forming or informal expressions not leading to permanent change. Much work lies ahead, but some narratives on emerging publics and public space have been told that can form a starting point in this future work. Finally, a focus on marginalized groups also can have the effect of stabilizing marginalization. It is not unproblematic to have groups representing marginalization and humble attitudes are needed. It is clear that a long-term building of trust is crucial.

Figure 14.7
Old artisan and new journeyman: stonemasonry and opinion expressing (left: public domain; right: Per Linde, CC:BY-NC).

Place can be said to be the experienced, lived, shared, and communally understood spaces in everyday life. Even "spaceless places" can give a feeling of place. This resonates well with parts of the thinking of de Certeau (1984, 97), who quotes Virgil: "The goddess can be recognized by her steps." De Certeau elaborates the example of the pedestrian appropriating a city by walking. Walking in the urban system is equivalent to what the speech act is to language. It allows a play with pre-defined systems. Referring to goddesses is actually a bit inappropriate, since de Certeau is concerned with power relationships and how the "weak" make systems designed by authorities their "own." The walker uses "tours" and "detours" as "tactical" strategies in an operation on space. By contrast, urban systems are developed through "strategical" tactics as the governing authorities infuse power programs in the city plan and its monuments. Mobile technologies, locative media, and place-centric strategies can support place-making from a variety of perspectives and in a negotiation of fluent ownership of public spaces.

References

Argyris, Chris, Robert Putnam, and Diana McLain Smith. 1985. Action *Science: Concepts*, *Methods*, and *Skills* for *Research* and *Intervention*. Jossey-Bass.

A. Telier (P. Linde, P. Ehn, T. Binder, G. de Michelis, G. Jacucci, and I. Wagner). 2011. *Design Things*. MIT Press.

Augé, Marc. 1995. *Non-Places: Introduction to an Anthropology of Supermodernity*. Verso.

Borden, Iain. 2001. *Skateboarding, Space and the City: Architecture and the Body*. Berg.

Butler, Judith. 1997. *Excitable Speech: A Politics of the Performative*. Routledge.

Castells, Manuel, Mireia Fernández-Ardèvol, Jack Linchuan Qiu, and Sey Araba. 2007. *Mobile Communication and Society: A Global Perspective*. MIT Press.

Chang, Angela, James Gouldstone, Jamie Zigelbaum, and Hiroshi Ishii. 2007. Simplicity in Interaction Design. In Proceedings of the First International Conference on Tangible and Embedded Interaction, Baton Rouge.

Crang, Mike. 1998. *Cultural Geography*. Routledge.

Cupers, Kenny, and Markus Miessen. 2002. *Spaces of Uncertainty*. Muller & Busmann.

de Certeau, Michel. 1984. *The Practice of Everyday Life*. University of California Press.

de Sola-Morales, Ignasi. 1995. Terrain Vague. In *Anyplace*, ed. C. Davidson. MIT Press.

de Souza e Silva, Adriana. 2006. From Cyber to Hybrid: Mobile Technologies as Interfaces of Hybrid Spaces. *Space and Culture* 9 (3): 261–278.

Di Salvo, Carl. 2009. Design and the Construction of Publics. *Design Issues* 25 (1): 48–63.

Fitzmaurice, Geraldine, and William Buxton. 1997. An Empirical Evaluation of Graspable User Interfaces: Towards Specialized, Space-Multiplexed Input. In Proceedings of the ACM International Symposium on Computer-Human Interaction. ACM Press.

Foth, Michael, ed. 2009. *Handbook of Research on Urban Informatics: The Practice and Promise of the Real-Time City*. Information Science Reference.

Galloway, Anne. 2004. Intimations of Everyday Life—Ubiquitous Computing and the City. *Cultural Studies* 18 (2/3): 384–408.

Halpern, David. 2005. *Social Capital*. Polity.

Halse, Joachim, Eva Brandt, Brendon Clark, and Thomas Binder, eds. 2010. *Rehearsing the Future*. Danish Design School Press.

Hermansson, Hans-Erik. 1988. *Fristadens barn: Om ungdomars livsstilar, kulturer och framtidsperspektiv i 80-talets Sverige*. Daidalos.

Högdahl, Elisabeth. 2003. *Göra gata*. Wallin & Dalholm.

Jarnäng, Marie. 2010. *Stadens odefinierade rum*. Sveriges Lantbruksuniversitet.

Kwan, Mei Po. 2004. Beyond Difference: From Canonical Geography to Hybrid Geographies. *Annals of the Association of American Geographers* 94 (4): 756–763.

Latour, Bruno. 2004. *Politics of Nature*. Harvard University Press.

Le Dantec, Christopher. 2012. Participation and Publics: Supporting Community Engagement. In Proceedings of ACM Conference on Human Factors in Computing Systems.

Lefebvre, Henri. 1991. *The Production of Space*. Blackwell.

Lieberg, Mats. 1992. *Att ta staden i besittning. Om ungas rum och rörelser i offentlig miljö*. Byggnadsfunktionslära.

Marres, Nortje. 2011. The Costs of Public Involvement: Everyday Devices of Carbon Accounting and the Materialization of Participation. *Economy and Society* 40 (4): 510–533.

Messeter, Jörn. 2009. Place-Specific Computing—A Place-Centric Perspective on Digital Designs. *International Journal of Design* 3 (1): 29–41.

Paulos, Eric. 2008. Citizen Science: Enabling Participatory Urbanism. In *Handbook of Research on Urban Informatics*, ed. M. Foth. IIGI Global.

Pinder, David. 2005. Arts of Urban Exploring. *Cultural Geographies* 12: 383–411.

Ragano, Dmitri. 2012. Growing Up in the Age of the Keitai (http://www.thefeaturearchives.com/topic/Archive/Growing_Up_in_the_Age_of_the_Keitai.html).

Redström, Johan. 2008. Tangled Interaction: On the Expressiveness of Tangible User Interfaces. *ACM Transactions on Computer-Human Interaction* 15 (4).

Turner, Victor. 1988. *The Anthropology of Performance*. PAJ.

Wakkary, Ron. 2009. Anything Is a Fridge: The Implications of Everyday Designers. *ACM Interactions* 16 (5): 12–17.

Wikström, Thomas. 2009. Mobilen och staden—Om mobilitet och konnektivitet i det nya stadslandskapet. MobiScape research report (https://idisk.mac.com/ptomasw//Public/files/MobiScape%20arbetsrapport%20layoutversion%2019%20dec%202010.pdf).

Zhang, Zhongyuan. 2006. What Is Lived Space? *Ephemera* 6 (2): 219–223.

15 Publics-in-the-Making: Crafting Issues in a Mobile Sewing Circle

Kristina Lindström and Åsa Ståhl

In this chapter we will explore the potentialities of *publics-in-the-making*—that is, publics that come out of making things together and that are continuously reconfigured by their participants, human and nonhuman. The potentialities of such public engagement will be explored through *Threads—a Mobile Sewing Circle*, a traveling exhibition in which people are invited to embroider a message received by means of SMS, either by hand or with an embroidery machine connected to a mobile phone with bespoke software. This is an invitation to stitch together different kinds of technologies, temporalities, materialities, practices, and participants. What makes participants gather in *Threads* is not that they necessarily know each other since before, neither that they necessarily have a shared problem that they want to address. What they do share is that they have responded to an invitation that, we argue, articulates an area of curiosity—ways of living with technologies—rather than a predefined problem. Our concern in this chapter is the co-articulations that result from a particular way of gathering and from particular ways of engaging with everyday technologies.

Threads—a Mobile Sewing Circle

The photo reproduced here as figure 15.1 shows some people gathered around a table. Some are engaged in handicraft. Others are talking. Overall they look pretty happy. If you look a bit closer you can see that someone has embroidered on the tablecloth. In the background there are more embroideries hanging on clotheslines. If you look even closer you can see that the man standing near the center of the photo is holding a mobile phone in his hand.

Threads has been traveling to public spaces, such as rural community centers and libraries, in Sweden. It doesn't have a set number of participants. To make its travels possible, substantial work has been put into making *Threads* more mobile by the two of us (Lindström and Ståhl, the initiators of the project) and by five partners: Swedish Traveling Exhibitions, Vi Unga (a youth-led organization for leadership, democracy, and entrepreneurship), the National Federation of Rural Community Centers,

Figure 15.1
An educational sewing circle in Åsgarn in 2011. Åsa Ståhl (CC:BY-NC).

Studieförbundet Vuxenskolan (a national organization that arranges study circles), and Malmö University. Together we worked to set up an emerging network that enabled *Threads* to travel around Sweden between 2010 and 2013.

The two of us hosted educational sewing circles during which we handed over some responsibilities to local hosts, who would then take *Threads* to their rural community center. The educational sewing circles lasted about six hours, and were based on learning by doing. The hosts were paid a small sum of money for their work by one of the partners.

All of the things that traveled with *Threads* fit into two cases that could be carried in the trunk of a car. Within a region, they were usually are transported between rural community centers by the local hosts. Transportation of the cases between regions was arranged and paid for by one of the partners. The schedule of the tour was announced on a website. There was only one set of equipment, so the sewing circles were consecutive.

Joint efforts and resources among the partners were also put into facilitating and supporting this emerging network. Each partner has had at least one paid representative who has worked part-time with the project and has contributed with resources and

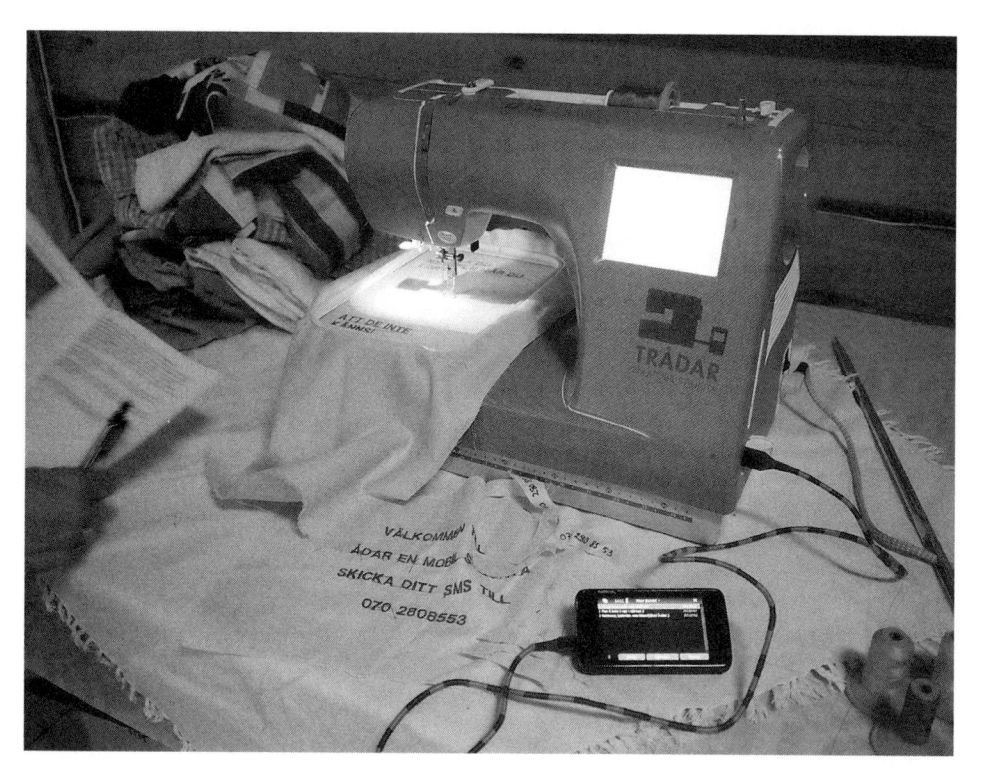

Figure 15.2
The invitation to *Threads* was to embroider messages received by means of SMS either by hand or with an embroidery machine connected to a specially programmed mobile phone. Kristina Lindström (CC:BY-NC).

facilities, such as local contacts and a place to host *Threads*. The two of us did this as part of our PhD studies, funded by public means.

About ninety sewing circles have been hosted. Some of the embroidered messages are now in a museum for cultural heritage,[1] and the Ministry of Culture has used the project as an example of collaboration between cultural institutions and civil society.[2]

The partners have various motivations for engaging with *Threads*. For example, one of the reasons for Swedish Traveling Exhibitions to join was that they wanted to explore how to design more participation-oriented exhibitions. The National Federation for Rural Community Centers wanted to reactivate rural community centers as meeting places. Studieförbundet Vuxenskolan was, among other things, interested in considering what a study circle could be. Although all the collaborating organizations had slightly varied main interests, they all shared an interest in participation and engaging the public. This interest made us set up *Threads*, where we invite the public

Figure 15.3
The two blue cases. Kristina Lindström (CC:BY-NC).

to engage with issues of living with technologies, new and old, digital and physical, through making things together.

Toward Publics-in-the-Making

Usually a sewing circle has a set number of participants who meet regularly in a domestic setting. Participants in *Threads* have likened sewing circles to other groups that gather to make or do things together: hunters, feather pickers, people who share a garage, and so on. To this list could also be added makerspaces and hackerspaces, which signal urban settings rather than rural ones. The reason for these groups or collectives to gather to make things differ. In some cases it might be because it is more fun to do things together. There might also be parts of the making, for example when repairing a car, that are difficult to do by oneself. The need for collective efforts might stem from a necessity of sharing knowledge, or joint investments in expensive equipment. As a consequence of the different kinds of makings, the conditions for socializing, talking, and so on also differ. The kind of belonging that is generated might also differ. Some are closed communities where the participants might know each other very well through sustained patterns of gathering; others are occasional get-togethers with less strong ties.

Waldén (2002) has helped us to understand sewing circles, as well as other groups that gather to make things, as sites of practicing democracy and creating publics. She has described sewing circles as hidden female publics, or shadow governments. In her description, handicraft is sometimes characterized as an excuse for women to gather in order to discuss matters important to them, something that was otherwise difficult for them to do. An important characteristic of these groups is, according to Waldén, that they were closed groups in which trust was built up over time. While the participants did not have access to formal decision-making forums, the sewing circles enabled them to make informed but informal decisions, which in some cases could be brought further to forums in which the matters were addressed formally.

We very much appreciate Waldén's work, but we are more interested in considering the potentialities of making things together as a kind of public engagement as something in itself, not necessarily an alibi for something more important, to talk. In other words, we want to explore how making, tinkering, and direct engagement with technologies and materialities can also become a way of understanding, negotiating, or imagining issues of living with technologies.

Marres (2005, 2012) uses the American pragmatism of John Dewey and Walter Lippmann, feminist technoscience, and Science and Technology Studies (STS) to argue for *material participation* as a specific mode of public engagement. The time of Dewey and Lippmann—the early twentieth century—was a time of technological development in communications, in transportation, and in the means of production. Much like today, technological development often resulted in complex issues that cannot easily be resolved by experts or institutions, but are left to the public to deal with. Although this can be seen as a threat to democracy, Dewey and Lippmann argued that this problematic entanglement, of being affected by an issue and not having a direct stake in the matter, is both the problem of the public and that which makes the public emerge. The constitution of a public is thereby characterized by being both inside and outside, which certainly is a problematic position. Marres fuses the positions of Lippmann and Dewey in this summary:

[T]he public's problem is that social actors are too involved in an issue to qualify as mere outsiders, who could leave the care for issues to other professionals. But at the same time they are too much of a stranger to the public affair in question to have access to the resources required to deal with them. (Marres 2012, 49–50)

In technological societies, where material entanglements continuously shift, it is not likely that these publics will map onto already existing groupings. Thereby these are rather unstable and ephemeral collectives that often lack a shared language, procedures, or locations. The kind of gatherings, or publics, described by Waldén, where the participants usually know each other well, thereby differ from Lippmann and Dewey's understanding of publics.

This position of being both inside and outside can be approached as a problem of representation, which for example is the case in liberal theory. Marres argues that it is more constructive to think of this simultaneous inside-and-outside position as a problem of relevance. This means that what an issue is, who is affected, and what procedures and institutions should be used to address it, is not a given. The challenge then becomes to articulate issues, actors, and their entanglements, or to establish relations of relevance. In line with Dewey and Lippmann, Marres points out that it should not be expected of a public to solve the issue that is in-the-making. The problem of relevance is a distributed problem, for the public, institutions, and others to care for. This is not simply done through talk or debate in political forums, but also through everyday practices such as when to turn on a washing machine or turn down the temperature in the house, what Marres (2012) describes as "material participation." What characterizes this participation is that material entanglements in issues and public engagement cannot be separated. In other words, Marres argues that use, and other ways of living with technologies, are potentially modes of participation in public affairs. This argument also implies that we cannot simply position the political in certain spheres, separated from the private or activities such as making or doing. It also invites us to think of the everyday as an environment for participation.

We align with Marres' argument that we become materially entangled, and possibly implicated in a range of issues, through mundane usage of technologies. What these issues are and who might be implicated in them is, however, not a given. Through the concept of publics-in-the-making, we want to explore and propose making as a means for co-articulations of issues. This means to acknowledge that issues are not just there, but always in-the-making as a joint effort between those humans and nonhumans who have the capacity to act in the given situation.

The focus on co-articulations through making also implies a critique against a separation between thinking and making as well as between public and private, which has been a dominant dichotomy in Western society. Similar thoughts can be found in works by Sennett (2008), Gauntlett (2011), and Ratto (2011a,b). Gauntlett (2011) argues for making as a mode of connecting ideas to other people and to our environment. With support from Ruskin and Morris, two main thinkers in the Arts and Crafts movement in Victorian England, Gauntlett argues for everyday creativity, that makes people happy. This should be understood in comparison to industrialization, which divided production into discrete tasks, and thereby also separated making from thinking.

Sennett (2008) also argues against the separation between thinking and making, but from an ethical position. He conceptualizes making, or craft, partly from the perspective of curiosity for what is possible to make and craft, and how to do it well. This curiosity is, however, not innocent. He means that we cannot allow the curiosity to run astray and judge in hindsight whether the outcome was beneficial or not. Without ethical considerations, curiosity might allow for the development of devastating innovations such as the atom bomb (ibid.). Instead of leaving the ethical question to the public, that only practices an after-the-fact ethics by responding to pressing issues, Sennett argues that we need to develop a craftsmanship that continuously asks ethical questions, in-the-making. This is a temporal and spatial shift which requires involvement rather than privileging distanced observers or representatives who can come and make a judgment afterwards. Curiosity, in Sennett's conceptualization, is then about the new, about what is possible to make, and must always be engaged with through ethical questions.

Ratto (2011a) works in more academic settings with making, in what he calls "critical making labs." In line with Sennett and Gauntlett, Ratto also aims to challenge the long tradition within Western society of separating thinking and making through highlighting "the interwoven material and conceptual work that making involves" (Ratto 2011b, 204). The reason for doing this is that Ratto and his colleagues have experienced that there is a gap between our "conceptual understandings of technological objects and our material experiences with them" (Ratto 2011a, 253). Critical making is an exploration of how people can critically connect society and technology with their own daily experiences, through investing in making physical creations and conceptual explorations. To do so, Ratto argues that the combination of making and social theorizing is preferred to external viewing: "… the ability of the participants to engage with the social theories presented to them and to develop and share new understandings was intimately related to the joint conceptual and materially productive work" (ibid., 258). As a potential of critical making, Ratto puts forward that investments made by those who participate in critical making can engender a caring for sociotechnical systems. We understand this as taking responsibility for the applied work, which might involve innovative technological or conceptual making, that one has created.

Marres' version of American pragmatism, combined with feminist technoscience and STS coupled up with Sennett, Gauntlett, and Ratto, leads us, instead of simply treating craft as an alibi for gathering, to consider the potentialities of making in terms of its gathering potential, and as a mode of engaging with our material entanglements. This is a move toward acknowledging co-constitution of humans and nonhumans, sometimes labeled the material turn (see, for example, Åsberg and Lykke 2010; Christensen and Hauge 2012; Hird and Roberts 2011), and a move away from the dominant discursivity, which has predominantly regarded the problem of the public as a lack or a deficit.

To explore the concept of publics-in-the-making further we will attend to *Threads*, and see how issues are articulated and made relevant through the making in *Threads*. But first we will take a closer look at the invitation, one of those things which makes people gather.

Invitation

Compared to a public that comes together because of being implicated in the same issue, or because of belonging to the same collective, *Threads* is related to, but differs from, both, in that it gathers as a response to a somewhat public invitation. The invitation is made through various means, for example through posters and flyers, using formal and informal networks of the collaborating organizations, through the project's website, and on a few occasions there have been ads in the local newspapers. Compared to the kind of sewing circles that Waldén has studied, *Threads* does not consist only of close friends, but of people who have responded to an invitation without necessarily knowing each other.

The invitation, in short, is to embroider a message received by means of SMS in a sewing circle, either by hand or with a machine, during one day. Without trying to make any scientific claims as to what motivates participants to join, it feels safe to say that there are multiple reasons for responding to the invitation. Several participants have expressed that they did not quite understand what *Threads* was or could be, but that the invitation made them curious. One woman said that for her, to come to *Threads* was a leap of faith. Another woman said that she was happy not to know too much because that puts pressure on her to prepare herself and perform. Others are very eager to prepare and bring, for example, embroideries or other handicraft.

It is also worth mentioning that the invitation doesn't only take place in advance, before the gathering, but continues throughout the day, through ours and other hosts' introduction of the day, through the setting in the room, through embroidered flyers with instruction about how to forward a message to the machine, and much more. In other words, invitations are made through talk and text as well as through material configurations.

Keshavarz and Mazé (2013) argue that through framing a design project, for example through the articulation of an invitation, a problem or issue is defined. To some extent this means that initiators of any kind of participatory project, more or less, in advance prevent the possibility for dissensus. One way of understanding this argument is that an invitation and who it is directed to, frames what the problem is, how to engage with it, and who are to be concerned. We certainly agree with Keshavarz and Mazé, that making invitations is a way of framing—and doing so is not innocent.

However, rather than refraining from making invitations or articulations, we want to explore the potentiality in making invitations that are more about articulating an area of curiosity, as opposed to defining a problem. The particular technologies and materials that are part of the invitation to *Threads* have normative capacities, but these are ambivalent (see more in Marres 2012). This means that we do not presuppose *what* might be an issue and *whom* it might concern. As we have mentioned, publics-in-the-making gather although we do not quite know the issue. However, the invitation to embroider a message received by means of SMS, which is articulated using a variety of means, in different locations and times, is, as we see it, a way of expressing an area of curiosity as well as a proposal about how to engage with it. The particular area of curiosity in *Threads* can be framed as meetings of old, new, digital, and physical means of communication. And the way we engage with this in *Threads* is through direct engagement with the technologies that the participants are entangled and engaged with in everyday use.

Co-articulations through Making in *Threads*

In this section we will introduce some examples of how issues are co-articulated through the making in *Threads*. These are responses to the area of curiosity, which is proposed through the invitation. Our accounts are based on material collected in connection with the educational sewing circles hosted by the two of us. The material consists of our field notes as well as images taken by us as well as other participants.

Although there was an atmosphere of joy and happiness on a crisp winter day, as can be seen in figure 15.1, some members of that particular group also had difficulties aligning themselves with all the things and practices introduced in *Threads*. Some, for example, were troubled by the embroidery machine and the mobile phone.

During the introduction of all the various materials and technologies that are part of *Threads*, an image was taken to learn how to upload images to the website (see figure 15.4) as a form of self-documentation. In this situation of learning-by-doing, a sense of non-alignment, separation and split was expressed when the participants saw the picture. One of them said that we should write not only "nya värdar" but also "skilda världar" (a bit of wordplay). With or without the 'l' in "värdar," "skilda värdar" is pronounced the same way. But depending on whether the 'l' is there, it can be translated to mean either "separate worlds" or "separate hosts." We are not speculating on which of all the possible splits this caption is referring to, but we take it as an acknowledgment of simultaneously belonging and being separate. *Threads* gather participants that are not all acquainted with each other. We have put lots of what can be taken to be contradictions into the setup of *Threads*, such as an embroidery machine and hand embroidery, smart phones and rurality. We have also invited curiosity toward how these contradictions could possibly be stitched together, or held separate. However, that is a matter of negotiations between the human and nonhuman participants. In this case the human participants responded to the image with playful resistance toward being taken as a simple unity of "new hosts," as if they had shared issues and ways of engaging with our multifarious invitation. In a coarticulation between humans and nonhumans, a non-specified difference was articulated.

The ambiguous feelings toward the relation between the familiar and unfamiliar, and the old and new was expressed by one of the participants through embroidering a phrase in Swedish: "Svetten lackar redan" (see figure 15.5). It was embroidered with

Nya värdar. Skilda världar?

Figure 15.4
"New hosts. Separate worlds?" Authors' translation to English of the caption for an image posted on www.mobilsyjunta.se during an educational sewing circle. Kristina Lindström and Åsa Ståhl (CC:BY-NC).

the machine on an apron that she had made by hand. The phrase cannot easily be translated but can be understood as both the anticipation of something coming up, and sweating because of hard work being done. She dealt with her anxiety toward the new technologies through actually using them in combination with something more familiar to her: a hand-woven apron. The making in this case was not only happy making but also rather demanding. First she had to ask for help to write and forward the text message to the embroidery machine. Then she had to go outside to send the message, since the reception at the rural community center was weak. In addition to these efforts, it is worth noticing that the making had actually begun even before that day, when she made the apron out of a linen towel. She was proud of having made the towel, but had put it in a hope chest and never used it until now. She did not follow the

Figure 15.5
Making an apron. Kristina Lindström (CC:BY-NC).

invitation to embroider a message received by means of SMS, but made something she found meaningful out of what she had at hand. Connections between past materials and ways of making and possible futures were made. Her concerns with the less known were, however, not settled.

During another sewing circle that was held in Stockholm, the capital of Sweden, several of the participants, who live elsewhere in Sweden, expressed how they experienced the capital as stressful. They exemplified with how people in the subway had been rushing and not looking at each other. The topic kept coming back throughout the time we spent together. A participant opposed herself to that urban/rural divide. She said that it was equally stressful in the countryside. While we would not say that her comment made any radical change to the conversation, or to the way that some of the participants experience Stockholm as stressful, there were further discussions during the days that dealt with ideas and ideals of well-being as being related to slowness and handicraft. One of the younger participants, who had moved to a ski resort in the Swedish mountains, expressed that it becomes stressful to allow oneself to take time for slowness without giving up other involvements and engagements. She was referring to having time to attend a sewing circle that she and her friends had initiated in her new home-setting. To her, there is a paradox in wanting to be part of many slow and relaxing contexts because it becomes stressful attending them all. Another participant mentioned hotels for sourdough, as an example of how the ambition of caring and allowing things to take time doesn't go well together with other commitments. At a sourdough hotel it is possible to leave the dough for someone else to do the work for you. Parts of this conversation were embroidered on a page in a textile file folder, to which the participants are invited to embroider parts of conversations that take place during the sewing circles (see figure 15.6).

Again, the makings in *Threads* enabled co-articulation of issues of living with technologies. The concern of having time to allow for slowness was, however, not settled.

At other times, text messages became cues to connect with experiences and people, outside of the sewing circle. At one sewing circle, one couple embroidered several text messages that they had received and sent just after the tsunami in Japan in 2011. The messages had to do with their daughter, who lived west of Tokyo. The father embroidered one message he had received, which said that the daughter would try to get to the Swedish embassy to pick up iodine, so her mother and father could wait a bit before sending iodine to her. The mother embroidered a conversation between the father and a friend of the daughter. The friend was not satisfied with the father's short replies, which resulted in the father calling the friend. This unsatisfactory SMS dialogue, in combination with the fact that they knew that the daughter was OK, became part of a discussion about the qualities—possibilities and drawbacks—of text messaging. Yet another message in the SMS-conversation between the friend and the parents was

Figure 15.6
"Sourdough hotel to have time to be slow." Authors' translation to English of an embroidered message in a textile file folder. Kristina Lindström (CC:BY-NC).

embroidered by the machine on a pillow case: "OK, but nuclear power seems insecure" (authors' translation).

The ambiguity in the machine-embroidered message could have been the cue for us to talk about the more elusive presence of electricity and energy sources, and make an explicit link between the use of electricity for the embroidery machine and the fact that energy has to be produced somewhere at that very moment, but we did not. Experiences of living far apart and feelings of being (dis)connected were shared and articulated through the process of making. Possible connections between our own use of electricity and the emergency that took place in Japan, were, however, not made. This doesn't come as a surprise since the concern about a daughter easily elicits strong feelings and is less politically charged than that about nuclear power and electricity supply.

Through everyday use of technologies, we become materially implicated in a variety of potential issues. As we have shown, some of these issues are co-articulated in the ongoing making in *Threads*. The co-articulations are not coherent or fixed, but are in themselves contradictory and ambiguous. Neither are they representations of issues that were already there to be represented, but in-the-making, and articulated between multiple actors, humans and nonhumans: how we have framed the invitation with embroidering an SMS as well as what we have brought in the blue boxes and what the participants bring.

It is also important to note that these co-articulations do not offer solutions to problems. However, the co-articulations do, at times, become interventions in, or reorderings of, the participants' everyday entanglements. For example, the apron is not only part of an articulation of something, but also a reordering of sociomaterial entanglements.

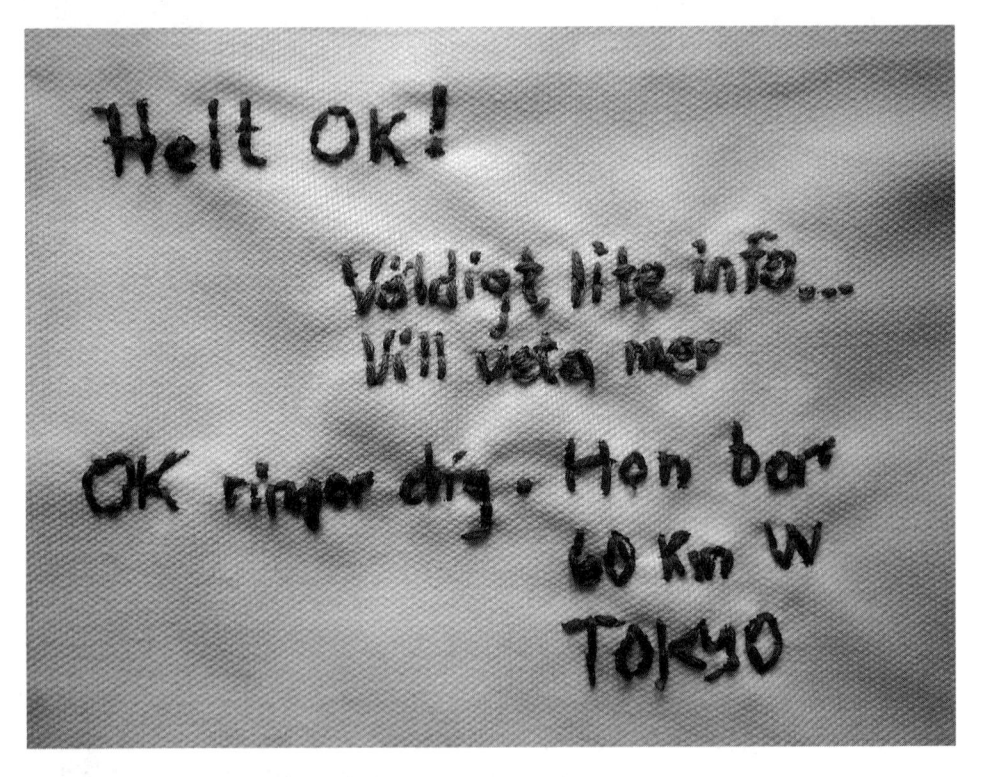

Figure 15.7
The embroidered representation of an SMS conversation between parents and a friend of a person in Japan just after the 2011 nuclear power plant accident in Fukushima. Authors' translation from Swedish: "Quite OK!," "Very little info. … Want to know more," "OK calling you. She lives 60 km W Tokyo." Kristina Lindström (CC:BY-NC).

This reasoning leads us over to the next section, which deals with the fact that the making that goes on in *Threads* is not only an intervention into the participants everyday entanglements; it also makes us entangled with making and work done elsewhere. As we will show, some of these entanglements are rarely included in the co-articulations of issues of living with technologies.

Absent Present Entanglements in-the-Making

In the last section we showed how one of the participant's making in *Threads* was interlinked with making done outside of *Threads*: the weaving of a linen cloth, which later on had been made into an apron. She could bring this making and work into presence since she was the one who had done the making. But, there is, of course, lots of other making done elsewhere that *Threads* as a collective is materially entangled with, although it is never articulated or in any other way brought into presence. We do, for example, not hear much about the making of the tablecloths that we set the table with. This work has so far remained absent present (Law and Singleton 2005) in *Threads*. By absent present we mean absent from conversations and shared experiences, but present through material entanglements. When looking at the tablecloths they have a tag saying "made by HEMTEX." Hemtex is the brand, so the tag highlights the company but obscures how, by whom, and under what circumstances the tablecloth was made.

The making in *Threads* has encouraged the participants to share experiences and articulate concerns, for example, related to unfamiliar technologies, stressing about having time for slowness, and living far away from loved ones. However, none of the participants have experiences of working at the assembly lines where the tablecloth, the mobile phones, or the embroidery machine have been produced. The woman's experience of weaving her linen cloth was made in a time and space which perhaps can make it possible to recognize that there is always hard labor involved in producing such a material, but it is not mirroring the conditions under which a linen cloth is produced today in other parts of the world. Nor does the HEMTEX tag help out very much.

Through our invitation, materials, and more, we do not manage to establish relations of relevance between these entanglements. Challenges with publics-in-the-making are thus that it relies on the experiences of its participants and that the materials seem to have little capacity to make certain stories present.

Concluding Discussion

In this chapter we have proposed publics-in-the-making as a specific mode of public engagement in issues of living with technologies (see also Lindström and Ståhl 2014). In short, publics-in-the-making refers to publics that come out of making things together, and that are continuously reconfigured by their participants—humans and nonhumans. In other words, what the issues are, are not pregiven but are in-the-making.

Other kinds of public-engagement projects could be when experts invite the public to be informed about the latest scientific and technological developments. This is an enactment of one-way communication, where experts are the knowledgeable ones. In other cases it can be that scientists or experts make some kind of audience studies or gather the publics' opinions in order to make use of them in their further development of science and technologies (see, for example, Mohr 2011; Bogner 2012).

Participatory design is an academic field that challenges the distinction between experts and laypeople. Participatory design has a long tradition of engaging the public in the design of new things and services. While some of the early participatory design projects took place mostly in workplaces, participatory design is today practiced in a range of contexts such as city planning, creative industry, and social innovation, which are also explored in this volume. Participatory design can be described as an attempt to democratize science and technology, since the aim is that those who are to be affected in the future should have a say in the decision-making process, which is recognizing that those who are affected have knowledge to contribute with (see, for example, Kensing and Greenbaum 2012). This reasoning can seem rather similar to liberal theory, in that it more or less assumes that what the issue is and who will be affected can be known in advance. In practice, we would, however, say that much work done in participatory design is about articulating issues, not as something given, but as something in-the-making, through prototypes (Ehn and Kyng 1991; Suchman et al. 2002), workshops, briefs, protocols and more. Similar reasoning can be found in Björgvinsson et al. 2012 and in Le Dantec and DiSalvo 2013, where participatory design is practiced as means of engaging publics, rather than an *a priori* community. This is, for example, done through infrastructuring, which suggests an ongoing engagement.

Through our proposal for publics-in-the-making we partly build on the democratic ambition of participatory design to engage publics in issues of how to live with technologies. In this chapter we have set out to explore potentialities of such an engagement, partly in terms of its potential to gather, and partly in terms of its potential as a mode of engagement. In practice, this is done through *Threads*.

As we have shown, *Threads* manages to gather despite the fact that the participants do not know each other from before, as in the case of a sewing circle, and despite the fact that the participants are not implicated in the same issue, as would be the case in publics as put forward by Dewey and Lippmann. The invitation to embroider a message received by means of SMS by hand or with an embroidery machine connected to a mobile phone with bespoke software is not a definition of a problem, but, as written earlier, an articulation of an area of curiosity, which we would frame as curiosity concerning ways of living with technologies. Since *Threads* has been attracting participants since 2009, with predecessors since 2006, we can claim that this invitation has managed to also create curiosity among its participants.

The invitation is, however, not only a way to make people gather, but it also suggests a way of engaging with the area of curiosity: through making.

More specifically, our invitation to embroider a message received by means of SMS is, as we see it, an invitation to engage with everyday entanglements. As we have shown, these engagements do at times result in co-articulations of issues of living with technologies. For example, through embroidering the specific words "Svetten lackar redan" on the specific linen cloth turned into an apron, there was a co-articulation between the woman, the materials, and the infrastructures about how to handle known and unknown issues of living with technologies. This co-articulation between various actors, including nonhumans, was an attempt at caring for familiar and less familiar entanglements as well as handling curiosity and anxiety in the same move.

When we say that this is a co-articulation rather than a representation we mean that the articulation is *in-the-making*. It was not simply there before to be represented, but was articulated during the making. Those that participated in the articulation were a woman, her textiles, the absence of an SMS, lack of reception and more. Furthermore, it is worth noting that these articulations are rarely solutions to a problem. And rarely do these co-articulations result in any kind of collective action to make change. This could easily be used to criticize the potentialities of *Threads* or, in more general terms, publics-in-the-making. In line with Marres, we would, however, argue that the problem of the public, the position of being both entangled in issues and not having access to institutions, forums, or other contexts where the matter is addressed, is also what makes the public come into being. Instead of expecting a public to offer solutions, we align with Marres, who argues that "the composition of the public—which entities and relations it is made up of—must be understood as partly the outcome of, and as something that is at stake in, the process of issue articulation" (Marres 2012, 53).

The composition of *Threads* is made through our invitation, as well as the multiple co-articulations that are in-the-making in *Threads*. Depending on what is included in these co-articulations, different stakes and stakeholders emerge.

In line with Sennett, Gauntlett, and Ratto, we can here see that thinking and making is closely entangled. Rather than treating making as something that should be separated from the public, we suggest that making can be a mode of engaging with possible issues, before they become pressing (see, for example, Perng et al. 2012) in the midst of an emergency. This should be understood as a caring approach, which doesn't come as after-the-fact ethics. Care, notably, requires ongoing engagement, which is not to be expected to be finished or solved (see, for example, Mol 2008; Mol et al. 2010; Puig de la Bellacasa 2011, 2012).

We take the co-articulations that are made in *Threads* to be articulations of issues of living with technologies. For example, how to handle the difficulties of a stressful life, whether it is in a rural or urban area, by trying to enact the promise of a slow and relaxing life by joining a sewing circle, or taking care of a sourdough. But then realizing that one has engaged in too many relaxing situations and too much slow cooking, and responding by insomnia and paying for somebody else to take care of one's sourdough at a bespoke hotel (which actually can be done in Stockholm).

What characterizes these co-articulations are that they most of all deal with issues that are of relevance in the participants' everyday lives. While we claim that the articulations are not representations of issues that were already there in advance, the participants' previous experiences of living with technologies are important parts of these co-articulations.

While one of the potentialities of publics-in-the-making is to relate to the participants' everyday entanglements, there is also a risk with this way of creating relevance through the mundane experiences of living with technologies, since more distant entanglements and distant effects of living with technologies are rarely made present or included in these co-articulations. Much like these more distant entanglements often remain absent in the participants' everyday lives, they also tend to be excluded from the co-articulations in *Threads*.

For example, *who* makes the tablecloth, the embroidery machine, and the mobile phones, out of *which* materials and under *what* circumstances, are not included in the articulations. These seem to require more care and perhaps it is a skill that could be practiced in the publics-in-the-making. But we also recognize that there is little potential in the publics-in-the-making to ask ethical questions in-the-making, when the making partly goes on at a distance from the gathering.

The co-articulations enacted in and through *Threads* show us that publics-in-the-making can contribute to establishing relations of relevance, but can also fail, depending on how caring curiosity is practiced in relation to the material entanglements that are brought into the present. What entanglements are brought into the present, or made part of co-articulations, matters. It matters since they are articulations of whose future and what consequences of living with technologies are cared for.

Notes

1. http://www.nordiskamuseet.se/artiklar/rekreation-och-revolution
2. http://www.kulturradet.se/Documents/publikationer/2012/kulturinstitutionerna_civila_samhallet.pdf

References

Björgvinsson, Erling, Pelle Ehn, and Per-Anders Hillgren. 2012. Design Things and Design Thinking: Contemporary Participatory Design Challenges. *Design Issues* 28: 101–116.

Bogner, Alexander. 2012. The Paradox of Participation Experiments. *Science, Technology & Human Values* 37: 506–527.

Christensen, Hilda Rømer, and Bettina Hauge. 2012. Feminist Materialisms. *Kvinder, Kön & Forskning* 21: 3–10.

Ehn, Pelle, and Morten Kyng. 1991. Cardboard Computers: Mocking-It-Up or Hands-on the Future. In *Design at Work: Cooperative Design of Computer Systems*, ed. J. Greenbaum and M. Kyng. Erlbaum.

Gauntlett, David. 2011. *Making Is Connecting: The Social Meaning of Creativity, from DIY and Knitting to YouTube and Web 2.0*. Polity.

Hird, Myra J., and Celia Roberts. 2011. Feminism Theorises the Nonhuman. *Feminist Theory* 12: 109–117.

Kensing, Finn, and Joan Greenbaum. 2012. Heritage: Having a Say. In *Routledge International Handbook of Participatory Design*, ed. J. Simonsen and T. Robertsson. Routledge.

Keshavarz, Mahmoud, and Ramia Mazé. 2013. Design and Dissensus: Framing and Staging Participation in Design Research. *Design Philosophy Papers 1*.

Law, John, and Vicky Singleton. 2005. Object Lessons. *Organization* 2 (3): 331–355.

Le Dantec, Chris, and Carl DiSalvo. 2013. Infrastructuring and the Formation of Publics in Participatory Design. *Social Studies of Science* 42: 241–264.

Lindström, Kristina, and Åsa Ståhl. 2014. Patchworking Publics-in-the-Making: Design, Media and Public Engagement. PhD dissertation, Malmö University.

Marres, Noortje. 2005. Issues Spark a Public into Being: A Key but Often Forgotten Point of the Lippmann-Dewey Debate. In *Making Things Public: Atmospheres of Democracy*, ed. B. Latour and P. Weibel. MIT Press.

Marres, Noortje. 2012. *Material Participation: Technology, the Environment and Everyday Publics*. Palgrave Macmillan.

Mohr, Alison. 2011. Publics in the Making: Mediating Different Methods of Engagement and the Publics These Construct. *Science and Engineering Ethics* 17: 667–672.

Mol, Annemarie. 2008. *The Logic of Care: Health and the Problem of Patient Choice*. Routledge.

Mol, Annemarie, Ingunn Moser, and Jeanette Pols. 2010. *Care in Practice. On Tinkering in Clinics, Homes and Farms*. Transaction.

Perng, Sung-Yueh, Monika Büscher, Lisa Wood, Ragnhild Halvorsrud, Michael Stiso, Leonardo Ramirez, and Amro Al-Akkad. 2012. Peripheral response: Microblogging during the 22/7/2011 Norway attacks. In Proceedings of Ninth International ISCRAM Conference, Vancouver.

Puig de la Bellacasa, Maria. 2011. Matters of Care in Technoscience: Assembling Neglected Things. *Social Studies of Science* 41 (1): 85–106.

Puig de la Bellacasa, Maria. 2012. "Nothing Comes without Its World": Thinking with Care. *Sociological Review* 60: 197–216.

Ratto, Matt. 2011a. Critical Making: Conceptual and Material Studies in Technology and Social Life. *Information Society* 27: 252–260.

Ratto, Matt. 2011b. Open Design and Critical Making. In *Open Design Now: Why Design Cannot Remain Exclusive*, ed. B. van Abel, R. Klaassen, L. Evers, and P. Troxler. BIS.

Sennett, Richard. 2008. *The Craftsman*. Yale University Press.

Suchman, Lucy, Randall Trigg, and Jeanette Blomberg. 2002. Working Artefacts: Ethnomethods of the Prototype. *British Journal of Sociology* 53 (2): 163–179.

Waldén, Louise. 2002. Textilens text. In *Tyg överallt*. Nordiska museets och Skansens årsbok.

Åsberg, Cecilia, and Nina Lykke. 2010. Feminist Technoscience Studies. *European Journal of Women's Studies* 17: 299–305.

16 Emerging Publics and Interventions in Democracy

Michael Krona and Måns Adler

Technological innovation, design, and development is often aimed at providing improvements for people and contribute to a progressive society, even though history tells us that fears of new technology are as common as the optimistic visions of the same. Discourses surrounding the development of radio, television, and the Internet have shared these dichotomous notions of what a new technology may portend. However, when the idea of democratizing live video broadcasting emerged and was implemented through Bambuser, visionary, idealistic, and optimistic notions set the tone. Bambuser was developed with the mission to democratize a technology that back in 2006 was available only to a lucky few. Innovative entrepreneurs with connections to the Malmö region shared the vision and realized the idea by aligning themselves with a strong Scandinavian heritage of participatory design. The focus was on the opportunity for citizens to broadcast live video from anywhere to anyone. At the time, only a major news corporation could afford a broadcasting van and transmit moving images. The vision was to see what happened if one could symbolically put a broadcasting van in everyone's pocket through the use of cellular phones and computers. In this chapter we enter the discourse of technological innovation through this type of visionary statements implemented in the design phase, but also through a critical notion of how this technology embraces a paradox in a societal context. When narrowed down to the political uprisings in the Middle East and North Africa in the years 2010–2013, this paradox surrounding media technology in general and the use of mobile communications and video broadcasting in particular can be witnessed in how both citizens and regimes use this technology in order to reach their respective objectives. These dimensions of access and use are vital parts of a rapidly evolving sousveillance society defining our time—a time in which boundaries of private and public have been dissolved and power relations are in transition.

This chapter starts in the design phase of Bambuser, puts the service and the use of it in present-day theoretical frameworks and empirical cases from the Arab Spring, and concludes with a wider discussion on the role and implementation of this technology in the societal context of increasing transnational sousveillance. By exploring both design and innovation behind the case of Bambuser, it contributes to obtain new perspectives on the creation of public discourses and making public spaces a matter for not only privileged but emerging new publics as well.

Digital divides, access, and social shaping of technology

Voices on how democracy best can and should develop, revitalize, and progress are hardly few. On the contrary, forums for dialogue and debate hold a variety of approaches in community discussions, and citizens have, more than ever before, the opportunity to use media technology to participate in a progressive way in discourses of public concern (Dahlgren 2009). It would be no exaggeration to say that these discourses are largely created and re-created by the public. However, the global distribution of infrastructural resources is characterized by a major inequality; the participation mainly derives from a Western definition of democracy and freedom of speech, and media technology as means for participation is sometimes taken for granted. The expansive technological revolution that has characterized most Western societies during recent decades has created a digital divide in relation to developing countries (van Dijk 2005). The continents and nations that are not included in this rapid development still have a long way to go in terms of infrastructure and network capacity. But the question of access to media technology involves a lot more than aspects of technical infrastructure, for example media literacy, which also has implications for political subsidiaries and cultural dimensions that need to be integrated in attempts to grasp this digital divide. Hence, the divide is defined on the distance that gradually grows as Western economies are still largely dominant in trade and create the information society as we know it. It is also fair to acknowledge that policy makers around the world define this as a technological phenomenon rather than a social one. This becomes problematic when the issue is discussed only in relation to the distribution of infrastructural resources and not in relation to social, cultural, and political implications. Much of the research on digital divides has focused on access, or what Riggins and Dewan (2005) call "first order effects." Little attention has been given to second-order effects, such as inequality in the ability to use and fully comprehend the nature of the technology. In line with this, we argue for a view on the digital divide as first of all a social problem in which the technological aspect is highly integrated. And it is within this social divide that Bambuser can provide opportunities to significantly alter the structure of public spheres and bring marginalized groups of citizens closer to a deliberative state of opinion creation.

One of the key factors in trying to decrease the gap between the Western world and nations in more undeveloped regions is the use and control of technology. This issue has been highly debated during the Arab Spring in particular and the ongoing uprisings in North Africa and the Middle East (Lynch 2011). The intellectual debate has above all focused on the use of media technology in order to achieve social change in the region, in other words, the debate has approached the role of technology predominantly from the users' perspective. The participatory function of media design is central to a comprehension of present-day media ecology; an ecology of digital networks as well as traditional media outlets. In this chapter we focus on the digital networks and what we define as democratization of technology, or in more specific terms the *democratization of the live video broadcast*. Bambuser, which was developed for this idealistic purpose, can to a certain extent be considered an example of how the relation between humans and media technology can intervene with democracy more explicitly than any traditional mass- and personal media ever managed throughout history.

Design and innovation within technology and communications must always be put in a societal context, positioning the innovation itself as a part of socio-political realities. Discussions of the role of technology sometimes seem to take a rather simplified direction in which the tool itself (technology) is solely defined as the main contributor to social and political change (Hofheinz 2011). This notion is also a statement in a larger intellectual debate on theoretical points of departure between Diffusion of Innovations Theory (DIT) and the Social Shaping of Technology (SST). These two oppositional perspectives, which share roots in an interactionist tradition connected to the Chicago school of sociology, differ substantially when it comes to the actual human intervention and use of the technology. It is within this intersection that the perspectives take oppositional directions. In the terminology of Boczkowski (2004) they can be classified as mediated impact and shaping explanations of technological development, respectively. The basic notion in the perspective of SST is that "technological determinism is an inadequate description or explanation of technological innovation and development" (Lievrouw and Livingstone 2006, 248). To talk about the impact or effect of technology in society would, within this perspective, be to accept a technological determinism. Instead the spotlight is directed on the pragmatic human intervention and choices within technological development.

Hence, our argument here is that the use of technology could, and should, be seen as contributing to changes in peoples' awareness and notions of citizenship rather than simply being a tool for political change. It is not the technology that changes society; it is people who use the technology. This argument is in line with the historical research on mass media and opinion making conducted in 1948 by Elihu Katz and Paul Lazarsfeld, who concluded that the mass media alone did not change peoples' minds. Opinions, knowledge, and awareness can be transmitted through media, but family members and friends then echo them through personal interaction in physical life. In this second and social step, the opinions are formed; hence, this is the phase in which media technology in general and social media in particular can make a difference. The present blurring of the boundaries between consumption and production within the media sphere has created possibilities for alternative voices and marginalized groups of society.

Democratic aspects of designing and implementing Bambuser

In the current construction of a new political modernity, citizens, through technology, gather around causes, shared values, and imagined communities in order to form opinions that opposes to the established structures that for decades have taught people how to be citizens (Howard 2011). This notion harmonizes with a perspective on design and innovation as a user-driven process with potentials in value production. In the case of Bambuser, the intersections between *design of the service, use, and involvement* as well as *the societal context of implementation* are important aspects of how to comprehend a democratization of technology.

Because Bambuser also is a service that derives from the Scandinavian tradition of participatory design, fundamentally as a result of challenging the use of technology and with ambitions to bring democracy and innovation closer together on several levels, it is adequate to theoretically frame this use toward a sociological trajectory of participatory communication (PC). Within the creation and implementation of PC processes, there are a number of principles that emerge as fundamental. Tufte and Mefalopulos (2009) discuss a number of these principles. In relation to Bambuser, two specific features of these discussions shed light on the user-driven design approach: (a) the creation of participatory spaces and (b) providing a voice to marginalized groups. Any society has gaps between social groups related to gender, ethnicity, religion, or class. Inclusion and exclusion in relation to public discourses and spheres is part of social life with or without technological development. However, when entering a critical discussion on innovation and design within communication and technology sectors, the question of access and inclusion becomes paramount. Access is not, and must not be viewed as, a matter of merely providing infrastructure through computers and Internet connections (Riggins and Dewan 2005). Accessibility also includes resources of physical, human, digital, and social nature. Education, literacy, and language all have to be taken into account when performing a societal analysis.

Bambuser—materializing the vision

Creating participatory spaces and platforms through community-based media, such as Bambuser or YouTube, can embrace progressive dialogue between individuals and groups. From this perspective, Bambuser can be viewed as a service with potential to provide an important arena for this dialogue (Löwgren and Reimer 2013). Access has in the design process been approached as a key concept regarding participation and stimulating dialogue. But as the design process evolved around the technical thresholds, there were two contextual dimensions that needed to be reflected upon: what people would choose to broadcast and what people would choose to watch.

In order to comprehend these dimensions one must first consider present-day financial and market incentives. Incrementally, in more economic terms the vision of Bambuser was to reduce production costs for traditional broadcasting and make it practically free for citizens. When the service was set up, the price for a second of broadcasting was equivalent to several U.S. dollars. The amount of viewers could then be used to finance the costs by letting them be exposed to commercials or through national public broadcasting fees.

Analyses of emerging trends in the technical ecology soon led to a strategic choice to integrate and enable the mobile phone as a symbolic counterpart to the broadcasting van. Three major trends were important. First, the processing power in mobile phones would grow exponentially, making them able to compress the video material faster to achieve higher quality. Second, the bandwidth within cellular networks was expanding rapidly, providing increased bandwidth to the phones and enabling better real-time broadcasts. Finally, and perhaps most important, as the cellular networks would grow in bandwidth capacity the cost of sending a megabit of data would decrease as a result of market competition, resulting in a close to flat-rate price. These emerging trends, which could be foreseen from any contextual analysis on the subject, resulted in design work that focused on cell phones. As Rheingold (2002) argues, information technology, and mobile communication in particular, empowers smart mobs to gather, initiate, and execute political action with the help of the mobilizing function of media technology. In this respect it is important to remember that the idea of Bambuser arose in the era of the Nokia N95, before Androids, iPhones, and app stores. However, the later emergence of these devices and phenomena and the rapid development of smartphones all worked in favor of Bambuser (Löwgren and Reimer 2013).

In late 2007 the video platform of Bambuser was launched. It was similar to other video platforms, such as YouTube and Daily Motion, but with the difference of live content. Bambuser grew steadily in Europe, backed by Norwegian venture capital and a so-called "freemium" business model. Users produced different material, from little league soccer games and union press conferences. Some people attached mobile phones to radio-controlled model airplanes. Through a normative assumption of contributing with an open-ended extension of the public sphere, people's increased possibilities to take part in opinion-building lectures, ask questions in real time, and watch public companies arranging press conferences on their phones were soon to be more frequent in larger political and social development contexts. That, however, required a re-design process that involved the user to a greater extent than before. In the beginning the technological and usability aspects were very simple. A user could just start a broadcast and give it a title. But as the user experience was continuously evaluated, it soon became clear that increased user-oriented convergence was necessary. Functionalities such as embeddable players that users could put on their own blogs and Web pages were soon added. Demand for metadata increased, and through the use of titles and GPS positioning viewers were given the opportunity to browse between broadcasts as they went live. Hence, by providing features that extended the experience of combining live video broadcasting with user-generated content, the number of users increased rapidly and the first sense of importance in providing the technology with a social dimension emerged.

Sharing the vision—social dimensions of the technology

The social implications and effects of new media technology have been discussed widely within the fields of media and communication studies and sociology (see Thompson 1995; Briggs and Burke 2009; Chapman 2005). These contributions share a macro-sociological approach in discussing how the printing press, radio, and television generated transformations in social life. Throughout history, cultural traditions and leisure have been transformed and integrated with different forms of media development. These social aspects of media, however, are not necessarily connected to more detailed social dimensions concerning user involvement and distribution—taking the social dimension of media to the actual interaction with the technology and not just the sociocultural implications. In the case of interactivity as part of digital media and culture, online video broadcasting through Bambuser holds a more specific approach toward placing technology in a social context.

It is important here to separate the previously mentioned contributions of social implications of the emergence of new media from what is argued here, namely the importance of providing the service or technology with a social dimension. This dimension can then serve as a participatory trigger of authenticity, making the user aware of the live feature and also be a co-director of the broadcast. Early broadcasts on Bambuser indicated a need for this type of interactivity. Viewers trying to overcome a lack of real-time interaction sent text messages to broadcasters telling them to film certain things. However, at the time most phones required the broadcaster to leave the Bambuser application in order to read the messages, which also meant stopping the broadcast. Soon a chat functionality was designed and implemented. This closer link between viewer and producer resulted in longer broadcasts. As viewers gained the opportunity to take part by typing messages and interact with the producer in real time, the participatory dimension seemed not only to remove the viewer from an observing position but also to increase the broadcasters ambitions and collaborative strategies. Aspects like these manifest the important role of user experience and behavior in the design process (Moggridge 2010). Traditional media organizations and journalists soon picked up on this and began setting up live interviews and to invite the audience to use the chat function to suggest questions.

Another aspect of this social dimension is the proximity and connectivity to upcoming social networks. The increasing popularity of social networks in 2006 and 2007 worked in the favor of Bambuser. Early in the design process the complex matter of publication platforms revealed itself. A need to address differences in platforms soon became evident. Luckily, real-time publication services such as Twitter, Facebook, and Jaiku were starting to take off at the time. Increasing the ability to easily share broadcasts to and through those services meant that the metadata of the transmission had a social context: an audience could be generated quickly.

With the chat functionality, the rise of social networks provided possibilities for instant feedback exchange between viewer and broadcaster as well as rapid distribution, and hence created opportunities for a larger and more interactive audience that could develop into a critical mass, especially in a context of socio-political turmoil (Krona and Bergknut 2011). This became clear during the uprisings and events in the Arab world in 2011.

Live video verifying events in Tahrir Square

In this section we discuss empirical events in relation to emerging publics and the implementation of Bambuser in order to enhance the understanding of the use in relation to the design of the service, but also to contextualize it theoretically through the concepts of emerging publics, participation, and public spheres.

On January 25, 2011, the main servers of Bambuser were running high as an increased number of broadcasts were coming out of Egypt. A similar rise of the number of videos had occurred a year before during the election in the country. This time, however, videos showed something different: huge demonstrations in Cairo's Tahrir Square. Traditional journalists were having a hard time trying to keep up with the rapid unfolding development in Egypt. A massive flow of tweets came out of the country with a purpose to convince international media and community of what was taking place. In Stockholm, journalists and editors on the national broadcaster Sveriges Television followed the flood of tweets from Cairo but had a hard time trying to verify the news. Lack of personnel on location made them unsure about what information they should broadcast. When live videos from Bambuser and other platforms reached the media institutions, the verification factor was put in another context. What journalists had failed to verify on Twitter was now unfolding live in front of their eyes. They were witnessing the events in Tahrir Square in real time and from multiple angles, as several Bambuser users were broadcasting with their mobile phones. Shortly thereafter, other international media outlets published news about the massive demonstrations in Cairo.

Journalists using only Twitter or other social networks primarily based on text messages weren't able to verify how many people were in the streets or assess the impact of the demonstrations. Videos on YouTube and images on Flickr or Facebook were also hard to validate, since it might as well be old videos or photos of former demonstrations that people were pushing again. Bambuser and online video broadcasting managed to overcome that uncertainty, and the element of live production was important. Through a number of verification points, among other things the integrated chat and the possibilities of both participation and authenticity it generates, the gap between medium and reality decreases. By typing messages into the chat the viewers can verify that something being screened is happening right now. Several Egyptian journalists wrote in the chat of some of the Bambuser broadcasts and asked if it was live and telling broadcasters to for example film to the right at a given point, hence participating themselves in the verification process. One could of course imagine that even though the technology was working fine, it was all a fake with people just acting. But the absurdity of having 100,000 "extras" in a square in Cairo fighting the police, multiplying truth claims and deliberately and strategically trying to obtain a specific purpose, seemed too far-fetched to be taken seriously.

Power and control—communication shutdown

The demonstrations taking place in January of 2011 in Egypt, and the struggle between citizens and the Mubarak regime, were the results of years of oppression. The digital revolution, to which Bambuser contributed, was certainly a new conceptual understanding of the huge change in power balances surrounding the public sphere and spaces for informing. Through Bambuser the tool to publish anyone's live story of the world was out there through a compatible mobile phone with an Internet connection. The leap was not only technological but also fundamentally changed ownership of the mediated public sphere, something that earlier was limited to major broadcasting companies and public broadcasters. The possibility of owning the tool of broadcasting real-time video changed the balance of power. Governments that earlier owned national TV broadcasting stations, such as the Egyptian government, lost control. In Egypt and in other countries, the relation between the state and citizens has been affected significantly by new information technologies (Osman and Samei 2012).

Power and control over technology and information have always been important dimensions to understand the socio-political implications of technology (Chadwick 2006), and during the Arab Spring the matter was clearly manifested. "Control of ... tools of mass information and persuasion" is, according to Monroe (1996, 8), "central to the idea of a commanding state." During the 1990s, with the emergence of satellite network stations such as Al-Jazeera and information technologies, several repressive states in the region already were faced with a dilemma. By stifling new technologies and channels, the regimes risked losing their potential benefits; however, permitting them might threaten the authority of those regimes (Kedzie and Aragon 2012). This

Emerging Publics and Interventions in Democracy 331

dilemma is still evident today, when the technological impact continues to increase in speed, reach, and usage.

On June 13, 2010, a lot of Egyptians went into the streets of Cairo to protest police violence that had resulted in the death of the young activist Khaled Saeed a week before. Khaled Mohamed Saeed died under disputed circumstances in the Sidi Gaber area of Alexandria on June 6 after being arrested by Egyptian police. Photos of his disfigured corpse spread throughout online communities and incited outrage over allegations that he was beaten to death by Egyptian security forces. "We are all Khaled Saeed," a Facebook group moderated by Wael Ghonim, brought attention to his death and contributed to growing discontent in the weeks leading up to the Egyptian revolution of 2011.

On June 13 the police started to use excessive force against the protesters. They arrested several hundred. To keeping the information scenario under control, they confiscated protesters' mobile phones and cameras. That day, Ramy Raoof, a well-known human rights lawyer, had equipped his mobile phone with Bambuser. The police erased hundreds of photos and videos from protesters' phones and cameras. On Raoof's phone they found nothing. Assuming that they had control of the information scenario, they denied having used excessive force. But since Raoof's broadcast had not only been broadcast to the Internet in real time but also stored on Bambuser's servers, it was available as evidence. Raoof was able to use the material as evidence against the police in a trial.

Figure 16.1
A screenshot from user Ramy Raoof showing demonstrations in Egypt.

Especially in Egypt, this event moved a lot of users toward using Bambuser rather than recording video and then uploading it to YouTube or some other website. The scenario also manifests how Bambuser steps in earlier in the process of recording videos. Whereas YouTube only receives already-recorded files, Bambuser records material in real time and thereby secures live material in a different way.

During the first weeks of the revolution in 2011, during the most intensive protests in Tahrir Square, tweets and other information stopped coming out of Egypt. The country "went dark" for 140-character broadcasted messages, even though Bambuser still received broadcasts. However, soon the service "went dark" in Egypt as the regime initiated a total shutdown of Web services and mobile communications, which became not only symbolic targets for the regime but highly strategic as well. But activists and demonstrators were able to get around the shutdown by combining physical and human interventions with using the technical infrastructure that still was available. One tactic used by activists was to put up tents in Tahrir Square with signs saying "Gathering Pictures and Videos" in order encourage people to compile footage and pictures from demonstrators and upload it online.

In these circumstances, the need for communication solutions, not only in order to get attention from the international community but also to find belonging, community, and identity during hard political and social situations, is evident, and the role of Bambuser is significant in both these aspects. When approaching this development through a sociological narrative of the public sphere, the current role of media technology can advantageously be discussed from a historical perspective. This also sheds light on the power structures of the public sphere as well as the forms of communication within.

Technology and a public sphere in transition

The conditions for the emergence of a common public space where citizens from different social classes could meet and conduct a dialogue on politics and society were most clearly idealized and described by Jürgen Habermas in *The Structural Transformation of the Public Sphere* (1962/1991). His ideal of a bourgeois public sphere is dated to eighteenth and nineteenth century Europe, however, as a result of significant changes in the political world, the social world, and the media world, the bourgeois public sphere is deconstructed at the end of the nineteenth century. With a capitalist ideological rampage in much of the Western world, the private becomes subject to economic and political interests. Habermas highlights how the communication context for a dialogic public (private citizens) was broken up and public opinion was turned to the informal opinions and also in large part to the publishing institutions of society that are driven by economic profit maximization. Citizens went from being involved in the shaping of public opinion to spectators to these journalistic institutions of formal opinion making. Even though Habermas has revised these notions during the last decade, the argument still reveals a critical attitude toward the modern mass media, their emergence, and their importance.

However, what is interesting in this matter is how media, design, and technological innovation during the last decade or so has altered the participatory form of communication (Rheingold 2002). Citizens' participation and possibilities for generating content within the media sphere is considerably different today and has empowered discourses on new media as a tool for alternative views and expressions toward established political interests (Hachten and Scutton 2006; Hofheinz 2005). In relation to Habermas' sociological perspective on public sphere and transformation, we can also apply the arguments on the current social and political state. Values and properties in the private (warmth, love, intimacy, passion, togetherness, community) are still valued in relation to the impersonal, cold, and aloof public life. A public life that is separate from the intimate sphere, with all the specific core values that it involves, is thus not very attractive. But the development that emerged at the beginning of the twenty-first century has led to what can be argued as a *reproduction of core values*, a re-introduction of high moral values in the public sphere. Understandings that enable citizens to have control and power over their own persona and role in society, which had previously been firmly linked to the private sphere, have now been incorporated also in the public life. This is a very interesting dimension of late modern society, made even more intricate by a notion that social change is no longer a narrow discussion in and of Western-oriented actors of society but is now a major global concern. Without making excessive claims to universalism or cosmopolitanism, it is necessary to emphasize the trends that appear to lead toward an increased supranational and international consensus on the political conditions that shape our time and history.

The role of media technology must be considered a major factor in this recent development. But instead of just considering technology as an indispensable trigger of a causal chain of events, we here put technology in relation to *emerging publics*, meaning that the appropriation of technology is considered one of several dimensions contributing to the emergence of new publics and behavioral changes toward more sustainable lifestyles. In the recent events in Egypt and Syria, citizens' use of technology (as opposed to the Habermasian notion of the role of mass media) has altered the form of the public sphere and to some extent revived the bourgeois ideal. Hence, the participatory design of Bambuser and other services is considered a key in trying to re-create an ideal of encounters on similar terms between citizens. New emerging publics, especially in the Arab world, are still far from being characterized by equality with free civic discussions on enhancing democracy, but rather are constituted by an initial phase of gathering around alternative views, expressions, and ideologies, and possibilities to make them visible (Lynch 2011). Hence, yet another shift of power has entered the discussion on democracy and public spheres of society. The diverse control of information, censored as well as user-generated, has changed the rules of engagement.

Local to public through live interaction

Aside from the fact that an important piece of information can be instantly moved from its locality to a global awareness, there is also a second effect that such a piece of information can have. Not only is the information available for later use; it is also available as it happens, which means that the public can act upon it. Watching a YouTube video has the inherent limitation that what you see on YouTube has already passed into history. Bambuser, because it operates in real time, opens up the possibility of interacting with, and taking action on the basis of, what is going on in the video.

A couple of months after the Mubarak regime stepped down, there was a demonstration at the Israeli embassy in Egypt against Israel's oppression of the Palestinian people. The police used tear gas, and as the activists tried to escape the gas the military awaited in ambush. Two hundred protesters were arrested. Between the time the police began to order the protesters to hit the ground and when a soldier grabbed him, a protester named Tarek managed to start a Bambuser broadcast with his phone.

The video was very dark during the first 90 seconds and only showed a couple of silhouettes, and the rest was completely black because Tarek put his phone in his chest pocket to hide it from the soldier. But the audio was clear, and what the soldiers and the police said to each other in Arabic couldn't be mistaken. The broadcast went on for nine minutes. By the time Tarek's phone was taken from him, 495 people were listening. Journalists among the viewers of Tarek's broadcast were quick to post the news

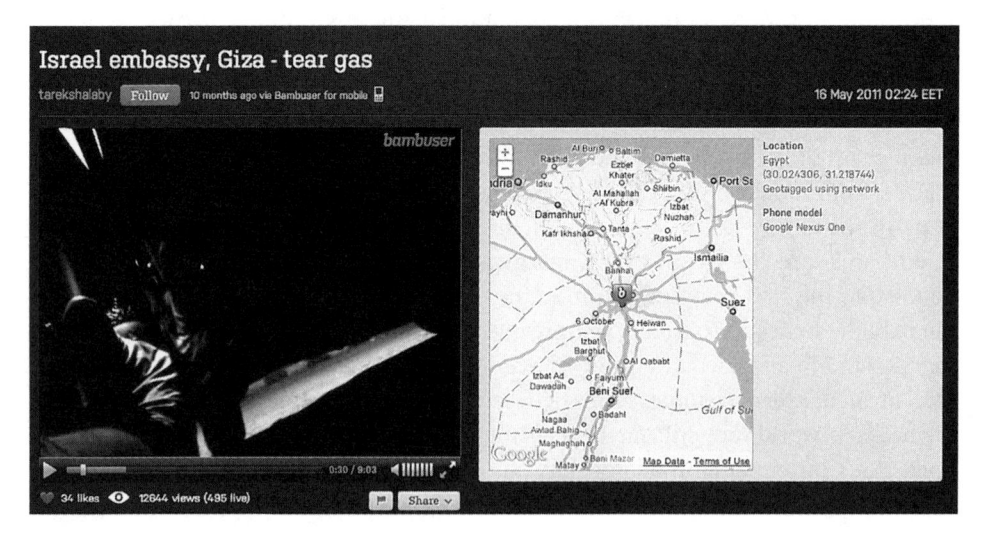

Figure 16.2
A screenshot from user tarekshalaby showing military excessive violence at demonstrations at the Israeli embassy in Egypt.

Emerging Publics and Interventions in Democracy 335

on various sites, extending its reach. The broadcast revealed how the military and the police harassed the protesters and raised questions as to why the police and the military were working together, since the military was supposed to be on the peoples' side.

On November 19, 2011, the streets around Tahrir Square became a war zone again after clashes between protesters and police on Mustafa Mahmoud Street. Ramy Raoof went to the front line of the protests, as he had done before, to document any excessive use of force by the police. With his mobile phone broadcasting live, he was shot twice in the stomach area. In the end of the 1.11-minute video one can see protesters throwing rocks at the police, who respond with rubber-covered steel bullets. The final seconds of the video shows Raoof screaming and running. He was lucky to have had several layers of clothes on, so the bullets made two large wounds but didn't pierce his stomach.

Bambuser was also used by the Egyptian police, perhaps in order to reconsider their ways of surveillance. The screenshot reproduced here as figure 16.3 is from a broadcast that was shot by the police.

This type of use illustrates the duality of accessible media technology and emphasizes the paradox mentioned in the introduction to this chapter; a paradox where citizens fight for freedom against a regime and the regime themselves use the same technology to fulfill their purpose. But the use of technology by authoritarian powers can also be more explicit compared to the case above. The next empirical example derives from Syria and problematizes this notion of the downsides of mobile transparency.

Figure 16.3
A screenshot from user A 7 m e D showing demonstrations in Egypt from the military's perspective.

Anonymity in the age of transparency

As the revolutions spread across the Arab countries after starting in Tunisia and Egypt, one of the states in which the aftermath resulted in a civil war is Syria. By early January of 2011, Bambuser.com had already been blocked within the Syrian borders. But during fall that same year, the blockade was seized and slowly an uptake in the amount of videos that were coming out of Syria was observed. The reasons for the blockade remain unclear, but among activists and users rumors went on saying that it was because the Syrian regime was ready to test a new tool for surveillance of Internet usage.

During the fall of 2011 several thousands of videos were broadcast from Syria, the majority of them similar. There was an image of a masked person on a rooftop. Hundreds of people in the street below were protesting with chants and songs. Why the camera wasn't down among the protesters seemed an obvious question, but the simple answer was that if the activists had shown their faces or if the video had shown any details suggesting the location the Syrian regime would have been able to pick individuals out and use the videos as evidence against them. It was important for the protesters to get their message out to the rest of the world, and to tell other Syrians that they are not alone in protesting, without compromising their own safety.

The screenshot reproduced here as figure 16.4 is from a video that came out of Syria during the most intense uprisings. The person setting up the broadcast is up on a rooftop, heavily masked in a scarf and sunglasses, and protesters down on the street are too far away for their identities to be revealed. It is an example of the use of analog

Figure 16.4
A screenshot from user Deerpresslive1 showing demonstrations in Syria.

strategies to create anonymity. The person in the broadcast is nearly identifiable but has disguised himself with glasses and scarfs. This is an illustrative example of how new and digital technology can be related to traditional and more analog strategies.

In this case, geographical position, both visible marks and the GPS coordinates of the broadcast, is problematized. The Syrian regime seeks to find out where livestreams are coming from. Even if some Syrian activists were using satellite Internet connection to make sure that the regime could not track them down based on cell tower triangulation or IP addresses, they also needed other kinds of methods to come around it. In February 2012 one user of the service started a broadcast from inside Syria showing an enormous plume of smoke coming from a gas pipe that had been bombed by the military. The live broadcast was picked up by Associated Press and then distributed to CNN, BBC, Sky News, and Al-Jazeera. It was re-mediated and broadcast in real time. According to Associated Press, it reached more than a billion viewers. But a couple of hours after this broadcast had been aired on all the major news outlets, Bambuser was blocked in Syria. The Syrian regime then tried to shoot down broadcasters on rooftops by triangulating the positions of broadcasts from well-known buildings that could be seen in the broadcasts.

Finding alternatives

After the blockade of Bambuser, Syrians kept trying to broadcast real-time video from their country, either through satellite Internet connections or by using SIM cards from Lebanon, Kuwait, or Jordan. Since many of Syria's large cities are close to borders with surrounding countries, several activists were able to use cellular networks in those countries to get around the blockade. That hadn't been possible in Egypt, because Cairo is in the middle of the country. People in Egypt had, however, recorded videos and then driven to the borders to upload them from there.

Realizing how hard it was to stop people from getting live video out of the country, the Syrian regime turned to other measures. One of these was turning the electricity off in opposition areas, making it impossible to charge technological devices and to use them to communicate. Another was to turn the electricity on and off irregularly. Another was to turn it off up to 15 hours a day so no one could charge devices or use the Internet, then to allow high voltage peaks to burn out devices that had been left plugged in.

Summary and concluding discussion

In any attempt to analyze or discuss the role of new media and technology in relation to political and social change, it is necessary to use specific concepts accurately. The extended use of information and communication technologies in the Middle East and

Figure 16.5
A screenshot from user example showing Syrian activists shining a gas lamp on a panel of solar chargers in order to charge cell phones during an electrical blackout.

Northern Africa has, at least during the last decade, been surrounded by an intellectual debate about contributing to the achievement of sociopolitical changes (Hofheinz 2011). However, it is our belief that scholarly contributions sometimes seem to focus explicitly on actual political change and politics, rather than critically highlight how new media can embrace, transform, and create dynamics in Arab public opinion, civic life, and political activism (Lynch 2011). We believe this focus limits the perspective in efforts of comprehending the role of media technology in sociopolitical change. Instead we have argued for a notion of technology as a mean to first and foremost, in the process of use, change people's awareness and by extension vitalize a public debate on social and political issues. Changes in continuous politics must be regarded as secondary in this process.

The purpose of this chapter is to describe, both theoretically and empirically, the role of media technology in peoples' struggle to achieve political and social change in Egypt and Syria during 2011 and 2012. Our main argument in this story has been that technologies hold different grades of significance depending on design processes, user involvement, and social implications. The case of Bambuser, an Internet and mobile application service that allows anyone to broadcast online video at any time for free, has been the center of attention. The service itself was designed with a specific purpose to democratize a technology and find answers to questions regarding what is important for people to broadcast and to view. This is here considered the first level of understanding the relation between user and the specific technology. The second level turns to the wider sociopolitical implications of the use. In a context of disturbing political contexts, as during political unrest in Egypt and Syria, what significance does the possibility to broadcast moving images have for activists and for political regimes? In order to find answers to these questions, we turned to a theoretical toolbox of public spheres and a perspective of social shaping of technology. The first one helped to conceive the retrospective importance of participatory design in the phases of development as well as implementation of technology, enhancing the traditional conception of public sphere. Initial notions on what Bambuser could and should be in relation to what it became, hold both similarities and differences. The vision that the service would help to democratize a technology, making it accessible for anyone with a mobile phone, not only stands but has also contributed to larger political implications in the specific region. Aspects of democratization in the design manifested itself in the continuous sensibility to user reactions and strategic development of enhancing the user experience. Designing Bambuser as a service providing both unique user experiences in real time as well as opportunity to affect political and social conditions enhances the interconnectivity between participatory design and communication. From the theoretical horizons applied in this chapter we argue that Bambuser, and other similar services, constitute a form of resistance against and a natural result of rationalization processes that for decades have signified political and social life, but also to some extent aspects of design and innovation. But resistance against what?

The need for formulating a theory of political transformation has never been more evident, due to the current interconnections between particular technological, political, and social concerns. In the reasoning of Andrew Feenberg (2002), as he states that there are ways of rationalizing society that democratize rather than centralize control, lies arguments on that modernity is characterized by an extent of rationality and therefore it takes oppositional and alternative rationalization processes to also reproduce alternative modernities. The type of rationality that has shaped society in general has also embodied the technological design of our days. And, when speaking of democratizing technology, it is basically a process of expanding the technological design in order to integrate oppositional (alternative) voices and interests. Originally we can find the predecessor for this theoretical trajectory as far back as to Max Weber's sociological theory of modernity, in which he argues for capitalism's focus on formal rationality, leading up to a differentiation between technology and social spheres of society. In other words, the emerging modernity has throughout history proved to be achieved at the expense of a transformation based on moving away from a private sphere (substantive relations) to a public sphere of impersonal and formal relations of modernity. A capitalist society demands this shift and adopts formal rationality to expand production and profit. Just as Theodor Adorno and Max Horkheimer argue on the rationalization of cultural industries, within the legacy of the Frankfurt Institute, one can apply the discourse of rationality in relation to this Weberian theoretical framework (see Adorno and Horkheimer 1947).

The rationalization of society can take different forms of manifestation, including technological processes. Bambuser, because it challenges former structures and enables alternative voices and marginalized groups to be heard (Tufte and Mefalopulos 2009), can be considered an alternative form of expression. The progressive view on both technology and citizens' use of it also encapsulates a more balanced approach to the sociological implications of media technology in late modern society. Even if services like Bambuser are to extend the public sphere and put new rules of engagement in it, the same technological impact must be framed toward related critical dimensions for this extension. Habermas' (1962/1991) ideal of a social and public sphere, in which participation and deliberation were to be equal, have in recent years been discussed by theorizing on Internet as forum for this equality, signified by free speech and accessibility. However this notion is easily challenged due to hierarchical structures and resource (both human and infrastructural) inequality. In this chapter we have outlined both the challenges associated with digital divides and possible contributions to decreasing it. Aspects of democratizing a technology, as the case of Bambuser illustrates, is considered a realm of this process. The technology itself doesn't achieve democratic reforms or political change but can rather trigger citizens in terms of awareness, community building, organization, and mobilization (Krona and Bergknut 2011). And when approaching this from the perspective of participatory design, hence involving users on several levels, the implementation of the technology may have wider democratic impact in comparison with top-down design and implementation as earlier media technology development bear witness of.

However, the progressive features of this development simultaneously lead to necessities of critical reflection on the both proven and hypothetical downsides. The Arab uprisings showed that the use of video as a monitoring tool has shifted decisively. Throughout the 1990s and 2000s, civil libertarians worried about governments and corporations slapping up surveillance cameras on public places. The fear was that they would be used as tools of oppression.

But now those tools are being democratized, as we are witnessing an emerging culture of "sousveillance"; providing opportunities for emerging new publics. The difference from before is that technology opens up for the monitoring function to be offered to more stakeholders, that is to say that there are no longer only states or regimes that monitors its citizens in various ways, but also citizens who can monitor their oppressors. The Orwellian Big Brother-society is though certainly nothing new. Jeremy Bentham's historical consideration of the panopticon and a social system where the monitoring and observation made people aware of the fact that they might be monitored, although didn't know. This impact was found, according to Foucault, to implicate that monitors through the both symbolic and pragmatic use of the panopticon within a specific social context (such as a prison) could influence people to think and act in a certain way based on the fear that they could be monitored, thus given rise to opportunities for social control. The panopticon was part of the industrial revolution which embraced a need for industrial monitoring where owners and other people in power could monitor public places, not just prisons and factories, or, as Foucault (1980, 71) put it, "panopticism was a technological invention in the order of power, comparable with the steam engine."

Since then the monitoring devices have been more integrated with everyday life and currently also been put in the hands of everyone. "Sousveillance" is the monitoring of events not by those above but by citizens, from below. Steve Mann, a pioneer in wearable computing at the University of Toronto, coined the neologism and in the 1990s he rigged a head-mounted camera to broadcast images online and found that it was great for documenting everyday malfeasance, like electrical-code violations. He also discovered that it made security guards uneasy. They would ask him to remove the camera and when he refused they would escort him away or simply tackle him.

The perhaps most famous example of this feature could be when a Los Angeles resident named George Holliday videotaped police officers assaulting Rodney King in 1991 after stopping him for a traffic violation. From the voyeuristic images a debate on police brutality emerged and the officers were put on trial. The example manifests an unplanned sousveillance, opposite to the cases being put forward in this chapter on the Arab Spring. In this latter case the technology is primarily used by citizens through a conscious implementation in real time often with specific purposes. But the purposes aside, the current society being balanced between surveillance and sousveillance technology is no longer a utopian vision but an implemented reality. Since the attempts from regimes in Egypt, Syria, and other Arab countries to control the technology and integrate the same technology that has empowered citizens to resist and mobilize protests in their own operations, present-day society must be considered technocratic in the sense that control and strategic use of technology during these circumstances is an extremely important feature for stakeholders on both sides. The struggle over information control has been going on for a long time but currently we are witnessing how contextual power balances have been evened out, much due to the technological design and innovation supporting democracy, citizens, and free speech. The future is not written but there is no reason to believe that the technological development, especially within the media sector, will stop from further rise according to peoples' struggle for freedom and participation in the public spheres of society.

References

Adorno, Theodor, and Max Horkheimer. 1947. *Dialectic of Enlightenment*. Fischer.

Boczkowski, Pablo. J. 2004. *Digitizing the News: Innovation in Online Newspapers*. MIT Press.

Briggs, Asa, and Peter Burke. 2009. *A Social History of the Media*. Polity.

Chadwick, Andrew. 2006. *Internet Politics: States, Citizens and New Communication Technologies*. Oxford University Press.

Chapman, Jane. 2005. *Comparative Media History*. Polity.

Dahlgren, Peter. 2009. *Media and Political Engagement: Citizens, Communication and Democracy*. Cambridge University Press.

Feenberg, Andrew. 2002. *Transforming Technology: A Critical Theory Revisited*. Oxford University Press.

Foucault, Michel. 1980. *Power/Knowledge: Selected Interviews and Other Writings, 1972–1977*. Harvester.

Habermas, Jürgen. 1962/1991. *The Structural Transformation of the Public Sphere*. MIT Press.

Hachten, William, and James F Scutton. 2006. *The World News Prism—Global Information in a Satellite Age*, seventh edition. Blackwell.

Hofheinz, Albrecht. 2005. The Internet in the Arab World: Playground for Political Liberalization. *Internationale Politik und Gesellschaft* 3: 78–96.

Hofheinz, Albrecht. 2011. Nextopia? Beyond Revolution 2.0. *International Journal of Communication* 5: 1417–1434.

Howard, Philip. N. 2011. *The Digital Origins of Dictatorship and Democracy: Information Technology and Political Islam*. Oxford University Press.

Kedzie, Christopher, and Janni Aragon. 2012. Coincident Revolutions and the Dictator's Dilemma: Thoughts on Communication and Democratization. In *Technology, Development and Democracy: International Conflict and Cooperation in the Information Age*, ed. J Allison. SUNY Press.

Krona, Michael, and Amanda Bergknut. 2011. Social Media Mobilization in Arab Nations during the Uprising of 2011. Paper presented at annual Nordmedia Conference, Akyreyri, Iceland.

Lievrouw, Leah, and Sonia Livingstone, eds. 2006. *The Handbook of New Media*. Sage.

Löwgren, Jonas, and Bo Reimer. 2013. *Collaborative Media: Production, Consumption, and Design Interventions*. MIT Press.

Lynch, Mark. 2011. After Egypt: The Limits and Promise of Online Challenges to the Authoritarian Arab State. *Perspectives on Politics* 9 (2): 301–310.

Moggridge, Bill. 2010. *Designing Interactions*. MIT Press.

Monroe, Edwin P. 1996. *Television, the Public Sphere and National Identity*. Oxford University Press.

Osman, Amr, and Marwa A. Samei. 2012. The Media and the Making of the 2011 Egyptian Revolution. *Global Media Journal* (German Edition) 2(1): 1–19.

Rheingold, Howard. 2002. *Smart Mobs: The Next Social Revolution*. Perseus.

Riggins, Frederick, and Sanjeev Dewan. 2005. The Digital Divide: Current and Future Research Directions. *Journal of the Association for Information Systems* 6 (12): 298–337.

Thompson, John. B. 1995. *The Media and Modernity: A Social Theory of The Media*. Polity.

Tufte, Thomas, and Paolo Mefalopulos. 2009. *Participatory Communication: A Practical Guide*. World Bank.

van Dijk, Jan A. G. M. 2005. *The Deepening Divide—Inequality in the Information Society*. Sage.

Contributors

Måns Adler

Kaospilot. Founder, Bambuser.

Erling Björgvinsson

PhD in interaction design. Senior lecturer, School of Arts and Communication, Malmö University. Björgvinsson's research interests are in participatory design, participatory cultural production, and democratic innovation.

Karin Book

PhD in urban geography. Senior lecturer, Department of Sport Sciences, Malmö University. Book's research interest in the intersection between urban planning and sport studies encompasses spatial planning for sport and leisure activities and redefinitions of activity spaces and sport strategies in city marketing.

David Cuartielles

MSc in telecommunications engineering. Lecturer, School of Arts and Communication, Malmö University. Co-founder, Arduino.

Pelle Ehn

Professor, interaction design, School of Arts and Communication, Malmö University. Ehn's research interests are in design, information technology, democracy, and participation.

Anders Emilson

PhD student, interaction design, School of Arts and Communication and Medea, Malmö University. Emilson's research interests are in design for social innovation and sustainability, designing networks, democracy, and participation.

Per-Anders Hillgren

PhD in interaction design. Senior lecturer, School of Arts and Communication, Malmö University. Hillgren's research interests are in collaborative design and social innovation.

Mads Hobye

PhD in interaction design, Medea, Malmö University. Co-founder of Illutron collaborative interactive art studio. Hobye focuses on how digital material can be used for exploring social transformative play situated in the context of everyday life.

Michael Krona

PhD in media and communication studies. Senior lecturer, School of Arts and Communication, Malmö University. Krona's research interests are in media technology and social change. He is working on articles on social media activity during the Arab uprisings and on a book about the interplay between media technological development and political revolutions during the twentieth century.

Per Linde

PhD in interaction design. Senior lecturer, School of Arts and Communication, Malmö University. Linde's research addresses ubiquitous computing, mobile interaction, participatory design processes, and Living Labs.

Kristina Lindström

PhD in interaction design, School of Arts and Communication, Malmö University. Lindström works in a long-term research and art practice with Åsa Ståhl. They explore materialities and meanings of information and communication technology. They also intervene in and reconfigure publics through crafting and making things together.

Sanna Marttila

PhD student, new media, School of Arts, Design, and Architecture, Aalto University. Marttila studies participatory culture, especially in the context of audiovisual media. As a designer, she is interested in supporting and facilitating open and collaborative design activities.

Elisabet M. Nilsson

PhD in educational sciences. Senior lecturer, School of Arts and Communication, Malmö University. Nilsson's research interest concerns the dialectic relationship between social change and technological development, and how the introduction of new technologies and mediating tools evoke new patterns of behavior and thinking. In recent years she has primarily been engaged in research projects exploring co-design-oriented activities and tools and methods to support collaborative learning.

Contributors

Anna Seravalli

PhD in interaction design, Medea, Malmö University. Seravalli investigates how collaborative design processes can be used to explore production practices in which use value, human capital, and social capital are generated, with environmental limits kept in consideration. She is actively involved in the running of the maker-space Fabriken.

Pernilla Severson

PhD in media and communication studies. Senior lecturer, School of Arts and Communication, Malmö University. Severson's research interests are in media development, aspects of communication, innovation, and learning.

Åsa Ståhl

PhD in media and communication studies, School of Arts and Communication, Malmö University. Ståhl works in a research and art practice with Kristina Lindström. They explore materialities and meanings of information and communication technology. They also intervene in and reconfigure publics through crafting and making things together.

Richard Topgaard

BA in media and communication studies. Digital media strategist, Medea Collaborative Media Initiative, Malmö University.

Lucy Suchman

Professor, anthropology of science and technology, Lancaster University. Suchman's research interests are in critical innovation, feminist technoscience studies, and relations between humans and machines.

Laura Watts

Associate professor and ethnographer, IT University of Copenhagen. Watts' research in the field of science and technology studies is concerned with the effect of landscape and location on how futures are imagined and made—how different landscapes make different futures. She has worked in the Orkney Islands, in the mobile-telecoms industry, in the renewable energy industry, and in public transport.

Index

Accountability, 10, 65, 77, 80, 81, 178, 180, 215–217, 242, 243, 247, 252
Actor-Network Theory, 8, 191, 199, 228–231, 235
Agonism, 20, 28, 29, 36, 63, 64, 69, 81, 178, 183, 232, 272, 273
Agonistic democracy, 9, 273
Agonistic design, 64, 65, 68–70, 74, 80
Agonistic spaces, 36, 71, 76
Arab Spring, 275, 323, 324, 330, 341
Arena analysis, 190, 201, 203
Artistic experimentation, 133

Bluetooth, 278, 284, 285
Boundary objects, 8, 188, 199, 218, 274

Capacity building, 44, 45
Civic media, 227
Co-creation, 3, 27, 205, 206, 275, 278
Co-design, 19, 24, 27, 35, 40, 41, 91, 102, 216, 227–229, 232, 240, 248, 251, 252, 289, 298, 299
Collaborative consumption, 91
Collaborative design, 2–5, 19, 28, 51, 87–91, 180, 181, 233, 240, 248
Collaborative production, 91–94, 99, 105, 109
Collaborative prototyping, 7, 8, 69
Collaborative services, 4, 5, 20, 23, 24, 35, 91
Commons, 5, 9, 85, 87, 92, 94, 100, 103–112, 115–122, 126, 182, 191–193, 200, 203, 206, 207, 214, 218

Commons-based production, 88, 89, 94, 100, 103–106, 109, 111
Communities of practice, 7–9, 274
Community-based media, 326
Creative class, 1–6, 9, 37, 38, 173–176, 179, 181, 203, 257, 265
Creative Commons, 90, 134, 153, 163, 165, 187, 192–196, 199, 203–207, 214–220
Creative communities, 4, 36
Creative industries, 5, 6, 28, 29, 65–70, 74–82, 257, 258, 261, 264, 265, 299
Crowdfunding, 3, 189, 207, 208
Crowdsourcing, 3, 229
Cultural commons, 5, 9, 187–192, 214, 218, 219

Democracy, 3, 5–10, 22, 53, 64, 66, 69, 77, 78, 81, 88, 99, 111, 157, 174, 178–184, 187–190, 195, 199, 200, 214–217, 227–232, 248, 252, 257, 261, 265, 269–278, 284, 303, 307, 318, 326, 333, 338–341
Democratic design, 8, 18, 28, 88, 111
Design for politics, 28, 80
Design for social innovation, 36, 41, 45, 46, 56
Design things, 8, 10, 20, 28, 29, 36, 278–280
Design thinking, 3, 25
Digital divide, 324, 340
Digital material, 133, 137, 139, 143, 145, 147, 150, 151
Digital sketching, 147–149

DIY (do-it-yourself), 9, 10, 88, 115–118, 158, 167, 188, 193, 194, 199, 208, 214, 219, 286
Durable commons, 106–109, 117, 120, 192, 218, 219

Economies of scope, 108, 109, 122

Fab labs, 5, 91, 99, 109–111, 122, 154
Feminist technoscience, 7, 307–309
Framework projects, 35, 40, 55, 56
Free/libre and open-source software (FLOSS), 87–90, 103–106
Friendly hacking, 9, 29, 36, 42–51, 56–58
Future-making, 4, 7, 173, 174, 178, 181, 183, 188, 189, 211, 214, 228, 252, 257–262, 265, 270

Games, 241, 278, 289
GNU project, 90, 153, 159
Governance, 1, 8, 9, 28, 29, 64–70, 74–82, 92, 93, 174, 189–192, 210, 228, 271, 272, 280
Grassroots communities, 36
Grassroots initiatives, 46, 49, 70, 101, 246
Grassroots innovation, 99
Grassroots journalism, 1, 5, 227, 232, 241, 250
Grassroots media, 228, 230, 238–243, 247, 249, 251
Grassroots movement, 25
Grassroots organizations, 5, 36, 49, 63, 76, 79, 242, 246, 299

Hackathon, 123
Hacker community, 109, 114, 119, 123
Hacker movement, 156
Hackerspaces, 91, 99, 109, 110, 136, 154, 156, 306
Handicrafts, 303, 307, 310, 314
Hip-hop, 6, 71, 234–238, 241, 244, 283, 284

Incubators, 5, 25, 29, 63–65, 70–81, 111, 229
Infrastructuring, 8–10, 28, 29, 36–40, 51, 54, 56, 70, 73, 109–112, 123, 181, 190–193, 211, 214–218, 234–241, 244, 247–252, 274, 275, 318
Interactive installations, 131, 133, 136, 138
Internet of Things, 111, 153

Knowledge alliances, 64, 77, 78, 82

Lead users, 37, 124
Learning by doing, 304, 311
Living labs, 8, 9, 19, 22, 28, 35–37, 40, 51, 55–57, 63, 65, 70, 126, 180, 184, 187, 190, 193, 194, 199, 211, 215, 229, 248
Local media, 241
Locative media, 281, 300

Maker community, 155, 156
Makerspaces, 5, 9, 91, 94, 99, 101, 110, 126, 156, 306
Making, 8, 10, 132, 143, 145, 150
Mass media, 227, 228, 241, 244–247, 250, 251, 325, 333
Matchmaking, 36, 40, 56, 73
Material participation, 307, 308
Media ecology, 325
Media sphere, 325, 333
Media technology, 323–340
Mobile gaming, 274, 278, 289
Mobile-media broadcasting, 227, 232, 243
Mobile technologies, 6, 232, 245, 272, 278, 281, 284–290, 297, 300

New media, 37, 71, 180, 197, 227, 233, 241, 248–251, 271, 275, 278, 280, 289, 328, 333, 337–338
Non-governmental organizations (NGOs) 2, 7, 9, 19, 25, 35, 41, 42, 46–51, 67, 70, 73, 76, 99, 101, 102, 118–122

Online sharing communities, 150
Open design, 90–94, 106, 163
Open innovation, 4, 5, 35, 174, 184, 187, 190, 228–230, 240, 248, 252, 270

Index

Open-source hardware, 5, 153, 158, 159, 164

Participatory culture, 271
Participatory design, 4–7, 10, 18–20, 24–28, 64–71, 76, 80, 87, 88, 157, 163, 174, 181, 187–190, 216, 231, 232, 318, 323, 326, 333, 339, 340
Participatory urbanism, 282
Peer-to-peer file sharing, 187, 194–197
Peer-to-peer production, 87, 88
Personal fabrication machines, 93, 106, 109
Place-making, 274, 278, 280, 297–300
Political design, 28, 80
Prosumers, 124, 228,
Prototypes, 20, 43, 53, 54, 69, 81, 145–149, 164, 166, 183, 184, 233, 235, 275, 278, 282, 286, 288, 299, 318
Prototyping, 7, 19, 20, 25, 28, 29, 41–44, 51, 54, 88, 91–94, 110, 113, 145, 147, 166, 167, 183, 188, 228, 240, 242, 248, 251
Publics, 2–6, 27, 76, 174, 228, 269–273, 277–281, 284–289, 299, 309, 310, 317–320, 324, 329, 333, 340
Public space, 6, 7, 150, 174, 271–275, 278–284, 288, 290, 296–303, 324, 332

Reflective practice, 41, 55, 148
Robotics, 133, 158, 159, 162, 168

Science and Technology Studies (STS), 6, 7, 307, 309, 318
Self-produced media, 278, 284
Service design, 23, 24, 81
Sewing circles, 272, 304–310
Short Message Service (SMS), 275, 285, 289–290, 303, 310, 314, 316–319
Smart cities, 277, 278
Smartphones, 272, 328
Social capital, 38, 54, 57, 103, 115, 126
Social design, 23, 26–28
Social innovation, 5, 6, 9, 17–29, 35–37, 41, 44, 46, 49, 56, 63–77, 81, 91, 289, 318

Social interaction, 278, 282
Social media, 196–199, 294–298
Social networks, 91, 329
Social production, 103, 118
Sousveillance, 276, 323, 340
Street journalism, 241, 242, 247, 250
Sustainability, 1–6, 21–24, 28, 37–39, 51–54, 64, 77, 87–91, 103, 108, 113, 116, 121, 122, 151, 333

Things, 4, 8–10, 64, 65, 68–82, 230, 231, 250
Third industrial revolution, 99, 102–105, 125, 126
Transformation design, 24, 56
Transmedia, 211, 214

User-centered design, 3, 27
User-driven innovation, 3, 4, 8, 104

Video blogging, 235, 236, 249
Video broadcasting, 6, 323, 328, 330

Wireless, 274, 275, 278, 284, 285